CISTERCIAN STUDIES SERIES: NUMBER FORTY-FIVE

pachomian koinonia I

The Life of Saint Pachomius

Pachomian Koinonia

The Lives, Rules, and Other Writings of Saint Pachomius and his Disciples

CISTERCIAN STUDIES SERIES: NUMBER FORTY-FIVE

pachomian koinonia

Volume One

The Life of Saint Pachomius and his Disciples

Translated, with an introduction by,

Armand Veilleux
Monk of Mistassini

Foreword by

Adalbert de Vogüé
Monk of La Pierre-qui-Vire

Cistercian Publications Inc.
Kalamazoo, Michigan
1980

Translation of the works contained in this volume
was made possible by a translator's grant from the
National Endowment for the Humanities,
Washington, D.C.

Typeset by the Carmelites of Indianapolis

Third Printing
1996

Library of Congress Cataloging in Publication Data

The Life of Saint Pachomius and his disciples.

(Pachomian koinonia; v. 1) (Cistercian studies series; 45)

1. Pachomius, Saint. 2. Christian saints—Egypt—Biography. 3. Monasticism and religious orders—Egypt. 4. Monasticism and religious orders—Early church, ca. 30-600. I. Veilleux, Armand. II. Series. III. Series.

BR1720.P23P3 vol. 1 281'.3s [281'.3'0924] [B] 80-21796

ISBN (hardcover) 0-87907-845-6 (v. 1)
(paperback) 0-87907-945-2

CONTENTS

FOREWORD

THIS COLLECTION of materials, carefully and invaluably assembled by Father Armand Veilleux, contains the archives of a great event: the origin during the fourth century of communal religious life within Christianity. The consequences for Church and society of this event, still continuing to unfold, cannot be measured. It occurred in Upper Egypt at the initiative of a certain Pachomius, a young Copt who had recently been baptized and who knew neither Greek nor Latin. Marginal to the great centres of civil and religious life in the Roman Empire, this phenomenon was quickly marked by an impressive magnitude: nine, and later twelve, gigantic monasteries totalling thousands of monks, followed by more or less spontaneous outbursts of similar experiments in less remote areas. Before the end of the century, the pachomian *Koinonia* had sister-houses in Pontus and Cappadocia, in Syria and Palestine, in Italy, Africa, and Gaul—to mention only those which are best known to us through their literary remains.

The first fruit of this spiritual outburst, pachomian cenobitism was in many respects the most distinguished. It is an interesting fact that, from the beginning, christian community life attained there a degree of vigor difficult to rival. Analogous to the rich harvest produced from virgin soil, the *Koinonia* formed by the sons of Pachomius experienced an extraordinary growth among a semi-pagan people, in a Church which had previously known nothing of this kind.

This astounding vigor was experienced not only in terms of numbers—and the egyptian communities were to become proverbial in Christianity—but more importantly in the organizational model which incorporated these multitudes, maintained a high level of spirituality among them, and formed them into an intense communion. The word *Koinonia* has probably never carried so vibrant a meaning as it did in this community surrounding, and surviving, 'Our holy Father, Apa Pachomius'. Here were thousands of men united in sharing all their goods in common, with absolute equality in their use, completely submitting themselves to a rule and to a hierarchy instituted by the man of God. Certainly, these traits were not without parallel before or after Pachomius, in jewish or christian monasticism. But what made them quite distinctive in this setting was the perfect integration and centralization of the whole organism, both temporally and spiritually. Transcending the many local communities, the *Koinonia* was one and the same in every locality. A single bursar-general oversaw its property and its work. A single Father guided it, governed it, and led it to God.

Under a multiform hierarchy—every monastery was subdivided into houses, each directed, as was the monastery itself, by a master and his 'second'—this first monastic arrangement in Upper Egypt was at once the most numerous, the most solidly structured, and the most closely united that has ever been seen. In the fourth century, in any case, nothing even dimly resembled it in its grandiose, yet compact, plan: neither the greek brotherhoods directed by Basil, nor the monastery of Hippo established by Augustine, nor the eighty monks gathered around Martin at Marmoutier.

The difference, I repeat, was not merely quantitative but qualitative. From Basil we have an *Asceticon* in several layers, some letters on the monastic life, and a eulogy by Gregory of Nazianzen. From Augustine we inherit a small rule comprised of two brief but substantial texts, as well as various writings or statements concerning monks, and a biography by his disciple, Possidius. By Sulpicius Severus we have the famous *Life of Martin* which is completed by his Dialogues. In comparing these writings with the nearly contemporary literature of the Pachomians, we immediately become aware of the grandeur and singular richness of the last, in spite of the poverty of it cultural setting.

The works of Basil and Augustine certainly lack neither teaching based on the Word of God and discreetly imbued with a high cultural level nor the ability to direct persons on their spiritual journey, nor a sensitivity to and experience of community life. To someone desirous of deepening the theory and practice of cenobitism, the nourishment they offer is far more palatable and succulent than the meagre fodder provided by the pachomian texts. But the uniqueness of Pachomianism, and the thing which gives it its incomparable force, is its faith in a person chosen by God, a person who draws the hope and love of thousands of hearts: 'Our holy Father Pachomius who first founded the *coenobia*'.

This cult of the founder does not appear, obviously, in his own works, apart from the titles of the four collections of rules in Jerome's version. But it springs up on nearly every page of the writings of his successors, Theodore and Horsiesios, and it inspired the great anonymous *Life of Pachomius* available to us in Coptic, Greek, and Arabic. These varied documents disclose the same intense veneration felt by the entire group, and by each member of it, for the man to whom they knew they owed everything.

In effect, it was Pachomius who assembled the *Koinonia* in God's name. It was he who gathered together all these souls to bring them to a knowledge of God and to salvation. They did not hesitate to call him the 'mediator of God and the saints', those saints of the Old and New Testaments with whom he was so often associated as an equal or a successor. Pachomian monks saw in him an authentic heir of the prophets and apostles, someone who had written with them a page worthy of the finest pages of salvation history. Even after his death, he remained their guide through the rules he had established in God's name for the salvation of souls. He was the intercessor who watched over the *Koinonia*, the Father around whom his sons would once more flock after their death, as they had gathered around him during their life together here.

The fact that this portrait of the saint took definite shape only after Pachomius' death, under his early successors, speaks for itself. The acute crisis which swept over the *Koinonia* five years after he died, the superiors' interests, the administrative concerns, doubtlessly all contributed to promote a cult essential to the group's survival. But the image of their saintly founder could not have been so prominent had it not been powerfully impressed upon the conscience of the community while Pachomius was still alive. Theodore and Horsiesios' efforts to develop this image imply a deeply-felt conviction shared by everyone.

For that matter, without this conviction, there would have been no crisis, not even any difficulties after Pachomius. The notion that the *Koinonia* was about to be shattered and dissolved, obedience rejected, rules abandoned or mitigated, would not have revolted the monks' consciences so, if they had not perceived these events as a destruction of the work for which the Father had suffered so greatly. If the *Koinonia* was to be maintained in its original vigor and fervor at all costs, this was because Pachomius had wanted it that way, and so it was God's will, manifested through him, for all time.

The most beautiful element in pachomian literature is this ardent veneration which fostered the unity of the *Koinonia*. This faith in the man of God engenders a human warmth which has no parallel in the other monastic circles mentioned above. Whether we read Basil's funeral eulogy, the Life of Augustine, or even that of Martin, we do not find this spirit of total interdependence between the monastic community and its founder. These three saintly monks were also bishops, and the first two were great teachers as well, while the third was a missionary who extended himself well beyond his own diocese. Within their vast ecclesiastical horizons, the communities of monks they founded or directed could occupy only a limited place. Their panegyrist or biographer was a friend, an admirer or at most a disciple, and could not be—as in the case of the pachomian hagiographer—an anonymous son immersed in the large filial community whose devotion and grief he gave voice to.

Pachomius, for his part, was simply the founder of the *Koinonia*, and nothing more. He belonged entirely to this work to which he had given his life. Reciprocally, the *Koinonia* knew that, after God, it owed him everything. As Theodore said one time, everything which gave the *Koinonia* its singular place in the monastic world, its originality, and its value, it had received from Pachomius. This awareness evoked in all hearts a deep feeling of gratitude and fidelity. There was a total mutuality between Pachomius and the *Koinonia*.

From this stems the uniquely moving nature of pachomian hagiography, especially conspicuous as it retraces in the appendix to the *Life of Pachomius*, the vicissitudes of the congregation under Horsiesios and Theodore. Theodore's tenderness toward the Father, echoed by the entire community and its scribes, gives these pages a charm which is missing in the otherwise valuable biographies of a Basil, an Augustine, or a Martin. We can make the same observations regarding the *Life of Antony* by Athanasius or Gregory's Life of Benedict. Neither the famous bishop of Alexandria nor the great pope of the sixth centry enjoyed this same relationship of son to father, of the member of a religious community to the founder who had conceived of it through God's inspiration and had given birth to it at the cost of personal suffering.

Moreover Antony, for his part, established no community, properly speaking. Gregory, who had other aims in mind, has left us completely ignorant of his relationship with Benedict. Eugippius, the biographer of Severin and the author of the *Lives of the Fathers of Jura* (and one of their sons) was in a better position to express the sentiments of a community towards its founder. Yet nothing in those estimable works can compare with the warmth of the pachomian writings.

Paradoxically, the gigantic pachomian monasteries were much more a family than the basilian fraternities which seem to have had the advantage of being more family-sized. But the pachomian *Koinonia* had a father capable of binding it together, one who radiated the grace of fatherhood to the superiors of each monastery and each house. The father image is not absent in the basilian texts, but neither is it dominant. Although they sometimes refer to the model when speaking of the local superior, there is no saintly personality which dominates and draws the whole group together. Neither Basil, who was a director more than a founder, nor—for quite different reasons—his master Eustathius, adopted this role.

As far as we know, the monks of Pontus and Cappadocia spoke, and thought, of no one as having revealed to them the way of pleasing God as did the brothers of Pachomius' *Koinonia*. The 'answers' given by Basil in his *Asceticon* impose themselves by their solid scriptural basis and the rigorous logic of their austere demands, but they were never considered inspired commandments in the sense that the pachomian rules were. These were seen not merely as conforming to the Scriptures but as similar to them because of the authority of the man of God who had promulgated them. The brotherhoods of Asia Minor never considered the keeping of their rules as an act of fidelity to a well-beloved Father and as a way of repaying him for his efforts and his pains by striving to observe what he had enjoined upon them so he could be happy and proud of his work before the Lord.

This way of conceiving of the observance of the rule, as Horsiesios preached it in his Testament, should be present in the modern reader's mind when he surveys the minute regulations in the *Praecepta, Instituta, Judicia,* and *Leges*. Given for the most part by Pachomius himself—according to the most recent critical studies—this legislation can seem terribly dry, niggling, and spiritless. Nevertheless the breath of the spirit is very much present in the pachomian observance. Without theorizing and reflecting, the rule sets up in a very realistic fashion a doctrine of personal renunciation and communal charity flowing out of the Gospel. In addition, these 'holy rules' were considered by everyone, including (it seems) their authors, as the expression of divine will authentically transmitted by his servant. The faith, gratitude, and filial veneration which 'Our Father Pachomius' inspired permeate the observance of the Rule with a warmth which is both human and religious.

To return to Basil: it is significant that this great witness to and theorist of early monasticism in his later years aspired to unifying the brotherhoods under his care. At the end of his *Long Rule 35*, where he was combating the attempts at secession which threatened some of his communities, he expressed as a kind of impossible dream the wish that 'many of the brotherhoods which are located in various places might be placed under a single authority to be exercised by capable men in the unity of the Spirit and the bond of peace'. This somewhat ineffectual desire eventually took more concrete shape in *Long Rule 54*, where Basil instituted periodic meetings of superiors. But this great bishop-monk had something in mind which undoubtedly went beyond the idea conveyed in these simple conferences. What he longed for, without having a clear concept of it, had been realized forty years earlier in Pachomius' group and was at the time still flourishing in the distant Thebaid under his third successor. Besides having the two annual meetings at Easter and in August, the *Koinonia* enjoyed daily a common direction, material as well as spiritual, which made it a splendid vision of peace and unity.

When Basil aspired to a common government for his brotherhoods, he was thinking of the primitive Church, where five thousand new converts were of one heart and mind, living together, holding everything in common under the single collegial authority of the Twelve. It was this same model to which the Pachomians looked. For them the *Koinonia* was the 'apostolic life', the Church of the Apostles reviving in their midst after several centuries. Among them, however, authority was personal rather than collegial. Pachomius and his successors alone exerted this authority in its fullness; the other members of their administration only participated in it to a degree or had some of it delegated to them. Rather than the model of the Twelve at Jerusalem, the unique position of the pachomian superior general recalls Paul's role in the churches he founded, where he alone was the father. Horsiesios, moreover, was referring to the pauline texts when he spoke of the 'tradition' and the 'deposit' which the *Koinonia* had been given by its founder.

This sacred legacy from the Father, embodied in the kind of life he had established, constituted the solid axis around which the *Koinonia* was built and maintained. We must never forget this fact when we quite rightly admire the fraternal spirit inherent in pachomian cenobitism. This fraternity proceeded from a paternity. By Pachomius himself at times accepted, at times rejected—in the complex manner of the New Testament—the title Father was,in any case, the one unanimously given him by his disciples. As such, the man continually engendered communion among those innumerable brothers. Again, from this point of view Pachomius' role is analogous to that of the Apostles as it is described in Acts. In the well-known summation which recalls the early days of the Church (Acts 2:42), 'communion' (*koinonia*) comes only after the 'teaching of the Apostles'. If the brothers of Tabennesi, like the new converts in Jerusalem, were united in a community of goods and feelings, this was because Pachomius, like the apostles, kept them united by the Word of God and by the example of a life in the Spirit.

Indeed, teaching held first place in Pachomius' quasi-apostolic mission. As surprising as this seems when we consider the feeble echoes and remnants of his preaching, this is what he and his sons considered his essential work. Pachomius was, before all else, a harbinger of the divine Word, a teacher, even an exegete. Characteristic, in this regard, is the story told of Theodore, his favorite disciple. What first attracted this young monk from Latopolis to Tabennesi was not the enticing image of the *Koinonia*, nor even the fame of its founder's virtues. It was simply an account of a scriptural explanation which Pachomius had given in a conference one evening. Pachomius' interpretation of the Epistle to the Hebrews, which holds Christ up as God made man and the christian people as the 'holy of holies' in the new covenant, seemed so new to Theodore, and so interesting that he left his own monastery to join the school of the unknown exegete whose conference he had heard about.

Later on, when Pachomius had appointed him to be the head at Tabennesi, Theodore would walk each evening the half hour's distance which separated this monastery from Phbow to hear the Father's teaching and to repeat it to his own monks. No constraint or flattery induced him to do this. Doubtless he had faith in the grace of the Father who spoke in God's name; but was he not also moved by a real spiritual hunger, drawn just as he had been that first day by Pachomius' words? After Pachomius' death, Theodore continued to repeat to his brothers everything he had heard from him.

Teaching was the primary task of the Fathers who succeeded him, as it had been for Pachomius himself. In the beginning, poor Horsiesios filled this role without distinction, offering in lieu of anything better the short parables that Pachomius had commended to him. But even then, as the Father, he had the mission and the grace of interpreting Scripture. When Theodore, still on the sidelines, was questioned in this area, he effaced himself and left the matter to Horsiesios, the rightful exegete. When Horsiesios' strength began to fail and he appointed Theodore as his colleague, Theodore threw himself into this ministry, 'nourishing' the brothers with biblical doctrine in the manner of Pachomius.

Thus the *Koinonia* of his sons unfolded in the grace which Pachomius had received and then transmitted to his successors. It was a grace unprecedented in early monasticism. The *Greek Life* does mention a certain Aotas who had tried something similar before Pachomius, but only to chronicle his failure. As for the contemporary communities which appeared on the margins of the pachomian exploit—many of them affiliated to it—though we scarcely know what elements in their constitutions and usages distinguished them from the *Koinonia*, we see clearly that a considerable gulf separated them from it in everyone's eyes. In his own cenobitic undertaking Pachomius seems to owe them nothing. All we can say is that in those first decades of fourth-century coptic monasticism, the idea of community was in the air.

However true it is that the foundation of the *coenobia* was a real beginning, its historic roots cannot for all that be overlooked. At the beginning was Pachomius, but he was a follower of Palamon, and Pachomius had been an anchorite with Palamon. Cenobitism was not born in the apostolic age, as Cassian would have us believe. It appeared three centuries later in the wake of anchoritism. Antony and the first hermits were not the products of ancient *coenobia* founded in apostolic times. Instead, it was they who preceded, stimulated and formed the early cenobitic fathers, especially Pachomius.

The *Koinonia's* anchoritic background as it is revealed in the *Life of Pachomius* is of great historical interest. Born some forty years before Pachomius, and dying ten years after him, Antony overshadows the entire life of the *coenobia's* founder. Or, to take a contrasting and truer image, we can say that it was in the light of the antonian experience that Pachomius, the disciple of Palamon, undertook his cenobitic task. And just as these two pioneers succeeded one another in their respective endeavors, so also did the biographer of the one precede, influence, and we might even say, stimulate the biographer of the other. The *Life of Antony* written by Athanasius was the model which the hagiographers of the *Koinonia* used, at Theodore's invitation, to write the *Life of Pachomius*.

Cenobitism, then, emerged from anchoritism. Has this significant fact been sufficiently highlighted and explained? Perhaps anchoritism had to open the way, drawing persons out of the world and from the Church which dwells in the world. Possibly these individual separations needed to precede and prepare for the formation of monastic communities, themselves separated from the churches while still united to them. In any case, the communitarian inspiration of the primitive Church as it is depicted in the opening chapters of Acts, did not immediately or of itself provoke the birth of cenobitism. It was in the train of the anchoritic exodus and it was among the anchorites themselves that cenobitism took shape, as if the extreme self-denial inherent in this form of asceticism served as a catalyst to the great collective renunciation of the *Koinonia*.

Pachomius' dependence on Palamon and on the anchoritic

movement should not, however, conceal the deeper and more personal roots of his undertaking. Long before he entered the school of the aged anchorite of Šeneset, Pachomius had wanted to serve humankind. This was his initial vocation at the very moment of his conversion, and the vision that followed his baptism revealed that divine grace, passing through his hands, would flow out onto the earth. In conformity with his original vow, the first three years of his christian life were spent serving the surrounding villages in every possible way. Only after this apprenticeship to charity did he embrace the monastic life, and his entire career as a founder demonstrated his persistent ineradicable desire to give humble physical service as well as spiritual direction.

Such a decided line of conduct reveals Pachomius' very personal charism, which preceded his monastic initiation and was preserved by it. From all the evidence, this initial orientation to the service of humankind lay at the origin of the *Koinonia*, a society in which Pachomius united the brothers to serve them himself and to teach them to serve one another. Before Palamon the anchorite, Pachomius had had another master whose unforgettable lesson provided the primary motivation for his entire work: the charity of the Christians at Thebes. Their generosity in helping strangers for the love of God became above all else the model for the *Koinonia*.

Yet, important though it was, this example did not sufficiently build the personality of the great founder. Another influence was necessary to prepare him for his mission. Simple social service left Pachomius disquieted and dissatisfied. Monasticism attracted him as a spiritual good which he could not do without and in his time this implied anchoritism, the only form of monasticism available. He became a disciple of Palamon. Fasting and vigils, reading and continual recitation of Scripture, prayer and the struggle against demons, humility and obedience to the elder—all this asceticism practised under the aged anchorite molded him for the work he was to undertake. Every detail and episode in the description of the time he spent with Palamon finds its counterpart in the history of Pachomius, the founder of the *Koinonia*.

Thus, pachomian cenobitism has two sources: the secular church and anchoritism; the charity of Christians at Thebes and the monastic *ascesis* of Palamon. The first provided the initial impulse; the second carried that thrust to its highest level as it passed from social service to the ministry of the Spirit. Without ever giving up his mission of serving his brothers in the most concrete possible manner, Pachomius assumed their spiritual direction both on the level of the community of which he was the organizer and master, and on the level of the individual souls over whom he watched in order to bring them one by one to salvation.

The originality of pachomian cenobitism over against eremetism has been pointed out more than once in the past thirty years, and with good reason. Perhaps there has been less frequent mention of everything Pachomius owed to Palamon: asceticism, the experience of spiritual kinship, orthodoxy, and—at the heart of eremetism—communion with the Church.

Asceticism. There is evidence on more than one page of Pachomius' story that he remained an extremely vigorous ascetic his entire life. No doubt, in the *Lives* there are also warnings addressed by him to those false ascetics who were proud or excessive, whether they were anchorites or cenobites. Doubtless again, his community rules were moderated because of, and for the benefit of, the brothers' great numbers. But the impressive austerity he practiced on his own was something other than individual eccentricity or the vestiges of his pre-communal way of life. The words 'cross', frequently found in pachomian texts, and 'martyr', which is applied to Pachomius himself, indicate well the height and spiritual depth of this self-denial.

Not only did his own personal renunciation reach an heroic degree, but the Father maintained that physical mortification was absolutely necessary for everyone. He suffered at times when he saw his sons not mortified enough and he was not even afraid to hurl challenges at them: let us remember his night vigil along the Nile, and the next one at Thmoušons. The image of a Pachomius who was 'awesome and sad', in contrast to the 'charm' of

Theodore, is not an invention of the *Greek Life* but a true reflection of the characters of the two men, the one formed in the hard school of Palamon the hermit and the other brought up from childhood in the milder life-style of the community.

In Pachomius' asceticism, however, bodily austerity did not count for everything, nor was it the principal element. The continual guard over one's thoughts, the battle against the suggestions of the enemy, the 'meditation'—or oral repetition—of Scriptures learned by heart, prayer so frequent it became incessant: these were the most important points. All of these Pachomius had learned from Palamon. And the simple fact of *learning* them from another provided the main lesson for him. From it he developed his idea of the role of the Father in the *Koinonia*. As a disciple of Palamon, Pachomius experienced with him the father-son relationship which he later lived out with innumerable monks in his monasteries. The humble and loving obedience which he had practised for seven years with the old anchorite was to become a universal pattern for all that disciplined multitude, beginning with the type of the disciple, the young, fervent, and well-beloved Theodore.

Ascesis and spiritual fatherhood: Besides these essential elements which were to find their place in the foundations of the *Koinonia*, Palamon bequeathed Pachomius a sound faith and ecclesial communion, values which were infinitely precious and without which cenobitism would never have found a place in the Church. The portrait of Theodore given in the *Ammon's Letter* draws our attention to this cardinal point. Orthodoxy did not go unchallenged in the christian setting in which Pachomius was baptized. The meletian schism, the marcionite error, and other heresies are mentioned by Ammon, and they naturally recall the gnostic writings recently discovered at Šeneset-Chenoboskion. All these sectarian movements lay across Pachomius' path and beckoned him from near or from afar. In selecting Palamon as his master, an ascetic from the larger church, he chose orthodoxy. This link of fidelity to the bishop of Alexandria he and his congregation maintained throughout the arian crisis.

This fact was of great importance for the Pachomians because it assured them of the two-fold nourishment of Scriptures and the Eucharist. The Word of God which they heard continually read in their Offices and explained in their conferences, which they repeated in unceasing 'meditation' during their work and their leisure time, that Word was provided and guaranteed by the authority of the Church. And in the body and blood of Christ they received the sign of communion in unity with the Church. As sons, they awaited this spiritual bread from the bishops and priests sent by her. In the light of this continual filial submission, the dispute at the Council of Latopolis, as grave as it was, represented only a passing blot and resulted in but a restricted breach. In theory and in fact, pachomian cenobitism was to be not a branch cut off from the Church, but its most beautiful blossom. Rather than forming one more sect, this community set apart was to be at the heart of the Church's communion.

Though he was marked by Palamon with several essential traits, the founder of the *Koinonia* reached pastoral maturity only through the painful experience of failure. The *First Sahidic Life* alone has preserved this poignant and singularly instructive account. It was only after four or five years of wasted effort at giving a monastic bent to the group of men whom he served that Pachomius discovered the necessity of having a compelling rule and an authority capable of imposing it. His own moral influence, his simple example of service and self-denial were not in themselves enough to spread his own spiritual fire. To the men gathered around him, he had not succeeded in communicating his religious spirit.

This unsuccessful attempt demonstrated that Pachomius was not called to be a spiritual father in the anchoritic mode, that is, through simple moral authority and personal influence. If he was to direct souls, to form monks, to accomplish his mission, his desire for self-effacement and service had to be coupled with a frank acknowledgement of his own role as legislator and master. The common rule, to which he first of all submitted himself, became the foundation of his authority while at the same time satisfying his personal need for humility. This instrument would provide the basis for his influence on others as well as his own abasement at the feet of all. This rule and the hierarchy it set up, and through which it was maintained, would establish a communal life-style, a society endowed with the structures of the Church in which the perfect *Koinonia* of apostolic days could be re-established.

So it was that Pachomius' work evolved from a failure through which he learned the social and ecclesial conditions of his vocation as a Father. In fact, the *Koinonia* always understood itself as a church, applying to itself all the biblical images of the Church. It knew itself to be, and wished to be, the 'body of Christ', the spiritual 'temple', the 'vine of saints', the 'people of God'. As we have already seen, its rule was a 'tradition' and 'deposit', its founder had been sent by God as had the Apostles. Its masters had the mission of 'governing the Church of God' like the presbyters of Ephesus, of 'pasturing the sheep' of Christ like Peter himself.

In union with the one Church and founded on its model, the pachomian *Koinonia* appeared at the precise moment when this Church was experiencing a change in its social status. This coincidence was surely not fortuitous, although it is not easy to interpret. According to the *Lives*, it was by decree of Constantine that Pachomius was mobilized, snatched from his family, and thrown on the pathway where he would meet Christ. Historians may raise their eyebrows, arguing that the mobilizing prince was not Constantine at all but his colleague Maximian. The fact remains that Constantine and Pachomius had something to do with one another. Converted within a few months of each other, they worked interdependently, in both opposing and complementary ways. Pachomius introduced a society into the Church; Constantine introduced the Church into society. The one put an end to martyrdom; the other instituted its continuation. At the moment when the first christian emperor was inaugurating a new era by opening the world to the Church and the Church to the world, the founder of the *coenobia* was establishing in Christianity a community withdrawn from the world, one by which was reproduced —as it never had been from the time of its birth—the Church of the Apostles.

It is worth noting that the beginnings of anchoritism coincide with the end of the persecutions, and the origins of cenobitism with the establishment of peace for the Church. How is one to interpret the relationship between these two phenomena? Was it a question of numbers—that cenobitism alone was capable of incorporating the great throngs, or the result of a relaxation, as if cenobitism became to anchoritism what the constantinian Church was to the Church of the martyrs? Or was it simply that it had become possible to found monastic societies that were publicly recognized or tolerated? Whatever the case, the Spirit of Christ raised up this *Koinonia* of renunciants at the heart of the Church just when the aspects of renunciation and communion were about to lose their lustre among a christian people who were becoming more and more identified with secular living.

The relationship between the pachomian movement and the Church of its day is not, however, to be limited to these analogies and distinctions. In an active manner, it incorporated itself into the great movement of conquest which carried forward the Christianity of its time. Pachomius himself was a pagan convert and his attainments proved that men born as pagans could, through the grace of Christ, reach the highest perfection. As a monk, he prayed for the whole Church, he asked God for the salvation of all men, he built a church for the poor of his area and personally read them the Scriptures in the liturgy. Each year at Easter, at the central monastery at Phbow all the catechumens who had entered the various pachomian communities were baptized.

Metanoia—conversion. This was the name given at the end of the century to the monastery founded by the pachomians near Alexandria. This foundation, made in response to Archbishop Theophilus' request, was situated on the site of the former pagan sanctuary of Canopus. Such a name gave appropriate expression to the double victory of the Church and of monasticism, allied for the kingdom of God, over Egypt's secular idolatry and pagan way of life.

Yet this note of exultation from a conquering people, so resounding in Athanasius' *Life of Antony*, is not the dominant tone of pachomian literature. On the contrary, the plaintive mood occurs more and more as one advances in the *Lives*. Pachomius' *Life* had already given more than one sinister prediction of the *Koinonia's* destiny after his death. With the serious crisis which occurred five years later under Horsiesios, with the mitigations which crept in towards the end of Theodore's leadership, those menaces became painful reality. The crisis was overcome by the accession of Theodore, of course, and long after his death the *Testament* of Horsiesios depicts a congregation which was, on the whole, peaceful and flourishing despite a constant struggle against various abuses. It is none the less true that the Pachomians were keenly aware of the fragility of their beautiful edifice. Conscious of the greatness of the *Koinonia*, they were even more cognizant of the inadequacies of their own human fraility. In their anguish, they turned unceasingly to divine aid, to the example of the Fathers and especially to the intercession of Apa Pachomius himself.

Were these first cenobites of Upper Egypt deceiving themselves as to the *Koinonia's* chances of survival and of death? Along with his distressing forebodings, we are told that their Father Pachomius had received promises of perpetuity for his work. These divine promises, like so many others, were realized in a mysterious and unexpected manner. The rules and traditions, organization and hierarchy, monasteries and congregation all disappeared, and the faint literary or institutional traces of Pachomianism left to the monastic world—particularly in the latin West—would of themselves constitute only a pitiable survival. But in truth, the *Koinonia* of the sons of Pachomius has not ceased to exist. It is found wherever brothers gather together in the love of Christ to live in total sharing, perfect charity, and the renunciation of self-will 'under a rule and a father'.

Adalbert de Vogüé
Abbaye de la Pierre-qui-Vire

Translated by Denyse Lavigne
Santa Rita Abbey

translator's preface

THE VARIOUS DOCUMENTS of pachomian cenobitism are well known to specialists through excellent critical editions. The Coptic texts were published by L.-T. Lefort, the Greek by F. Halkin, and the Latin by A. Boon. Other documents discovered more recently have been published by H. Quecke. In the absence of a critical edition of the Arabic Lives, those published by E. Amélineau can still be used.

A few good publications have stressed the importance of pachomian spirituality and several scientific studies have analyzed the complex technical problems raised by the interpretation of the sources. Various translations have also made these sources accessible to the French-speaking public. The Coptic *corpus* was translated by L.-T. Lefort, the *Pachomiana Latina* by the monks of Solesme and the First Greek Life by A.-J. Festugière. The Testament of Horsiesios (*Liber Orsiesii*) has also been translated into German and Spanish. But apart from a provisional translation of the First Greek Life published by the Scholars Press of the University of Montana, practically nothing of the wealth of pachomian literature has been available for the English-speaking readers until now. An English translation of the pachomian *corpus* was therefore long overdue.

More than that. There was also a great need to gather into a single publication a few dozen documents published in various scientific series or journals through the years, and to produce a homogenous translation of that *ensemble*. These sources have come down to us in different versions—Sahidic, Bohairic, Greek, Latin—each ancient translator adapting the terminology to his taste and to the customs of his time. And that diversity has sometimes been accentuated by modern translators. By taking the pachomian *corpus* as a whole and translating all the texts according to the same principles and—as much as possible—using a consistent terminology, we hope to help the readers to penetrate more deeply into the understanding of one of the richest and least known traditions of ancient monasticism.

None of our documents is a masterpiece of literature. The Greek Life is written in the language of the koinè and the *Pachomiana Latina* are not in Jerome's best Latin. The genius of the Coptic idiom is very different from that of our western languages. Since a good part of the message is conveyed through the style itself, we have tried to follow closely the original texts while making a readable English translation. And while aiming at clarity in our own text, we have maintained in the translation the occasional obscurities and ambiguities of the original, reserving our interpretation for the notes.

The terminology used for the various officers, the parts of the monastery, the community exercises, etc. varies largely from one source to another, and even within the same document. We have made every effort to translate each Coptic, Greek, or Latin term always by the same English word. And refusing the temptation to harmonize the terminology in order to help the reader, we chose to be consistent in respecting the inconsistency of the sources. The *Glossary* and the notes should permit the reader to understand in each case who is who and what is what.

To that rule we have made an exception, however. For each name of person or place we have adopted one single form, usually the one closest to the Coptic original. Many of these names have several forms, even in the same language. For example, we always call the fourth Pachomian foundation Thmoušons, (which is the Bohairic form), although we find in Sahidic: Tmounešons, Tmoušons and Tmounšons, and in Greek: Μόγχωσις, Μογχοσή, Μώνχωσις, Μουχονσίς, Μονχοσή, Μόνχωσις, Μούνχουσις, not to mention the Arabic, Syriac and Latin forms. We made an exception for the places having completely different names in Coptic and in Greek, like Šmin-Panopolis or Šeneset-Chenoboskion. For biblical names, we have followed the spelling of the Jerusalem Bible.

The spiritual life of the pachomian monks was constantly nourished by the Scriptures. This is reflected in their writings, which are often long series of biblical quotations. The text of the Scriptures they use is evidently closer to the Sahidic version of the Bible or to the Septuagint than to the Hebrew of the Old Testament or to the Greek of the New. They also quote freely, adapting the original text to the context. We have always translated the biblical quotations as they are in our documents. A very interesting study could be done of the utilization of the Scriptures by the Pachomians. To facilitate such a study, we have placed at the end of the third volume a very elaborate biblical index covering all the documents translated.

There are still many unsolved problems concerning the relationship between the various pachomian Lives, the interpretation of some documents and especially the chronology of Pachomius and Theodore's life. We have not attempted to solve all these problems, either in our Introduction or in our notes. We have simply tried to help the readers by offering them some information based on the present stage of research. For the questions of chronology and dates, we have relied largely on the well-documented studies of D. J. Chitty.

The manuscripts of some of our Coptic fragments are in a very poor state. In his critical editions Lefort has very carefully indicated with brackets the parts of the texts that he restored. We have translated the Coptic texts as they have been restored by the editor, without indicating in our translation all the words and sentences so restored, except in the cases where the restoration was extremely hypothetical. On the other hand, we have signaled with angular brackets (‹ ›), and justified in a note, each correction or addition made to the original text. The square brackets ([ ]) in our translation indicate the words we have introduced for the sake of clarity, the most frequent case being the substitution of a person's name for a personal pronoun. The abuse of personal pronouns is a characteristic of the Coptic language.

We have numbered the paragraphs of all the documents in order to facilitate their utilization. When a document had already been numbered by the editor we have respected that numbering, except for a few paragraphs in the Appendix to the Bohairic Life, where this has not been possible. We have also given a title to each paragraph. These titles are not adequate summaries of the content of the paragraphs. They are simply a tool meant to help the readers in consulting the sources, especially in finding a passage they may be looking for.

Our publication is divided into three volumes. The first is composed of the various versions of Pachomius' Life. The second is divided into two parts: a) a collection of historical documents related to the Life; b) the legislative texts of the pachomian community. The third volume contains a collection of writings (instructions, letters, etc.) by Pachomius, Theodore and Horsiesios.

The various documents forming the last third of the Bohairic Life (SBo 115 to the end) have been translated by Father Mark Sheridan of St Anselm's Abbey. We have re-arranged them into a continuous text and we have slightly edited the translation to bring it into harmony with the rest of the *corpus*. For Horsiesios' Testament (*Liber Orsiesii*), in our third volume, we have used a translation made by Father Philip Timko of St Procopius Abbey. We have retouched it for the sake of consistency with the other documents. In both cases we have added the notes. We are grateful to Father Mark and Father Philip for their co-operation, which has permitted us to concentrate our efforts on the other documents.

The translation of such a series of texts from various ancient languages into an idiom which was not my mother tongue was a challenge I could not have dared to face without the help of many friends. I am particularly indebted to Dr Rozanne Elder and Father Adalbert de Vogüé. Rozanne persuaded me to undertake that task in the first place, and she has never ceased to bolster my courage through her cheerful and constant attention to the slow progress of the work. She has also edited the entire manuscript for style and literacy in English. Father Adalbert has very charitably read the manuscript with great attention, and his several corrections and suggestions have allowed me to improve my translation in very many points. He has also agreed to write the foreword. His brotherly support was an encouragement to go on when the work seemed to be without end.

Thanks to the kindness of Mrs D. J. Chitty and of Father Kallistos Ware, I have been able to consult an English translation of the Greek documents (First Greek Life, *Paralipomena* and Bishop Ammon's Letter) made by the late Derwas J. Chitty. It was a very literal but extremely faithful translation that the great scholar had made for his personal usage and that was probably not meant for publication. It has been a very great help to me, especially in many passages that were particularly difficult.

Among the many other persons who have helped me in various ways and at different stages of the work are Father Frederic Daly of our Abbey at Mistassini, Sister Denyse Lavigne of Santa Rita Abbey, Brother John of Crawley Monastery, Father Jerome Ebracher and Father Martinus Cawley of Our Lady of Guadalupe Abbey. And I owe of course a last word of thanks to my brothers of Mistassini Abbey in Canada who supported me in this work as well as to my brothers of Divine Providence Community in Kumasi, Ghana, among whom I have realized it.

Armand Veilleux
Monk of Mistassini

Our manuscript was at the printers when we became aware of the publication of 'Une vie inédite de saint Pachôme,' by F. Halkin in *Analecta Bollandiana* 97 (1979) 5-55, 241-287. It is basically an abbreviated form of G^2 with a few additions from the H.L. and the Rule of Pachomius-A.V.

CRITICAL EDITIONS

of the texts translated in this volume

The Bohairic Life has been translated from:

L.-T. Lefort, *S. Pachomii vita bohairice scripta, CSCO 89.* Louvain, 1925; rpt. 1953.

The Sahidic Lives have been translated from:

L.-T. Lefort,*S. Pachomii vitae sahidice scriptae*, CSCO *99/100*. Louvain, 1933/34; rpt. 1952.

The First Greek Life has been translated from:

F. Halkin, *Sancti Pachomii Vitae Graecae, Subsidia hagiographica 19.* Brussels, 1932.

To restore a few passages missing in the Coptic documents, texts from the following sources have been used:

Vatican cod. arab. 172. L.-T. Lefort, 'Vies de S. Pachôme (Nouveaux fragments).' *Muséon* 49 (1936) 219-230.

L.-T. Lefort, 'Glanures pachômiennes,' *Muséon* 54 (1941) 111-138.

E. Amélineau, *Monuments pour servir à l'histoire de l'Egypte chrétienne au IVe siècle.—Histoire de Saint Pakhôme et de ses communautés. Documents coptes et arabe inédits, publiés et traduits par E. Amélineau, ADMG 17* T. II Paris, 1889.

A *lacuna* in the published text of G^1 has been filled with a complement from:

Athens, cod. gr. 1015.

INTRODUCTION

SHORTLY AFTER PACHOMIUS' death, his *Life* was written by brothers who had known him and had learned about the beginnings of the *Koinonia* through the accounts of Theodore and of the founder's other early disciples. Collections of his instructions to the brothers and various short narratives had probably been assembled even before then.

That *Life of Pachomius* was often copied, translated, rearranged and combined with other sources into various types of compilations. It has been transmitted to us in very many forms. Along with a few primitive Sahidic fragments, the main recensions of the *Life of Pachomius* that we presently know are the *Bohairic Life*, the *First Greek Life* and an unpublished *Arabic Life*.[1]

1. THE BOHAIRIC LIFE (SBo)

We owe our knowledge of the various Coptic recensions of the Life of Pachomius to the patient research and the scholarly publications of L.-T. Lefort. When he undertook to prepare a critical edition of all the Coptic pachomian fragments, he grappled with an almost impossible task. The fragments found in the East in the last century, belonging to several recensions and compilations, had unfortunately been scattered in several libraries around the world. At times bits of a single folio were preserved in different countries. Over a period of more than a quarter of a century Lefort patiently identified, classified, and published all this material.[2]

Before Lefort's publications, part of this material was known through the useful but unscientific edition by E. Amélineau of the *Bohairic Life*[3] and a few Sahidic fragments[4] belonging to the same recension. Some fragments were also known through the publications of Zoega[5] and W. E. Crum.[6] In 1925, Lefort produced a new critical edition of the *Bohairic Life*, and a Latin translation of the same appeared eleven years later.[7] In 1933-34 he published the critical edition of the *Sahidic Lives*.[8] A few other fragments found later were published in 1936 and 1941.[9] Finally, in 1943, a French translation of all the Coptic texts crowned an immense work undertaken in 1912.[10]

Sahidic, the Coptic dialect of Upper Egypt, was the idiom of Pachomius and his disciples. The *Coptic Life* of Pachomius was evidently written in that dialect. But it is in a translation into Bohairic, the Coptic dialect of the Delta, that the most popular and, as it were, 'standard' *Coptic Life* has been preserved in its most complete form. The *Bohairic Life* is in fact a translation—at times a little clumsy[11]—of the recension represented by the fragments S^4, S^5, and S^{14}. The *Arabic Life* at the Vatican (Av) is a good translation of the same *Sahidic Life*, and S^{3b}, S^6, and S^7 belong also to the same group, although some explanations will be necessary about these. To this whole group of documents, transmitting basically the same *Life*, we give the siglum SBo.

There are however notable differences between these documents. While S^7 and Av end with Pachomius' death, Bo and S^5 add a long *Appendix* covering the government of Theodore and Horsiesios. As for S^6 and S^{3b}, they contain only that *Appendix*. The present state of S^4 and S^{14} does not permit us to know at what point of the Life they stopped. It also remains uncertain whether that *Appendix* belonged to the original Life or was added at a later period.

There is a great affinity between that *Coptic Life* and the *First Greek Life* (G^1), and discussions have been going on for almost a century among scholars in order to determine which of them is the original. In other words, the question is: Was the first *Life of Pachomius* written in Coptic or in Greek? For Amélineau both the *Bohairic Life* and the *First Greek Life* were translations and abbreviations of an original, longer, *Sahidic Life*; but the Sahidic fragments he knew belonged, in fact, to the group SBo.[12] P. Ladeuze considered, on the contrary, that G^1 was the source of all the documents of pachomian hagiography.[13] L.-T. Lefort[14] and the Bollandists,[15] while stressing respectively the importance of the Coptic and the Greek *Lives*, have expressed more qualified views and have looked in the direction of a lost common source for all the *Lives* we know. More recently A.-J. Festugière has made a careful comparison of all the paragraphs of SBo and G^1.[16] His analysis confirms the view, now generally accepted, that, in their present state, neither can SBo be the source of G^1 nor G^1 be the source of SBo. They are two independent witnesses of a same tradition, each having its value and its weaknesses. But their affinity is such that they must have had a common written source. Whether that source was Coptic or Greek is still open to discussion.

SBo is longer than G^1. To complete its immediate source, it had recourse to other Coptic documents that are preserved, partially in Sahidic fragments, and more fully in an Arabic translation (Ag). We will analyze more fully the relationship between SBo, G^1 and that *Arabic Life* below.

Our translation is based on the Bohairic text. Nevertheless in many instances we had recourse to the Sahidic fragments and occasionally to the Arabic translation to correct mistakes of the Bohairic translator or to restore the text where the Bohairic manuscript has some *lacunae*. Each case is clearly indicated in our notes. For the first part of the *Life*, the restoration did not present real problems. But for the *Appendix*, where Bo is more fragmentary and the other witnesses less homogenous, we have been obliged to do a type of reconstruction that in some points remains hypothetical. We thought, however, that it was the best way to provide the reader with the integral content of that *Appen-*

dix. In that section, it has not always been feasible to respect the numbering of the fragments of S^5 by Lefort, and we have adopted the one used by J. Gribomont in an Italian translation of the *Bohairic Life* soon to be published. The following table shows how we have reconstructed that *Appendix*:

SBo 124-138	S^5, VS, p. 174-187	(S^5 118-132 in Lefort)
SBo 139-142a	S^6, VS, p. 268-280	(Cf. VC, p. 324-330)
SBo 142b-144a	Bo, VB, p. 155-158	(Bo 165-167 in Lefort)
SBo 144b-145a	S^6, VS, p. 278-280	(Cf. VC, p. 331-332)
SBo 145b-155a	S^5, VS, p. 189-197	(S^5 145-155 in Lefort)
SBo 155b-180a	(missing)	
SBo 180b-210a	Bo, VB, p. 159-215	(Bo 180-210 in Lefort)
SBo 210b	S^{3b}, VS, p. 302, B, 25-303, B, 14	(Cf. VC, p. 348, 6-25)

2. THE FIRST GREEK LIFE (G^1)

A critical edition of the Greek *Lives* of Pachomius, prepared by F. Halkin, was published by the Bollandists in 1932.[17] The most important piece of that *corpus* is the *First Greek Life* (G^1), on which all the other Greek *Lives* depend in various ways. It had been published for the first time by Papebroch in 1680, in the *Acta Sanctorum* (Tome III of May).

Halkin's edition is based on Ms. XI,9 of the *Biblioteca Laurentiana* of Florence (Ms. F.), which was copied in 1021 in the monastery of Apiro in Southern Italy, and had also been the basis of Papebroch's edition. Halkin used as well another manuscript, the MS *Ambrosianus* D 69 *sup*. (Ms.A.) of which only fragments are extant. The text of this manuscript slightly modifies the text of the *Florentinus* from a stylistic point of view, without altering its content. It can be used at times to correct wrong readings of the *Florentinus*. Unfortunately, Halkin was not able to make use of a third manuscript, the MS 1015 of the National Library of Athens (Ms. Ath.), the existence of which he discovered too late.[18] This manuscript, which also contains the *Paralipomena*, has an almost complete text of G^1 and is clearly related to the *Ambrosianus* of which it could be a copy.[19] Like the *Ambrosianus* it permits us to correct the *Florentinus* at times and especially to fill its gap of two folios in ¶¶ 31-33.

A Latin translation of G^1 can be found, along with the Greek text, in the *Acta Sanctorum*. A French translation was made by A.-J. Festugière in 1965[20], and an English one by A. N. Athanassakis published in 1975.[21]

Amélineau and Grützmacher[22] attached only a secondary importance to G^1, judging it inferior to all the Coptic and Arabic *Lives*. Against that radical position Ladeuze tried to demonstrate that G^1 was the primitive *Life* on which all the others, oriental or occidental, depended;[23] he was followed in this by Heussi.[24] More recently, the discussion was resumed by L.-T. Lefort[25] who stressed the weaknesses of G^1, and by D. J. Chitty, who showed its great qualities.[26]

In any case, as we have seen above, G^1 cannot be considered either as the source of SBo or as its translation. Both depend on some common written source which they complete and independently modify. G^1 has kept one important story, the painful account of the Synod of Latopolis, that we find in the *Arabic Life* but that all the witnesses of SBo have for obvious reasons suppressed.[27] In a few other cases G^1 has preserved its source better than SBo.[28] But in other cases it has summarized it to the point of being incomprehensible without recourse to the Coptic parallel.[29]

To complement his source, the author of G^1 had access to collections of stories about and instructions by Pachomius as well as to the Pachomian Rules.[30] All the clear allusions to the text of the Rules are indeed peculiar to G^1. Two passages of the *Life* imply that the last redactor of G^1 was writing after Athanasius' death (†373) and even after Horsiesios' death († after 387).[31] The language he uses in his additions betrays that he was not conversant with the traditional pachomian terminology and customs.[32]

In our translation we have followed Halkin's text. We have occasionally corrected it with a better reading from Ms. Ath. 1015, from which we have also translated the section corresponding to the gap of two folios in G[1] 31-33.

3. THE ARABIC LIFE OF GÖTTINGEN (Ag)

If we have good critical editions of the *Coptic Lives*, that is not the case for the *Arabic Lives*. The important *Life* of MS 116 of the Universitätsbibliothek Göttingen is yet unpublished.[33] However, the great Arabic compilation published by Amélineau (see below) contains an almost identical Life to which large sections of an Arabic translation of the *Third Greek Life* have been added. In the absence of a critical edition of Ag, we may use—although with prudence—the parallel text in Am:

Ag 5 Am 337-599 (except: 365,17-369,13; 373,15-380,9; 382,9-384-12)
Am 644-651

That *Arabic Life* has great affinities with SBo and G[1]. The Coptic form of the nouns of persons and places, as well as the structure of the sentences, leaves little doubt that it was translated from Coptic; it cannot therefore be a translation of G[1]. Could it be a translation from SBo? No, because although SBo and G[1] usually agree in their mode of relationship to Ag, there are cases where G[1] is closer to Ag than SBo.[34] In order to understand the relationship between Ag on the one hand and SBo-G[1] on the other, we must analyze the internal structure of Ag.

We can distinguish three sections in Ag. In the parallel text of Am, they correspond to the following pages:

A : pp. 337-386 (without the passages from G[3])
B : pp. 386-552
C : pp. 553-599; 644-651

If we consider the order of the paragraphs, we realize that in section A and C the order is very similar to that of SBo-G[1]. But the stories we find as a block in section B of Ag are scattered through all parts of SBo-G^1. In the hypothesis that Ag depends in some way on SBo-G^1, it is impossible to imagine any type of logic according to which all these stories would have been extracted from different parts of SBo-$G^1$and gathered here in one block. It is much more probable that someone revised the original order of Ag by distributing these stories through the *Life* according to chronological order, and that such an adaptation was the common source of SBo-G^1.

Now if we turn to the text or the content of the narratives, we find the same difference between the three sections of Ag. In sections A and C Ag translates a Coptic text very close to what must have been the common source of SBo-G^1. But in section B the correspondence is less strict. The divergence can usually be explained much more easily by assuming that the source of SBo-G^1 summarized and combined various stories of Ag, rather than the other way around.[35] In fact the *Arabic Life*, in this section, is a close translation of a Sahidic recension that has been partially preserved in the fragments S^{10}, S^{11}, and S^{20}.[36]

All this leads to the conclusion that two distinct documents have been merged in Ag. In fact, the sections A and C form a short and well-constructed *Life of Pachomius*. We learn about his youth, his conversion, his withdrawal to Šeneset, and his years of formation under Palamon's guidance. Then he settles in Tabennesi and the first disciples arrive. When their number grows he builds a church in the monastery having previously built the one in the village, and organizes the system of 'houses' in the community. Then Pachomius makes his eight other foundations and, after the painful incident of the Synod of Latopolis, commends his soul to the Lord. About Theodore we learn little: his vocation, his fault of ambition, and his long penance. In previous studies we have called that document the *Vita Brevis* (VBr).[37]

That *Vita Brevis* (VBr) was cut into two parts and a long series of stories forming section B was added to it. The author of these stories wanted to show that Pachomius and his disciple Theodore were men especially enlightened by God and gifted with clairvoyance, and that the brothers must have total faith in them. Theodore has a prominent place in this section. His obedience and faithfulness to Pachomius are stressed; his fault and his great penance are explained away. At the beginning of this section the compiler of Ag writes: 'We must begin the story of our father Theodore before we finish that of our father Pachomius. . . .' On the basis of that indication, and considering the prominent place held by Theodore in this document, we have called it a *Life of Theodore, Vita Theodori* (VTh), in our earlier studies.

The hypothesis that a *Life of Theodore* was one of the two sources of Ag has met with the opposition of some critics who could not see the possibility of a *Life of Theodore* in which Pachomius played no important role, and *vice versa*.[38] This argument is not without some strength and, in fact, the document from which this long section comes, and which corresponds to at least a large part of S[10], could as well be a larger version of the original *Life of Pachomius* or—more probably—a distinct collection of stories about Pachomius and Theodore. In any case, the important place given to Theodore in that document shows that it was written by Theodore's disciples. It often smells of an apology.

The publication of Ag along with a good translation would permit us to push the analysis further and to determine with more accuracy the nature of its sources. In the meantime we still use the siglum VTh although it may be partially inaccurate. And even if the hypothesis of an independent *Life of Theodore* may repose on too weak a foundation, a careful analysis of Ag and its relationship to SBo-G[1] permits us to maintain with a high degree of probability that: a) Ag combines two distinct documents; b) the order of the paragraphs of Ag and sometimes the stories themselves have been rearranged by a later compiler; c) this new version of the Coptic original of Ag has been the common source of SBo and G[1].[39]

4. OTHER COPTIC LIVES

A. *The First Sahidic Life.* We possess in a few fragments a Sahidic parchment manuscript from the sixth century through which we probably reach the most primitive pachomian tradition. Its accounts have a much more vivid and original flavour than the corresponding narratives in other recensions.[40] In particular, it tells us in detail Pachomius' first attempt at founding a community with the people who had come to live around him at Tabennesi, and his failure. Ag-SBo-G^1 have only vague, embarrassed allusions to that incident.

Only sixteen full pages and two half-pages of this valuable codex are extant. But the large compilation S^3 has integrated large sections of S^1 along with sections of SBo; and so it is possible to restore part of S^1 from fragments extant in S^3. Since S^3 does not seem to have had other sources than S^1 and SBo, the prologue that we find both in S^8 and S^3 comes probably also from S^1. What we translate in this volume under the title of *First Sahidic Life* (S^1) is the text of S^1 restored in the manner as given in Table 1 on the following page.

B. *The Second Sahidic Life*. The twenty odd pages that remain of S^2 are too few to permit us to situate it clearly in the pachomian *corpus*. Lefort considered it as one of the primitive documents, along with S^1,[41] but this is very doubtful. The character of S^2, fond of visions and miracles, is very different from that of S^1.

There is a long section in S^2 that corresponds to SBo. Lefort took for granted that S^2 was here the source of SBo. But what we know of the relationship between SBo and Ag makes us consider it much more probable that it is S^2 which has copied SBo. In fact, the exact parallel between S^2 and Av permits us to use it to restore the Coptic text of SBo 113-116. On the other hand, some points of affinity between S^2 and S^3 make us wonder whether S^2 borrowed directly from SBo or through the great compilation S^3. Or perhaps S^3 could have borrowed from SBo through S^2. The fragments of S^2 are too few to permit us to answer these questions.

In our translation of S^2 we have omitted the passages having an exact parallel in SBo.

The First Sahidic Life

From codex S[1]		From codex S[3]	
page of codex	edition	page of codex	edition
[1-3]	...	3-4	VS, 253,A, 12-254,B,36
...	...	...	...
[?]	...	37	VS, 102, A,1-30
...	...	...	...
[43-44]	...	41-42	VS, 106, B,25-107,B,23
45-48	VS, 1,1-2,21	42-44	VS, 107, B,23-109,B,1
48-51	VS, 2,21-3,24	...	...
51-53	VS, 3,25-4,23	65-66	VS, 112, B,25-113,B,23
53-59	VS, 4,24-7,14	[67-68]	...
59-60	VS, 7,14-28	69	VS, 114, A,1-34
[61-62]	...	69-70	VS, 114,A, 24-115,B,38
...	...	...	...
[?]	...	75-76	VS, 116-117
...	...	...	...
[?]	VS, 8-9	...	...
...	...	...	...
[?]	...	147-148	VS, 118-119
...	...	...	...
[?]	...	389-390	*Muséon* 1941, 113-115,A,15

Table 1

C. *The Tenth Sahidic Life*. This recension is represented by three fragmentary manuscripts (S^{10}, S^{11}, and S^{20}) which we may consider as one *Life*. If we except the first few folios of S^{10}, to which we have no parallel, everything that survives of that *Life* has its exact correspondent in the *Arabic Life* of Göttingen (Ag), and in the same order. Through the fragments that we possess, we can follow the correspondence between S^{10} and Ag–Am from Am 391 to 459 and in Am 552-553. It is probable that such a correspondence went from Am 386 to 553, that is, through the whole section B of Ag.[42]

Some of the stories of this recension have passed into SBo–G^{1} almost unchanged; others have been shortened or modified. In our translation of S^{10} we have selected only the passages that are either absent from SBo–G^{1} or are found there in a different form.

D. *Other Coptic fragments*. The *Third Sahidic Life* must have been the longest Coptic compilation. The thirty-odd pages that remain from that *codex* of some four hundred large pages show that the author integrated almost all the sections we know of S^{1} and much of SBo into his compilation. He may have used other sources as well, but everything that still exists of S^{3} seems to come either from S^{1} or SBo.[43] The interest of this *Life* lies in the fact that it always copies its sources faithfully, as we can verify whenever there is a parallel text. For example, in its borrowing from SBo, it is closer to the excellent *codex* S^{5} than to the Bohairic translation. It also has the story of $S^{5\,93}$, absent from Bo.

The *Eighth Sahidic Life* is the only Coptic *Life* of which we have the very beginning. But its prologue, inserted in S^{3}, probably comes from S^{1}. Apart from that it gives us only a short story that we find in a different form in SBo.

The other fragments published by Lefort (S^{1a},S^{9},S^{12},S^{19}) are too mutilated to deserve a translation or to permit an analysis. Nor have we translated the few other texts having a vague relationship with Pachomius or the Pachomians that Lefort published under the sigla S^{15}, S^{16}, S^{17}, S^{18}, and S^{21}.

5. OTHER GREEK LIVES

A. *The Second Greek Life* (G^2). This *Life* was by far the best known during the Middle Ages. The manuscript tradition is very rich[44] and many authors, like Paul Evergetinos, have borrowed from it.[45] Before the publication of Halkin's *Sancti Pachomii Vitae Graecae*,[46] this *Life* was found only in its Latin translation, made in the sixteenth century by Hervetius and published by Lippomano and Surius,[47] and in the German translation of H. Mertel.[48] Both these translations were made from the excellent codex Vat. 819 (Ms V), which was also used by Halkin as the basis of his edition. Hervetius' translation cannot be used without caution, for it contains a number of serious mistakes.

There is a close relationship between G^2 on the one hand and G^1 and the *Paralipomena*[49] on the other. That relationship has been the subject of some discussion. For Ladeuze, G^2 was a literary adaptation of G^1 which combined it with the *Paralipomena*.[50] But the Bollandists put forward the hypothesis that the author of G^2 might have been using a primitive *Greek Life* that did not contain the passages of G^1 that we do not find in G^2.[51] Chitty came back basically to Ladeuze's position and the conclusion that emerges from his careful comparison of the order of the two *Lives* is that the author of G^2 did indeed use a text of G^1 similar to the one we have and combined it with almost the whole of the *Paralipomena*, while leaving aside large sections of his main source.[52]

In any case, G^2 does not offer anything new to our knowledge of pachomian monasticism, since everything we read in it is already known either from G^1 or from the *Paralipomena*. Its language is purer than that of its sources and its style more pleasant, but its author, who was not a pachomian monk and probably not an Egyptian, manifests an ignorance of Egyptian geography and of pachomian terminology.

B. *The Greek Life translated into Latin by Denys* (*Den.*). The *Latin Life* of Pachomius must be mentioned in connection with the

Greek *corpus* because of its close relationship to G^2. It was translated by Denys (Dionysius Exiguus) at the beginning of the sixth century. An excellent critical edition was published by H. van Cranenburgh in 1969, with the Greek text of G^2 facing the Latin version.[53]. Before that publication, the only edition available was that published by Rosweydus in his *Vitae Patrum* and reproduced in Migne's *Patrologia Latina*.[54] There is also an old French translation made from that edition by Arnauld D'Andilly during the seventeenth century.[55]

Was Den. translated from G^2 or was the Greek original of Den. the source of G^2? This is another point that has been discussed among specialists for almost a century. Ladeuze considered Den. an abbreviation of G^2.[56] Nau on the contrary, saw in G^2 a new edition of Den., with a few modifications and many additions.[57] Following Nau, Lefort, too, wanted to see in the lost original of Den. not only the source of G^2 but probably the most ancient *Greek Life* of Pachomius.[58] After a careful comparison of G^1, G^2, and Den., Chitty arrived at the conclusion that Den. is probably a translation of G^2, and his arguments seem very convincing.[59] In the introduction to his critical edition, van Cranenburgh analyzes the arguments for each position and, without arriving at a definitive solution, inclines toward a priority of Den. over G^2, pending a more detailed philological study of the Greek and Latin texts.[60] We find some difficulty in accepting that conclusion when we consider as a whole the relationship between G^1, G^2, and Den. From beginning to end, G^2 follows faithfully the order of G^1 in all the paragraphs it has in common with it; and the middle section of G^2 (39b-58a) without correspondent in Den. does not interrupt that fidelity to the order of G^1. It is easy enough to understand Den. abbreviating G^2 by leaving aside a whole section of its source (although some other difficulties remain to be explained); but it is quite difficult to imagine that the author of G^2, using Den. as his source, would in his additions to Den. have kept the order of the stories taken from G^1, while mixing them with stories from the *Paralipomena* and respecting the order of these as well.

In any case, whether G^2 depends on Den. or Den. on G^2, both of them are compilations from which we learn nothing that we did not already know from G^1 and the *Paralipomena*.

C. *The last five Greek Lives* (*G*^{3},*G*^{4},*G*^{5},*G*^{6},*G*^{7}). All the other Greek *Lives* are late compilations without real importance to the knowledge of pachomian monasticism. Let a few words suffice about them.

G^3 and G^4 were practically unknown before the publication of Halkin's *Sancti Pachomii Vitae Graecae*. G^6 was published by F. Nau in 1907 in the *Patrologie Orientale* with a French translation of the Syriac version of the *Paralipomena* facing the Greek text.[61] In the same publication we find a few fragments of G^5.[62] Halkin published G^3 according to the only known manuscript, no. 9 of the monastery of St John at Patmos (Ms.P.). But since G^3 copies G^1 almost without change in many of its passages, Halkin did not publish those passages separately but simply indicated the readings of the Patmos MS. in the critical apparatus of G^1. Of G^4, published by Halkin, a few chapters were already known through a German translation made by H. Mertel.[63] Since G^5 is nothing else than the juxtaposition of the first two-thirds of G^4 and the last three-quarters of G^3, Halkin simply indicated its variants in the critical apparatus of G^3 and G^5. Although the edition of G^6 by Nau was not entirely satisfactory, Halkin did not make a new one. Finally, we give the siglum G^7 to the short *Life of Pachomius* published in 1978 by Halkin and which is simply an abbreviation of G^2.[64]

The author of G^3 had a complete copy of the pachomian *corpus* and he tried to do a complete work himself. He must have had a document similar to the *Atheniensis*, where he could find G^1 and the *Paralipomena*. He also had access to extracts from Palladius' *Lausiac History*. But since he inserts his borrowings from Palladius at the places where Den. does in his . . 21 , 25 and 28, we may suppose with Lefort that he had also under his eyes the Greek *Life* translated by Den., and this is confirmed by the presence in G^3 of important variants of G^2-Den. Finally the compiler added three other stories that we also find in the *Apophthegmata*, from which he probably took them. He was not very familiar with pachomian monasticism, as is proved by his borrowings from the *Lausiac History* and the fact that he assumed Pachomius was a priest. One interesting thing about this *Life* is that it was translated in Arabic. From a stylistic point of view, G^4 is the most polished of these *Lives*. The author knows well the rules of the hagiographic genre and of the Greek language, but he falls easily into affectedness. Halkin thinks that he can recognize in his translation the methods of Symeon the Metaphrast. In any case, he was not a pachomian monk. His two sources were G^1 and the Palladian chronicle.

The author of G^5, without being as good a stylist as the writer of G^4, has the same literary preoccupations. For the part of his *Life* that he borrows from G^4, the work of a purist, he simply transcribes his model with only a few minor modifications. But in the part that comes from G^3, the Greek of which is not particularly elegant, he constantly corrects his model and even recasts almost all the sentences, not without introducing a few unfortunate modifications.

The strangest and least important of the compilations, G^6, is the simple juxtaposition of the following disparate pieces: a few chapters borrowed from the *Lausiac History,* including the Rule of the Angel; almost all the stories of the *Paralipomena,* according to the textual tradition of the Syriac-*Atheniensis* group, but without the peculiarities of G^2; and finally another series of stories from the second part of G^2.

As for G^7, we have already mentioned that it is only a *résumé* of G^2.

In conclusion, all the Greek *Lives* of Pachomius can be reduced to two basic documents: The *First Greek Life* and the *Paralipomena*. We give the translation of the *First Greek Life* in the present volume. The introduction to the *Paralipomena* and their translation will be found in our second volume.

6. OTHER ARABIC LIVES

Although the Arabic *corpus* is much less well known than the Coptic and the Greek ones, we can divide the Arabic *Lives* into three categories.

A. *Translation from Coptic.* Apart from Ag, which we have studied above, the other manuscript of this category is the Arabic codex no. 172 of the Vatican Library (Av).[65] We have already mentioned that it is a faithful translation of a *Sahidic Life* of the group SBo, and for a short section (SBo 111-112) it is our only witness of that recension.

B. *Translation from Greek.* There are many manuscripts in this category. The most important one is MS 261 of the Bibliothèque Nationale in Paris (Ap).[66] An edition published in Cairo in 1891 by a monk of the monastery of al-Baramūs was probably based on a very similar manuscript.[67] The Greek text that served for these Arabic translations was that of the *Third Greek Life*.

C. *Arabic compilations.* All the manuscripts of this category are modern and the problems of textual criticism they pose remain obscure. They are MSS 4783 and 4784 of the B.N. in Paris, respectively of 1886 and 1834, and MS Or. 4523 of the British Museum, published by Amélineau with a French translation.[68] This is a copy made in 1816 of an original from the monastery of St Antony.

As we mentioned above, this compilation integrates an Arabic Life identical to that of Göttingen (Ag), translated from the Coptic, and a large section of an Arabic translation of G^3. Further studies will tell us whether the compiler translated that section directly from the Greek text or used one of the existing translations, like Ap or Ac.

Current research in the rich treasury of Arabic manuscripts in western and eastern libraries will perhaps give us new pachomian documents.[69]

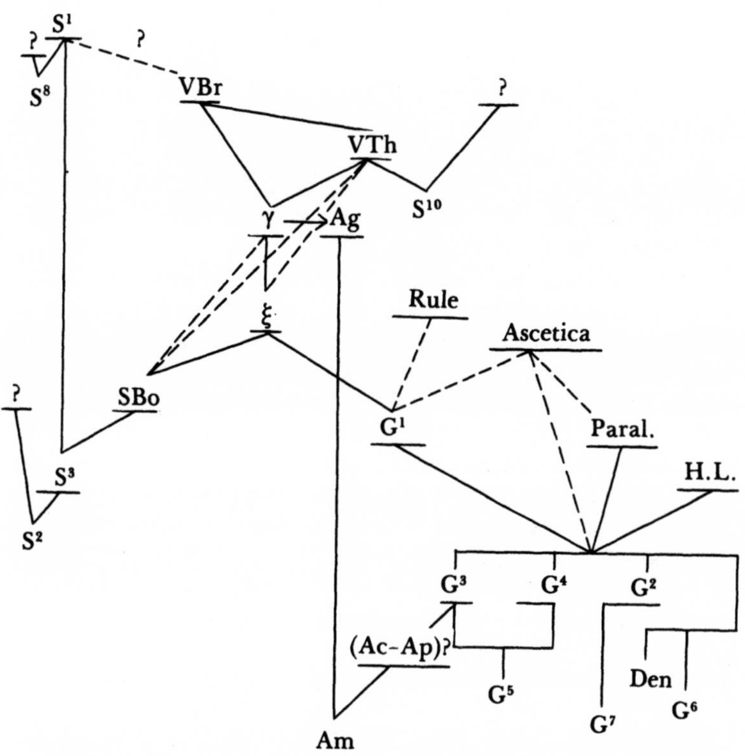

7. GENEALOGICAL TABLE OF THE LIVES OF PACHOMIUS

a) Very early, during Theodore's superiorship or immediately afterwards, a first *Life of Pachomius* was written, probably by compiling already existing collections of stories and instructions. Our fragmentary S^1, of all the texts we knows is certainly the closest to that source. S^8 has copied the prologue of S^1, but has also used other sources.

b) To the *Coptic Life* translated in Arabic in the MS of Göttingen, we give the siglum γ. We consider that the author of that *Life* used two sources, one of which was a short primitive *Life of Pachomius* (VBr) and another document, in which Theodore held a prominent place (VTh), that forms most of what we possess of S^{10}, which used also other sources.

c) A compiler made an adaptation of γ, rearranging the order of the paragraphs, merging some of the stories and shortening others. The result of that adaptation (ξ) was the common source of SBo and G^1. SBo completed its immediate source by reintroducing some of the stories either from γ or from VTh. G^1 completed its immediate source by borrowing from the Rules and from collections of narratives and instructions (*Ascetica*).

d) On the Coptic side, S^3 is a combination of S^1 and SBo; S^2, as far as we can see is a combination of texts from SBo, probably through S^3, and of other source(s).

e) On the Greek side, all the other *Lives* are rearrangements of G^1 combined with other texts from the *Paralipomena*, the *Lausiac History* and collections of *Ascetica*.

f) The *Third Greek Life* was translated into Arabic. The Arabic compilation published by Amélineau is a combination of the text of Ag (a translation of the Coptic model γ) and of part of G^3 translated into Arabic, probably borrowed from a *Life* of the type Ac and Ap.

The two great *Lives* and the few fragments that we translate in this volume are really at the heart of all the pachomian hagiography. Was the first *Life of Pachomius* written in Coptic or in Greek? Perhaps it is not possible to answer such a question. But one thing is clear: both SBo and G^1 depend on documents we know through an Arabic translation from Coptic and through Sahidic fragments, and of which no trace of a Greek version is extant.

NOTES

[1]For a more elaborate description of all the pachomian sources, see the general introduction of our book: *La Liturgie dans le cénobitisme pachômien au quatrième siècle*, Studia Anselmiana 57 (1968) pp. 1-159. In the shorter presentation that follows here we have modified our positions on a few points, taking into account the various studies of the last decade.

[2]On the magnitude of Lefort's contribution, see the issue of *Le Muséon* dedicated to him in 1946; especially the article of P. Peeters, 'L'édition critique des Vies coptes de s. Pacôme par le Prof. Lefort', pp.17-34, and that of J. Vergote, 'L'oeuvre de L.-T. Lefort', pp. 41-62.

[3]E. Amélineau, *Histoire de Saint Pakhôme et de ses communautés. Documents coptes et arabe inédits...*, *ADMG* 17 (Paris, 1889) I: 1-334. The *Bohairic Life* was then called the '*Memphitic' Life*.

[4]E. Amélineau, *Monuments pour servir à l'histoire de l'Egypte chrétienne aux IVe, Ve, VIe et VIIe siècles, MMFA* 4 (Paris, 1895). The *Sahidic Life* was then called the '*Theban' Life*.

[5]Cf. *Bibliotheca Hagiographica Orientalis*, no. 825-827.

[6]W. E. Crum, *Catalogue of the Coptic Manuscripts in the British Museum* (1905); and *Theological Texts from Coptic Papyri*, (Oxford, 1913).

[7]L.-T. Lefort, *S. Pachomii vita bohairice scripta*, *CSCO 89* (Louvain, 1925); Translation in *CSCO* 107 (Louvain, 1936).

[8]L.-T. Lefort, *S. Pachomii vitae sahidice scriptae, CSCO* 99/100 (Louvain, 1933/34).

[9]L.-T. Lefort, 'Vies de S. Pachôme (Nouveaux fragments)', *Muséon* 49 (1936) 219-230; and 'Glanures pachômiennes', *Muséon* 54 (1941) 111-138.

[10]L.-T. Lefort, *Les Vies coptes de saint Pachôme et de ses premiers successeurs, Bibliothèque du Muséon* 16 (Louvain, 1943; rpt.1966). Parts of these Coptic texts were also translated into French by R. Draguët in *Les Pères du désert*, (Paris, 1949) 87-126.

[11]Cf. L.-T. Lefort, 'Littérature bohairique', in *Muséon* 44 (1931) 115-135.

[12]E. Amélineau, *Monuments*, Introduction.

[13]P. Ladeuze, *Etude sur le cénobitisme pakhômien* 45-51.

[14]L.-T. Lefort, *Les Vies coptes*, p. LXXX.

[15]See the Introduction of F. Halkin, *Sancti Pachomii Vitae graecae*.

[16]See the Introduction to *La première Vie grecque*. This comparison is weakened, however, by Festugière's failure to realize that a large part of Amélineau's *Arabic Life* is a translation of G^3, and not an independent document.

[17]*Sancti Pachomii Vitae graecae. Ediderunt Hagiographi Bollandiani ex recensione Francisci Halkin, Subsidia Hagiographica* 19 (Brussels, 1932).

[18]This manuscript is yet unpublished; we have used a microfilm copy kindly sent to us by the *Centre National de la Recherche Scientifique* in Paris. A few indications about it can be found in Lefort's review of Halkin's edition in RHE 29 (1933) 424-428. See also A. Ehrhard, *Überlieferung und Bestand der hagiographischen und homiletischen Literatur der griechischen Kirche* III, *TU* 52 (Leipzig, 1952) 903-904. The manuscript is not complete: the first three folios are missing; and the pagination, which is modern, did not take into account the absence of other folios between fol. 9 and 10, between fol. 20 and 21 and between fol. 37 and 38.

[19]For the relationship of the *Ambrosianus* to the *Florentinus*, see Halkin, *Sancti Pachomii Vitae graecae*, pp. 12*-17*.

[20]A.-J. Festugière, *Les Moines d'Orient*, IV/2: *La première Vie grecque de saint Pachôme. Introduction critique et traduction* (Paris, 1965).

[21]A.N. Athanassakis, *The Life of Pachomius* (*Vita Prima Graeca*). *Translated by Apostolos N. Athanassakis. Introduction by Birger A. Pearson.* (Missoula, Montana, 1925).

[22]O. Grützmacher, *Pachomios und das älteste Klosterleben*, (Fribourg, 1896).

[23]P. Ladeuze, *Etude sur le cénobitisme pakhômien* 4-73.

[24]K. Heussi, *Der Ursprung des Mönchtums* (Tübingen, 1936) 115-131.

[25]In his introduction to *Les Vies coptes*, pp. XXXVIII-L.

[26]D.J. Chitty, 'Pachomian Sources Reconsidered', *JEH* 5 (1954) 38-77; *Idem*, 'Some Notes, mainly Lexical on the Sources for the Life of Pachomius', in *Studia Patristica* V, *TU* 80 (Berlin, 1962) 266-269. See Lefort's answer to the first article, in L.-T. Lefort, 'Les sources coptes pachômiennes', *Muséon* 67 (1954) 217-229.

[27]G[1] 112; see SBo 96, note 3.

[28]V.g. G[1]; see SBo 113, with note 1.

[29]V.G. G[1] 28 (note 2); see SBo 26 with note 2. G[1] 29 (note 3); see SBo 25. G[1] 116 (note 2); see SBo 122.

[30]G[1] 99 and 142 seem to refer to such collections of stories and instructions; see SBo, note 2. For dependence on the Rules, see G[1] 58-59.

[31]See G[1] 94 with (note 2) and G[1] 149 (end).

[32]See G[1] 54 (note 2); G[1] 77 (note 2); G[1] 134 (note 2).

[33]See a few brief notes about that manuscript in W. E. Crum, *Theological Texts*, p. 176 and L.-T. Lefort, *Les Vies coptes*, pp. XVI-XVII.

[34]For example G[1] 86 and G[1] 96a-97 correspond to two distinct stories of Ag (Am 440, 19-442, 10 and Am 471, 6-17) that SBo 72 has merged into one.

[35]V.g. SBo[75] (= G[1] 92) combining Am 454,3-14 and 455,14-458,8; also SBo 79 combining Am 458.9-459,13 and 449, 10-15.

[36]Through the few fragments of S[10] and S[20] that we have, we can follow the correspondence between that Sahidic recension and Ag from Am 391 to Am 553; see table in A. Veilleux, *La liturgie*, p.60.

[37]See A. Veilleux, 'Le problème des Vies de Saint Pachôme', *RAM* 42 (1966) 293; *Idem*, *La Liturgie*, 61-63.

[38]See D. J. Chitty, 'Pachomian Sources Once More', in *Studia Patristica X* (1970) 56; A. de Vogüé, 'La Vie arabe de saint Pachôme et ses deux sources présumées', *AnBoll* 91 (1973) 380-390. But Chitty had not read our demonstration in *La liturgie*. . . at the time he wrote his article, and de Vogüé analyzed only one part of our argumentation.

[39]Nobody has been able to propose any other explanation of the nature of the relationship between Ag and SBo-G[1].

[40]See L.-T. Lefort, *Les Vies coptes* p. LXXII; and 'Les sources coptes pachômiennes', *Muséon* 67 (1954) 217-229.

[41]See *Les Vies coptes*, p. LXXIII.

[42]See A. Veilleux, *La liturgie*, 59-61.

[43]*Ibidem*, 43-47.

[44]See Halkin, *Sancti Pachomii vitae graecae*, 45*-55*.

[45]*Ibidem*, p. 45*, note 6.

[46]Pp. 166-271.

[47]*De Prob. SS. Vit.*, III.

[48]H. Mertel, *Leben des hl. Pachomius*, *BKV* 31 (Kempten, 1917) 779-900.

[49]The *Paralipomena* are a collection of pachomian stories much used by the compilers of the late Greek lives. For an introduction to, and a translation of, that document see Volume II.

[50]P. Ladeuze, *Etude sur le cénobitisme pakhômien*, 16.

[51]F. Halkin, *Sancti Pachomii vitae graecae*, 97*-99*.

[52]D. J. Chitty, 'Pachomian Sources Reconsidered', 55-65.

[53]H. van Cranenburgh, La vie latine de saint Pachôme traduite du grec par Denis le Petit, édition critique, *Subsidia hagiographica* 46 (Brussels, 1969).

[54]H. Rosweydus, *Vitae Patrum* (Antwerp, 1615; Lyon 1617[2]; Antwerp 1628[3]. In the edition of 1618, the *Vita Pachomii* is found on pp. 111-138.

[55]Arnaud d'Andilly, *Les Vies des Saints Pères des Déserts* (Lyon, 1663) 175-276.

[56]P. Ladeuze, *Etude sur le cénobitisme pakhômien*, 6-13.

[57]J. Bousquet and F. Nau, *Histoire de saint Pacôme*, 416-418.

[58]L.-T. Lefort, *Les Vies coptes*, pp. XXVII-XXXVIII.

[59]D. J. Chitty, 'Pachomian Sources Reconsidered', 55-65, especially p. 59.

[60]H. van Cranenburgh seems not to have known Chitty's study.

[61]J. Bousquet and F. Nau, *Histoire de saint Pacôme, PO - IV, 5* (Paris, 1907) 425-503.

[62]*Ibidem*, pp. 504-511.

[63]*Leben*, cited above in note 48.

[64]F. Halkin, 'La vie abrégée de saint Pachôme dans le ménologe impérial (BHG 141b'. *AnBoll* 99 (1978) 367-381.

[65]This manuscript was described by W. E. Crum, *Theological Texts*, 177-183.

[66]See Crum, 173-174.

[67]See Crum, 174-176 and in *ZDMG* 68 (1914): 181-182; see also H. Coussen in *Festschrift Eduard Sachau* (Berlin, 1915) 53-61, and more recently K. Samir, 'Témoins arabes de la catéchèse de Pachôme...', p. 505, note 2.

[68]E. Amélineau, *Monuments pour servir à l'histoire de l'Egypte chrétienne au IVe siècle...* (Paris, 1889). Arabic text with French translation, pp. 337-711. About the manuscripts used by Amélineau, see Crum, *Theological texts,* 176-177.

[69]A.S. Atiya, *The Arabic Manuscripts of Mount Sinai*, (Baltimore, 1955), mentions four manuscripts connected with Saint Pachomius (No. 356, 411, 536, and 541). A few years ago Mgr. J.-M. Sauget of the Vatican Library informed us of the presence of pachomian stories in the Arabic *Paterika* of which he was preparing an edition; some of these stories corresponded to our fragments of S^1.

the life of our father pachomius

the Bohairic Life
(SBo)

THE WORD OF GOD, who made all things, came to our father Abraham and ordered him to sacrifice his only son.[1] He said to him, *I will shower blessings on you, I will make your descendants as many as the stars of heaven; all the nations of the earth shall be blessed in your seed.* After our father Abraham, he spoke to Moses, his prophet and servant, and to all the prophets; then he appeared and spoke as man and as the seed of Abraham, for he had promised to him a blessing for the nations, and he commanded his disciples, *Go and teach all the nations, baptizing them in the name of the Father and of the Son and of the Holy Spirit.* *G[1] 1.* **Prologue** Gn 22:17-18. Mt 28:19.

Then, as his Gospel spread throughout the whole world, by God's permission and to put faith in Him to the test, pagan emperors stirred up a persecution against Christians everywhere. Many martyrs, offered themselves to various tortures unto death and received the crown, the last of them being the courageous Peter, patriarch of Alexandria. Then faith increased greatly in the holy Churches in every land, and † 24 Nov. 311.

monasteries and places for ascetics began to appear, for those who were the first monks had seen the endurance of the martyrs.[2] Therefore they revived the conduct of the prophet Elijah and of those of whom the apostle Paul said, *They were afflicted, maltreated; they wandered over deserts*
Heb 11:37-38. *and mountains, in caves and ravines of the earth.*
Then they offered their souls and bodies to God in strict *ascesis* and with a befitting reverence, not only because they looked day and night to the holy Cross, but also because they saw the martyrs take up their struggles. They saw them and imitated them.

G[1] 2a. **Beginning of monasticism** 2. [1]Such was the virtuous life of our holy father
Apa Antony, like that of the great Elijah, of Elisha, and of John the Baptist. We heard that of this kind was also the life of our holy father Apa Amoun, father of the brothers living on the Mountain of Pernouč, and of Theodore his faithful disciple.[2] We know that because *instead*
*Is 35:10;50:11. *of sorrow and lamentation** *grace has poured*
†Ps 45(44):2. *forth from the lips of*† the blessed one who
‡Eph. 1:3. blesses‡ all—for *he visited the earth** and made it
*Ps 65(64):9. drunk—admirable fathers of monks existed in
every land, as we have said earlier, whose *names*
Ph 4:3. *are written in the book of life.*[3]

In Egypt and the Thebaid there had not been many of them. It was only after the persecution
AD 284-305 under Diocletian and Maximian† that the con-
†305-306. version of the pagans increased in the Church.
With the bishops leading them to God according to the teaching of the Apostles, they brought forth virtues, fruits of the Holy Spirit, and they became lovers of Christ.

3. There was a certain Pachomius in the diocese of Sne.[1] Born of pagan parents, he received from the great mercy of God the grace to become a Christian in the diocese of Diospolis, in a village called Šeneset.[2] It appeared that through his progress he became a perfect monk. We ought therefore to recount all the details of his life from childhood for the glory of God who from all sides *calls* all men *from darkness into his wonderful light.*

G[1] 2b.
c. AD 292.
Pachomius' birth and call

1 P 2:9.

4. As a child his parents took him with them somewhere on the river to sacrifice to those [creatures] that are in the waters. When those [creatures] raised their eyes in the water, they saw the boy, took fright and fled away. Then the one who was presiding over the sacrifice shouted, 'Chase the enemy of the gods out of here, so that they will cease to be angry with us, for because of him they do not come up'.[1] At once his parents reproached him, 'Why are the gods angry with you?' The boy sighed after God and went away home. Another day they brought him with them to the temple, where they were going to offer a sacrifice. After the sacrifice they gave him a drink of the wine they had poured out for the demons. But at once he vomited it out vigorously. And his parents were distressed about him, because their gods were hostile to him.

G[1] 3a.
Pachomius' childhood

5. Still another day, his parents gave him a cauldron of antelope meat to take to the laborers working somewhere. As he went along the road the devil set on him a crowd of demons under the form of dogs bent on killing him. But the boy raised his eyes to heaven and wept. At once they scattered. Right away then the devil assumed the

Other story from Pachomius' childhood

form of an old man and told him, 'If you are so bothered on the way, it is because you are disobedient to your parents'. The boy blew his breath into his face, and at once he disappeared. Coming to the place where he had been sent,[1] he gave the cauldron of meat to the laborers. And he had to sleep in that place that evening. The owner of the place had two very pretty daughters, and one of them took hold of him saying, 'Sleep with me'. But he was horrified because he hated that, considering it an impurity and a wicked sin before God and men. He said to her, 'Let me not commit that impure act! Have I a dog's eyes that I should go and sleep with my sister?' So God saved him from her hands. Then he fled, running away to his home.[2]

G[1] 3b.

How the demons do not know the future

6. After he became a monk, he recounted these things to the brothers so that they too would be on their guard. And concerning the interpretation of this story, he told them, 'Do not think that the demons, who do not know the good, had me driven out of that place because they knew beforehand that I was later going to receive mercy by the true faith. Rather they saw that I hated evil even then—for *God made man upright.*[1] And it was for this reason that they moved their servants to chase me out of that place. Just as anyone will say about a field that has been cleared, "Probably the field that has been cleared of all darnel is going to be sown with good seed."'[2]

Qo 7:29(30).

G[1] 4,5a.

Pachomius, made a conscript, meets Christians for the first time

7. A little later, after the persecution, the great Constantine became emperor; he was the first Christian among the roman emperors. And he had not been reigning long when a tyrant of the Persians attacked him, wishing to take the empire

away from him.[1] At once he sent orders throughout his whole empire to induct big and sturdy conscripts to go to war against the enemy of God. The potentates of the palace, dispatched to all countries with the imperial decree, recruited sturdy [conscripts] in cities and villages. Young Pachomius, who was then twenty years old, was also recruited. Although he was not too sturdy, they took him in with the others because of the great number they recruited. c. AD 312.

As he was led away to the boat with his companions, he raised his eyes to heaven and sighed, saying, 'My Lord Jesus, *may your will be done*!'[2] They got on board and [the boat] sailed north with them. When they arrived at Ne,[3] capital of the ancient empire, the men were brought into the city and thrown into prison. In the evening, some citizens of that city brought bread and victuals to the prison, and they compelled the recruits to eat, because they saw them sunk in great affliction. When young Pachomius saw them, he asked the men who were with him, 'Why are these people so good to us when they do not know us?' They answered, 'They are Christians, and they treat us with love for the sake of the God of heaven.' He withdrew to one side and spent the whole night praying before God saying, 'My Lord Jesus the Christ, God of all the saints, may your goodness quickly come upon me, deliver me from this affliction and I will serve humankind all the days of my life'. The next morning they were led out and put into the boat, and they travelled until they came to the city of Antinoe. When his companions went ashore to the cities to buy food[4]—it was taken out of the im-

Mt 6:10;26:42.

perial provisions—they would often constrain him and drag him to evil places for worldly pleasures. But he rebuked them because he loved that purity which God and the holy angels love.

G[1] 5b.

Pachomius becomes a Christian

8. While they were still detained in the prison of Antinoe, the godloving emperor Constantine, with God's help, defeated his adversaries. At once he issued an edict all over the world that the conscripts should be discharged. As soon as they were set free, each one returned to his home with great

AD 313.

joy. Young Pachomius too went south until he arrived at a deserted village called Šeneset, scorched by the intensity of the heat. And he began to think about the place, in which there were not many but a few inhabitants. He went down to the river, into a small temple the ancients called Pmampiserapis. There he stood and prayed.[1] The Spirit of God seized him; 'Struggle and settle down here'. The thing pleased him and he settled down there, growing some vegetables and some palm-trees in order to feed himself or some poor man of the village or again some stranger who should happen to pass by in a boat or on the road. It was his custom to converse with lots of people, and they would give up their homes to come and live in that village because of his way of encouraging them. It was really because of his attitude that many men made their dwelling in that place.

After he had spent some days there, he was

c. AD 313.

brought to the church and baptized[2] that he might be made worthy of the holy mysteries, that is to say of the body and blood of Christ. On the night he was baptized he had a dream. He saw the dew of heaven descend on his head, then condense in his right hand and turn into a honeycomb; and while he was considering it, it dropped onto the earth and spread out over the face of all the earth. As he was still disturbed, a voice came to him from heaven, 'Understand this, Pachomius, for it will happen to you in a short time'. He made progress in that place by his charity for all. He was encouraging toward anyone who came to him, and his renown went out to many people, who came to live in that village because of him.

Pachomius ministers to the people of Seneset

9. Some time later, there was a serious outbreak of pestilence in that village, and many people died of it. He would go out to serve them; he would distribute to them a great quantity of wood that he carried from the forest. There was in fact a great and abundant forest of acacias nearby. In short, he served them until God should grant them the favor of healing. When they had been cured of their sickness he said to himself, 'This service of the sick in the villages is no work for a monk. It is only for the clergy and the faithful old men. From this day on, I will no longer undertake it, lest another should put his hand to this task and should be carried away by the scandal of my example, and lest the written word be applied to me, *A soul for a soul.*[1] For it is also written, *Pure and unspoilt religion in the eyes of God our Father is this: to visit the orphans and widows and to keep oneself uncontaminated by the world.*'[2]

Ex 21:23; Lv 24:18.

Jm 1:27.

G[1] 6.

Pachomius comes to Palamon

10. After three years spent in that place, he realized that he was surrounded by many people to the point of being much inconvenienced, for they would never let him have a moment's peace.[1] Then he sought to become a monk and to give himself up to the anchoritic life. While he was

thinking of moving away from that place for this purpose, he was informed of an old man, an ancient ascetic called Apa Palamon. He was a great monk who had settled a little way from the village and had become a model and a father for many in his vicinity. At once Pachomius gave his place to another old monk who was to look after the few vegetables and the palm-trees for the needs of the
c. AD 316. poor. Then he went to the place of the holy old man Apa Palamon.

He knocked on the door of the cell. Immediately [the old man] looked out through the window, saw him, and said roughly, 'Why are you knocking?'—for he was abrupt in speech. Pachomius replied, 'Father, I wish you would allow me to become a monk in your company'. The old man Apa Palamon said to him, 'That thing which you seek is not so simple; for many men have come here for that [very] thing and could not bear it; but they turned back to their
Cf. 2 P 2:21. shame, for they were unwilling to labor at virtue. Yet Scripture in many places commands us to do so, adjuring us to labor in fastings, in vigils, and in numerous prayers that we may be saved. Now go settle down in your cell, hold on firmly to what
Cf. Rv 3:11. you already have, and you will be honorable before God. Or else, try yourself in every point to find out whether you can be steadfast; then you will come back to us again. When you come back we will be ready, in so far as our weakness allows, to labor with you until you get to know yourself.[2] In any case, we are going to show you what the measure of monastic life is; you will go away, you will examine yourself first, and you will see whether or not you shall be able to stand the

thing. The rule of monastic life, according to what we have learned from those who went before us,[3] is as follows: We always spend half the night, and often even from evening to morning, in vigils and the recitation of the words of God, also doing manual work with threads, hairs, or palm-fibres, lest we be overcome by sleep. [We do this work] for our bodily subsistence also; and whatever is above and beyond our needs we give to the poor, following the words of the Apostle, *only let us remember the poor.* Eating oil, drinking wine, Ga 2:10.
eating cooked meats are something quite unknown among us. We always fast until evening, [eating] daily during the summer,[4] while in winter every other or every third day. As for the rule of the *synaxis*, it is sixty prayers during the day and fifty during the night,[5] not counting the ejaculatory [prayers] we make so as not to be defaulters,[6] since we are commanded to *pray without ceasing*, and it is also written, *If any one* 1 Th 5:17.
of you is in trouble, let him pray. Our Lord Jesus Jm 5:13.
Christ likewise commands his disciples, *Pray, so as not to enter into temptation.* Prayer is indeed Mt 26:41.
the mother of all virtues. So, I have told you what the law of monastic life is. Now, go, try yourself in every point. If you are able to do what I have taught you and if you do not timidly turn back, then we will rejoice with you on every count.'

[7]When Pachomius heard the old man Palamon say this and saw him, he answered humbly, 'I have been trying myself in everything for days before coming to your charity'. Then Palamon came down, opened the door, gave him a pure kiss and said to him, 'Do not think, my son, that all that I said to you about *ascesis*, prayers, and

vigils, I said out of human vainglory. Do not think either that we are imposing on men; we are only teaching you how to work at your salvation, so that you may have no pretext [against us], for it was written for us, *Every pure thing is luminous*, and it is by doing violence to yourself that you shall enter the kingdom of heaven. Now I want you to return to your dwelling and test your soul for a few days, because what you ask for is no small thing.' Pachomius answered, 'I have already tried my soul in all things, and I am confident that with the help of God and of your holy prayers, your heart will be at rest concerning me'. The old man answered, 'Very well'. At once he received him with joy and he kept him in his company for days, to try him with prayers, vigils, and fasting. When they ate their bread, the old man let him eat alone to one side. After the old man had tried him for three full months and had seen his courage and his firm determination, he took a monk's habit with the belt and he placed it before the altar, and they spent the whole night praying over them. Then he clothed him with it at daybreak, and they celebrated the morning prayer together with joy.

[8]They lived together as one man, practising a hard and exhausting *ascesis.* As soon as Pachomius had become a monk, Palamon wanted to try him by vigils from evening to morning in prayers, recitations and numerous manual labors, to judge his measure of sleep and to see if he would hold out without getting sick. When evening came they took their frugal meal; the old man addressed young Pachomius, 'Soak for us some reeds, palm leaves and fibres, enough to last the

night, for it is the rule that we should keep vigil from evening to morning on Saturday night.' Pachomius did with great obedience what his father Apa Palamon had commanded. Then, shortly after sunset they rose to pray and continued to keep vigil, blessing God and carrying out their manual labor without stopping. If sleep was weighing them down at work, they would change to another manual work, thus getting rid of the heaviness of sleep. And if they saw that sleep was still overtaking them they would go out to the mountain outside their cell, and carry sand in baskets from one place to another, giving their bodies labor so as to stay awake to pray to God.[9] And when the old man saw the young man tottering with sleep, he comforted him, saying, 'Stay awake, Pachomius, lest Satan tempt you, for many have fallen asleep in their affliction because of the heaviness of sleep.' When the old man saw that he held out until the time of the *synaxis*, he was very glad of his obedience and of his progress and he rejoiced at his salvation.

Cf. Mt 26:41; 1 Co 7:5.

Cf. Ac 20:9.

G[1] 7.

Palamon's fasting

11. On the day of the Closing of the holy Passover,[1] the old man Apa Palamon said to him, 'My son Pachomius, since today is a great day, prepare our meal, and let us eat a little bit at midday; when evening comes we will again eat a little.' At once he got up and prepared the meal; and after their prayer they sat down to eat. Looking at the salt, [the old man] saw a bit of oil that [Pachomius] had put in it. He struck only his face[2] and said, 'My Lord was crucified for me and am I to eat that which would give strength to my flesh! Let us either eat some vegetables without oil or vinegar or let us put ashes in the salt before

eating it; let us ⟨not⟩ [3] abandon the law of our fathers, and let us not eat something which gives strength to the flesh!' At once he retired, not to eat until the next day. Young Pachomius overturned the salt with a little oil in it and brought some that contained ashes. Then with great humility he begged [the old man], 'Pardon me, my lord Father, get up and eat!' Then the holy old man swore that, 'but for the holy sanctuary lamp and the work with bristles, I would not have tolerated that creature, oil, in my cell.'[4] Pachomius replied, 'My holy father, pardon me, it is I who am at fault.' Then he got up; they sat down and took their frugal meal while tears flowed down their cheeks.

Pachomius' vision

12. Having got to know the courage of the old man Apa Palamon, young Pachomius made it a habit to leave his cell and to go often to tombs filled with dead [bodies] and to pass the whole night there, praying before the Lord Jesus from evening to morning. And the spot on which he stood would grow muddy from the abundant sweat that poured from his body.

c. AD 320.

After four years, Pachomius again saw the vision he had had before:[1] the dew from heaven coming down on him, falling and filling all the earth's surface. He likewise saw some keys that were being given to him secretly. The next morning he informed the holy old man Apa Palamon of the vision he had had. The latter was quite puzzled and said, 'There is a deep meaning to the interpretation of this affair, O my son Pachomius; but *may the Lord's will be done*!'[2]

Mt 6:10;26:42.

13. One day, on the feast of Epiphany, Pacho-

mius on returning from the acacia forest saw the old man boiling something in a pot. Astonished, he wondered to himself, 'What is the old man cooking today?' Shortly afterwards, the old man said, 'Pachomius, bring the dish here quickly!' When he had brought the dish, [Palamon] uncovered the pot and emptied it into [the dish]; it was only some hard figs! For there was in that place a large fig-tree which they used to water by hand for the eventual needs of the sick. Then they got up, prayed and ate, thanking the Lord, for *the hungry throat finds all bitterness sweet.*

Other example of Palamon's fasting

Pr 27:7.

14. Another day, while they were seated on either side of a burning fire, working together at their manual labor and reciting the holy Scripture by heart, a brother who lived in a cell near theirs appeared at the door. Right away Pachomius got up and opened the door to him. The other, once inside, spoke with pride; at the sight of the coals, the devil filled his heart, and he said to them, 'You pride yourselves on having a great way of life before God! So now, whichever of you has faith, let him stand on these glowing coals and recite the Gospel prayer!'[1] The holy old man Apa Palamon answered him very angrily, saying, 'A curse on the demon who tossed that evil idea into your heart. And now, that should be enough for you!' But he did not obey the holy old man. On the contrary, thanks to the one whose pride was acting in him, he stepped on the glowing coals and said the prayer, and his feet were not burnt. At once he very proudly walked away and retired to his cell.

G¹ 8.

Story of a boastful monk

Cf. Mt 6:9.

Cf. Pr 6:28-29.

Then Pachomius said to the old man, 'My lord

Father, the Lord knows that I was in awe of that brother who got up on that fiery mass without getting his feet burnt!' The blessed Apa Palamon answered, 'O Pachomius my son, do not admire that man, for doubtless it is the Lord who, by a demonic intervention, allowed his feet to be unscathed; as it is written, *To the devious God*
Pr 21:8. *will send devious ways.* Believe me, my son, if you knew the tribulations that are going to overtake that man you would weep over his wretchedness.'

And a few days later, as [the brother] was in his cell with his great pride, he was noticed by the demon who had earlier deceived him and filled him with pride. [The demon] then took the form of a beautiful woman and came knocking on the door of his cell. He went briskly to open the door. Then the demon, having the appearance of a woman, said to him, 'I beg of you, my lord father, take pity on me and let me come in until morning; truly I am tormented because of a loan, and I have not the wherewithal to repay my creditor.' And because of his blindness of heart, he did not discern at all that he must not let her in. On the contrary, he let her in and was very happy to bring her into his cell. Then the devil
Cf. Eph 6:16. began to dart at his mind evil fleshly desires;[2] and he inclined to sin with her. Suddenly the demon struck him, and tormented him grievously until the next day.[3]

When he came to his senses again, he ran to the holy old man Apa Palamon and, throwing himself at his feet, he entreated him, saying with an abundance of most bitter tears, 'My lord father, may your holy prayers uphold me. And pray to the Lord for me that he may have pity on me in that situation which I myself chose. Help me in my misery, for I am in torment. Yes, I am the cause of my own ruin, for you have taught me again and again what was useful to my soul, but my pride kept me from listening to you and being saved; and now woe to me, wretched man!' The holy old man Apa Palamon and Pachomius, seeing his great dejection, wept in great affliction, then took him in and got him over his great distress. While they were praying together, that demon once again knocked him down and tormented him some more. They stood over him and in tears prayed to the Lord for him until he recovered and was on his feet before them. But as they were taking hold of him to put him in a solitary place until the Lord should be pleased to heal him of that unclean spirit, he—by the strength of the demon dwelling in him—snatched up a big log to kill the two of them. They were unable to get hold of him, and straightaway he ran northward over the mountain until he entered Šmin,[4] threw himself of his own accord into the open furnace of the bathhouse, and was miserably burnt to death.

The old man Apa Palamon was very sad about that wretched man's soul, and many times he would speak of him to Pachomius, to all the neighboring brothers, and to those on all that mountain, for he was their father and comforter. In their presence he would often bring up the memory of that wretched man, instilling fear in them through Scripture, 'To him who gave way to the impotent spirit, see what the latter has done, not only to his poor soul, but also to his wretched body!' On hearing these terrifying words from their father Apa Palamon, the brothers were powerfully moved to keep themselves with great courage in the future and to save themselves. Their dread was greater still at contemplating his example, for he bore in his flesh at all times the Cross of Christ.

G[1] 9, 11.
Pachomius' ***ascesis***

15. As for Pachomius, he gave himself up ever more and more to important exercises,[1] to a great and intensive *ascesis*, and to lengthy recitations of the books of Holy Scripture. He had his heart set on reciting them in order [and] with great ease. He would mainly practise his mortifications in those deserts, in the acacia forest that surrounded them, and in the far desert. If thorns happened to pierce his feet he endured them without removing them, remembering the nails that pierced our Lord on the cross.[2]

G[1] 13a.
Palamon's illness

16. The old man Apa Palamon was in contact with all those who had settled on that mountain. They admired him and the courageous behavior he carried out with steadfastness and without flinching. But the old man Apa Palamon contracted an illness of the spleen as a result of his manifold *ascesis* and above all because he took no respite in his old age from his exercises. His immediate neighbors as well as some ancients coming from afar saw him when he was afflicted by his disease and they brought him a famous doctor, thinking he could perhaps apply a remedy to it. After seeing him, the doctor said to them, 'It is no matter for a doctor at all; he is simply exhausted from his *ascesis*. Now, if he will agree to take a little appropriate food, he will get well.' With many prayers the brothers counselled him to do so. He obeyed them and ate some of the

dishes it is customary to give the sick. When he had eaten this food for some days, he understood that he would not get well, and he said to the brothers, 'Do not think that healing comes from perishable foods. No, healing and strength come through our Lord Jesus the Christ. For if members were cut off from Christ's martyrs, or if they were beheaded, or burnt to death, and if they endured till death through the faith they had in God, well then, is it not fitting I should be made weak by a little sickness? Although I obeyed you and did as you wished and ate the dishes that are thought capable of strengthening the body, nevertheless I got no alleviation.' And thus he went back once more to his *ascesis* with great mortifications, until the Lord saw the constancy of his courage, provided him with an alleviation, and cured him of his illness.

Cf. Heb 11:33-37.

G[1]12.

Col 3:10, 12.

Pachomius' vocation to build a monastery

17. Young Pachomius strove to imitate him in every work that *he put on himself*.[1] One day he set out, according to his custom, across that desert to the large acacia forest. Led by the spirit, he covered a distance of some ten miles and came to a deserted village on the river's shore called Tabennesi.[2] Then he felt inspired to go in and pray there a little and he followed the one who gave him that inspiration. He came into that place, stretched out his hands and prayed to the Lord Jesus Christ that He might teach him His will. And as he lengthened his prayer, a voice came to him from heaven, 'Pachomius, Pachomius, struggle, dwell in this place and build a monastery; for many will come to you to become monks with you, and they will profit their souls.' Then at once he returned to his father the

old man Apa Palamon and told him about what he had heard.

[Palamon] wept and said to him, 'Is this it, that after these seven years you have borne with me with such obedience you too are now going to leave me in my old age? However, *may the Lord's*
Mt 6, 10; 26:42. *will be done* always! For I hope that the dream you have seen a first and a second time is going to become reality for you in this affair the Lord has imposed on you.[3] Now, my son, let us go south-
c. AD 323. ward and let us put up a small cell for you. We shall visit each other, you and I in turn, until the Lord shall visit me.' And so it was that they both went and built the cell; they would go and mutually pay each other visits with joy and the love of God, [Palamon] counselling [Pachomius] on many points.

G[1] 13b.

Palamon's illness and death

18. Actually that situation had not lasted long when the old man fell ill. Immediately the brothers sent south for Pachomius.[1] He left with great haste and came north, and he ministered to him until the Lord visited him in peace, at the
c. AD 323. tenth hour of the day, on the twenty-fifth of Epip. They spent the whole night reading and chanting psalms around him, till the hour of the *synaxis*. They offered the Eucharist[2] for him, and they brought him to the mountain[3] at a little distance from his cell. They buried him and prayed for him; then each one returned to his cell, remembering with sadness the consolation they used to receive from the holy old man Apa Palamon. For many of them said, 'We have become orphans.' As for Pachomius, he returned to the south to his cell. He blessed God [but] with sadness and sighing, because of the holy man's death.

Again he gave himself still more to great and numerous ascetic practices.

19. When John, his elder brother, heard that Pachomius was in a place alone, he got on a boat and came north to him. They had not seen each other, in fact, since the day he had been taken to be made a conscript. When he met him at Tabennesi, he embraced him. At once [Pachomius] spoke the word of God to him and made him a monk with him. They practised together a great *ascesis*, carrying the Cross of Christ according to the word of Paul, *At all times we carry the death of Jesus in our body, so that the life of Jesus may be manifested in our mortal flesh.*

G[1] 14, 15.
c. AD 323.
Coming of John, Pachomius' brother, and their life together
2 Co 4:10-11.

They lived in great renunciation, for they gave away everything they earned through their manual work except what they absolutely needed. They bought a monastic garment, that is, a tunic, and they divided it in two parts; with it they made clothes for themselves, because those they were wearing were worn out. They likewise bought hoods, and they owned also a small mantle for the two of them. Every time their tunic was dirty, they put on the little cloak in turn until [the tunics] were washed and they put them on again.[1] They both lived in great renunciation. They kept nothing but two loaves of bread daily and a bit of salt.

They also put on hair garments and went to very hot places where they prayed from evening till morning. They mortified themselves during their prayers, moving neither their feet nor their hands, which they kept stretched out lest sleep overtake them. To fight sleep, they rarely knelt down during the whole night. Therefore their feet were swollen by the pain because they stood on them all night long. Likewise their hands were covered with blood because they did not withdraw them from the crowds of gnats which bit them.

If they needed a little sleep, they would sit down in the middle of the place where they prayed, without leaning their back against any wall. And if the sun and the intense heat fell on them when they were doing some physical work during the day, they would not move to another place unless they had finished the work they were doing. Thus they fulfilled the word of the Gospel,
If anyone wants to come after me let him deny
Mt 16:24. *himself, take up his cross and follow me.*[2]

One day, as they were building a part of their dwelling, Pachomius wanted to extend it because of the crowds that would come to him, but John's mind was that they should stay alone. When Pachomius saw that John was spoiling the wall they were building, he said to him, 'Stop being foolish!' Immediately John got angry and grew sad. Pachomius said to him, 'Forgive me, for I got angry with you.'[3] Toward evening Pachomius went down [to an underground place][4] and prayed from evening till morning.

And he said, 'Alas for me, for the mind of the
flesh is in me. I am going to die; indeed, as it is
Rm 8:6, 13. written, *The carnal thought is death.* Whether I
am put to the test unjustly or for good reason,
have mercy on me, Lord, lest I be lost. If the enemy finds, little by little, a place for himself within
me, he will overcome me in the end;[5] for, *If a*
man keeps the whole of the law but fails in one
Jm 2:10. *single point, he is responsible for it all.* I believe
that if your abundant mercy helps me, I will learn
how to walk in the way of the saints, *stretch-*

ing out toward what lies ahead; for they indeed have put the enemy to shame, with your help. How indeed will I teach those you will call to this life with me, if I do not begin by overcoming carnal thoughts.' Ph 3:13.

He kept praying like this from evening till morning. Then he came out from that place; he called his brother and they made the prayer together. And Pachomius mortified himself till the end of the prayer; then he humbled himself saying, 'Forgive me, for I got angry with you'.[6]

John witnesses Pachomius' faith

20. [1]Another day they were both throwing a few reeds into the water to wet them. Suddenly a crocodile rose up at that place. John took fright, ran away toward the shore, and cried to his brother, 'Quick, come to the shore for fear the crocodile grab you and gobble you up'. Pachomius laughed and said to him, 'John, do you think wild beasts are their own masters? Not so!' Then once more the crocodile came to the surface, daringly close to him, hardly farther from him than three cubits.[2] Pachomius filled his hand with water and hurled it in the crocodile's face saying, 'May the Lord condemn you never again to come back here!' At once the crocodile submerged. When Pachomius had come up out of the water his brother John ran up to him, kissed his mouth, his hands and his feet with great joy and said, 'The Lord knows, my brother, that every day I used to say that I am your elder by the flesh, that was why every day I would call you my brother. From this day forward I will call you my father because of your firm faith in the Lord'. As for John, he performed great exercises and a great *ascesis* till the day of his death.

G[1] 18,19,22.

Pachomius is tempted by the demons

21. Pachomius endured a great many temptations by demons, with God's permission and for his own training as well as for the benefit of others. They began to attack him openly. Sometimes when he was going to bend his knees during his prayer, [the demon] would apparently make a sort of pit in front of him, to frighten him into praying no longer to the Lord. But understanding the wiles of the tempter, he would kneel with faith and would bless God, thus giving thanks to Christ and putting the demons to shame. At other times, when he would be setting out to go about one of his tasks, they would march in front of him in double file like soldiers marching before commanders, while saying to each other, 'Make way for the Man of God' with the intention of tricking him into looking at them.[1] But the Man of God, through his hope in God, would not look at them, but instead would mock them as powerless creatures. And at once they would vanish from his face. Still other times they would shake his cell to make him afraid that it would collapse on him. At once he would say, *Our God is our shelter, our strength, a help in the afflictions that try us exceedingly. So we shall not be afraid when the earth is shaken.* Another day, when he sat down to work, one demon took the form of a cock and crowed in his face. He shut his eyes, did not look at it, and was not moved a bit. When the evildoers realized that they were powerless to deceive him, they fetched an object in the form of a tree leaf and a long, thick rope, as if they were a group of men doing some very tiring work. They pretended as if they had tied their rope to a big stone to drag it and bring it

Ps 46(45):1-2.

somewhere. Doing this, they shouted loudly in order to overcome him should he look and laugh. At once he stretched out his hands and prayed, sighing, until they vanished and withdrew from him. Still many another time, when he sat down to eat his bread, they would come to him in the form of naked women and sit down to eat with him. The Man of God would close his eyes and his heart until they vanished away and dissolved into thin air.

He asked the Lord to keep sleep away from him and that he sleep no more until he had put to rout those who were warring against him, as it is written, *I will not turn away till my enemies have been wiped out.* The Lord granted his request for some time and they were chased away by him in shame, and feared him.

Ps 18(17):37.

22. He was alone one day ⟨on an island⟩,[1] gathering some few rushes for his manual labor. Once, as he was keeping vigil there, as was his custom, an angel of the Lord appeared to him and said to him three times, 'Pachomius, Pachomius, the Lord's will is to minister to the race of men and to unite them to himself.'[2] When the angel of the Lord had gone away, our father Pachomius began to reflect, 'This comes from the Lord.' And when he had finished gathering his few rushes, he went back to his monastery.[3]

G[1] 23.

Pachomius' other vision about his vocation

23. By God's providential design, three men came to him, that is, Pšentaesi, Sourous, and Pšoi, and said to him, 'We want to become monks in your company and to serve Christ'. He talked with them to know whether they would be able to renounce their parents and follow the Saviour. Then he put them to the test and, hav-

G[1] 25a,24,25b.

Pachomius receives his first disciples and makes himself their servant

c. AD 324.

Lk 14:26-27.

ing found they had the right intentions, he clothed them in the monks' habit and received them as his companions with joy and God's love. Once they had joined the holy community, they gave themselves over to great exercises and many ascetical practices.

They saw him laboring alone in the work of the monastery, whether tending the few vegetables or getting their food ready; or if someone knocked at the door of the monastery, it was again he who went to answer it. If any of them was sick, he ministered to him until he got well, telling himself with regard to his three companions,[1] 'They are neophytes who have not yet attained that stage which would allow them to serve each other'. Therefore he exempted them from any labor, telling them, 'For your salvation endeavor *to hold fast** to that to which you have been called.'†

*1 Co 11:2.
†1 Tm 6:12.

They also said to him, 'We are saddened, O our father, to see you wearing yourself out alone around the monastery.' He replied, 'Who yokes his beast to a ⟨water wheel⟩ [2] and does not care until it falls down and dies? So then, if the Lord sees that I am tired, he will send us some others able to help us in every good work.'[3]

In fact he established for them an irreproachable life-style and traditions profitable for their souls in rules [which he took] from the holy Scriptures: absolute equality in their clothing and food, and decent sleeping arrangements.[4]

G[1] 26a.
Other disciples come; he expels some of them

24. The renown of his piety went out over all the land of Egypt. In a certain place were five brothers leading the anchoritic life; they were

men valiant in the work of God. Their names are: Apa Pecoš, Apa Cornelios, Apa Paul, Apa Pachomius, and Apa John.[1] Having learned about his sound faith, they set out and came to live with him, and he accepted them, rejoicing in the Spirit. Still fifty others, who lived up-river in a place called Thbakat and had likewise heard of him, came to him. He accepted them likewise, but discovering they had a carnal mind, he expelled them from his dwelling.[2] After that, the Lord was at work in many others who came to him; and he accepted them, building them up in the law of God.

G[1] 29,26b,27.

Pachomius builds a church in the village and, later on, one in the monastery

25. When he saw that a lot of people had come to live in the village,[1] he took the brothers and went to build them a church where they could assemble. Besides, there were a lot of people all around that place. He took care of their offering because they were in a state of great poverty.[2] He would take the brothers and would go out there on Saturday to receive the sacraments. He did the reading for them; and he kept close watch on where he directed his gaze, according to the words of the Gospel, *He who looks at a woman with lustful intent has already committed adultery with her in his heart.*[3] When the brothers came to number one hundred, he built a church in his monastery so they might praise God there. But he would still go to the village for the celebration of the Eucharist on Saturday evening while the clergy would come to celebrate it for them at the monastery on Sunday morning, because no one among them had clerical rank in the holy Church.[4] Indeed, our father Pachomius did not want any clerics in his monasteries, for

Mt 5:28.

fear of jealousy and vainglory. Very often, indeed, he would talk to them on this subject; 'It is better not to seek after such a thing in our *Koinonia*, lest this should be an occasion for strife, envy, jealousy and even schisms to arise in a large number of monks, contrary to God's will. In the same way as a spark cast into the threshing floor, unless it is quickly quenched, will destroy a whole year's labor, so it is with a thought of grandeur at its outset. It is better to be subject respectfully to the Church of God, so that he whom we shall receive at a given moment and who has been established by our fathers the bishops should suffice for that office.' If someone from the clergy came to him and wanted to become a monk, and if he saw that he was righteous, he would accept him and make him a monk. He would respect his rank but he would make him walk willingly in the rules laid down for the brothers, like anyone else.

G[1] 28.

First organization of the community

26. He appointed some from among the capable brothers as his assistants to take care of their souls' salvation. [He appointed] one [of them] at the head of the first house, that of the lesser stewards, with a second to help him in preparing the tables and in cooking for [the brothers].[1] [He appointed] another brother also, with his second—men who were faithful on every score—to look after the food and the care of the sick brothers. If anyone wanted to abstain from what was served at table or from what was served to the sick, there was no one to prevent him from doing so.[2] And at the doorway [he appointed] other brothers whose *speech was seasoned with salt* to receive visitors according to each one's

Col 4:6.

rank. [These porters] also instructed those who came to become monks, for their salvation, until he clothed them in the monk's habit.[3] Similarly, [he appointed] other faithful [brothers] noted for their piety to transact sales and make purchases.[4] In each house the brothers in service were replaced every three weeks, and a new class was appointed.[5] They performed *in fear and trembling* the task assigned them by the housemaster. He appointed still others with a housemaster and a second to work at the shops and at mat-making, and to be ready for every obedience.[6] He likewise established three instructions a week: one on Saturday and two on the holy Sunday, while the housemasters gave some, if they wished, on the two fastdays.[7]

Ph 2:12.

G[1] 32.

Pachomius' sister founds a monastery for women

27. Pachomius' sister, whose name was Mary and who had been a virgin from childhood, heard about him and she came north to see him at Tabennesi. When he was told she had arrived, he sent the brother who watched at the door of the monastery to tell her, 'I see you have learned I am alive. Do not be distressed, however, because you have not seen me. But if you wish to share in this holy life so that you may find mercy before God, examine yourself on every point. The brothers will build a place for you to retire to. And doubtless, for your sake the Lord will call others to you, and they will be saved because of you. Man has no other hope in this world but to do good before he departs from the body and is led to the place where he shall be judged and rewarded according to his works.'[1] When she heard these words from the lips of the porter she wept, and she accepted the advice. When our father Pachomius had found that her heart in-

Rm 2:6-7.

clined to the good and right life, he immediately sent the brothers over to build a monastery for her in that village, a short distance from his own monastery; it included a small oratory.[2] Later on many heard about her and came to live with her. They practised *ascesis* eagerly with her, and she was their mother and their worthy elder[3] until her death.

When our father Pachomius saw that the number of [these women] was increasing somewhat, he appointed an old man called Apa Peter, whose

Col 4:6. *speech was seasoned with salt* to be their father and to preach frequently to them on the Scriptures for their souls' salvation. [Pachomius] also wrote down in a book the rules of the brothers and sent them to them through [Peter], so that they might learn them.[4]

If ever any of the brothers who had not yet attained perfection wanted to visit one of his relatives among [the sisters], [Pachomius] sent him through his housemaster's direction to the holy old man Apa Peter who in turn sent word to their mother to come out with her and another sister. They sat down together with great propriety until the visit came to an end; then they got up, prayed, and withdrew.[5]

When one of [the sisters] died, they brought her to the oratory and first their mother covered her with a shroud. Then the old man Apa Peter sent word to our father Pachomius who chose experienced brothers and sent them to the monastery with [Apa Peter]. They proceeded to the assembly room and stood in the entryway chanting psalms with gravity until [the deceased] was prepared for burial. Then she was placed on a bier and carried to the mountain. The virgin sisters followed behind the bier while their father walked after them and their mother before them. When the deceased was buried, they prayed for her and returned with great sorrow to their dwelling.

When their father, the holy Apa Peter died, Pachomius appointed for them another equally capable man called Apa Titoue. It was a marvel to see him and [to know] his temperament.[6]

28. After his appointment as archbishop of Alexandria, Apa Athanasius came south to the Thebaid with the intention of proceeding as far as Aswan to give comfort to the holy Churches. When our father Pachomius saw him with an escort of bishops walking before him, he also took the brothers and escorted him a long way. They chanted psalms while escorting him until they brought him inside the monastery, where he prayed in their assembly room and in all their cells. Apa Sarapion, bishop of Nitentori, grasped the archbishop's hand, kissed it, and said, 'I beg Your Piety to ordain to the priesthood Pachomius, the father of the monks, so that he should be set over all the monks in my diocese, for he is a man of God. Alas! he refuses to obey me in this matter.' At once Pachomius disappeared into the midst of the crowd so as not to be discovered. When the archbishop had seated himself, as did the great crowd that was with him, he opened his mouth to speak and said to Sarapion, 'Indeed I have learned about the renown of the faith of this man Apa Pachomius of whom you speak to me, since I have been at Alexandria and even before my consecration.' Then he rose, prayed, and

G[1] 30.
AD 328.
AD 329-330.
Athanasius' visit to the Thebaid

said to [Pachomius'] sons, 'Greet your father and say to him, "So, you hid from us, fleeing from that which leads to jealousy, discord, and envy, and you chose for yourself that which is better and which will always abide in Christ! Our Lord, therefore, will accede to your wish.[1] So now, since you have fled before vain and temporary grandeur, not only do I wish for you that that may not happen to you, but I will always stretch my hands toward the Most High that such a thing may never happen to you, and that never, never may you have a rank.[2] Nevertheless, if by God's will we come back to you, may we deserve to see your honorable Piety!"' Then at once he left them and went on south, accompanied by a number of bishops and an immense crowd with lamps, candles, and countless censers. After the archbishop had gone away our father Pachomius came out of the place where he had been hiding.

G[1] 34.

Theodore hears about Pachomius

29. One day a brother monk arrived, returning from the north. And as evening overtook him in the region of Tabennesi, he was obliged to ask for hospitality at the monastery. Our father Pachomius gave orders to the brothers to treat him with all brotherly love. And when the brothers had finished their meal and our father Pachomius took a seat and spoke the Word of God to them, commenting on the Scriptures, that brother also sat listening like all the brothers.

When that brother had returned south to his monastery in the diocese of Sne, the brothers assembled at evening as was their custom. For in all seasons, when they had finished their modest meal, it was their habit to assemble and for each one to pronounce what he knew of the holy Scriptures. That evening when they were seated, each one brought forth the saying he had learned or that he had heard from the lips of others. There was present a young man[1] called Theodore, son of a prominent family, who sat listening to what each one said with great attention and vigilance. He himself spoke not a word, but maintained a profound silence. The brother who had returned from the north spoke and said, 'Allow me, my brothers, to tell you the saying and its commentary which I heard from a righteous man. It was while returning south that I passed by Tabennesi and was put up there at Apa Pachomius' [monastery]. Toward evening [Pachomius] seated himself and spoke the Word of God to the brothers gathered around him. He spoke of the Tabernacle and of the Holy of Holies, applying them to two peoples: the first people is the outer Tabernacle, whose service consisted in sacrifices and visible loaves; the Holy of Holies, on the other hand, is the Gentiles' calling which, according to the Gospel, is the *fulfilment of the Law*. And all the objects that are found in this inner Tabernacle are filled with glory. For instead of animal sacrifices, there is the Altar of Incense; instead of the table, the Ark containing the spiritual loaves, that is, the fulness of the Law and all that is to be found there; and instead of the light of the lamp, the Mercy-Seat where God appears as *a comsuming fire*,[2] that is, God the Word made man who became remission for us by *appearing in the flesh*. The word Mercy-Seat means indeed the place of the remission of sins.'

Heb 9:1-5. Rm 13:10. Lv 16:12. Dt 4:24; Heb 12:29. 1 Tm 3:16; 1 Jn 4:2,10.

When the brother had finished his exposition

of that saying and its commentary, he said, 'I am confident that God will forgive me many of my sins because of the remembrance of that just man whose name I just pronounced here before you.' All the brothers uttered their admiration for the great knowledge that was in our father Pachomius, until it was time for each of them to return with joy to his cell.

The young Theodore also, when he returned to his cell, had a heart kindled as if with fire by what he had heard that evening about our father Pachomius. He rose at once and went to the other brother's cell and questioned him about Apa Pachomius. [The brother] told him everything: how he would receive everyone and would edify them in every work pleasing to the Lord. When Theodore had heard these words about our father Pachomius from the brother's lips, he returned at once to his cell and he prayed before the Lord in tears, saying, 'Lord, God of all saints, may it be your will that I should see that perfect man, your servant Apa Pachomius!' And he prayed in this way a long time before the Lord.

G[1] 35,36a.

Theodore's arrival at Tabennesi

30. Some time after that, our father Pachomius sent Apa Pecoš south for the service of the brothers.[1] In the course of his journey southward, by the disposition of providence, Apa Pecoš went to beg hospitality in the monastery where young Theodore lived. The brother who had heard the saying informed Theodore immediately, 'This great man come to us here is from Apa Pachomius' monastery.' At once Theodore asked Pecoš to take him along with him and bring him to our father so he might see him. The old man Apa Pecoš questioned the brothers

about him. Learning that he was a son of a prominent family in the city of Sne, he was afraid and said to him, 'I cannot take you along with me on account of your parents'. Theodore kept his idea in his heart and when they sailed northward, he set out and made his way parallel to them, so that he completed a long lap of the way north. From aboard the boat the brothers saw him and said to Apa Pecoš, 'There is the young man who said to you, "I want to go north with you"; he has been keeping an even way here with us since morning.' At once, he made them draw the boat to the shore and they took him on board. When they arrived up north, Apa Pecoš announced him to our father Pachomius. At once, [Theodore] embraced him, kissed his hands and his feet, and planted a kiss with utmost fervor on the door of the monastery. Then he turned his face away and wept saying, 'Blessed are you, Lord my God, because you have listened to the cry of my prayer.' Seeing him in tears, our father Pachomius said to him, 'Do not weep, my son, for I am a servant of your father.' In fact, it was God he referred to as 'your father'. Cf. Ps 18(17):2.

Later on he introduced him into the monastery. When he was in, he saw that the brothers were walking in uprightness; he imitated their good works and their virtues and he strove in his heart to keep these three things: purity of heart, a measured and graceful speech, and unquestioning *obedience unto death.*[2] Ph 2:8.

31. But now, for the glory of God, we must tell the story of his life from infancy.[1] Theodore was born into a prominent family, and was greatly loved by his mother. At the age of eight he was *G¹ 33.* **Theodore's childhood**

put in school so he might learn to write; and he became very advanced in wisdom. When he was twelve he gave himself up to great abstinence, eating no other food than that which it is customary for monks to take; he used to fast until evening every day, and at times he ate only every other day.[2] One day, on the feast of the
6 January Epiphany—which is the eleventh of the month of Tobi—on returning from school, he saw how his family was making a great celebration, and he was suddenly pierced by a very strong feeling: 'If you give yourself up to those dishes and wines, you will not see God's everlasting life'. Then he went away to an isolated room in his house. Falling on his face, he prayed and wept saying, 'My Lord Jesus the Christ, you alone know that I want no part of this world, but that it is you alone and your abundant mercy that I love.' When his mother learned that he had come back from school, and did not see him, she got up quickly, looked for him and found him alone somewhere in prayer. She looked at him, saw his eyes full of tears and said to him, 'Tell me, my son, who has vexed you so I may give him a hearty and stern rebuke. But get up and let us go and eat, for this is a feast-day, and we have been waiting for you since morning, I, your brothers, and all our household.' He answered her, 'Go, the rest of you, and eat, as for me I will not eat now'. When they had gone, he went on praying until morning without eating or drinking. When morning came he left his home and his city and went to a monastery in the diocese of Sne and led the anchoritic life with some pious old monks. He was fourteen years old. He stayed there, behaving

with great humility. After leading that sort of life for six years in that place, it happened that, by the disposition of providence—the Lord forgets not* those who *seek him with all their heart*† and with all their soul—the old man Apa Pecoš came south on a business of the brothers and Theodore went back north with him to our father Pachomius. He was then in his twentieth year.[3]

*Ps 77(76):9. †Ps 119(118): 2,10.

c. AD 328

32. When he arrived at our father Pachomius', [the latter] received him with joy because he saw what love he had toward God. When he had entered the monastery he gave himself up to *ascesis*, to fasts, and to vigils, and he was second to no other brother. He also strove to acquire great graciousness, with the result that, despite his age, he became the comforter of many, raising up by his soothing words whoever had fallen, for, as it is written, *the Spirit blows wherever it pleases*. Our father Pachomius, seeing that he was progressing ever more and more, realized in his heart that in a short while many souls would be entrusted to him by God who can always recognize his own.

G[1] 36b.

Theodore's progress in virtue

Jn 3:8.

Our father Theodore made fine progress of every kind, living a very courageous way of life. He was also growing up in the instructions he would hear from the lips of our father Pachomius, after whose image he was walking in all things. The brothers, seeing that he was growing up like Samuel and enjoying universal sympathy, began to imitate his example. And our father Pachomius would tell all of them as an answer to go and find [Theodore] and to get from him consolation in their temptations and tribulations. And they would go and see him, so much so that they called him the brothers' comforter. By the unction of his words he would restore calm to all. Often he would pray with many among them until the Lord put an end to their temptations.[1]

Theodore's desire to see God

33. One day, less than six months after his entry among the brothers, he came to our father Pachomius shedding copious tears. Our father Pachomius said to him, 'Why are you weeping?' For he had often been astonished at seeing this propensity to tears in him, although he was so new. He answered, 'I would like you, father, to declare to me that I shall see God; if not, what is the profit for me to have been brought into the world?' Our father Pachomius said to him, 'Do you wish to see him in this age or in the age to come?' He answered, 'I wish to see him in the age that lasts for all eternity.' [Our father Pachomius] said to him, 'Make haste to bring forth the fruit the Gospel speaks of, *Blessed are the pure in heart, for they shall see God.*[1] And if an impure thought enters your mind, be it hatred or wickedness, jealousy, envy, contempt for your brother, or human vainglory, remember at once and say, "If I consent to any one of those things, I shall not see the Lord."' When Theodore had heard these words from our father Pachomius, he made up his mind to walk with humility and purity, so that the Lord might satisfy his desire to see Him in the age which changes not.

Mt 5:8.

Theodore has his first revelation

34. One day, during his first year, Theodore was sitting in his cell plaiting ropes and reciting passages of the holy Scriptures he had learned by heart. And he would get up and pray every time his heart urged him to do so. While he was seated reciting, the cell where he was lighted up, and he

was quite surprised at it. And lo, two angels under the appearance of dazzling men appeared to him. Frightened, he ran out of his cell and scaled the roof, for he had never yet had a revelation. When he got to the roof, [the angels] likewise came there and delivered him from his fear; and the greater of them said to him, 'Put out your hand, Theodore!' He put it out as one does to receive the holy Mysteries, and the angel placed in his hands a large number of keys. When he had received them, he held them in his right hand; and while he was overcome with wonder at this event he suddenly looked up and saw the angels no more. Looking once more at his hands, he no longer saw any key. He did not dare to inform our father Pachomius of this revelation, as he had often heard him say, 'Keys have been given to me in secret,'[1] and he said to himself, 'Who am I to make myself equal to the Man of God, sinner that I am! For the important thing for me is rather to walk in humility all the days of my life, since we know that such is God's will.'

Theodore consults Pachomius about fasting

35. During the Forty Days [of Lent], he went to see our father Pachomius and asked him, 'Since the Passover numbers six days during which our remission and our salvation were accomplished, ought we not to fast the [first] four days in addition to the two [others]?' He answered him, 'The Church's rule is that we should only join together those two [days], so that we might still have the strength to accomplish without fainting the things we are commanded to do, namely, unceasing prayer,* vigils,† reciting of God's law,‡ and our manual labor about which we have orders in

*1 Th 5:17.
†Mt 26:41.
‡Ps 119(118):77, 92, etc.

the holy Scriptures and which ought to permit us
Pr 31:20. to hold out our hands to the poor.[1] Those who do things such as these, as well as those who withdraw into solitude, are free from human burdens which would harass them, but we often see them served by others worse off than themselves, and see that they are proud, or fainthearted, or vain in search of human vainglory.'[2]

G[1] 90.

Theodore consults Pachomius about a headache

36. He went to see him yet another day and asked him, 'What must I do with this headache I have?' Our father Pachomius answered, 'A faithful man should bear the sickness he has in his body for ten years before speaking of it to anyone, except for an obvious sickness he cannot hide.' When he had heard these words from our father Pachomius' lips, he resolved to endure everything with gratitude out of love for the Cross, whatever should come his way.

G[1] 37.

Visit of Theodore's mother with her son Paphnouti

37. After some time his mother obtained from the bishop of Sne a letter addressed to our father Pachomius that he might allow her son Theodore to come out and that she might see him. For she had heard that among them no one met his relatives again.[1] When she came north with her other son, Paphnouti, she had the letter brought to our father by the porter. When he had read the letter, he called [Theodore] and said to him, 'Doubtless you will go out to meet your mother and your brother, so that she may be satisfied? All the more because our father the bishop has written to us about that.'[2] Theodore replied, 'If I go out to meet her, will I not be found at fault before the Lord for having transgressed his com-
Cf. Lk 14:26. mandment which is written in the Gospel? If the answer is no, I will go; if that is going to be a

weakness [on my part], God forbid that I should see her. I would not spare her even if it were necessary to kill her, just as the sons of Levi of old acted by an order the Lord gave them through Moses. God forbid that I should sin against him who created me, because of love for parents according to the flesh.' Our father Pachomius replied, 'If you wish to obey the Gospel's commandment, am I going to make you transgress it? It would never occur to me to urge you to do that; but when it was announced to me that she was weeping at the door, I was afraid that you might hear of it and that your heart might be wrung over it. As for me, my whole wish is for you to be firm in all the commandments of life. For the rest, if the bishop who has written to us learns that you have not seen her, he will not be sad; on the contrary, he will rather rejoice at your intention, since [the bishops] are our fathers who teach us in conformity with the Scriptures.'

Cf. Ex 32:27-28.

Our father Pachomius gave orders that they should be well cared for in a special place, according to their rank.[3] And after they had spent three days there the mother was told, 'He will not come to you.' Then she began to weep very copiously. Seeing her in great affliction, the clerics of the church questioned the brothers, 'Why is that old woman weeping this way?' They told them she was weeping because her son Theodore would not come to her so she might have the satisfaction of seeing him. Then they informed her that Theodore would be coming out in the morning with the brothers, going to work; they got her to go up on the roof of a house. She set about waiting patiently until he came out with the brothers and she saw him.[4]

G[1] 65.

Theodore's severity toward his brother

38. Then his brother started running after him, weeping and saying, 'I too want to stay with you and become a monk'; for he was younger than [Theodore]. Theodore never once stopped to speak to him and did not treat him as a brother, even when he grew tired and kept weeping. Our father Pachomius was informed of the rough manner Theodore had used toward [his brother]. He called him aside alone, and told him, 'Theodore, don't you know how to condescend to them at the beginning as one does with a newly-planted tree? For we give it special care and we water it until its roots are firm; it is the same with these.' And so he gave orders to bring him in, and he became a monk. He led the same way of life as all the brothers.

As for their mother, she left to return south in deep affliction and weeping very bitter tears for her sons. For not only had Theodore not come to meet her, but her younger son, Paphnouti, had left her as well to become a monk along with him.[1]

G[1] 39.

Gift of wheat to the Community

39. It happened once that they were about to run short of wheat needed for their food; and the brothers grew as sad as death over their poverty.[1] Our father Pachomius consoled them, saying, 'I believe that our Lord Jesus Christ will not forsake us. However, here are two fine mats that someone brought with him when he came to the brothers; let us dispatch them and sell them for the price they fetch while waiting for the Lord to furnish what we need.' He spent the whole night watching and praying to God about it. And while he was reflecting on the situation at the first hour of the day, thanks to God's providence and to his

overflowing love for men, a councillor[2] knocked at the monastery door. He said to the porter who opened to him, 'Tell your father[3] that here is a little wheat I had promised to give to those working in the mines, for the salvation of my soul as well as those of my entire family. I have just been instructed in a vision that you need it. So now, send down and take it from my boat, so that you may keep me in remembrance.' The porter brought the news to our father, who was greatly astonished. He went out and addressed the man, 'We do need the wheat, certainly, but grant us a delay until by God's grace we can repay you'. The man then said to him, 'I did not bring it to you that you might buy it, but for my soul's salvation, and also because you are men of God.' Then [Pachomius] unloaded the wheat with the help of the brothers who accompanied him. After that he brought the man some little eulogies,[4] that is, a little charlock, some vegetables, and some loaves of bread; and he accepted them with great faith in God. Then our father blessed him and he left full of joy and with alacrity. Then our father Pachomius sat down and spoke the word of God to the brothers about the gift God had given them in such good times. And the brothers marvelled at how quickly God had sent them the wheat they needed because of his holy servant, Apa Pachomius.

G[1] 40.

Reception of visiting monks

40. There was after [the time of] the martyrs a certain confessor called Apa Dionysios. He was a priest of Nitentori, a godfearing man and a friend in God of our father Pachomius. He was greatly grieved when he learned that [Pachomius] no longer allowed outside monks

(who went about visiting the brothers) inside the monastery as previously, but had them stay on their own at a place by the gatehouse of the monastery.[1] He came to see him at Tabennesi to reprove him about this. When he had spoken to the Man of God, he replied to him, 'O Apa Dionysios, do not think that I want to grieve a man's soul, much less to grieve the Lord who said with his holy lips, *Inasmuch as you will have done it unto one of those little brothers who believe in*
Mt 25:40; 18:6. *me, you will have done it unto me.*[2] But you know that many kinds of men are to be found in the *Koinonia*: old and young men, and neophytes. That is why I declared that it is good to let those who come to us into the *synaxis* at the time of the prayer, and then to lead them to a place apart for their meal. And I likewise declared that they must not take to going through the monastery, seeing certain neophytes and becoming scandalized. That is why I took this step. In fact, the patriarch Abraham ministered to the Lord and those who were with him in a place apart near the
Gn 18:1-8. tree and outside the tent.' And when Apa Dionysios heard this, he was satisfied with the explanation.

G[1] 41.

Healing of a sick woman by Pachomius

41. There was a woman who had been suffering for a long time from a flow of blood; she was the wife of a councillor of Nitentori.[1] Learning that Apa Dionysios was going to see the Man of God Apa Pachomius, she went to him and made this request: 'I know that the Man of God Apa Pachomius is your friend; therefore I want you to lead me to him so I may see him; for I am confident that if I only see him the Lord will grant me healing.' He consented to her request, because he

knew the torment that was burdening her. They got her into the boat and they came north to our father Apa Pachomius. Apa Dionysios went in to him, and after having settled with him about the brothers kept in a place apart, he asked him, 'I would like you to get up and us to go out toward the gatehouse for a pressing matter that concerns us.' [Pachomius] got up and followed him outside the door of the monastery; then they sat down and conversed together. The woman came up behind our father and, in consequence of her great faith, as soon as she had merely touched him and his clothing, she was cured. The man of God Apa Pachomius was sad to death on account of that matter because he always fled from human glory.[2]

G[1] 42.

Story of a monk who wanted a charge

42. There was a small monastery about two miles to the south of Tabennesi. The father of that monastery would often come to see our father Pachomius because he was a friend whom he loved very much; and the words of God he heard from his mouth he would repeat to his own monks so that they too might fear God's commandments. It happened that a brother of his monastery asked for a certain rank, and he replied to the brother, 'Our father Apa Pachomius warned me not to do this because you are not yet worthy of that thing'. That [brother] grew angry and dragged him along, saying, 'Come, let us go to him, and he shall have to prove that to me'. The other followed him in amazement and sorrow, wondering what was going to happen.

When the two of them and one other came to him at Tabennesi, they found him busy building

a part of the monastery wall. [The brother] approached our father Pachomius and said to him very angrily, 'Come down and give me proof of my sin, O liar Pachomius!' The Man of God Pachomius, thanks to his long-suffering, gave him no word whatever in reply. The other went on and said to him, 'Who compelled you to lie, you who pride yourself on clear vision while
Mt 6:23. your light is darkness?' The Man of God Apa Pachomius understood the wiles of the devil who was in that man, and he said to him respectfully, 'I have sinned, forgive me; do you never sin yourself?' And at once his wicked anger calmed down.

Then our father Pachomius took the father of that monastery aside and questioned him, 'What happened to this brother?' He answered him, 'Forgive me, my lord father; the fact is that this man asked me for a thing that he does not deserve. I knew that he would not obey me; so, I quoted you to him by name so he might perhaps have nothing to say. For I know that nothing is hidden from you. And behold he has added an evil deed to his wickedness!' Then our father Apa Pachomius said to him, 'Listen to me, give him [the office] so that by this means we may snatch his soul out of the enemy's hands. For if we do good to a bad man he comes thereby to have a perception of the good. This is God's love, to take
Eph 4:2. pains for each other.' When they heard this teaching of our holy father Apa Pachomius, they went away very comforted and giving thanks to God.

When they arrived at their monastery, the father of the monastery gave the rank to the brother as he had asked, in accordance with our father Apa Pachomius' instruction. A few days later that brother came to regret his fault; then he went back to our holy father Apa Pachomius, kissed his hands and feet, and said to him, 'Truly, O Man of God, you are much greater than what we hear of you every day. For the Lord knows that if you had not been patient with me the day I insulted you, sinner that I am, and if you had spoken some harsh word to me, I would have rejected the monastic life and gone back to the world. Blessed are you, O Man of God, my lord father, for thanks to your patience and graciousness, the Lord has brought me to life.'[1]

G[1] 43.

Healing of a possessed girl

43. Another day a man brought to our holy father Apa Pachomius his daughter afflicted with a serious illness from the demon, wanting him to cure her. The brother in charge of the door announced him to [our father], and he sent word to [the man], 'Send me one of her garments that she has not put on since it was washed.' He sent him one that was quite clean. When he had looked at it he sent it back to her father with these words, 'The garment is hers right enough, but she does not keep monastic purity. So now, let her promise to watch over herself in future, and we believe that the Lord will grant her healing.' Her father was very disturbed when he heard these words. When he set about questioning her, she confessed what she had done, and promised to keep watch over herself thenceforth so as never again to sin as long as she lived. Then our father prayed over some oil and had it taken to her; and as soon as she had anointed herself with it in faith, she was healed in the name of the Lord.

G[1] 44.
Healing of a possessed boy

44. Another man brought our father Pachomius his son possessed by a stubborn demon, and he begged him to pray over him and to heal him. When our father Pachomius got back to the monastery, he dispatched the brother in charge of the door. 'Go get one of the brothers' loaves, take it and give it to the man whose son is sick; and you will say to him, "Give some of this bread to your son, and trust in the Lord who will heal him."' When the sick boy's father got [the bread] he kissed it three times. Then, when his son was hungry, he took some of the brothers' bread, mingled it with other bread, and offered it to his son. Sitting down to eat, the boy ate the other bread, but did not touch the brothers' bread. Later his father opened some dates and some cheese and put fragments of the bread inside them. Once again the boy, when eating, threw out the fragments of bread that were in them and ate only the dates and the cheese. Then his father left him two days without food or drink, until he became weak. Then he prepared some porridge for him with this bread. When he served it to him, he sat down and ate it like a man in the best of health. After that, he sent a little oil to our father Pachomius who prayed over it. When the sick boy lay down, his father anointed him with it in the name of the Lord Jesus; and at once he was healed. And thus he went back in peace to his home, full of gratitude to God and to the prayer of our holy father Apa Pachomius, the Man of God.

G[1] 45.
Pachomius' attitude toward miracles

45. The Lord did many other healings through him. But if he prayed over someone for his healing and was not granted his request by the Lord,

he was not afflicted at not being heard. On the contrary his prayer was always, 'Lord, *may your will be done.*'[1]

Mt 6:10; 26:42.

46. One day he sat down and spoke out to the brothers, 'Do not think that bodily healings are healings; but the real healings are the spiritual healings of the soul. So, if today a man who was blinded in his mind through idolatry is led to the way of the Lord, to the point of seeing plainly and of acknowledging his Creator, is that not healing and salvation for the soul and for the body before the Lord at once and forever? And if someone else is dumb from lying, not *speaking the truth*, but his eyes are opened for him and he walks in righteousness, again is that not a healing? And if another's hands are maimed through his idleness in following God's commandments, but his eyes are opened and he *does some good*, again is that not a healing? Finally, if someone is a fornicator and proud, but someone shows him the way and he comes to conversion, is that not again a great healing?'

G[1] 47.

Pachomius' teaching on spiritual healings

Eph 4:25.

Eph 4:28.

47. Once our father Pachomius was on ‹an island›[1] with the brothers to reap rushes. And Theodore was preparing for the brothers what they would need. One evening our father Pachomius came back with his body all bent double and he lay down. Theodore fetched a nice hair blanket and threw it over him. Then our father said to him: 'Take that blanket off me and cast a mat over me as over all the brothers until the Lord brings me relief.' [Theodore] did as he was told; then he took a handful of dates and offered them to him saying, 'Perhaps you will be able to eat some of these, my father, for as of now you

G[1] 51,52.

Pachomius refuses a special treatment during his illness

have not yet eaten.' He refused them saying to him in great sadness, 'Because we have to administer the labor and the needs of the brothers, do we have the right to give ourselves ease? Where is now the fear of God? Have you just now visited the huts of the brothers to see whether there was anyone in them who was sick? Do not think that the things you offered me are negligible; for *God*

Ps 50(49):6; cf. Ps 75(74):7.

himself is judge who examines all things.' He stayed sick in bed, and he spent two days without food. At intervals he would get up and pray because of the ardor of his heart and of his love for God. On the third day he recovered from his sickness, got up, and went out and even ate with the rest of the brothers.[2]

G[1] 53.

Pachomius' compassion for a sick brother

48. At another time he was again ill to the point of being in danger of death because of his excessive *ascesis*. So then they brought him to the place where the sick brothers lay, in order to get him to take a few vegetables there.[1] A brother was likewise lying sick there. He had been ill for so long that his body was mere bones. He had asked the brothers who were doing the service to be given a little meat to eat, but they refused to give him any, saying, 'Such a thing is not customary among us'. Seeing that they would not give him any he said to the brothers who were doing the service, 'Take me and carry me to our father.' They did, and when [Pachomius] saw him he was surprised at how his flesh had wasted away. Looking at him all the while he remained astonished. Just then they brought him the few vegetables to eat. He gave a sigh and said, 'O, you who are respecters of persons, where now is the fear of

Lv 19:18; Mt 19:19.

God? *You shall love your neighbor as yourself!*[2]

Do you not see that this brother is like a corpse? Why do you not give him what he asks for? The Lord knows that if you do not give him what he has mentioned, I will not eat or drink either. Is there no difference between a sick person and another? Are not *all things pure to the pure*?' Tt 1:15. And saying this, he wept. He went on and said to them, 'As the Lord lives, if I had been in the monastery when he asked for what he wanted, I would not have left him in this great affliction while he was so sick.' When they heard these things from the mouth of our father Pachomius, the brothers hastened to send out at once and to buy a little kid goat. They skilfully prepared it and offered it to the brother, who ate. Then they brought our father Pachomius his few cooked vegetables; and he too ate like any of the brothers of his monastery, giving thanks.

G[1] *54a.*

Foundation of Phbow

49. As the number of the brothers increased at the monastery of Tabennesi, he saw that they were cramped for lack of room, and he began to ask the Lord about it. He was told in a vision, 'Go north to that deserted village lying downriver from you which is called Phbow, and build there a monastery for yourself. It will become a base and a source of renown for you in all ages to come.'[1] At once, he took some brothers with him, c. AD 329. went north to that village and spent some days with the brothers until he had built a wall for the monastery. Later he built the little celebration room,[2] with the permission of the bishop of Diospolis, and he likewise built the houses. He appointed housemasters with seconds, according to the rules of the first monastery. He himself kept watch over the two communities day and night, as a servant of the Good Shepherd.[3]

G[1] 54b.

Foundation of Šeneset

50. After that, an ancient old man named Apa Ebonh, father of a community called Šeneset, heard of the fame of our father Pachomius.[1] He sent him a message to beg of him, 'I want my monastery to come under the jurisdiction of the *Koinonia* God has given you, and I want you to establish for us too the rules appointed for you from heaven.' Pachomius went there with some brothers accompanying him. He established the houses[2] with the housemasters and the seconds according to the rules of the other [monasteries]. He directed them himself, often coming to [visit] them and encouraging them in God's laws and the labors of saints.

G[1] 54c.

Foundation of Thmoušons and annexion of Pmampesterposen

51. Some time later, a great and capable old man called Apa Jonas, [1] who was father of a community called Thmoušons sent for [our father Pachomius]. The latter took three brothers along, and went to him.[2] After he had met him and embraced him, [Jonas] said to him, 'Since God has raised this great fragrance through you in our time, behold, I also want to be granted a share in that good fragrance.' Our father answered him, 'It is well'. Then he organized ⟨them⟩[3] according to the rules of the other [monasteries] in everything. And very often he came to visit them when they needed him for anything either material or spiritual.

He annexed as well the monastery where he had stayed when he was secular, that is, Pmampesterposen. He had their affairs submitted to the *Koinonia*. They took care of a few date trees that were there.[4]

(Cf. G[1] 83).

52. Some time after this, he was also told in a vision, 'You must also organize a community in

Tkahšmin, in order to gather a people for me there'. He rose at once, took the brothers and went there. With the brothers he built the monastery and the cells.[1] Then he established their housemasters with their seconds and all their dispositions and everything they might need, according to the rules of the other monasteries. He gave them a great and capable father to govern them, Apa Pesso. That [monastery] is called Tse. Our father Pachomius himself used to come often to visit them and he was attentive [to provide] them with the word of God and with what they might need.

Foundation of Tse

53. Hearing about [our father's] fame, a great and pious councillor who dwelt in the city of Kos[1] in Upper Egypt immediately brought up a boat he had; he loaded it with wheat and sent it to him. He also wrote to him the following letter: 'Having heard about the fame of your piety and how you go north and south to the other monasteries to visit your sons in God, my lord father, I am sending this little boat to your Piety, that you may receive its cargo and use it for the brothers. As for the boat, let it be at your disposal forever, that you may pray for me and that the King of heaven may have pity on me. For it is not I who give it to you, but the One of whom you and your famous community are servants.'[2]

A councillor gives a boat to the Community

54. After some time, an orthodox bishop of the city of Šmin,[1] an ascetic called Arios, sent our father Pachomius the following message, 'I beseech you to rise and to come to me and to organize a monastery at our place so that the blessing of the Lord may come to our land because of you.' He rose [and] took the brothers,

G[1] 81a.

Foundation of Šmin

including some of the ancients. They got on the little boat and went north. As soon as they arrived, the bishop appointed a place for them and gave them another little boat, saying, 'Here is this little boat; it will be yours for any need.' Our father Pachomius was building the monastery with the brothers, carrying the clay on his back like[2] all the other brothers.

Some wicked and envious people caused trouble for him many times. They would come during the night to throw down what the brothers had built up during the day. God gave him patience and he learned in a dream that an angel would surround the monastery wall as with a blazing wall. After this he worked cheerfully with the brothers till the monastery was finished. Then he established the housemasters with their seconds as in the other monasteries.[3]

G[1] 82,81c.

Visit of some philosophers

55. Some envious philosophers came to him to examine his sayings and they sent him this message: 'We want you to come so that we may talk with you'. The man of God recognized the snare set for him by the demon that was in them. He called Cornelios and sent him to them saying to him, 'Go out and answer to those senseless men who think only of the body whatever the Lord will put into your heart.' Cornelios went out to them with two other brothers. When the philosophers saw them, they told him, 'Where is your father?' Cornelios answered them gently, 'What do you want of him? His spirit indeed is upon us. Now speak your empty word.'[1] The greatest among them replied, 'You have quite a reputation for being great monks and for speaking wisdom. Now then, have you ever heard it said that some-

one brings olives to Šmin to sell them?'[2] Apa Cornelios answered, 'On the other hand, have you ever heard it said that one presses the olives in Šmin to make oil? Instead they salt them so they will not spoil. Well, we are the salt; we have come here to salt you, for you are more insipid than most people in the world. For you pride yourselves on being teachers and now what you say is vain. All discourse of this sort is very bad.' Hearing this, they retired, greatly put to shame, because by their vain learning they could not overcome those who possess the true knowledge of the Lord dwelling in them. When the philosopher returned to his companions he told them how he had been put to shame. The greatest of them all answered, saying to him by way of reproach, 'Was that then your only question? Well then, I will go myself to dispute with them about the Scriptures.'

Cf. Mt 5:13.

At once he arose, full of pride, with a few others. They went toward the place of the monastery and got themselves announced to our father Pachomius who sent Theodore out to them with two other brothers to make reply to their blindness. When they arrived outside, the philosopher said to them, 'I want your father, that I may converse with him about the Scriptures.' Theodore replied humbly, 'You have no business with the Servant of Christ; now utter your carnal words and he who is spiritual will answer you.' Then [the philosopher] said to him, 'You pride yourselves on knowing the Scriptures as well as their interpretation. So now, tell me who was not born and died, who was born but did not die, who died but did not decay.' Theodore answered,

'Oh you whose mind is like a leaking barrel,
dwindles like a breath and fades away! He who
died not having been born was Adam; he who
Gn 5:24. was born but did not die was Enoch;[3] while the
one who died and did not decay was Lot's wife
Gn 19:26. *turned into a pillar of salt* for the seasoning of
such insipid minds as yours that strut so stupidly!'

When the philosopher heard these wise words
of Apa Theodore the just man, he was greatly
troubled inwardly. And he said to Apa Theodore, 'Say to your father: "Oh, you who have
built your house on the immovable and ever un-
Mt 7:24. breakable *rock* that is in heaven, be blessed, you
Gn 12:3. and the spiritual generations you beget. You have
been granted a bright mind equal to the universal
demiurge; no one begotten of woman will hinder
your work, which will prevail, grow in strength,
and spread out to the ends of all the earth."'
After he had said that, the philosopher made a
bow to Apa Theodore and went back to his house
with his companions, full of wonder at the grace
of God who had spoken through Theodore.
When our father Pachomius heard Theodore's
story he was amazed and cried out saying, 'Blessed may you be, Lord my God, for having con-
Cf. Ps 129(128):5. founded Goliath and all who hate Zion!'

After that, his spirit went from strength to
Cf. Lk 1:80. strength and he worked with the brothers until he
had completed the monastery entirely in keeping
with the rule of the other monasteries. He appointed as their father Apa Samuel, a man who
lived by the Spirit of God. Then he commended
them to the Lord and he left. Many times he would
come to visit them, for he was a keeper of flocks
following Christ, the great Good Shepherd.

56. There was living at Čoč, in the diocese of Hew, a certain Petronios in whom the Spirit of God had dwelt from his parents' house.[1] His parents were persons of rank, possessed of great fortune; but as for him, he wished to withdraw from men. He set out to a place lying on his parents' lands and there built for himself a monastery called Thbew. And he gathered about him anyone who wanted to live in Christ. Having heard about the fragrance of the holy *Koinonia*, he sent word to our father Pachomius, 'Would I might deserve that Your Piety should come here to me, so that we too might dwell in the shadow of the holy *Koinonia* our Lord Jesus has given you!' Our father arose, went there with the brothers, and organized everything with housemasters and seconds, entirely in keeping with the rule of the other [monasteries]. As for Apa Petronios, he had a father called Pšenthbo and his own brother named Pšenapahi, godfearing men. He addressed them with the Word of God and made them monks with all their household; and they made a beautiful death.[2] Thereafter he donated to our father Pachomius' *Koinonia* all he had: sheep, goats, cattle, camels, donkeys, carts, and all he possessed, including boats.

G[1] 80.

Story of Petronios and foundation of Thbew

57. Later on, moved by Providence and the Holy Spirit, he again took the brothers, went north to the vicinity of the city of Šmin, and built there another monastery whose name is Tsmine.[1] He finished it well, like all the other monasteries. He took the pious Apa Petronios, the mighty man who was at Thbew, and set him there as father, following an inspiration he had had from God. He entrusted him besides with the care of the

G[1] 83a.

Foundation of Tsmine

other two monasteries near him, so his words might guide them, for his *speech was seasoned with salt.*[2] After that, he placed another excellent father named Apollonios at Thbew to govern the brothers in the way of holy Apa Petronios.

Col 4:6.

G[1] 83b,81b,81d.

Foundation of Phnoum

58. Some time later he was told in a vision to organize still another monastery, in the south. He arose, took the brothers and went south to the mountain of Sne to a place called Phnoum.[1] When he had begun building the wall of the monastery, the bishop of that diocese got a large crowd together; they set out and rushed at [Pachomius] to drive him out of the place. The man of God our father Pachomius withstood the danger until the Lord scattered them and they fled before his face. After that he built the monastery, a very large one, and finished it well, in full keeping with the rules of the eight other monasteries he had built. He brought in a good father called Apa Sourous and he placed at their head this man capable of confirming them in our Lord Jesus' commandments.

As for our father Pachomius, he would very often go round to the monasteries, comforting all [the brothers] by the word of God *as a nurse comforts her children* with her heart's affection.[2]

1 Th 2:7.

G[1] 55,60,61.

Pachomius teaches a lesson to two brothers and to Cornelios

59. One day, during the time when they were making their little loaves, he took two other brothers with him and got into a small boat to go to Thmoušons for a visit with the brothers. At evening they set about taking their frugal meal, and the two brothers, seating themselves ate of everything that was before them, cheese, olives, vegetables. Our father Pachomius kept his eyes lowered and shed tears, and he ate only bread.

After eating, one of them noticed that he was crying and he said to him, 'My father, at our mealtime why did you eat nothing but bread, and why are you crying?' Our father Pachomius said to them, 'If I cried, it was because the fear of God is not in you, judging by the unrestrained way you ate of everything that was before you. For it is important for a man who thinks of heavenly things to practise abstinence in everything, according to the words of the Apostle Paul. As for me, when I saw that the loaves had been soaked, I was satisfied with them alone.'[1]

1 Co 9:25.

Once again he spoke to them, 'Do you want us to keep vigil tonight?' They said, 'Yes.' Then he said to them, 'I learned three ways of keeping vigil from my father, the holy old man Apa Palamon.[2] In my turn, I am going to tell them to you so you may choose one of them. Either you pray from evening till midnight, then sleep till time for the *synaxis*. Or else you sleep till midnight and then pray till morning. Or finally you pray a little and then sleep a little, [doing that] from evening till morning.' They chose to alternate a time of sleep and a time of vigil. The Man of God undertook to arrange the times of sleeping and praying according to the way they had chosen. One of the brothers, overcome by drowsiness went off to sleep alone somewhere; the other persevered in prayer with our father till morning. At the time of the *synaxis*, they also woke the one who had gone to sleep and they made the *synaxis*. The one who had persevered till morning went off to the hold of the boat and slept in his turn. As for the one who had slept, he rowed with our father until they came to Thmoušons.

When our father arrived at the monastery, he embraced all the brothers and Apa Cornelios whom he had given them as a leader. Apa Cornelios asked the brothers who had come in the boat, 'What has our father been doing these days?' They answered, 'Last night he taught us a lesson.' He said to them, 'What weakness afflicts men of this age! Is it right to let that feeble old man outdo you, you who are young?'

At evening they went to take their frugal meal and our father Pachomius said to Apa Cornelios, 'Do you want us to stand up and say some prayers?' Apa Cornelios answered him, 'Do as you wish'. So they stood up and prayed. And they kept praying until the time of the *synaxis*. And when the signal was given for the *synaxis*, Apa Cornelios halted and said to our father Pachomius, 'My father, what have I done to you that you teach me such a lesson? You did not even let me drink a little water when I left the table at night.' Our father said to him, 'O Cornelios, is it right to let a feeble old man outdo you?' Apa Cornelios understood that Pachomius had heard through God when he had laughed at the brothers saying, 'You have let a feeble old man outdo you'. At once he bent low before him saying, 'Forgive me, my father, for I understand that I did wrong in not speaking as I should.' Then, they went to make the *synaxis*.

Paphnouti's appointment as Great Steward

60. When they left [Thmoušons], they went off toward Thbew. He visited the brothers, then quickly returned to Phbow. When he arrived there, he appointed Apa Paphnouti, Apa Theodore's brother, near him to take care of the administration of the monasteries, for he was a man of word and of deed and perfect in all the virtues of the Lord.[1]

G[1] 64.

Pachomius' abstinence

61. Once our father Pachomius was lying sick. They prepared for him a bit of very good broth so he might eat it, since he was sick. When he saw it, he said to Theodore, 'Bring me a jug of water'. When it was brought to him, he poured some water into [the broth] which he stirred with his hand until the oil that was in it was emptied out. Then he said to Theodore, 'Pour water on my hands so I may wash them.' He washed his hands, then cast water on Theodore's feet. After that, [Theodore] questioned him, 'What have you done, my father?' Our father Pachomius answered, 'By pouring some water on the dish of vegetables I did away with the sweetness of taste lest it call forth in me fleshly desire. You poured water on my hands as if you were washing them for me, and because you washed my hands, I in turn washed your feet. All this I did so that I might not be condemned for being served by you, when it is I who must be the servant of all.'

G[1] 66.

Theodore comforts a brother

62. There was a brother in the monastery whom our father Pachomius reprimanded frequently for the sake of his salvation. One day Theodore had a talk with him. And since his heart was dejected to the point of thinking of leaving the brothers, he said to Theodore, 'I cannot stay with that old man whose speech to me is so abrupt'. Theodore wishing to ease the brother of the burden that was weighing him down, answered him with an artifice that was full of wisdom, saying, 'Then you too have a heart that is full of sorrow?' He answered him, ‹'Yes.' Theodore went on,›[1] 'I am suffering more than you. But let us comfort each other until we test him once more. If he is good to us, we will stay

with him; but if not, we will go, only the two of us, to some other place.' Hearing this, the brother was greatly consoled because of what Theodore had said. Theodore went to our father Pachomius, unbeknownst to this brother, and gave him an account of the whole matter. Our father Pachomius replied, 'Very well! Now when night falls bring him to me, coming as if you were going to reprove me; and according to what God will put into my mouth, I will give contentment to his heart in what he wishes.' That night Theodore went to the brother and said to him, 'Let us arise and go to our father to find out how he will speak to you.' He followed him at once with joy; and when they came to our father Pachomius they began to speak. Our father Pachomius replied, 'Forgive me. I have sinned; are you able to bear with your father, as good sons?' Theodore began again to load him with reproaches as if he were really angry. The brother spoke up and said to Theodore, 'Stop! That is enough; I am greatly comforted.' And so Theodore through his good artifice benefitted that suffering brother.

G[1] 67,68.

Theodore accompanies a brother to his family

63. Among the brothers there was still another who set about asking our father Pachomius, 'If you do not allow me to go home and see my family, I will go home and become a secular again.' At once Pachomius called Theodore and said to him, 'I know your wisdom and how you sympathize with all those who are distressed. Now, you will take this brother in charge; you will go with him to visit his parents, and you will humor him in all things, so as to bring him back to us.[1] For, there is much that is excellent in him, and

we know above all that it is God's will that we humor all men in all things until we have saved their souls from the hands of the enemy warring against them. And God will give you the reward for your pains.' Theodore very humbly obeyed and went off with the brother. When they arrived there, they had to eat a frugal meal and to rest. The brother said to his parents, 'Prepare for us in a place apart some foods customary to monks.' When these were ready the brother said to Theodore, 'Rise and let us eat a little.' [Theodore] was loath to eat in a secular house because it was not his custom. But he noticed how the brother's face darkened and he realized that he was put out. Then he said to himself, 'Unless I go along with him in all things, he will never come back with me. Besides, no secular is going to see us eating and we are not eating anything but what monks eat.' So he ate a little, as if he was being offered as a sacrifice, humoring him in all things until he brought him back to the monastery. When they returned to the monastery Theodore reported everything that had happened to our father Pachomius, who did not blame him, since he knew that he had done this not of his own will but for God and his brother's salvation.

Later, Theodore took the brother aside and discussed the Scriptures with him in order to persuade him not to go again on visits to his parents, and he said to him, 'How do you understand this saying of the Gospel, *If any man comes to me without hating his father and mother*, etc.?'[2] The Lk 14:26.
brother answered, 'The Scripture has put its words quite high so that we might attain to a small part of them. For how can we hate our

parents?' Theodore went on, 'Is this truly the faith of the Tabennesiots?' The Gospel says one thing and you, on your own authority alone, say something else. Truly the Lord knows this. If this is your faith, then I will go back to the little monastery from which I came, for the old men I met there never denied the Gospels.' And having said that, he made a pretence of withdrawing and he hid somewhere for a little while. The brother came to our father Pachomius and informed him of everything. Then our father Pachomius said to the brother, 'Do you not know that Theodore is a neophyte, while you are an ancient in endurance? So now, hurry up and find him. If he leaves here we will not have a good reputation.' The brother went off in search of Theodore and attempted to change his mind with words. Theodore answered him, 'If you want me to stay here, promise me before the Lord and the brothers, "I will keep to the Gospels in all things."' The brother promised never again from then on to go to his parents. And that was how Theodore acted with a good artifice until he led the brother on to the perfection of the holy Gospel.

G[1] 69.

Obedience superior to fasting and psalmody

64. One day an angel of the Lord told our father Pachomius to teach a brother about his salvation. [This brother] was engaging in great practices and a harsh *ascesis*, but he was doing so not for God but for vainglory. Our father Pachomius took him aside and told him, 'It is written, *I have come down from heaven not to do my own will, but to do the will of the one who sent me*. Now obey me; when the signal is given at midday to call the brothers to eat, you shall go too and you shall eat a little. And whatever food

Jn 6:38.

they eat you shall take a little of it too, although without eating your fill. But at evening, when the signal is given again, let us go and eat properly. So obey me, for I see that the enemy envies you and wants to destroy all your labor.'[1]

The [brother] cheerfully obeyed the instructions [our father] addressed to him. Later, when the signal summoned the brothers for the midday meal, he got up too and went off to eat with the brothers. But once more he fell into his deception, saying to himself, 'Where is it written, "You shall not fast"?' And so once again he followed his vain judgement and did not go in to eat with the brothers.

Our father Pachomius was sad about this brother, and he called Theodore and sent him to him, saying, 'Go and see what that brother is doing. If you find him in prayer, hold him till I come, and vainglory will at once show itself forth in a lively manner in him.' Theodore arose and did as our father Pachomius had ordered him. And when he arrived where the brother was he found him busy praying, and he held him. At once [the other] grew angry like a devil; he seized a big stone to throw at Theodore's head and kill him, and said to him, 'Impious [Theodore], is it you who will keep me from praying to the Lord God?' Theodore rebuked him, and at once the demon who was living in him kept still. And the demon said, 'Do you want to know that I am the one who is at work in those who sing for pleasure?[2] If you do not believe me, listen to that brother who is singing. He is going to say that verse nine times.' There was a brother in a cell, who was singing the beginning of the Canticle of

Moses with these words, *Let us sing to the Lord, for he has been exalted gloriously.* Theodore pricked up his ears, and what the demon had said happened. Reflecting on the devil's devices, he was awestruck, and wondered if the man would be able to escape a lot of trouble. While Theodore was seated near the brother and watched over him, our father Pachomius came. He stood, as did Theodore, and they prayed together over him. The Lord healed him; he opened the eyes of his heart so that he could understand how he must behave, *not as a fool but as one wise.* And he gave glory to God.

Ex 15:1.

Eph 5:15.

G[1] 70.

About a murmuring old brother

65. One day our father Pachomius took the brothers and went down into the monastery cistern to clean it. There was an old man who had lived long in the world, and had been a monk for only a short time. This man began to murmur, saying, 'Is this old man taking the children of men down into that cistern in order to kill them?'[1] That night he had a dream. He saw himself as it were standing over that cistern. He was looking down into it and he saw a man shining with glory in the midst of the briskly working brothers. He said to them, 'Receive, all of you, a spirit of obedience and strength, and you, the old man, a spirit of faithlessness toward the holy men.' At morning, that day, he came in the midst of the *synaxis*, and falling on his face before all the brothers, he confessed this thing.[2]

G[1] 71.

Pachomius' vision concerning the future of the Koinonia

66. Once our father Pachomius was engaged with the brothers in cutting rushes. One day they were on their way back to the boat, all loaded down with rushes, following our father Pachomius and reciting the Holy Scriptures. Half way

there he looked up to heaven and received great revelations. Then he put down his load of rushes, as did the brothers, and they remained standing and praying. The man of God Pachomius remained stunned for a long time by the frightening vision he had seen. He lay face down and kept weeping copiously, the brothers likewise shedding abundant tears with him.

When he got up from his prostrate position the brothers asked him, 'Father, tell us what you saw.' He sat down, addressed them with God's word and said to them, 'I saw the whole community of the *Koinonia* in great pain. Some were surrounded by great flames they could not pass through. Others were in the midst of thorns whose points would pierce them, having no way out. And others, on the bottom of a great, deep, ravine, were struggling desperately, unable either to climb up because of the steepness of that precipice or to throw themselves into the river, for there were crocodiles lying below in wait for them. Now, my children, woe is me, for I think that after my death all this will happen to the brothers ‹and they will not find the one who can comfort them in their tribulations.›'[1] Then he got up, prayed and took up his load of rushes. The brothers likewise took up their loads, reciting until they reached the boat.[2]

G[1] 72,73,75.

Theodore does not understand an order from Pachomius

67. After they returned to the boat an ancient anchorite brother living in that place came up to [our father] to pay him and all the brothers a visit. [Our father] embraced him and said to Theodore, 'Go and prepare a meal and give this brother who has come to us something to eat'. Theodore left him and sat down, thinking that he

had told him, 'Let me speak to the brother.' Afterwards he sent another brother, who also did not understand what he had said and who went out and sat down too. Our father Pachomius understood that this was a work of the spirits. He himself prepared the food, gave the brother to eat and dismissed him. Then he called Theodore and said to him, 'If your father according to the flesh told you something, would you have disobeyed him? Then why did you not obey my commandment to give the visiting brother something to eat?' Theodore answered, 'Forgive me, I thought that you told me "Withdraw, that I may speak to the brother."' He called the other one, who also answered the same thing. Our father Pachomius sighed and said, 'I understand it was an evil spirit hindering a good deed. But blessed be the Lord who has *granted* wisdom and *patience** to all *those who love him.* †

*Is 57:15.
†Si 1:10.

'For, often I have heard evil spirits speaking among themselves of the different evils they inflict on men. One day I heard a demon saying sadly to another demon, "These days I am busy with a man who is hard to deal with in all he does. When I suggest an evil thought to him, he stands at once, prays and weeps before the Lord; as for me, I go out ablaze." In turn the other demon said, "As for me, every counsel I give to the one in my charge, he swiftly carries out, and even much more." Therefore be on your guard against evil thoughts.

'Imagine a house today in which there are a hundred rooms. If someone today buys one room from the master of the house, can anyone possibly prevent him from entering it, even though it is the furthest one of all in the house? So, too, a faithful man, even if he has all *the fruits of the Spirit* and is negligent of one of them, will he not be weak before the enemy's face because of that fruit? Perhaps too, if he does not mend his ways the enemy will defeat him also in another [fruit]. Ga 5:22-23.

'For there is not just one measure in God's service. There are spiritually rich commanders; there are captains of fifties, of hundreds, and of thousands, and a perfect king like our father Abraham who was told, *You are a king from God,* and not an ordinary king, but a king *the King of kings* is with.' Gn 23:6. 1 Tm 6:15.

Our father Pachomius said all this while in the hut on the shore upstream from the boat, putting fear into the brothers for the salvation of their souls.[1]

G[1] 76.

Story of Mauo

68. The next day at morning he took the brothers and set off to gather rushes because they needed some more. Among their number was an ancient old man[1] who was a housemaster, called Apa Mauo. He had not set out with the brothers that day but he had gone to bed in the hut as if he were ill.[2] He was not ill, but quite indignant over the instructions he had heard in the evening from our father Pachomius. He said, 'Why these long lectures the old man gave us in the evening? Are we in danger of falling every hour?' While he was sunk in these thoughts, God's goodness willed to restore his calm.

At that moment a bishop sent our father Pachomius a letter and a monk wearing a hair garment, with another brother. He wrote to him in these terms, 'I am here sending you this old man. This man, who used to have a great way of life, has been caught by us in the act of stealing. We have sent him to you for you to judge him because he is a monk.' When [these two monks] came to the spot where the boat and the huts were, they asked for our father Pachomius and learned that he had gone off with the brothers to gather rushes. The old man Apa Mauo embraced them and said to them, 'Sit down for a while until our father comes in.' Then he said to Theodore, seeing that he was getting the food ready for the brothers, 'Make haste to get food ready and give the brothers who have come to see us [something] to eat, for I can tell by the aspect of that great man that he is pious.'

At evening our father Pachomius arrived, loaded with rushes, with the brothers. And when he had embraced the visitors, they gave him the letter the bishop had written to him. When the Man of God had read the letter, by the discernment of the Holy Spirit that was in him, he at once reprimanded [the monk] concerning the fault he had committed. This latter entreated our father Pachomius weeping and confessing his fault with great humility. Our father Pachomius
Jm 3:2. replied to him, '*We all fall very often.* But let us pray to the merciful God and, if we watch over ourselves in future, he will heal us.' After these words, the [old man] left with the brother who accompanied him, greatly consoled by the light penance our father Pachomius had laid on him.

When the old man Apa Mauo heard these words about that [other] old man, he was astonished and glorified God for the firm words he had heard at evening from our father Pachomius. Our father Pachomius said to him,

'O Mauo, because you are firmly seated on the unshakable rock, do you think that everyone is going to find that way? Let us pray the Lord full of mercy and pity that he may save us from the ambushes of the evil one and the wicked devil.' The old man Apa Mauo replied, 'Forgive me, my lord father and man of God, for in the ignorance of my heart I dared to insult the Holy Spirit which is in you.'[3]

Cf. Mt 7:24-25.

G[1] 77,78a.
Theodore's first instruction

69. That day, a Sunday, our father Pachomius called Theodore and said to him, 'When the brothers come out from table in the evening, give your ministry to another brother and come to the place where we assemble for the instruction.' Theodore did so; and when he came to [our father] who stood speaking God's word to the brothers, Pachomius immediately took him by the hand in the midst of the brothers and said to him, 'Stand here and speak to us the holy words of God'. Although unwillingly, he began to speak in front of all the brothers who stood, including our father Pachomius who listened too like the brothers. Immediately some among them, out of pride, were angry and returned to their houses without listening to the Lord's word. They said, 'He is a young one while we are ancients, and it is to him that he gives the order to instruct us!' In fact, Theodore was thirty-three the day our father made him stand to give the instruction, knowing that he was farther advanced than they.[1]

When our father Pachomius found out that some among them had gone away without listening to God's word from Theodore's mouth, he sat down and said to [the brothers], 'What is the meaning of this great [fuss] among you, because

I have appointed a young man to give us the instruction? What great and foolish madness! The words that he spoke, were they not those of the Lord of the universe? Indeed we hear the Lord say about a little one, *Anyone who receives a little one like this in my name receives me.*[2] [Mt 18:5.] And was I not standing with you, just like any one of you? And I tell you, I did not only pretend, but I was listening with all my heart, as one thirsty for cool water[3] [Cf. Pr 25:25.] in summertime. For worthy indeed of all acceptance is the word of the Lord, as it is written.[*] [*Cf. 1 Tm 1:15; 4:9.] Wretched are those who went back[†] [†Jn 6:67; Ps 44(43):18.] and estranged themselves from God's mercy and kindness. Yes, I swear to you, unless they repent of their pride their life will be [nothing but] suffering; for *the Lord is close to those contrite in heart, and he will save the humble of spirit.'* [Ps 34(33):18.] After these words, he rose, prayed and dismissed the brothers, each to his cell. And when he had finished gathering rushes, he returned to the monastery.

G[1] 78b.

Theodore becomes steward at Tabennesi

AD 336-337.

70. Having found out that Theodore was capable in the spirit of the Lord, he appointed him steward at Tabennesi, to govern others. Our father Pachomius himself stayed at the monastery of Phbow where the administration of the eight other monasteries was.[1] Although Theodore had been appointed at Tabennesi, it was as if he had not been appointed at all, for there was no fleshly desire in him. For, *the word of God had proven him through fire*[2] [Ps 105(104):19.] and strengthened him to *mind the things which are in heaven and no longer the things that are on earth*;[3] [Col 3:2.] and his whole effort was to *love the Lord his God with all his heart*[4] [Mt 22:37.] in conformity with the

commandment He has given us in the Gospels. He made good progress in profiting the brothers, for his word was full of grace in every way.

G[1] 83c.

Appointment of the Great Steward at Phbow, and assembly of the month of Mesore

71. As for Paphnouti, [Theodore's] brother, he established him near him at Phbow; it was he who received the [fruits of the] manual labor of the other monasteries and who provided them with all their needs.[1]

Twice a year they would come to Phbow. [They came] to celebrate the Passover together in the word of God. And again at the season of the harvest they would come on the twentieth of Mesore[2] to render their accounts to the Great Steward. And if one or the other needed to receive an ordinance, our father Pachomius would give it to them, then each would go back very peaceably to his place.[3]

13 August.

G[1] 96,86,97.

Pachomius is corrected by a young brother and corrects another one

72. Once, our father Pachomius went again to Tabennesi for a visit to the brothers and because of a slight transgression one brother had made.

As soon as he arrived at the monastery he made haste first of all to weave his mat in his usual manner. While he was working on it a young man entered; he was the weekly server in the community. Seeing our father Pachomius working on the mat, he said to him: 'That is not the way we are working at present; for our father Theodore gave us orders not to weary the plaits, so that the mats may sound well[1] and be good to look at!' Our father Pachomius got up at once and said to the brother, 'Come, sit down and show me!' After the young brother had taught him, he sat down again to work with joy because he had vanquished the thought of pride. And he did not rebuke the little young man for speaking out of turn.

When he had finished his mat he seated himself and spoke the word of God to the brothers from morning till evening. Then he said to them, 'I was sent here today because of a man's welfare, and I found that for which I came here in an earthenware vessel.' By that figure he meant the offence of a man. And when he spoke, there was present a brother called Elias, a simple man. He had gathered five figs to eat them after the fast. When he heard the fearful words of our father Pachomius, he understood that the accusation lay upon him. At once he rose quickly, went out, brought the vessel with the figs into the midst of the brothers and revealed the fact, saying, 'My lord father, forgive my offence. The Lord knows that these here are all that I have taken; see, now I have revealed my fault to you.' The brothers marvelled at the Spirit of God which was in our father Pachomius and at his perfect clairvoyance. After that, he arose, ⟨prayed⟩[2] and went back to Phbow without having eaten or drunk.

G[1] 88.

Pachomius has a terrifying apparition

73. After his promotion at Tabennesi, Theodore had the habit of coming to Phbow every day after his manual work in order to listen to the word of God from our father Pachomius. He would then return to Tabennesi the same day so as to repeat it to all the brothers of Tabennesi. And he did so for a very long time.[1] Once Theodore came as was his custom to hear what our father Pachomius would say, and as he did not find him, he went up on the roof of the assembly room[2] to recite. Our father Pachomius was at prayer in the assembly room; but Theodore did not know it. In his prayer our father Pachomius had some terrifying apparitions and revelations,

and the assembly room suddenly shook like water. When Theodore noticed that the roof was moving, he was afraid; he grew troubled and hurried to come down. He went into the assembly room to pray because of his fright. He stretched out his hands in prayer, but he could not stand because of the fright in that place. Then he sat down immediately; but when he was seated, he felt oppressed like a man wedged between two walls and so he quickly fled away out of the assembly room. During all this, he did not know that our father Pachomius was inside the place.

This is the revelation that our father Pachomius saw in his prayer. Looking toward the east wall of the sanctuary, [he saw the wall] become all golden; and on it there was a large icon, like a large picture [of someone] wearing a crown on [his] head. That crown was glorious in the extreme; all around its sides were multicolored images which resembled precious stones and which are the fruits of the Holy Spirit: faith, goodness, fear, mercy, purity, humility, righteousness, patience, kindness, gentleness, temperance, joy, hope, and perfect charity.[3] Before the icon were Ga 5:22-23.
two great and very august archangels, motionless and contemplating the Lord's image that had appeared in the assembly room. While watching that great revelation, our father Pachomius went on praying and imploring [God] in these terms: 'Lord, may your fear descend on us all forever, so that we may not sin against you all our life long.' And he went on repeating that same prayer. Then the angels said to him, 'You cannot endure the fear of the Lord as you request'. He answered, 'Yes, I can, by God's grace.' And at once the ray

of fear, after the manner of the sun rising on the entire world, and without leaving its place, moved gradually forward toward him. That shining ray was very green and its sight wonderfully terrifying. When fear touched him, it pinched all his members, his heart, his marrow, and his whole body; and at once he fell to the ground and began to writhe like a living fish. His soul grew very sad and he fainted away toward death. The angels were watching him with part of their faces without in the least averting their eyes from the image of the Lord that was appearing to our father Pachomius. They said to him, 'Did we not tell you that you could not stand the full shock of the Lord?' He cried out, 'Have mercy on me, my Lord Jesus Christ!' At once the ray of fear retreated gradually until it returned to its place. Then the sheen of mercy moved toward him like a rich holy chrism. When mercy reached him he was comforted; he rose at once to his feet and blessed God until the time when the brothers do the *synaxis*; and he rested a while.

After the morning *synaxis*, Theodore found our father Pachomius relating these things in private to some ancient fathers, saying to them with sighs and tears, 'I nearly had my soul torn out of me last night when I went into the assembly room to stretch out my hands before the Lord. And while I was in distress of soul, a bold man came in, and was close to having his soul torn out of him too because of the fear which he saw.' Theodore said, 'That was me, my holy father. I came north in the evening to pay you a visit and get your blessing, but when I did not find you, I went up on the roof of the assembly room. After a short time, while I was meditating, the assembly room shook and I fled away in fear and I came down. Then I tried to go into the assembly room and my body quaked; so I quickly fled outside, badly frightened.' Our father Pachomius said, 'The Lord knows, O my son Theodore, that it is by a great mercy that you fled quickly from that place.' When the ancient old men heard these things, they were greatly struck with fear and they said, 'These holy men are like those of heaven in their just thoughts about our Lord Jesus Christ.'

G[1] 89,91.

Breach of silence in the bakery

74. Another day, Theodore came to Phbow to visit our father Pachomius, who was very weak in body. When he arrived, [Pachomius] said to him at once, 'Go and investigate this transgression, find out how many men talked at evening in the bakery.' Theodore went, inquired, and found that five brothers had talked, and he came back to report it to our father. Then our father Pachomius said, 'Theodore, do those men think that these are human things? I assure you that if a commandment is given even about a slight matter, it is nevertheless important. For that great multitude spent seven days marching around Jericho in silence, obedient to the commandment they had been given. Then, when they received the commandment to do so, they shouted; obedient again, they fulfilled the will of God proclaimed by the man who had given the orders. Now, let these [brothers] be careful in the future and they will be forgiven for what they have done. If indeed this commandment had not been profitable to their souls, I would not have arranged the matter thus.'[1]

Jos 6:1-21.

Pachomius would often send Theodore to the other monasteries to visit them. And often in the midst of the brothers he would say to them, 'Theodore and I fulfill the same service to God. And he has power over everything, as father and as master.'

G[1] 92.

A brother falsely accused of stealing

75. Another day Theodore went off to a monastery to visit the brothers, and straightway they brought him a brother they accused of having stolen something, that he should expel him from among the brothers for this reason. The culprit, however, was not this brother, but another who passed for a faithful man among all the brothers. But they were accusing the former because he was somewhat negligent in their view. When the thief realized that he had not only committed the first fault but that, moreover, because of him they were going to drive the other brother away from the monastery, he went to see Theodore privately and said to him, 'Forgive me, my father; I am the one who committed the theft'. Theodore said to him, 'The Lord has forgiven you the fault you have committed, for clearing the innocent in our presence.' Then he called the one who had been falsely accused and said to him: 'I know that you are not the perpetrator of this fault. But even if the brothers affliced you a little for the fault you have not committed, nevertheless do not be proud of your innocence in this case. For you are doubtless indebted to the Lord for other faults you have committed. Therefore, give him thanks and be in fear of him all your life long.' Then he said to the brothers about this matter, 'Have you not entrusted me with judgement so that I might pass

sentence? Well, it is God's will that he should be absolved. Indeed, we are all in need of God's mercy.'

Another vision of Pachomius and Theodore

76. There was in the community of Tabennesi a brother tempted by a demon. Theodore mounted him on a donkey and brought him to our father Pachomius at Phbow so he might pray over him. When he was about to arrive, our father Pachomius saw him from afar, while he stood addressing the word of God to the brothers for their soul's salvation. Straightway he left the brothers and went out to meet Theodore. Some of them grew angry saying, 'We are elders and he left us in order to meet Theodore, who is a young man, as soon as he caught sight of him.' Those who were angry were again those who had been upset before, when [our father] assigned [Theodore] to give the instruction to the brothers for their soul's salvation. He embraced Theodore and said to him, 'Before you arrived here today I had word of you by a command of the Lord. So now, turn over to someone else this sick brother you have brought with you and join me quickly in the assembly room.' Our father Pachomius prayed for the brothers and dismissed them; and each of them returned to his cell.

When Theodore came back to our father Pachomius, he took him along and went into the assembly room. They remained standing and prayed from the second to the ninth hour. While they were praying they saw appearing above them as high as a tower a great throne on which the Lord was seated under the form in which he chose to be seen by them. At times the throne would be raised so high that they would cease to see it; at times it would come down to them so low that they could all but touch it with their hands; and the throne continued this process for about three hours. When the throne came low, our father Pachomius would lay hold of Theodore as if he was carrying him in his hands and would present him to the one who was seated on the throne, saying, 'Lord, accept this gift from me'; and he went on doing so a great many times while repeating those words, until he heard a voice, 'Your prayer has been answered, be manly and brave.' After that, he dismissed Theodore, who brought in the sick brother, and together they prayed over him. Thus the Lord healed him of his sickness and along with Theodore he returned southward to Tabennesi as if he had never been sick at all.

Cf. 1 Co 16:13.

Another breach of silence in the bakery

77. One day our father Pachomius was with the brothers at Tabennesi to make up the little loaves they needed for a year's supply at Phbow, as there were as yet no bakers there. He had given them the commandment that no man should speak in the bakery, but all should recite God's word together; and if those who were kneading had need of a little water, they should beat on the kneading-trough with their hand.[1] Once while the kneading was going on, one of the brothers who was kneading spoke out to some ministers, 'Give me a little water'. Our father Pachomius was standing some distance away, but forthwith an angel of the Lord beckoned to him while the others were still talking among themselves, 'See how those men are behaving; they have disobeyed the commandment you gave them. So now, if Theodore comes to you and raises his hands to

you, will you hold him excused?' He answered, 'No'.

At morning, our father Pachomius summoned Theodore, who was the father of the monastery of Tabennesi and had responsibility for the bakery as well as for the bakers. He said to him, 'Go and find out who disobeyed the commandment in the bakery last evening'. He made a thorough investigation of the matter and found out that eighteen men were involved in the disobedience. Quite shamefaced, he came in to our father Pachomius and raised his hand to him ⟨saying⟩,[2] 'Since when? Till when?' When our father Pachomius saw him raise his hand to him, he remembered the words the angel had spoken to him; and straightway he laughed in his face with great anger. Theodore, seeing the nature of his laugh, was still much sadder. Some of those present spoke to him, 'Why are you crying? What did he say to you?' Our father Pachomius said to them, 'Let him be. Let him cry about the negligence he committed before God.'

Theodore turned over the command of the bakery to another brother and withdrew to a place in the community according to our father Pachomius' will. He fasted two days at a time[3] with sighs and groans, and he prayed with tears night and day about what the brothers had done. After he had practised that great *ascesis* for three weeks, our father Pachomius said to him, 'Stop, that is enough; but take care that you never again hereafter be negligent and that no transgression occur among the brothers, lest you be found guilty of sins before the Lord Jesus Christ.'[4]

78. When our father Pachomius saw that

Theodore becomes Pachomius' assistant in Phbow

Cf. Jos 1:1.

Theodore was making progress in the work of the Lord, he took him away from Tabennesi and replaced him with another, named Apa Sourous the Young, as their father. He brought Theodore to Phbow and kept him at his side as a helper—like Joshua, son of Nun, at Moses' side.[1] Then he would very often send him to the monasteries to visit the brothers and encourage them by the word of God. It was he who would accept in each community those who came to become monks; on the other hand, when it was necessary to expel some of them by the order of God and of our father Pachomius, he it was again who expelled them.

A brother who ate too many leeks

79. Another day it happened that [Theodore] was somewhere working with the brothers. In the evening, when they had finished work, he caused a meal to be prepared for them. While they were eating, Theodore stood by to wait on them, and he noticed one of them at table eating a lot of leeks. He was a sturdy young man come among the brothers not very long before. When Theodore had finished serving the brothers their meal, he went off by himself and leaned his back against the wall, for he was fasting two days at a time[1] and it was very warm outside. Then he said to the brothers concerning the one he had seen eating many leeks, the same being present and hearing, 'A monk must not eat many leeks, for that invigorates the body and makes war on the soul'. While he was speaking, our father Pachomius arrived among them, wishing to see the place where he was working with the brothers. When he saw Theodore with his back against the wall he said to him sadly, 'Is it the wall that is

going to carry your body?' Theodore straightened up immediately and humbly made a prostration before our father Pachomius. In everything he humbled himself without ceasing so as to become perfect in the law of the Lord.

Theodore was very sad over the brother he had reproached for eating many leeks, because it was perhaps not God's will that he should speak thus. He said to himself, 'Why did I not wait for the Lord to move him in his free choice, and for him to learn from those who have a good way of life how to constrain his body by virtue?' As for this brother, having heard these words, he never again attempted to eat leeks till the day of his death. And when Theodore noticed that this brother did not try any more to eat leeks, he too refrained from eating them till the day of his death, fearing that God would condemn him for not having himself abstained from a thing he had made the subject of reproach to another.

Theodore is reproached for being too inquisitive

80. One day encountering one of the brothers returning from somewhere wearing his cloak thrown over his shoulder—the superior[1] of that community had sent him out for a service—he said to him, 'Where are you coming from?' Our father Pachomius, some distance away, heard him questioning [the brother]. After the latter had gone on, he called Theodore and said to him, 'Theodore, make haste to be master of your heart with all moderation, so as not to form habits and so as to avoid asking anyone, "Where are you going," except solely to question him about his soul's salvation.' Having heard these words, Theodore took them to heart all his lifelong, saying, 'Whether that is a small or a

great thing, never again will I undertake to do it'.[2]

Another vision of Pachomius and Theodore

81. Another day, at the seventh hour of the day, when the heat was very great out of doors, our father Pachomius called Theodore and said to him, 'Let us go and eat a little bread, for we are going to proceed quickly to the monastery of Thmoušons for the sake of a brother catechumen, who is at death's door'. Theodore said, 'As you wish'. They went at once to the refectory. At that moment there was no one in the refectory but the two of them alone. When they had placed their loaves in water, he said to Theodore, 'Let us pray while we wait for the loaves to soften'. They had begun to pray when a great fear came down on them. They saw a man standing before them shining with light and holding out his hand to them ⟨saying⟩,[1] 'Give me your sweet-smelling prayers that I may bring them before the Lord'. Immediately they bowed down to the ground and cried out to the Lord, saying with many supplications and tears, 'Lord our God, *may your mercy be upon us*!' Then they went on praying until evening. Our father Pachomius made many supplications concerning the brother catechumen, that the Lord might leave him in the body, so they could see him before he died. At evening, they sat and ate, then got up quickly and set out on the road. They spent half the night on the road before they reached Thmoušons.[2]

Ps 33(32):22.

As soon as they arrived there they went in to the sick brother. The leader of the place spoke to our father Pachomius, 'He has been sick for two days. We were afraid to pick him up and take him south to be baptized, lest he die on our hands along the way.' It was indeed a custom with them to bring all the catechumens of the monasteries to Phbow during the Forty Days to baptize them. Our father Pachomius said to him, 'Since you saw his condition was worsening, why did you not baptize him here?' The leader answered, There is no priest here to baptize him'. While they were conversing, and before the brother gave up the spirit, our father Pachomius' and Theodore's eyes were opened; they saw the angels who had come to fetch him secretly baptize him before he left his body.

G[1] 93b.

Vision concerning the fate of souls at the time of death

82. Here is the way the angels of light visit the good brothers, as the thing was many times revealed to [Pachomius] by the Lord. If the dying man is good, three angels whose rank corresponds to the measure of the dying man's conduct come to fetch him. If he is of a high rank by his practices, angels who are outstanding are sent to conduct him to God. If on the other hand he is a little one in virtues, angels of lower rank are sent to come for him. God acts thus so that those [angels] who come ⟨to visit⟩[1] the man may lift him out of his body with proper patience, and lest some high-ranking [angels], being sent to take someone who is of low rank by his practices, should treat him according to the custom of earthly authorities. These [authorities] act with partiality, impressed by the riches and empty glory, and treat those who are despised or poor according to their condition of scorn and poverty.[2] But the divine powers act in all things in accordance with right judgement, in conformity with the Lord's command and with the merit of the works that have been accomplished.

The three angels sent to fetch a man are in ascending rank, and the one of lower rank always obeys the one whose rank is higher. At the moment when the man is about to breathe his last, one of the angels stands by his head, another by his feet, in the attitude of men who with their hands would anoint him with oil until the soul should leave the body. The third spreads out a large spiritual cloth on which[3] to receive the soul with honor. As for the soul of the holy man, it is beautiful to see and white as snow. After the soul has emerged from the body onto the cloth, one of the angels seizes the two upper corners of the cloth, the other the two lower ones, after the manner of men on earth lifting a body. The third angel sings in front of the soul in a language no one knows; even the others, namely our father Pachomius and Theodore who were having this apparition, did not understand their singing; they only heard the angel making resound the word *Alleluia*. And thus they proceeded through the air toward the east with the soul; they did not proceed as men do on foot, but advanced with a gliding movement like flowing water; for they are spirits. They proceeded on high with the soul so it might see the boundaries of the universe from one end to the other, that it might see all creation and glorify God whose creation it was.

After that, they let him know the place in which he will rest by the Lord's order so that, having once entered the place of his rest earned by his good works, he may realize what torments he has escaped and may thus the more bless the Lord for saving him from all those sufferings through the goodness of our Lord Jesus Christ.

Then they bring him to the feet of the man of God who taught him the fear of the Lord and nourished him with his law. He in turn carries him like a gift to the feet of the Lord. Then he blesses the Lord outspokenly saying, 'I will bless you, my Lord, with all your saints.' After that they Cf. Ps 150:1.
lead him to the resting place the Lord assigned him according to the measure of the works he accomplished. ‹At the time the soul is about to be presented to the Lord,›[4] it is authorized to come near—or to stay at a distance—in accordance with the merit of the good works it accomplished on earth. For whoever has merited everlasting life doubtless also sings and blesses the Lord before entering the resting place prepared for him by the Lord. ‹And when they bless the Lord›,[5] there are some who see the Lord and bless him, thanks to their purity of heart, saying, *Blessed are the pure in heart; they shall see God.* For whoever is negli- Mt 5:8.
gent in his practices has not deserved to see God in the glory of his godhead, because his purity of heart is not perfect. Nevertheless if he deserves simply life, he sees the flesh of the Son of God, that is, his humanity, which is one with his divinity in which it exists inseparably.

According to the merits of each of the dead, the saints come toward those who have done God's good pleasure to meet them solemnly, by the Lord's command. They come toward some of them as far as the door of life and embrace them. They come toward others a distance proportionate to their merits. Others they let come near them before getting up and embracing them. Others have not even enough merit to be embraced by

the saints; they merely inherit life in the measure
of their littleness. When they come forth to meet
them, the just wear crowns brighter than those
which the person they come out to meet has won
in combats on earth in which he fought against
the devil, except *the crown of justice* which on
resurrection day he will receive from God *the just*
2 Tm 4:8. *judge*, as Paul says.[6] When the soul of the just
comes close to the door of life, the Lord puts
David's words into his mouth so he may repeat
them saying, *Open for me the gates of righteous-*
Ps 118(117):19. *ness so I may enter and glorify the Lord*. And the
angel who keeps the door of life answers saying,
This is the gate of the Lord, the righteous ones
Ps 118(117):20. *will enter there*. If it is the souls of some who were
disciples of perfect men, the angels who accom-
pany them exclaim when they arrive at the door,
Open the gates! Let in the people that keep
righteousness and that keep justice and peace, for
Is 26:2-3. *they have hoped in you, Lord,* as it is written in
Isaiah.[7]

Our father Pachomius had this great revelation in the monastery of Thmoušons on the occasion of the brother catechumen who was secretly baptized before dying. After seeing how the righteous leave the body, he asked further how the soul of the sinner leaves the body; and the angel said to him, 'The Lord will give you entire satisfaction. If it is a soul with an evil way of life, two merciless angels come to fetch it at the time it is to be visited. When the man is at the point of death, when he no longer recognizes anyone, one of the merciless angels is placed near his head, the other at his feet; and thus they begin to thrash him until his wretched soul is on the point of going up. Then they thrust into his mouth a hooked object, a sort of fish-hook, and they yank that wretched soul out of his body; it is dark and shady. Then they tie it to the tail of a spirit-horse—for [the soul] also is a spirit—and thus they take it away and pitch it into torments or else to the bottom of hell, according to its works' deserts.[8]

'In fact, there are also many good men who pass through these sufferings during their last illness and at the moment of breathing their last. It is because they resemble cooked meat that still needs to be cooked a little longer before being eaten. It is the same with the faithful who are so tried in their latter days before dying as to be free of everything and pure before the Lord. We know likewise that some holy men were made to undergo sufferings at the time of their death, for instance, saint Stephen, all the martyrs, and those who can be likened to them. Job, too, David, and many other holy men sustained great suffering and many tribulations in the course of their lives, some on their deathbed. In fact, many sinners die quietly without having undergone sufferings in this world because of the tribulations and the punishments awaiting them, as it is written, *The wicked man is kept for an evil day.* That is why, Pr 16:4.
having seen this sort of people, Ecclesiastes said, *The same end will come to the righteous and the wicked, the pure and the impure, the good and the bad.* Indeed we see our Saviour, the Lord of Qo 9:2.
all, hung on the cross with two thieves, one on the right, one on the left, and the Lord in between.' Mt 27:38.
These things were taught to our father Pachomius at Thmoušons. And he was very happy

that the brother catechumen had entered into the resting place of the holy men of the Lord. And when that brother had been carried to the mountain and buried beside the brothers, our father went south quickly with Theodore to Phbow, grateful to the Lord for what he had seen.

G[1] 93a.

Vision of a soul escorted by angels into heaven

83. Another day, as Theodore was sitting somewhere in the assembly room, he heard in the air angel voices singing a melodious song. He rose at once and went to our father Pachomius, who said, 'It is a righteous soul that has left its body with which they are passing over above us; and we also have had the grace of hearing those who are blessing God in front of it'. While they were speaking together they looked up, they saw the one who had been visited, and they knew who he was.[1]

The Lord often opened their eyes. And they saw the angel of God at the altar in the sanctuary dispensing to those who were worthy the sacred mysteries by the hand of the priest or the bishop who was dispensing them. And if someone who was unworthy or defiled came forward to receive the sacred mysteries, the angel would withdraw his hand, and it was the celebrant alone who dispensed them to him.[2]

(Cf. G[1] 96).

Another vision of Theodore

84. Still another day our father Pachomius, accompanied by a brother, set out for a monastery on a matter concerning a soul. And he had ordered Theodore to look after the brothers until he should come back. Once Theodore arose in the night and went through the community to watch over the brothers. He stood somewhere and prayed. While he was praying an esctasy

came over him, and this is what he saw in a vision: All the brothers were lying down like resting sheep, and an angel was in their midst guarding them. Theodore, seeing [the angel], arose as if to approach the angel; the latter beckoned to him and put what he wanted to say to him into his mind before he said it with his mouth. He said, 'Who is watching over the brothers? Is it you or is it me?' Immediately Theodore was troubled and returned to his place saying, 'Truly we only appear to be; in reality it is the angels who are our shepherds and watch over us, sheep of the spiritual flock of Christ. It is they again who keep us safe from the wicked snares of the enemy.' The form of this angel's habit[1] made him resemble a king's soldier; in his hand he held a very bright and fiery sword; he was dressed in a *sticharion* (for at the time he was wearing not his *chlamys*, but the *sticharion*); large medallions adorned this very shiny and very fine *sticharion*; and his belt was a palm's breadth in width, it was bright red and sent out innumerable rays.[2]

Theodore hears Pachomius' teaching from a long distance

85. Still another day our father Pachomius sent Theodore to a monastery at Tkahšmin for a visit to the brothers and for a pressing matter of theirs. While he was praying near a fig tree in this monastery, he looked far off and saw our father Pachomius at Phbow, eight *schbo* away,[1] sitting and speaking the word of God unceasingly to the brothers. And Theodore also heard the words he was saying to them. When he returned south, he came to our father Pachomius and told him that he had seen him praying at Phbow,[2] and the words he had heard from his lips while he was speaking them to the brothers. Our father Pacho-

mius told him, 'Theodore, what you heard is exactly what I said'.

Pachomius receives more revelations

86. Still another day, while our father Pachomius was praying somewhere alone, he fell into an ecstasy: all the brothers were in the *synaxis* and our Lord was seated on a raised throne, speaking to them about the parables of the holy Gospel. In the vision he saw on that day, he could hear the words He was saying, as well as their interpretation, while He was pronouncing them with His mouth. From that day on, when our father Pachomius wished to address the word of God to the brothers, he would occupy the place where he had seen the Lord seated and speaking to the brothers. And if he repeated the words and their commentary which he had heard from the Lord's mouth, great lights would come out in his words, shooting out brilliant flashes; and all the brothers would be terribly frightened because of our father Pachomius' words, which resembled flashing lights coming from his mouth.

Theodore corrects a brother who did not follow a good inspiration

87. Still another day Theodore was at work somewhere with the brothers and toward evening, when work was over, they took their meal. Theodore had had prepared for them a bit of porridge, since many among them had the custom of not eating bread. One of them, named Patlole,[1] was a young man of robust body constantly at war with the passions of youth. When the desire came over him to eat a bit of porridge, at once the Spirit of God admonished him, 'That substance has been cooked for those who need it, but you have no need of it, for thoughts of the flesh are assailing you.' But he did not obey the thought prompted in him by the Lord; on the contrary he

went up, sat down, ate, and took besides the steward's bowl to eat from. When the brothers had finished eating, they retired to the hut as was their custom to hear the words of God ‹Theodore would›[2] address to them. And they put questions to him to get him to say wherein they had been at fault. To certain of them he made the reproach, 'You are faint-hearted'; to others, 'You are quick to get angry'; to others, 'You are hard in speech' and 'I see one among you who puts all his hope in a cooking pot'. At once the brother understood that this riddle was addressed to him, and he quickly bowed down to the ground in the midst of the brothers, saying, 'Pray for me, for I disregarded my conscience knowingly; because I disobeyed the good suggestion that came from my heart, the Lord has rebuked me in public.'[3]

Vision of the punishments of sinners after death

88. Still another day, by the Lord's command, our father Pachomius was carried away that he might contemplate the punishments and the torments to which the children of men are subject. Was it in the body that he was carried away, was it out of the body?—God knows that he was carried away.[1] Having been brought to the north of the paradise of delights, far from this world and from the firmament, he saw rivers, canals, and ditches filled with fire; in them the souls of sinners were being tormented. And while he walked with the angel, contemplating the torments, he saw those above where he was now going suffering much more than those he had seen at the start. They were delivered up to torturing angels of a very frightening aspect and holding fiery whips in their hands. If some of the souls

Cf. 2 Co 12:2-3.

they were tormenting lifted their heads above the fire, they would whip them hard and thrust them farther into the fire. They would sigh desperately without being able to cry out because of their exhaustion and because of the way they were suffering the great number of torments weighing on them. The souls being tormented were very numerous, even innumerable.

He likewise saw wells and cisterns filled with fire which burned more fiercely still. He looked in and saw that there was only one soul in each cistern. That soul's two feet, which had the appearance of the flesh it wore in the world, were set one on each side of the cistern. And fire was consuming, one by one, the members with which it had sullied itself in the world. On looking attentively at one of the cisterns, he recognized the one who was being tormented in it; it was one of those who are marked out in the world, and whom the Scrip-
Cf. 1 Co 6:9 tures call effeminate.[2]

He likewise saw monks subjected to punishments in that place, and he questioned the angel who was walking with him, 'What evil have these done to be brought here?' The angel answered, 'Those whom you see are quite pure as regards the body, but they are idlers who go about in places where brothers live as anchorites. They speak evil of the other brothers living near [those they are visiting], knowing that the latter are not on good terms with the former, and thus they think they will find favor on account of their slanders, with a view to getting food and drink. And when they leave these [brothers] and go away elsewhere, in turn they speak ill of those they have been flattering in the ears of those they had just been slandering, again with a view to being well-received by these others. And so for their slanders they have been cast into these hard torments that never cease.'

The torturing angels were quite filled with joy and gladness. They rejoiced as an administrator rejoices to see his master's wealth increasing; for the Lord had created them pitiless, that they might not feel sorrow for the wicked men turned over to them to be tormented. And if the souls they Cf. Si 39:28. are tormenting beg them to have pity on them, they are full of anger toward them and punish them more with fierce torments. When souls are brought in and turned over to them, they are overjoyed—like one who has made an immense gain—happy over the downfall of the wicked.

As our father Pachomius was looking at the punishments with the angel who accompanied him, one of the torturing angels tugged at him and said joyfully, 'Come, Pachomius, let me show you these other wicked punishments'. Our father Pachomius, seeing himself gaily dragged by him to look at all these punishments, was amazed at the nature of these pitiless angels and at the way they rejoiced over such evil torments. As for him, he was very sad at the sight of the sufferings in which were found the wretched souls of impious men that were being tormented.

When he had gone on a bit he saw an innumerable crowd of souls of all ages being roughly bustled along by the pitiless torturing angels. Once more he asked his accompanying angel who these souls were and he was told, 'These are the souls of sinners who died today throughout the world, and they are being classified for punishment according to their deserts.'

Having gone on once more toward the west with the angel who was accompanying him and showing him the punishments, he saw down below an opening at the gate of hell. Hell itself is very deep; it is dark and sends out heat like a hearth. This place is the Lord's prision. When men are brought in, they are hurled into it; they utter loud cries, 'Woe is me for not knowing the God who created me that I might be saved'. Then they cannot speak at all because of the heat and the thick mist of the place. And they no longer recognize each other because of the darkness and the distress that grips them.

Going further on, toward the southwest, he saw there other harsh punishments, of the sort which he had previously seen to the north and by which the souls were being punished. He was further shown a kind of large house of stone whose length, breadth, and height were enormous. It was full of fire. Into it were thrown all the young people who in this world have sullied their bodies with impurity, unbeknownst to their parents; that is why they are enduring these fierce torments for evil and impure acts which are wicked before God and before men.

It happened that when the angel had finished showing our father Pachomius all the punishments and the sufferings of the torments they entailed by command of the Lord, he counseled him urgently in these terms, 'Pachomius, bear witness to the brothers of all that you have seen, so that they may strive not to fall into such evil punishments. God has sent me to you to show you all this; in turn bear witness of it to the brothers and to the whole world, that they may do penance and be saved.' From that day on when our father Pachomius assembled the brothers for the instruction, he spoke to them first on the Scriptures because they are the main thing and the breath of God; then he would inform them about all the punishments he had seen and about the sufferings they entailed, and concerning which the angel had given him instructions from the Lord, so that they might have the fear of God and might avoid sinning and falling into such punishments and into the tortures which he had seen.

G[1] 94,95a.

Vocation of Theodore the Alexandrian

89. In fact, the fame of our father Pachomius and of his charity reached everyone. His name was heard even abroad and among the Romans, and they came to become monks with him. And the man of God Pachomius treated them well with every word and with every doctrine, *like a nurse comforting her children.* 1 Th 2:7.

There was living at Alexandria a young man called Theodore, who was twenty-seven years of age.[1] Born as a pagan and carefully watched over by his parents, he was moved by the Spirit of God to become a Christian. Then he made a resolution in his heart, 'If the Lord leads me on the way that I may become a Christian, then I will also become a monk and I will keep my body without stain until the day when the Lord shall visit me.' Some days later he went to see the archbishop, Apa Athanasius, and told him about everything that was in his heart. The [archbishop] at once baptised him, made him a lector, and arranged a place for him to live in the church, where he gave himself up to *ascesis*. He met no women at all, with the sole exception of his mother and his sister. When he read the lessons in church, he would strive not to let his eyes rove over the people, fearing the Gospel maxim that says, *He that shall look at a woman to lust after her has already committed adultery with her in his heart*; and again, *Avert my eyes, so they may never at all see vain things*. He led a great way of life as far as his strength allowed, finding himself near the source of fresh and living water, that is, the apostolic archbishop Apa Athanasius. After twelve years spent as lector in the church of Alexandria, he noticed that those who were in the church with him, that is, the clerics, had discussions that were vainglorious, ate often, and were proud. When Theodore saw them behaving this way he would send up sighs to God with supplications and tears saying, 'Lord, show me a man leading a life that agrees with your holy will; then I will go to him to know you well by means of that servant of yours.'

Mt 5:28.

Ps 119(118):37.

While he was speaking and praying in his heart about this, he heard some monks singing the praises of the *Koinonia* which, out of his love for men, God had founded through our father Pachomius. Having heard these words, Theodore called upon God saying, 'I pray you, my Lord Jesus Christ, make me worthy of seeing this your holy servant, of getting his blessing, and of living with him.' Some time later our father Pachomius sent some brothers to Alexandria with a little boat to visit the archbishop and to buy a few things for the needs of the sick brothers. When he saw the brothers in the church talking with the archbishop, who was asking them after their father Pachomius, Theodore was overjoyed. He went up to them and while someone acted as interpreter for him he spoke to them, 'I, too, wish to go south with you to see your father, the Man of God, and to have his blessings.' They replied to him, 'We cannot take you with us because of your parents[2] and because of the archbishop.' At once he obtained leave from the archbishop to be taken along with them.

Having come south to our father Pachomius, he embraced him with the kiss of peace. Our father received him with joy because he saw that he was humble, and especially because the archbishop had written him about [Theodore asking him] to receive him cordially. At once he assigned him to a house in which an ancient old man lived who, as he understood the Greek language, could converse with him and comfort him. He made fine progress and advanced in all good works and according to the rules of the brothers.

One day our father Pachomius, with the interpreter's help, questioned him on the faith of those who lived as anchorites in Alexandria, and about their *ascesis*. He replied, 'Thanks to your holy prayers, my lord father, they are quite firm in the orthodox faith of the holy catholic Church of Christ. There is no one who can shake them in it, for they fulfill the word of the Scripture, *Be firm, you will not be changed in your faith*. As regards their food, there are plenty of good things on their table, they eat and drink well, walking in accordance with what is written, *These things God has provided for his faithful that they might partake of them with thanksgiving*.' Then our father Pachomius said, 'Is it possible for them to eat and drink without measure and for all that still keep their purity?' Theodore replied, 'In everything their purity is great, and their know-

1 Co 15:58; 16:13.

1 Tm 4:4.

ledge is a match for anyone'. Our father Pachomius had in his hand at the moment a small stick. He struck the ground with it twice, saying, 'If this ground is watered and if it is manured, will it not produce plants? It is the same with the body; if we gladden it with abundance of dishes, of drinks, and of rest, it will not be possible for it to keep its purity. For, holy Scripture says, *Those who are of Jesus the Christ have crucified their flesh with its*
Ga 5:24. *passions and its desires.*[3] When Theodore had heard that, he was confounded.

Some time later the brothers went off to Alexandria as was their custom. When they returned south Theodore asked them about certain brothers living as anchorites there, 'How are they doing at present?' They informed him that some of them had been caught in impurities and that others were held in evil repute by lay-people for their foul behavior. Hearing that, Theodore was in admiration at the words he had heard from the mouth of our father Pachomius, in the comparison between the soil and monks who eat their fill.

Theodore rose immediately, bowed to the ground and kissed our father Pachomius' feet, out of admiration for the high divine knowledge in him and for the way in which he had foretold that it was impossible for those who eat and drink to practise perfect purity. And thus he had still a greater way of life, thanks to the firm teaching he heard from the mouth of the man of God, our father Pachomius.

When our father Pachomius noticed that Theo-
AD 333(or 343?). dore had made progress in divine knowledge, he

appointed him housemaster for the strangers who were also coming to become monks with him. And our father Pachomius made efforts to learn Greek, so as to exhort them often according to Scripture and to teach Theodore the way to govern the brothers placed under his authority.[4]

90. One day he told him privately, 'It is a mighty thing when you see someone of your house negligent of his salvation if you do not busy yourself with him and if you forbear to instruct him for his reform and his soul's salvation. If once he gets angry, be patient with him, waiting for him to be touched by the Lord. It is just as when someone wants to extract a thorn from somebody's foot. If he draws out the thorn and it causes bleeding, the man has relief. On the other hand, if he does not succeed in removing it but it goes in deeper, he applies some salve; and thus, with some patience on the man's part, the thorn comes out gently by itself and the man is healed. It is the same with a man who is angry, if the one who is instructing him crosses him. If on the contrary, [the instructor is] patient with him, he will profit greatly. But if the offence is serious, report it to me, and we will do as God will inspire me. Take greater care of the sick than of yourself. Practise continence at all times. Bear the cross more than they do, since you hold the rank of a father. Be also an object of edification to the brothers and their model in everything. And if there is anything else you want to discern and you do not know how, inform me, and with God's grace we will go at it together until we find the exact answer and put it in practice.'

G[1] 95b.

Pachomius' advice to Theodore the Alexandrian

Cf. Dt 1:18.

Cf. Mt 10:38.

91. One day Theodore questioned our father

G[1] 111,95c.

Question of Theodore the Alexandrian to Pachomius

Pachomius about Apa Cornelios, 'I have heard he has purified his heart to such a point that in the *synaxis* he has no idle thought during the whole *synaxis*. As for me, I have tried very often, and among a multitude of prayers I make hardly three of them warding off the thoughts that assail my heart in many ways.' Our father Pachomius said to him, 'Theodore, I am going to fulfill your wish concerning this by means of a parable, to give you greater courage. If today a slave sees a man who is free though poor, he longs nevertheless for freedom for himself like his fellow; again in the same way, if a poor man sees a commander, he too longs to be a commander; and again if a commander sees a king, he longs to become like the other, a king too. Such too is the case with Cornelios who struggled until he had acquired all the fruits of the Holy Spirit with the grace God gave him in every good work. As for you, Theodore, emulate his good example and always be grateful to the Lord, keeping his commandments with your whole heart, and you will never again succumb in any way.' Theodore, hearing these words and these parables of our father Pachomius, was awestruck by his great knowledge of God.

Thanks to his steadfastness and to his intelligence he understood the Egyptian language.[1] At the time when our father Pachomius was speaking the word of God to the brothers, Theodore would be watchful and athirst[2] for what he would hear from his mouth; and on returning to his house he would repeat it in Greek to those he served as interpreter. *Like a nurse comforting her children*, he comforted them with

1 Th 2:7.

the words of life of our father Pachomius, with which he instructed them and which he recommended they put into practice and keep carefully in their hearts.

The first spiritual fruits of his house were,[3] among the Alexandrians, Ausonius the Great, another Ausonius, and one other called Neon. Among the Romans there were Firmus, Romulus, and Domnius the Armenian. As for the cityman Theodore, he performed the functions of housemaster for ⟨thirteen⟩ years,[4] up to the death of our father Pachomius. He translated all the teachings he heard from his mouth, and he did the same in Apa Horsiesios' time up to the day God visited him.

92. There were at Phbow ten ancient brothers who, although they had a great way of life and were pure in body, often used to murmur against our father Pachomius because of the words he addressed to them for the salvation and the healing of their souls. The man of God Pachomius took upon himself for their benefit vigils, supplications, and fasts before the Lord until they repented of all their errors and corrected them. One after another they all died in the peace of God, amen.

G[1] 100.

Story of ten ancient brothers who indulged in murmuring

93. Still another day one of the brothers died. Our father Pachomius did not allow the brothers to sing psalms for him or to bless him. On the contrary, he burned his clothes and his habit in the midst of the brothers gathered near him, instilling in them fear lest they disregard their own soul. How he put up with him in a like state of sin until he died we do not know. But this we do know, that men of God do nothing without good

G[1] 103.

Pachomius refuses psalmody to a bad monk after his death

cause, and their severity as well as their goodness are solidly based on a perfect knowledge which is pleasing to our Lord Jesus.[1]

G[1] 106, 107a.

Theodore's great trial

AD 344.

94. One other time it happened that our father Pachomius was ill, so ill that he was in danger of death. Then all the fathers of the communities[1] and all the brothers who were at Phbow gathered about Theodore and said to him, 'Promise us that, if the Lord visits our father, you will place yourself at our head and you will become our father in his stead. We must not become wretched and scatter like shepherdless sheep. For no one exists among us who knows his virtues as you.' But he made them no reply at all, because out of his great humility he did not want the rank of a father or this world's glory. They proceeded to beg him again until he gave them his consent.

This matter that they arranged among themselves did not escape our father Pachomius; and when he got a little better from his illness he said to the brothers, 'Let each of you tell his shortcomings; as for me, I am often negligent in visiting the brothers'. In turn, Theodore replied, 'For seven years now I have been with you and you often send me to the monasteries to visit the brothers; and like you, I establish rules about everything. The thought never came into my heart that I should become their father after you. Now, as the brothers were urging me in this matter, I consented. Should I deny it and assert that I have not given them my consent, I would be a liar in your presence all the days of my life, and there would come upon me the word of Scripture

Ps 5:6.

which says, *The Lord will destroy whoever tells lies.*' Our father Pachomius replied and said to

Theodore in the presence of all the brothers, 'I tell you this: from now on you no longer have any authority over anything at all concerning the brothers; but go to a solitary place and pray to the Lord until he forgives you for consenting to this.'

Theodore went off to a solitary place where he fasted often and wept day and night before the Lord with a great many tears and sighs without number. He was not crying over his loss of rank, but because of the wicked thought he had made room for in his heart.

Seeing him shed so many tears and in such great affliction, one brother said within himself, 'It must not happen that he cut himself off from the brothers and go away as a result of this affliction!' When, during the night, Theodore would come out of his retreat for some need, this brother followed him as if to watch him lest he go away somewhere. The thought of leaving the brothers never entered Theodore's heart, and when he came back into his retreat, he would pray to the Lord over this brother saying, 'Lord God of our father Pachomius, deliver that brother from the wicked thought about me that has entered his heart, which is that I might leave the brothers because of a slight reproach from my father. May such a thing never happen to me!' Later, when the signal was given for the *synaxis*, Theodore came forward in the assembly room, in the midst of the brothers, saying, 'Pray for me so that my Lord Jesus Christ may forgive me; for I have got drunk with the wine of abomination Cf. Rv 17:2.
which I drank of ⟨without⟩ knowing it.' Having said this, he bowed down to the ground and wept.

And seeing the abundance of his tears, all the brothers too wept a great deal along with him. When he had finished making his prostration, he went back to his retreat and went on weeping and afflicting himself day and night before the Lord in conformity with our father Pachomius' command. Actually many brothers as they went past his retreat heard him weeping and would themselves weep greatly over him.

Many ancient brothers also came to him in order to encourage him. They would say, 'No doubt you are afflicted and you weep because our father Pachomius has taken from you the rank you held!' But he let none of them speak fleshly words to him; instead he would say to them in all humility, 'It is not for the thought the devil has suggested to you that I am weeping but because of the sin I have committed before the Lord.' Then they began to criticize our father Pachomius in his presence, thinking they would encourage him in that way. They said, 'What was your fault, that our father should treat you in this manner? Is it not plain to see that you are going to be his successor? Then why does he now take your rank away from you?' When Theodore heard these words he became, because of his great humility, like one who is being sacrificed, for why were they criticizing the Man of God at all in his presence? Theodore would try to convince the brothers with these words, 'Do not think that our father has done this to me without my deserving it. No, whatever he has done to me he has done for my soul's salvation, that I might be worthy of the Lord.' When he had convinced them by his great humility, they left him, giving glory to God who was in him, and having found great profit in his words.

After them another devout and ascetic brother called Apa Titoue came also and encouraged him saying, 'Do not be afflicted, Theodore, over what our father has done to you. The Lord knows that if you persevere in this humility, thanking the Lord for what has happened to you, you will also be blessed like Job, the just man of old.' He also spoke many other encouraging words to him and then he left him and went back to his house. Theodore took profit from Titoue's words and considered them as coming from the Lord. At once he got up, prayed[2] and took up a book that was there; on opening it, he happened on this passage that was there written, *After that, I will come back, and I will rebuild David's tent that had fallen in; what has collapsed I shall rebuild, what was overturned I shall set right again*, etc., Am 9:11; Ac 15:16.
and at once Theodore was consoled by the way the Lord had encouraged him through the prophet.

One of the brothers who considered himself a great man had the wicked thought, inspired in his heart by the devil, of saying to himself, 'Would our father Pachomius have removed Theodore if he had done nothing wrong? Doubtless he caught him doing wrong; that is why he removed him.' So this brother in whom Satan was came to see Theodore to put him to the test, saying, 'Is the saying true that I have heard about you from the lips of our father Pachomius? I have in fact heard him say, "I did not remove him on this account only, but because I caught him being impure."'

When Theodore heard these words, he wept at once and groaned in affliction. He thought the matter over and said to himself: 'If I say I have done nothing of the kind, I will make a liar of our father, according to the brother's statement of having heard him speak these words. Neither is it right, on the other hand, to answer this brother that what he said is true, or I will turn liar myself, since I have never done anything of the kind since I was born.' He began again to shed tears without stopping, and he answered him not a word. The other, seeing that [Theodore] said not a word to him and wept without stopping, got up and, greatly embarrassed, left him. At once Theodore got up and prayed saying, 'I will put you to shame, O devil, for planting your evil thoughts in this brother whom I greatly love; for your intention in making him say that was to uproot from my heart the love I have for the Man of God who saves me from your evil snares which are full of guile in every way.' Then he got up and entered the place where our father Pachomius was; having come up behind him, he took hold of his head and kissed it many times. Our father Pachomius, not knowing who it was, said to those around him, 'Who is the one who kissed my head?' They answered him, 'It is Theodore'. At once he called him, 'Theodore, come up close to me and sit down!' Theodore said to him, 'Him whom I was
Cf. Sg 3:2. seeking have I found, O my father!' And thus he left him and went back to his retreat, telling no one why he had kissed our father's head, and without having been asked by him, 'Why did you do that?'

G[1] 107b, 108. 95. While Theodore was still doing penance,

Theodore is comforted by angels on his way to Thmoušons

our father Pachomius was told in a vision, 'Make haste to send Theodore to one of the surrounding monasteries; for by that means he will be comforted and will find rest.' Our father Pachomius called him and told him, 'Theodore, make haste and set out for the monastery of Thmoušons and visit the brothers to see how they are doing!' He left him at once with great humility and set out as he had been commanded.

On reaching Šeneset he sat down on the bank to wait for the ferry to take him over westward.[1] As he sat, two angels also arrived in the guise of two old monks and sat down near Theodore. One of the angels started praising and congratulating him, 'You are fortunate, Theodore my son, to have taken refuge at God's feet and for having renounced the world and its idle cares.' The other, as if annoyed, replied, 'Give up pouring out all that praise on this wretched man, for he has not yet reached the measure where he would deserve all the praise that you heap on him. But when you see him grown up to the full measure of the man with the basket,[2] heap on him all the congratulations and all the praise he really deserves.'

Then the angel said to his companion angel —both appearing in the guise of old monks seated with Theodore—'What is the measure of this basket that you extol in such exalted terms as you speak of it? Do tell me what is meant by it, since you are greater than I!' Then his companion said to him, 'Listen to me, I will explain it to you as I myself have learned of it from others. For the story goes, concerning a farmer, that he was a man harsh in his work and in all things. Every man who came to work under his orders as a

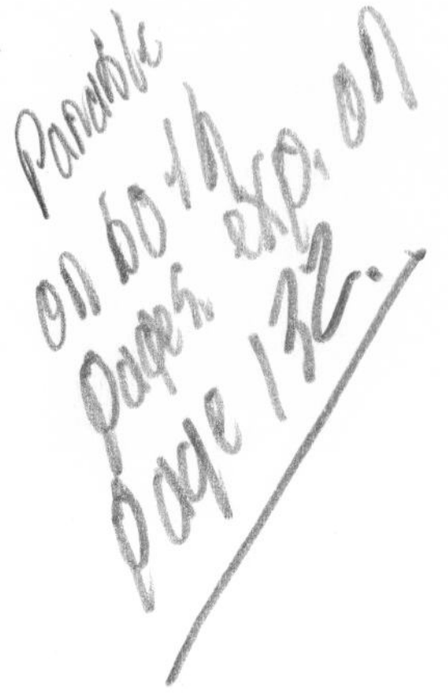

laborer, after spending the great part of the year, or even almost the whole year at the work, would make his escape and work with him no more; for he used them so harshly that they went away. After a while there was someone who made a courageous resolve saying, "Since no man is able to round out a single year of work with that farmer because he is hard on them, well, I will go and work with him in such a way that I will put in a full year. I will go along with him in everything he commands me to do until I get to know how he works." Then he got up, came to him and said, "I want to work with you this year." The farmer answered the man, "With pleasure; and my wish is that everyone should work with me, on condition he understand me in my method of work." Then he worked with him in all patience.

'When the time came to go to work in the field, the farmer said to the man, "Now we are going out to work in the field; I do not work the water-wheel[3] during the day to irrigate the field, but at night." The man replied, "All right. That is an idea of great wisdom; for if we do not irrigate during the day, neither bird nor beast is going to come and drink from our ditch, but we will save all our water and it will penetrate easily in our field." When the time came for plowing, the farmer said to him, "Let us sow one furrow of wheat, another of lentils, another of barley and so on with the other seeds; that is the way we will sow the field." The man answered him, "This bit of wisdom is even greater than the first one; for if we proceed in that way, our field will be outstanding in its beauty through the great splendor of all its flowers." After they had finished sowing

the field, when the shoots had come up from the sowing, while they were still green and had not reached maturity, the farmer said to the man, "Get up, let us go and harvest our field, for it is ready for the harvest." The man replied to him again, with great condescension, "Oh, but there is no limit to your great wisdom! In fact, if we do as you said in your heart and if indeed we harvest our crop before it dries out, not a single ear will fall to the ground; on the contrary, they will all be saved." When they had taken in all the crops, they flailed them on the threshing-floor; and only chaff was left on it. The farmer said to the man, "Let us fetch a basket; we shall measure the chaff with it, and use it as well to carry the chaff to its place, so as to find it at the time when it will be needed for our work." The man once more replied to the farmer, "This cunning is far better than all you had thought out before; indeed, if we carry on diligently in this way, the chaff will be preserved in our storehouses." After submitting him to all these trials, and seeing that he was not fainthearted and did not turn back, but on Cf. Jg 7:3.
the contrary put up with him till the year's end, [the farmer] marvelled at him and said to him, "Now I have really understood that you are capable of staying with me always, because you acted in all things in accordance with my wishes; the two of us have become like one man." And that was how the man remained working with him all the time. They lived peaceably together till the end of their days.'

When one of the angels in the guise of old monks had finished telling this parable, the other one said to him, 'You have told me today a great

parable; but please likewise give me its interpretation.' The other angel said to him, 'The real farmer is God; the rough usage he employs are the trials and tests to which he subjects those who want to serve him well; he puts them to the test so that they may be able to endure him when he opposes their will in everything in order that his own will may be realized in them at all times. So now if there is anyone who says to himself, "I am his servant," he will gratefully put up with him when he is in any way put to the test by him, and to him he will be as one of his elect. How shall such a man be able to bear all the tribulations and trials which he will meet unless he says to himself, "I am a fool in everything before all men"? For I have heard that a passage of the Scriptures says, *Let him among you who wants to be wise become*
1 Co 3:18. *a fool, so as to be wiser in the Lord's eyes.*[4] So then, if this monk bears up with everything that his father tries him by, he too will become an elect, and blessed before the Lord Jesus Christ.'

While the two angels of the Lord in the guise of old monks were thus conversing, Theodore remained seated not far from them, his head resting on his knees[5] as he listened to them talking together; and he did not know they were angels. He was comforted by what they said about him.

A few moments later the ferry came to shore. They all boarded together and when they reached the landing place, Theodore did not see the two old monks; at once he understood that they were angels of God, and he went on his way until he reached Thmoušons, weeping because of the sweetness of the words he had heard from the angels' lips. When he arrived at the brothers', they all embraced him with great cheerfulness while congratulating him; he visited them according to our father Pachomius' command, then returned to Phbow greatly consoled. Nevertheless he was still in affliction and cried unceasingly saying, 'I have sinned by letting such vainglory enter my heart.'

G[1] 109a,113.

Trip of Theodore and Zacchaeus to Alexandria

AD 345.

96. When the small boat was about to cast off for Alexandria, an ancient old man called Zacchaeus, who was the head of the boatmen, came in to our father Pachomius. He begged him to send Theodore to Alexandria with him to minister to the boatmen, and also that he might be a little comforted in his distress, for it was to be feared that his eyes might suffer as a result of much weeping. These words pleased our father Pachomius. He called Theodore and sent him to Alexandria on the boat with [Zacchaeus]. He also wrote a letter to our holy father Apa Athanasius, the archbishop.

On the boat, Theodore's attitude to the others was very humble, his head was bowed, and he submitted to them all like a little child. When they sat down at table to eat, they would yield place to him so he should serve himself first; but he would refuse to serve himself until all had done so; then he too would eat, reciting God's words without ceasing. In fact, many times he would spend the whole night reciting the Scriptures.[1] Every time they had to moor in the course of the trip to Alexandria, it was he who jumped out on the bank first to tie the boat to the stake. And yet again, when he was sent ashore to a village on an errand with another brother, he would make a recommendation to the brother, saying, 'If you want to do me a favor, be the one to answer if anyone comes to us and greets us!' And, knowing that this was his wish because of his great humility, the brothers would consent to him in this. When he came to Alexandria, the archbishop saw him and marvelled. He wrote a letter to our father Pachomius in which he praised Theodore because he had often heard of him and wanted to see for himself what he was like.

When the boat returned south, our father Pachomius embraced Apa Zacchaeus, Theodore, and all the brothers, and said, 'How is the Church?' They answered him, 'Thanks to God's help and to the raising of your hands, peace has begun to exist'. For he was grieved for the Church at that time, because the Arians had risen up like bandits against it. He prayed to God for the peace of his catholic Church, afflicted as he was over the people ⟨of God being so wronged and deprived of their archbishop Athanasius, the

AD 339-346.

Christ-bearing.⟩[2] He would say, 'The Lord has

Cf. Dt 32:43; Si 7:16-17; Lk 18:8.

permitted this to happen in order to put the faithful to the test, for God will certainly take speedy revenge on the evildoers as they deserve.'[3]

G[1] 109b.

Theodore's rehabilitation

c. AD 345-6.

97. After that, he spoke again to the brothers about Theodore, saying ⟨'My brothers, do not think that⟩[1] Theodore suffered a diminution before the Lord because he was publicly demoted before men. In no way. On the contrary, he has grown in his progress far beyond what he formerly was, because of the humility with which he patiently endured it. Take note that the word of the Gospel will be fulfilled for him, *He who humbles*

Mt 23:12.

himself will be exalted.[2] Actually Theodore and I

carry out this same ministry together and in this same spirit,' [Theodore] followed in [Pachomius'] footsteps to the day he was visited. When [Pachomius] sent him to visit the brothers, he would sit down and speak the word of God to them.[3]

98. When the brothers would see [Pachomius][1] seated on the ground or in an uncomfortable place they would bring him something to sit on, but he would not consent to it and would tell them, 'While my body is still free from illness I will not do that; for I am afraid of being a servant in the age to come in the presence of all who see me, for having sought ease for my body. For thus it is written in the holy Gospels, *He who wants to be great among you shall make himself the servant of all.* And again, *The Son of Man did not come to be served but to serve and to give his life as a ransom for many.* Therefore, we ought to become one another's servants and not make others wait on us.'

(Cf. G[1] 21).

Pachomius' endurance

Mt 20:26.

Mt 20:28.

He had instructed the brothers not to lose confidence ‹if they trod›[2] on snakes, scorpions, and other wild beasts, and he had said, 'I know all that I did before knowledge was revealed to me'. After that day, if a scorpion stung him while working with the brothers and made him suffer, he would not stop working and would look on that suffering as one of the sufferings he accepted for Christ. If he was stung toward evening, he would remain standing and would pray until he was healed, saying, 'There is no effective remedy other than the name of the Lord.'[3]

One day, while he was standing in the *synaxis* at the morning hour and was addressing the word of God to the brothers, he looked toward the entrance and perceived a spirit of darkness standing there. Over him there was a vent closed by a mat on which two bricks had been placed. When one of the brothers pulled the string attached to the [mat] to open the vent to let light into the place, the bricks then fell on [Pachomius]. The brothers took fright and cried out, thinking his head must be broken. The Man of God, who understood that something was going to happen to him through the one he had seen standing near the door, swiftly covered his head with his hands and underwent with gratitude the shock of the bricks.

⟨At once he made a sign to the brothers to keep silent.⟩[4] Soon after, the brothers questioned him, 'Is your head not broken?' He answered them, 'Before this happened, my head was aching, whereas now it leaves me in peace.' In replying that, he had been mindful of the Apostle's words,
1 Th 5:18. *Give thanks in all things*;[5] and at the same time
he knew that nothing would happen to him without God['s permission].

Being at the harvest somewhere with the brothers when evening came, he spoke the word of God to the brothers. While he was speaking, two snakes came and wound themselves around his feet. But he did not look at them at all, nor did he move his feet from where he was standing. When he had finished talking, they prayed so that each might return to his dwelling. After that he asked for a lamp. When it had been brought he saw the beasts wound around his feet; then he killed them at once and gave glory to God *who*
Ps 16(15):7. *saves those who hope in Him.*[6]

G^{1} 101,84. 99. During that night there was a certain Paul,

Story of a brother stung by a scorpion

a great ascetic, who stood reciting. A scorpion stung his foot, but he did not stop reciting from dusk till daylight. As the pain caused by the poison seized his heart, he almost gave up the spirit. But he cried out before the Lord saying, 'I will not desist from praying to you until you give me rest and cure me of the wicked poison from that beast. For even if I was made to suffer the afflictions of the persecutions I would never deny you because of torments.' Thus he stood firm. He made a recommendation to some brothers placed under him, saying, 'Take care to tell no one what has happened to me lest I should be compared with our father and lose the reward prepared for me by the Lord after my death.' But one of the brothers revealed the matter before everyone. When morning came all the brothers assembled[1] and saw the scorpion that had stung him lying dead at his feet, and they marveled.[2]

Pachomius fasts and prays during a famine

100. Another day it happened that the brothers went out for a service. They informed our father Pachomius that a great famine and a contagious disease were raging in the world to the point where the earth was threatened with destruction. When he was informed of this, it was the second day he had gone without eating, and he went on not eating until the next day saying, 'Neither shall I eat while my fellow-members go hungry and find no bread to eat.' All the while the famine lasted outside he mourned and mortified himself the more by fastings and abundant prayers, fulfilling the words of the Apostle, *If one member suffers, all the members must suffer with it.*[1] He also prayed the Lord with great insistence to cause the level of the waters of the river to rise

1 Co 12:26.

to a good height so that abundance might prevail on the earth and that men might find bread, eat, live, and bless [the Lord], doing His will.[2]

Cf. Ps 30(29):9.

Pachomius' prayer for the whole of mankind.

1 Tm 2:2.

101. Every time he prayed he would remember the recommendation of the Apostle, *Pray for everyone: either for the emperor or for* orthodox *men of rank, so that we might lead a calm and quiet life in all honor and devotion.*[1] That was why our father Pachomius when he prayed would pray for the whole world in kind. In the first place for monks and virgins, that the Lord might grant them means of fulfilling the promise they pronounced with a resolute heart, he would say, 'Lord God Almighty, blessed God, grant us to carry through this service my fellow-members and I have begun, that we may be worthy of you; that you may dwell in our bodies, in our souls, and in our spirits; and that we may always be perfect in your love, walking before you according to your good pleasure. May we not sin against you or put to the test your *Holy Spirit in whose name we have been sealed.*[2] May we, on the contrary, be pure and spotless before you all the days of our life in this world; so that through your mercy we may deserve the goods of your heavenly and everlasting kingdom, O friend of men!'

Eph 4:30.

He would pray also that those in married life might keep his commandments, which are in his holy Gospels, so as to be given everlasting life. Likewise he would pray for three classes of men: first, for those who began to do what is good, but afterwards[3] were unable to complete it because of the vain cares of this world which kept them from doing it; that the Lord might grant them the means of doing what is good by freeing them

from all concern for this vain world—save solely
for the needs the body imposes—and that thus
they might do God's will, escape torments, and be
heirs of the eternal kingdom. He would pray for
those who cling fast to the works of the devil, for
all the heathen and for those who without knowing it are deluded by heresies, having been led
astray by others; that God might grant them
understanding, that they might understand and
bring forth worthy fruits of repentance, having in Mt 3:8.
mind above all the good he always does them.
Thus it is that he makes the sun to shine for them
on earth by day, enlightening them while they
carry on their craft, each at his own work, to provide for their life's necessities. The moon and the
stars shine for us by night. The *seasons of fruit-
fulness, the rains*, the dew and the winds destined Ac 14:17.
to make grow the harvests that have been sown in
the fields, all things that are necessary to men
and to all the creatures have been created by God
for man's needs, as the psalmist David says, *At
your command there was the day*; and again, *All* Ps 119(118):91.
things are at your service. *Ibid.*

Again he would pray for kings and men of rank
on earth, thus fulfilling the words of Solomon, *By
me kings rule*; that God in his mercy might keep Pr 8:15.
them lovers of God and of men, that they may
render justice to those who suffer injustice. [He Ps 146(145):7.
prayed] that they too might appear in the midst
of all the saints who have ever done God's good
pleasure and that they might say with the prophet
Isaiah, *The Lord is our God, the Lord is our
judge, the Lord is our ruler, and the Lord it is
who gives us life.*[4] [He also prayed] that they Is 33:22.
might hold in contempt this world's royalty which

lasts only for a time, so as to become heirs of the heavenly kingdom which lasts forever; and that they might resemble the just kings, namely David, Hezekiah, and Josiah, and those like them
Cf. Heb 11:33. who practised righteousness.

Again, he prayed for the clergy of the catholic Church, saying, 'Although they are my fathers, it is nevertheless a duty for me to remember them and to pray for them, because the holy Apostle invites us to do so, saying, *Brothers, pray for us as well, so that God may open for us the door for the*
Col 4:3. *Word.*' Such was the way he used to pray for all.

Story of ten negligent brothers

102. There were ten brothers at Phbow who lived negligently; their hearts were full of wicked thoughts which Satan put there at every moment. As a result of the impure thoughts they were full of, they had no faith in the teachings our father Pachomius would set forth to the brothers, and they would oppose him openly on many points. Our father Pachomius was grieved on their account and used to pray to God for them day and night that their souls might be saved. He remembered the troubles he had gone to for them since their youth, and above all he knew that they had so far in no way defiled their bodies by a wicked act. Then, while he was praying for their salvation, God sent down a wrath that surrounded all the brothers because of these others. Some avenging angels even thrust out at our father Pachomius; while he was praying, they wanted to snatch his soul away on the others' account, because he was praying for these men who made light of the teachings he would set forth to them for their salvation.

One of the ancients spoke to our father

Pachomius and said to him, 'Why are you taking so much trouble for those men? Here you are, going to be chastised on their account! Indeed you would do better to drive them out of our midst than to see God angry with you for their sake because you are patient with them while they do no penance to avert this wrath.' Our father Pachomius replied to him, 'O wretched man of narrow mind! What means this word that you have uttered, "Drive them out"? Have you never heard what Moses did in bygone days—for the saints are models for us—how he gave up his soul for the people which had sinned, and said, *So now, Lord, you are going to blot them out! Rather, blot me out from the book that you have written!*'[1] Such was the way in which our father Pachomius toiled for them in order that they might repent, do penance, and work at their soul's salvation. Ex 32:32.

After some time our father Pachomius happened to meet one of these ten brothers and with a cheerful face said to him, 'My son, how are you at this time, and how are your brothers?' The brother replied, 'Grace be to the Lord and to your holy prayers, ⟨at this time my heart is at rest.'⟩[2] Again the Man of God spoke to him, 'During the days you believed you were suffering because of us, the demons were fighting against you because they found in you no place to rest. Indeed it is just like a soldier who wants to enter a house and make his quarters there. He causes a lot of trouble to the house[3] he wants to enter, when he cannot do it because the door is well barricaded. But if those inside the house fear him and open to him, once he has got in he no longer makes trouble, but rests there comfortably. It is the same with you; the unclean spirit was formerly troubling you because you were not carrying out his work; but now you have opened your door to him, he is dwelling in you, you are filled with him *from the tips of your toes to the hairs of your head*, and thus it is still possible for him to cause you annoyance because you have accomplished his whole will.'[4] Once again the brother said to him, 'Is it still possible for the wicked demon to leave me, that I may do God's will and escape the punishments in store for the kind of sinner I am?' Our father Pachomius replied to him, 'I tell you that [even] if you fast two days at a time and if you pray from evening until morning, this demon will not leave you as long as this unbelief remains in you. But if you believe that the words I am speaking to you are true and come from God, I assure you that by midday today the demon will have left you and you will be at peace.' When the brother had heard that, he left him and went away. For a time he fasted two days at a time, but he did not give up his lack of faith in the man of God our father Pachomius, till the day of his death.[5]

Cf. Dt 28:35; Jb 2:7.

G¹ 102.

Vision of Pachomius

103. Upon another day it happened that the Lord sent our father Pachomius a vision. He looked and saw the aspect of a dark and gloomy hell, in the midst of which stood a pillar. Voices were heard from ali sides making an outcry and saying, 'Here is the light, here close to us'. The men in that place were groping their way, for great was the darkness of that gloomy place and very frightening. Then when they would hear 'Here is the light, here close to us', they would run

there seeking the light and wanting to see it; but when they ran forward they would hear another voice behind them, 'Here is the light, over here'; and at once they would turn to the rear seeking the light because of the voices they had heard. He saw also in the vision some of those who were in the darkness, as if circling a pillar and thinking they were going forward and drawing near the light, not realizing that they were only turning around a pillar. He looked again and saw in that place the whole community of the *Koinonia* walking one after the other, holding fast to each other for fear of getting lost by reason of that deep darkness. Those who were in front had a small light like that of a lamp to light their way; only four of the brothers saw that light, while all the rest saw no light whatever. Our father Pachomius watched their way of progressing; if one let go his hold on the man in front of him, he would lose his way in the darkness, along with all those who came after him. He saw one of them, called Paniski and a great man among the brothers, refusing with a few others to walk behind the man in front showing them the way. Then the man of God Pachomius called them each by name in his ecstasy before they should give up, saying, 'Hold to the man in front for fear of going astray!' The small light that went before the brothers continued in front of them until it reached a great opening through which a great light on high was coming; they climbed up to it. This opening was fitted with a great trap to keep the light from falling below and to keep those who were in the dark from going out by it.

After he had seen this our father Pachomius

was likewise instructed on the interpretation of the vision by the one who had shown him all this; 'The image of the hell that you saw is this world; the gloomy darkness that reigns there are all the stupid errors and vain cares. As for the men who are there, they are the souls without knowledge; and the voices crying "here is the light, here close to us", are the heretics—and the schismatics —each of which says, "Ours is the right opinion". The pillars[1] around which they walk in circles are the authors of error the simple ones trusted in because they said, "We are they who save; they are those who lead astray." The brothers showing the way are all those who love the Lord and walk in the right faith as it is written, *For all of you are*
Ga 3:28. *one in Christ.*' He was told besides, 'Those of the brothers who let go their hold stand for bishops who are in the right faith of Christ, but are in communion with the heretics and mislead many of those they teach and especially men who know no malice; they neglect those who behave well and give scandal to many. As it is written, *Woe to*
Mt 18:7. *him through whom scandal comes.*[2]

'‹The small light guiding the brothers is the Gospel, divine truth; truly he who is deluded by himself and by his passions is not pure, as it it written, *Among them God has blinded the hearts of the faithless ones of this age that they might not see the light of the Gospel of Christ who is the*
2 Co 4:4. *image of God.*›[3] That is also why that light is small, for in the holy Gospels it is written about the kingdom of heaven, *It is like a mustard seed,*
Mt 13:31-32. *which is small.* As to the flood of light coming in on high through the opening, it is the word spo-

ken by the Apostle, *Until we shall all have come to that same notion of faith and to the knowledge of the Son of God; to the perfect man, to the exact measure of the fullness of Christ Jesus.*' Eph 4:13.

When our father Pachomius had seen this, he called the brothers whom in his vision he had seen letting go their hold and advised them to struggle in the fear of the Lord and to live. And when they had left him, they did not pay heed to getting rid of their negligence and their contempt; on the contrary, they persevered in their former attitude so that they became strangers to the brothers and to the everlasting life of the Lord Jesus.[4]

(*Cf. G[1] 58,59*).

Organization of the *Koinonia*

104. Our father Pachomius was diligent ⟨to instruct them⟩[1] in the knowledge of the saints, and was working at the salvation of the brothers' souls as at a vineyard cared for by a good and industrious gardener. [Such a gardener] is zealous in keeping his vineyard with all firmness and care, looking after its wall or its hedge against thieves and beasts; he likewise sets scarecrows for the birds, lest they spoil his harvest. So it is written, *The vineyard of the Lord of hosts is the house of Israel.*[2] For he gave them laws and traditions; some were committed to writing, some others were learned by heart, after the manner of the holy Gospels of Christ. He also recommended to all the brothers in each monastery that if someone transgressed the commandments given them for their salvation, he should receive a punishment proportionate to the offence, so that the Lord might forgive him for the negligences he had committed by disobedience. He also recommended to those in charge of the brothers' exter-

Cf. Mt 21:33.

Is 5:7.

nal ministry not to bring back to the community any news whatever about worldly matters. If someone entrusted them with a message for a relative, or gave them something for him, they must not, when they rejoined the community, go to that man or say a word to him. They should instead go to the father of the community and tell him about the matter. The latter must examine the matter: if the recipient might draw profit from hearing of it, he must then be told; if not, he must not be told of the matter.

Among the brothers there was no clashing voice in their midst; but their way of life was conformable to the holy laws. With them there was no care for this world; on the contrary, they were as if transported from earth to heaven as a result of the quiet and of the way of life they persevered in.

Teaching of Pachomius

105. Another day, while passing through the community our father Pachomius heard someone whose thoughts were fleshly speaking with others and saying to them, 'This is the grape season'. On hearing him, the Man of God grew angry and rebuked him properly, saying to him, 'O wretched man, do you not know that the false prophets are dead but their spirit is still abroad among men trying to find a place in them—in these, for example? Why then have you made room for such a demon, that he would dwell in you and speak through your mouth in such a way that some ignorant men now hearing you name that fruit will be tormented by the wish to have some of it, and that you become a stranger to God for having scandalized their souls, as it is written, *A soul for a soul?*[1] Have you not heard the Apostle

Cf. Mt 7:15.

Ex 21:23; Lv 24:18.

say, *Let no evil word come from your mouth; but let every good thing give pleasure to those who hear it,* and at the same time to those who speak it? Do you not know that this word which you uttered just now will be a matter not of edification for your brothers but rather of ruin and perdition? ‹Then, wretched man, why did you say it to them?›[2] For, this I warrant you: every idle word of this kind, or unbecoming remark, or foolish word, or stupid saying, is a defilement of the human soul before God. Eph 4:29.

'By means of a parable I am going to show you how God's wrath will descend on the man who uses shameful or scurrilous speech in the midst of the brothers. It is like a rich man who invited some other persons to his banquet that they might eat and drink and be gay. Once they were at table, they wantonly got up and threw down the vessels in his house. So he got angry with them and rebuked them saying, "Ungrateful wretches! I invited you to my house to eat and drink well, why then have you, in the wantonness of your souls, thrown down the dishes that are in my house and eaten with ingratitude?" Such is the case of anyone who lives under the yoke of monastic life and speaks scurrilous things. The Lord will bring his wrath to bear on them and [say to them], "You too were called to this holy vocation, and you want to ruin ‹your souls and the›[3] souls of those I have brought together for their salvation! Are you going to bring on their ruin by your scurrilous words?"[4]

'I will show you as well that the honor and the glory of the men of the *Koinonia,* who have a good way of life together with the excellence of

the toils they impose on themselves, are superior to those of men who lead the anchoritic life. I will show you also that the ruin, the falls, and the loss of those who do not walk aright in the *Koinonia* give rise to greater scandal than among those who lead the anchoritic life. Indeed, it is like a trader who sails on the sea and rivers in all kinds of weather. If he escapes the sea's danger he will get very rich; but if his boat goes down, not only will his wealth be lost, but his life too and his remembrance will be lost forever. At the same time, listen to the interpretation: he who makes progress in the *Koinonia* with purity, obedience, humility, and submissiveness, and puts no stumbling-block or scandal before anyone by his words or by his acts, that one will grow rich forever in imperishable and enduring riches. But should he be negligent, and should a soul be scandalized by him and perish from it, woe to
Cf. Mt 18:7. that man; not only has he lost his soul and the troubles he took on himself, but he also will have to render an account to God for that soul he scandalized.

'About those who lead the anchoritic life, listen, and I will teach you their parable. It is like a merchant selling bread or vegetables or anything else of that kind in the market-place. He is not going to get rich on such a daily gain, but neither will he be in want of any of this world's material things. So it is with an ascetic leading the anchoritic life. He does not bear the responsibility of other ascetics, but neither does he see those who practise exercises—a thing which would incite him to imitate their actions and the excellent practices they perform in order to do the same himself. Well, such a man will not rank high in the kingdom of heaven, but neither will he be deprived of eternal life, because of the purity of the *ascesis* he has practised. The reward for the fasts, prayers, and exercises he has performed in Christ's name and for the love and the fear he bore him will be paid him by Christ tremendously multiplied in the age to come, in his kingdom.

'Again I will instruct you by a parable about the brothers who are the lowliest in the *Koinonia*, who do not give themselves up to great practices and to an excessive *ascesis*, but walk simply in the purity of their bodies and according to the established rules with obedience and obligingness. In the view of people who live as anchorites, their way of life does not seem perfect and they are looked upon as the lowliest. Truly, it is like favorite servants of the king and his favorite eunuchs: they have greater freedom of movement in the palace than the powerful who are under the king's orders and who cannot get at the king unless they have themselves announced to him by the eunuchs. So it is with those others who are considered the lowliest in the *Koinonia*, and will be found perfect in the law of Christ[5] because of their steadfastness. They practise exercises in all submissiveness according to God. They are also far superior to those who live as anchorites, for they walk in the obligingness the Apostle walked in, as it is written, *By the love of the Spirit, be servants of one another in a kindly spirit and in all patience before our Lord Jesus.*'[6]

Cf. Ga 6:2.

Cf. Ga 5:13; Eph 4:2,32.

Vision of Pachomius about the sinful brothers

106. On another day it happened that our father Pachomius, being in prayer somewhere, was given in a vision a revelation concerning

those who went aside from their own resolution and became darnel. As it is written in the holy
Mt 13:38. Gospel, *The darnel is the sons of the evil one,*[1]
Cf. 1 Co 11:7. that is to say, those who defile the image of God.[2] Then he did not omit to separate those of this sort from the good grain, for he knew the suppression of men of this sort would bring about an increase in those who are upright.[3] When he found that the one who had been deceived by a son of the evil one was a little one, and if he knew ‹that no one was informed›[4] about this little one, he would nurse his soul and heal it. Besides, when he found out someone who had fallen into sin, and he knew that this one would do penance, he would make haste in his mercy to save him from the devil's grasp, remembering the Apostle's recommendation, *My brothers, if one of you falls into sin, you who are spiritual should set him right in a kindly spirit; and examine yourself, lest you be tempted*
Ga 6:1. *as well.* On a balance, those he knew had become sons of the evil one he would strip of the monastic habit, dress in worldly clothes and expel from the midst of the brothers. Quite often, too, before they had realized the desire they had conceived in their hearts to carry out, he would know of it, thanks to the spirit of God that dwelt in him; he would question them at great length until they would confess by word of mouth what they had thought in their hearts to do, and then he would likewise expel them from the midst of the brothers.

Story of a brother who had lived in impurity before coming to the monastery

107. One day the brothers had come to Alexandria with a few mats, to sell them there and to purchase what is necessary for the sick brothers. It happened as they were about to leave for the

south, that three men desiring to become monks boarded the boat with them and came south to the monastery of Phbow. When our father had embraced all the brothers, he questioned them concerning the peace of the holy catholic Church of Christ. Then he said to the superior[1] of the brothers, 'Why have you brought with you this darnel, <saying to me>,[2] "make him a monk"?' The brother said to him with great humility, 'Holy father, do you think that I have the gift the Lord has given you of knowing which men are good and which bad?' Then he told him, 'By his deeds this man has been darnel since his childhood because of the many impurities he has committed before God. It is hard indeed for men of this sort to live, unless they undertake great toils, many fasts, long prayers, a great many ascetical practices and numerous vigils. But since you have brought him, we will let him in with the other two, lest by sending this one away we discourage the other two and they give up. As for him, we will watch over him and will show him the way he can be saved, lest he take up again in our midst the evil practices he used to indulge in before you brought him to us. If he becomes converted and does penance we will receive him well and will make a place for him among us; but if he does not do penance for his sins, we will send him back to the place you brought him from. Were we to decide to expel him now, the other two would grieve over it and would retreat; on account of him their souls would suffer harm by our doing and the Lord would blame us for it.

'What need is there to gather with us evil men who have not resolved in their own hearts to do penance before God? Actually, those we have turned away from us this year number about a hundred'—the number of the brothers of the whole community of the *Koinonia* hardly reached three hundred and sixty men at the time.[3] The brother said to him, 'If you had not sent away from us those men you spoke of, the brothers would have increased and the *Koinonia* would have developed amply and peacefully'. Then our father Pachomius said to him, 'No, on the contrary, if I had let them stay, the brothers would have diminished in number; for when evil men increase in number side by side [with good men], God's anger likewise comes down on the others who are good and all come under the curse, as Scripture says, *Sin brought it about that the tribe grew less under the curse of the Lord; but when they drove the wicked out from among the Lord's people, the blessing of the Lord came down on all the people which multiplied greatly and bore fruit to God.*'[4]

Then the brother spoke to him again, 'I wish you would teach me the full meaning of the word you spoke, "This man is darnel". Is it that their nature is evil from birth, as men affirm? If such is the nature with which this man was born, what can he do?' Again our father Pachomius said to him, 'Every man whom God has created out from Adam possesses the power to choose between good and evil. And even if there exists someone whose nature is evil from infancy, doubtless he got it from his parents' evil nature. But the Lord cannot be reproached with that, because that man is free to conquer himself against the passion which harasses him. If there exists a multitude of women who have conquered their own nature by giving themselves up to *ascesis* in virginity till the day of their death although their nature is not virile, how much more surely should a man, whom God created after his image and likeness by giving him a virile nature, even if this kind of passion harasses him as men affirm, be able by an act of his own will and the judgement of his reason to master the passion which harasses him and to cast it far from him![5]

Cf. Gn 1:26-27; Ws 2:23.

'Scripture teaches us that man created by God is upright,*[6] but of his own volition he has turned aside toward evil thoughts† and has angered God who created him.‡ Then of his own volition he has turned his heart toward wicked and impure thoughts, abominable desires, shameful talks and mockery, as Solomon says, *I saw how man was upright, but for his part he has sought out wicked reasonings in his heart before the Lord.* Even if someone is a bad offspring of his parents, it is possible for him to change by his own will and judgement, whatever his nature may be.[7]

*Cf. Qo 7:29.
†*Ibid.*
‡Dt 32:18-19.
Qo 7:29.

'The prophet Ezechiel provides confirmation of this statement for us when he says, *If an iniquitous and blood-thirsty man begets a son and if that son, seeing his father's iniquities, is fearful and walks not in that way, but on the contrary deals righteously before the Lord of hosts, he will certainly live and shall not die in the sins his father committed.* On balance, should a man who has not got such a character or, to put it briefly, is without passion at all, wish to cultivate honorably the virile nature God created him with, he will commit no abominable iniquities. If he walks instead in the fear of the Lord and hon-

Ez 18:10,14,17.

estly, he will live in the purity of marriage and will not give himself up either to whoring or to adultery; he will on the contrary be content with
Cf. Gn 2:24; Eph 5:31. only his wife. If he is also zealous for perfection according to the words of the holy apostle Paul
1 Co. 12:31. who said, *Be zealous for higher gifts*,[8] he will live in the purity of the angels. Then the Holy Spirit will dwell in him and sanctify him; he will go and become a monk and serve the Lord in all purity and uprightness.'

When our father Pachomius had said these words the brother replied and told him, 'My lord and father, now you have contented me from the Holy Scriptures about the question I put to you. Now I wish you to tell me why, of that multitude of men who come to us with the desire of becoming monks, you send the great number away and refuse to accept them as monks. What moves you then not to accept men of this sort, and to say about them, "There is no repentance for them"? And why do you also say about them, "They have not come with all their hearts to become monks"?' Then our father Pachomius said to him, 'Did you think to yourself that I disregard God's image? Not so; God forbid that I should in any way lack esteem for men! But all those I do not accept are darnel like the one who I told you was darnel. For men of that sort it is difficult indeed to be saved in the *Koinonia* because of the passions that dominate them. For it is impossible for anyone, unless it is someone in whom the Lord dwells, to correct them in such a way that they are afraid of the sins and abominations they have committed.

'I assure you that if I revealed their deeds to the brothers that they might pray for them before the

Lord, not only would they not pray for them, but they would despise them, make fun of them, and refuse to eat and drink with them. That is why we do not accept them, lest one of the brothers fall into their evil actions, that his heart be hardened by any of them, and that he get caught in the snares of the devil.

'For my part I sometimes accept one or two men of that kind and struggle with them very hard until I save them from the enemy's grasp. I must go to them often, night and day, until they are safe or else until the Lord visits them and they repose in Him. This I do in order to fulfill the words of the holy Apostle, *Take pains with one another so that you may be saved.* Cf. Eph 4:2; Ga 5:13; Jm 5:16.

'As regards those whom I do not accept, I am afraid to do as the farmer who wants to clear all his fallow, sandy and thorny land while leaving his good land fallow because he cannot work both of them. Such is my way of doing. Indeed I tell myself that I must not go about busying myself with impure men while perhaps so neglecting to visit the brothers who are pure that they succumb to impurity. On the contrary, with the grace of Christ I train the pure souls in the commandments of everlasting life. And those among the others whom I will succeed in restoring to life, I hasten to get to pass from their bad behavior to the service of the Lord.

'As to those men whom I send away, I tell them, "Since you have committed these sins out of blindness of heart and ignorance, there is repentance for you, but you cannot be saved in the *Koinonia*. Go off alone somewhere, lead the life of an anchorite and undertake a great many

Eph 4:18.

lengthy ascetical practices; fast and pray before the Lord night and day with abundant tears because of the sins you have committed, that he may pardon you. Keep careful watch on yourself lest you find yourself once more in these impurities, and do not consent to the wicked thoughts the devil will sow in your heart for you to carry out." These are the words I speak to each man of that kind so that I may be innocent of their blood*[9] before God on the day of his great just judgement,† and so that they may not say, "You did not give us room for doing penance unto the Lord".'

*Cf. Dn 13:46; Mt 27:24.
†Cf. 2 Th 1:5.

The man from Alexandria, of whom he had said that he was darnel, he took apart, and when he had introduced him among the brothers, he laid lengthy ascetical practices and exercises on him, so that by performing them he might escape torments. He strongly recommended that he fast until evening every day and eat nothing cooked. He told him, ‹'Should you someday happen to fall sick›,[10] do not believe [you are sick] unless you had warned me first[11] and I had examined the situation [to find out] whether the thing came from God or from devils who set a snare for you, desiring to master you through the things into which you have fallen before in the world. If I find that it is a sickness sent by God, I will order the [brother] who has care of the sick to take good care of you until you are well. Only, keep your soul and body entirely pure from this day forward and do not yield to the impure thoughts the devil sows in your heart. Make haste to keep watch, praying to God and shedding tears with all your strength, so that the evil spirit for whom you have been an abode may depart from you. Be humble of heart and say, "When I shall have finished observing all that I have been commanded, I shall scarcely have deserved to live and to escape the fire that cannot be put out and the undying worm of punishment."[12] Should some brothers see your *ascesis* and praise you for it without knowing the iniquities you have committed, say to yourself at once with tears, "My Lord Jesus, if they knew the impure deeds I have done night and day before you, as well as the uncleanness and the abominations that even now I am guilty of,[13] they would not only not address me with words of praise, but they would not even wish to look on my face because of the stench of the sins I have committed before the Lord." Watch and keep guard on yourself! Let no proud or vain thought enter your mind, lest you add still more to your sins and you be cast into unending punishments. Should someone insult you or hurt you, bear it with gratitude and say to yourself, "Many times I have angered God with my impure and abominable actions". Likewise, be submissive and obedient with the brothers in all humility, meekness, and be without murmuring, in accord with the rules imposed on us in the *Koinonia,* so that God may *see* your *humility and* your *efforts, that he may forgive* you *the sins,*[14] the iniquities and the abominations you have committed in his presence night and day, and that he may not cast you forever into harsh and enduring punishments. Whatever you do do in the fear of the Lord. Do nothing for human glory, for fear your efforts should be for nothing.

Cf. Lk 17:10.

Cf. Is 66:24: Mk 9:44.

Ps 25(24):18.

the devil should dominate you once more, and you should be again his servant.'[15]

Having heard all this from our father Pachomius' lips, that man so gave himself over to great *ascesis* that all the brothers marvelled at his *ascesis* and at the efforts he made. For none among the brothers knew that it was on our father Pachomius' recommendation that he practised such an *ascesis*; they thought he was doing it of his own accord. Neither was there any one of them who knew what he had been like in his unclean actions committed before becoming a monk, save our father Pachomius and the brother who had brought him from Alexandria. Our father Pachomius, truly a just man, had forbidden the brother who brought him from Alexandria to inform any brother about the sins and impurities [this brother] had committed in Alexandria. This Alexandrian was young and had a strong build; he spent nine years carrying out a great *ascesis* well, but not in the fear of the Lord or in repentance; he was still addicted to the works of his evil passions and to his abominable pleasures.

After practising *ascesis* with steadfastness for nine years, it happened that, with his bent for impurity, he once more set a snare for a soul to ruin it. Our father Pachomius, who knew about it through the Holy Spirit of God abiding in him, saw the demon in this man who had accepted his wicked thoughts and who had then begun to carry out a great piece of very detestable iniquity on the advice of his father, the devil. Then our father Pachomius summoned him to the midst of all the brothers and began to question him concerning the thought he had taken into his heart to carry out without fear of the living God. The man grew troubled as a result of the fear of God he saw on the face of our father Pachomius, and at once confessed the sin he had consented fearlessly to commit. At once [our father Pachomius] expelled him from among the brothers; and when they learned of this matter, all the brothers were seized with a great fear for the grace of God that dwelt in our father Pachomius, and they gave glory to God.

Pachomius expels a sinful brother

108. Another day it happened that our father Pachomius went south with some brothers to gather rushes. When they reached the community of Tabennesi, he wanted to visit the brothers there. He went in with the brothers while reciting with them. And having embraced all the brothers, he saw that one of them had been wounded by a diabolical sin. The following night he prayed to the Lord about this, saying, 'Lord God Almighty, *Father of our Lord Jesus Christ,* you who are blessed, who have assembled this holy place, namely this holy *Koinonia* which was established from the beginning by our fathers, the holy apostles whom you have chosen and loved[1] and upon whom you later established us that we might live in all purity, that we might glorify and bless your holy name for ages unending, amen; we pray to your Goodness and to your Charity, O God, for this wretched man in our midst. He has shown ingratitude toward your Goodness and your Bounty. He has himself chosen to become the devil's vessel rather than *a vessel of election* and the dwelling-place of the Holy Spirit who saves every person. He has committed murder of

Eph 1:3.

Rm 9:21-22.

another in your holy house by consenting to these wicked thoughts instigated in his heart by the wily demon whose son he has become. And yet he is not ignorant of the Scriptures to such a degree that I should pray to you for him, since he is acquainted with your true knowledge, and himself teaches others to walk in the ways of your holy will. Actually, the sins and the impurity he teaches others to shun are exactly those he lives in, commits, and irreligiously carries out; that is why he deserves death. But I cannot do him any harm unless it is your holy will. Therefore, Lord, God of all the saints, just as you have revealed to me his abominable iniquities, teach me as well what I must do with him.'

While he was still praying, an angel of the Lord, very terrifying, appeared to him, having in his hand a fiery sword unsheathed. He said to our father Pachomius, 'Just as God *has blotted out his*
Cf. Ex 32:32-33; Ps 69(68):28. *name from the Book of Life,* just so do you drive them[2] out from the midst of the brothers, for they are not ignorant. Indeed even to the ignorant impurities of this sort seem like abominations before God.' When it was morning he put them in worldly clothing and told them, 'Go and do as is fitting to the clothes whose practices you have made your own.' And he expelled them from among the brothers. The words of the prophet were fulfilled about them, *I will drive them out of*
Ho 9:15. *my house,*[3] *and I will love them no longer.*

After that, he sat down and spoke the word of God to the brothers; he instilled fear in them by means of the negligence of those he had expelled, while shedding very many tears for the unhappy lot that had overtaken them on account of the abominations they had committed night and day before God. Then he rose and prayed with them all. After that each went back to his house, calmly reciting the word of God. As for our father Pachomius, he left too with the brothers who had come with him to gather the rushes. They recited the word of God until they came north to Phbow.

Pachomius heals a possessed man

109. The next day some people brought to the door of the monastery a man possessed by a demon and suffering a great deal. When these people had got themselves announced to [our father Pachomius] and had entreated him, through the brother on guard at the monastery door, he arose quickly and came out to them accompanied by two brothers. When he had come up to the sick man, he asked the people who were accompanying him, 'What is his name?' The possessed man replied, 'My name is Hundred.' Our father Pachomius then said to him, 'You good for nothing, where did you learn what a hundred is worth?' Turning his face toward the ground he told our father, 'By that speech you have put me to confusion.' Our father said to him again, 'Where did you drink water?' He answered him, 'I drank from the sea'. Our father said to him again, 'Unclean spirit, tell me the truth; where did you yourself drink?' Humbly he then said, 'I drank from the sea, at the bottom.' Our father said to him again, 'Tell me, who gave you power to go into this man to torment him?' The unclean spirit told him, 'He who was crucified; he it is who has given me power over this man.' Our father spoke to him for the fifth time, 'Wicked spirit, since it was he who gave you this power to dwell in him, show me the nails which were driven into

him who was crucified on the cross.' At once the demon gnashed his teeth saying, 'With that you have again beaten and put me to confusion.' Then our righteous[1] father stretched out his hands and called on the Lord with many prayers and floods of tears saying, 'I pray to you, my Lord Jesus Christ, for this your servant, that you, O lover of men, in your pity and your abundant mercy might cast your eyes on him, because he is your image and likeness, and heal him from this wicked demon, for you alone deserve glory, honor and power with your Good Father and your Holy Spirit now and forever and for ages unending, amen.' When he had said 'amen,' he signed him in the name of the Father and of the Son and of the Holy Spirit. Then he rebuked the unclean spirit, who at once came out of the man, who was restored by the power of Christ and the prayers of our father Pachomius. At the sight of that, which had come about quickly, all the persons who were with him gave glory to God and to our father Pachomius.

Pachomius heals a possessed brother

110. They likewise brought to him from a monastery a brother who was being tried by a demon. When our father Pachomius spoke with him, he answered well as one who is in no way tried by demons. He said to the brothers who had led him to him, 'I assure you, this demon is hiding in him and will not speak to me by this man's voice; but I am going to examine his whole body till I find out which of his members he is hiding in.' While he was examining his whole body he came to the fingers of his hands and said to the brothers, 'Here is the way the demon got in by, I have found it in the fingers of his hands'. Then

when he came to his neck, the place where the demon was, [the demon] made a great outcry and the man gave a violent jerk, and four men were hardly able to hold him. Our father Pachomius took hold of the place where the demon was and prayed to Christ for [the brother] that He might cure him. While he was praying the demon came out of the man who was immediately restored, thanks to our father Pachomius' prayers. All the brothers who had seen what had happened gave glory to the Lord for his mighty works which he shows forth through his saints. Cf. Si 38:6.

A brother tormented by the demon is not healed

111. It happened again that a man came to the gate of the monastery to become a monk. This man had in himself a demon who often agitated him, but he was an honorable man and very humble. Having looked at him face to face our father Pachomius saw the demon that was in him; immediately he took him aside and prayed to the Lord for him that He might cure him of this demon. The unclean spirit answered saying, 'You, Pachomius, what have you to do with me? And are you seeking to drive me out of this man? Cf. Mt 8:29. Am I hindering him in any way from doing the whole will of God? The Lord gave me this dwelling place to keep till the day of this man's death; but if you go after me to drive me out of him, know that I will not disobey you. But I will kill him and come out of him; for power has been given me to deal with him this way.' On hearing that, our father Pachomius began again to pray for him to the Lord that He might cure him of this wicked demon. While our father Pachomius was praying for this man that the Lord might take pity on him, cast the wicked spirit out of him

and cure him,[1] the angel of the Lord appeared to him and told him, 'Stop praying for this man, Pachomius. The Lord has sent this illness to him for his salvation; if he were healed of it, he would regret it very much.' After his prayer, [our father Pachomius] called the brother aside and told him, 'Do not be grieved about this [illness], because the Lord has sent it to you for your soul's salvation. Now, give him thanks for everything
Ps 18(17):46. saying, *Blessed be the Lord of my salvation.*'

From that day on, when people came to him with that illness and he knew that they would not profit from being healed, he would tell them, 'This is [for] your salvation; give thanks to the Lord in order to acquire life'.

Another sick brother who is not healed

112. There was a brother in the community of Phbow who fell sick every third day. He came to our father Pachomius and besought him with tears, 'You heal many people from the world, and, behold, you have not prayed for me, that I might be healed from this difficult illness.' He answered him, 'Those people are healed in their bodies through their faith but they tend to evil because of the respite they receive from their illness. But the servants of God will receive unfailing rest in the other age, a rest without illness or toil. They walk valiantly in the way of the Cross, according to what is written in the Gospel, *He who loves his soul loses it; but he who hates his*
Mt 16:25; Mk 8:35; Lk 9:24. *soul in this world will find it in the eternal life.*' When the sick [brother] heard this from the man of God, he was greatly comforted.

Some time later, seeing that his illness continued, he took with him some of the great men of the monastery and came to [our father Pachomius] to beseech him to pray over him, that God might give him rest. When the man of God saw that they compelled him, he wanted to satisfy them. Immediately he took with him a God-loving monk, one of the great ones who were beseeching him, and they went somewhere to pray for the sick man. When they had begun to pray, a voice came from heaven, saying, 'Do not ask for rest for this man. God has sent this trial to him in order to save him from the snares of youth that the devil sets for him, that he may be saved.' Immediately he stopped praying and came out with the [other] brother. He thought that those outside had heard the voice that had come to him. When he had come out, the brothers came to him and said, 'Why did you come out so soon, and did you not pray over the sick man?' He answered them, 'Did you not hear the voice that came?' They said, 'No'. The other brother who had been praying with him also said, 'I did not hear anything either.' He told them all that had happened to him, and how the voice had come when he was praying. When the brothers had heard this, they marvelled saying, 'Great is the work of the Lord for he is good and cares for those who seek him; without him nothing would exist.'[1]

113. It happened one day as he was sitting and working at a mat that a demon appeared to him in the aspect under which the Lord used to appear to him. From afar, [the demon] told him, 'Greetings'. When he saw him, he thought in himself, 'What kind is this one?' Then he recognized him by this: 'Behold, I have thought as usual.'[1] When the demon saw that he was

G[1] 87.

Discernment of apparitions

thinking, he began to take the thoughts away from his mind. Again Pachomius said to himself, 'How is it that I do not think any more? My thoughts have gone away.' Immediately he jumped and stood up, according to the Lord's inspiration. He took the hand of the phantasm of the demon and straightway blew in his face, which became dark. The demon's hand gradually disappeared from his own hand like smoke. Then, after [the demon] had disappeared, he stood up and prayed to God saying, 'Blessed are you, Lord God of all the saints and my God, who have delivered me from every tribulation and from every snare of the enemy.'[2]

Pachomius' trip to heaven

114. It happened once that he fell sick and he suffered so much that those sent out to fetch him snatched his soul away and he died. Then he was brought to the other age. But as he was approaching the gate of life, an order came from God to bring him back to his body once more. He was sad when he learned this, because he did not want to come back to his body again. Indeed he saw that the light of that air was wonderful and of such beauty as to be indescribable because of its splendor. As he was sad, a man who stood at the door to guard it turned toward him to look at him. The face of that man shone like a great painting because of its splendor, and the appearance of his body was all light. That man said to him, 'Go, my son, return to your body, for you still have to suffer a small martyrdom in the world'. When he heard this word he was very happy, for he greatly desired to be a martyr for the Lord's name. The angels who rejoiced with him informed him that, 'This man who is speaking to you is the apostle Paul'.

As soon as they brought him to the place where his body was, the soul considered its body; and behold, it was dead. It happened that when the soul approached the body, all the members of the body secretly opened up; the soul took its place again and the body became alive. While [Pachomius'] soul had been carried away, the brother who was with him slept.

After this, he was carried away to Paradise many other times. In what manner? God knows; as the Apostle says, *Either in the body, I do not know; or without the body, I do not know, it is God who knows; and so it is that that one was caught up to the third heaven and he heard secret words which man*[1] *is not allowed to repeat.* So 2 Co 12:2,4.
also our father Pachomius was carried away to that place, and he saw the cities of the saints, of which it is not possible to describe the constructions, the monuments, and the good *things that the Lord has prepared for those who love him.*[2] 1 Co 2:9.
When he saw those cities, he remembered what the Lord says in a parable in the Gospel, speaking to the servants whose talents had produced ten and five talents, *Enter into your master's happiness,*[3] and again, *He said to one, 'Be in charge* Mt 25:21,23.
of ten cities'; and to the other, 'Be in charge of five.' Lk 19:17-19.

The climate of that age is very even and its surface without limits. The fruit trees and the vineyards produce a spiritual food and are incorruptible, so that the fruits of the trees of this age are like unworthy and contemptible things compared to their variety. No tree or plant growing in paradise is ever deprived of fruits profusely giving out great fragrance. A man cannot bear that fra-

grance without passing out, unless the Lord gives him the grace. That age is above this earth and outside the firmament. That land is far above the mountains. The lights that are in the firmament and lighten the earth are not those that lighten that age, but it is the Lord that lightens it, as Isaiah says, *It will not be the light of the sun that will lighten us during the day, neither the shining of the moon that will lighten us by night, but the*
Is 60:19-20. *Lord will be our everlasting light*. There is no day or night in that age, but it is lightened by an abundant and unceasing light. So great are its boundaries that this world is nothing in comparison. A little outside the paradise there are many fruit trees and vineyards totally like those of this world. When our father Pachomius saw them, he thought within himself, 'Perhaps Noah took some of them and planted the world again after the flood.' He was thinking of the word written in [the book of] Genesis, *After they came out of the ark, Noah and his sons began to be farmers and*
Gn 9:20. *planted a vineyard*. That age was also surrounded by a great and thick darkness full of tiny insects, so that no one can enter there unless he is led there by an angel of God.

Story of a late vocation

115. [1]After that a man arrived at the gate of the monastery wanting to become a monk. Our father Pachomius went out to see him and asked him, 'You want to become a monk?' He answered, 'It is a thing I wanted in the past, but my negligence made me drift into the works of this vain world. Today as I walked along the road I heard a voice above me calling me by name. I answered, "What is it, Lord?" The voice spoke to me again, "How long will you be negligent and

refuse to do penance for your sins? So now arise, go and become a monk under Pachomius of Tabennesi and strive to look after your soul before you die and are cast into torments because of your sins." So now, my lord holy father, here I am, I come to you wanting to become a monk.' Our father Pachomius said to him, 'We rejoice along with you over the fact that you want to be saved in accordance with the voice you heard from the Lord. Now, when we see that you have walked in the way I am going to propose to you, I shall then be disposed as a father to take good care of you in everything your salvation calls for. Only, have no other care in this world than to keep in your heart the thought and the fear of God alone and to work solely at your soul's salvation.' The man spoke to him again, 'When you try me, God will, I think, put your mind at rest in my regard thanks to your holy prayers, O my lord father!' Our father Pachomius made him a monk very readily.

Once he had entered the community, this man saw the brothers' zeal, their godly humility, and their love for God. He too gave himself over to great ascetical practices, protracted exercises, frequent nights spent in vigils, and many fasts, humbling himself like a simple and innocent child. If anyone chided him harshly to his face, struck him or insulted him, he would not grieve over it or get upset about it at all. He would say to himself, 'The time was when I too vexed the Lord with the evil actions I used to commit; he did not retaliate,[2] ⟨but instead he did⟩ good to me, bringing me back to the path of life; and now I would not suffer a slight affliction or rebuke he directs at me! I would not ‹be able to suffer that my brother do that to me!' When he saw some brothers quarrelling or having an argument, he went to them humbly saying, 'Forgive me, brothers, I am the one at fault.'› Straightway those who were quarrelling would laugh and end their quarrel. He led this way of life for four months and then he died.

Story of a spiteful monk

116. [1]There was in the community, at that time, a brother ‹who had been a hermit. He lived among the brothers and used to fast for two days at a time.› He wore a sackcloth tunic throughout his life and would eat nothing at all except bread with salt. On the other hand, if a brother somehow offended him, he would hate him and nurse his anger against him so as to repay him evil for evil.

Once, after these had died, our father Pachomius was transported into the other age, as we have related previously.[2] He saw the guileless young man who had spent four months living the ascetic life in great gladness and joy. When the latter spotted our father Pachomius walking with the angel who was teaching him about the splendor of the other age, he rushed toward him. He tugged at him, saying, 'Come, my holy father, and see the inheritance which the Lord has given me because of the excellent teachings in which you taught me to walk.' He showed him his spiritual gardens and their imperishable fruit; he showed him his entire dwelling place as well as the mansion built in it. And their beauty was unutterable, filled as they were with the glory of the Lord. When he had shown him his entire dwelling place, the man of God was filled with great joy for him.

Afterwards, when they were a little way outside the delightful paradise, they saw the old ascetic in a scorching hot place, fastened like a dog to a tree laden with fruit. He was living off its fruit but was unable to move away from that tree. When he saw them, he bowed his head in shame until they passed him. When they saw him, they gazed at him very sadly and the guileless brother said to our father Pachomius, 'You have seen the old ascetic whom you labored to instruct. He did not obey you and did not walk humbly. See now what sort of punishment the Lord has inflicted upon him for his wicked disobedience!'

Pachomius refuses a special treatment during his illness

117. One day our father Pachomius became ill. He did not inform any of the brothers that he was ill nor, as usual, did he believe in his illness,[1] but because of his strong will, he had gone with them to the harvest. (In those days the brothers were reaping.) While he was reaping, he fell on his face in their midst. The startled brothers ran to him and lifted him from the ground. They discovered that, because of the sickness, he had a high fever in his body. They brought him to the monastery where he lay down upon the ground with his belt fastened. They pleaded with him to get him to unfasten it on account of the fever and to lie down on a bed like all the [other] sick brothers. However, he did not obey them in this but remained lying on the ground. Someone sat fanning him with his hood. Many had succumbed to the sickness in those days,[2] for the sickness which had struck them was severe and pestilential. One of those who came to inquire about him said to the brother who was fanning him with his hood, 'Could you not find a fan

with which to cool him?' When [Pachomius] heard this, he was unable to answer because of the severe illness which had worn him down, but with a movement of his finger he said to him, 'Is this whole crowd not sick? Are you going to find a fan for each one so that one can be found for me as well?'

Pachomius' last illness

118. His illness was protracted. It was during the Forty Days of the holy Passover. In the last week of the Forty Days of the Lord's Passover, when all the brothers of the monasteries were gathered at Phbow to celebrate the Passover together, an angel of the Lord came to him and said, 'Prepare yourself, Pachomius, because the Lord will take a great offering from your house on the day of the Feast.' He thought to himself, 'Perhaps the Lord will visit me on the Saturday of the Lord's Feast.' He spent the four days of the Passover without eating,[1] grieving and sighing within himself, so that the unity of the *Koinonia* might not be dissolved.

On Friday evening, the third day he had not eaten, he gathered all the brothers about him and spoke to them as Samuel had spoken to the people of his time, telling them all the ordinances. He likewise spoke with them, saying, 'I think, my brothers and my sons, that the time has come for me *to go the way of all the earth*[2] like all my fathers. You are well acquainted with my whole mode of life, how I have walked with all humility and renunciation in your midst. You know that I never sought after an easier life in any respect than anyone of you. ⟨On the contrary, we were all in our life like one single man; I was not hidden from you⟩[3] in any thing in this holy

1 K 2:2.

place. For the Lord is a witness to my conscience, that I have not said these things out of vanity or pride. And indeed, I am not going to speak to you of those things I do which are evident to you in order to persuade you, but, on the contrary, I am going to speak to you of those things which have not been manifested so that your hearts may thus be satisfied. Before God and men, I have not given any scandal to you. Likewise, the Lord knows that if you do not observe all the laws which I have laid down for you, and if you do not put them into practice and carry them out, you will not see any place of rest for your souls. I say this because I do not know what is going to happen to us. For the Lord commands us in the Gospel, saying, *Watch, because you do not know the day or the hour when the Son of Man will come.* Mt 25:13; Lk 12:40.
You know [what has been] my aim: I never corrected any one of you as the one having authority except for the sake of his souls's salvation, nor did I move any of you from one place to another or from one occupation to another unless I knew that it was to his advantage according to God that I do it. Nor did I ever repay anyone evil for evil. Nor did I ever curse anyone who had cursed me in impatience and anger, but on the contrary I used to teach him patiently so as not to let him sin against God, saying to him, "Now even though you have sinned against me, a man like you, take care not to sin against God who created you." I never became angry when someone reproached me justly, even if he who reproached me was a little one. But I would accept his reproach for God's sake, as if it were the Lord reproaching me. Nor when I was about to go somewhere or to a com-

munity, did I ever come to say, as one having authority, "Give me a donkey to mount". But I used to go on foot gratefully and humbly. When one of you with the donkey pursued me to make me mount it after I had set out on foot, if he caught up with me on the road when I knew that my body was sick and I needed the relief, I would accept it from him. But if I knew that I was not sick, I would not accept it. With regard to eating, drinking, anointing, and the other means of refreshing the body, you are not ignorant of [my use of] each one of these, as I have told you previously.'[4]

While he was saying these things, Theodore was sitting a little distance away weeping with his face down between his knees.[5] Many of the brothers were also weeping, knowing his ceaseless service to everyone and his great humility when he acted as the servant of each one of them in the fear of the Lord; as Paul says, *We became like little ones in your midst. As a nurse warms up her children, so we greatly wished to give you not only the Gospel of God but even our souls because you*
1 Th 2:7-8. *have become dear to us.*[6] But as our father Pachomius asserted all these things to the brothers he was lying sick; it was the third day he had not eaten. They were all weeping because of the calamity which would fall on them should the Lord visit him.

G[1] 114a.

Outburst of plague and death of Paphnouti

119. Apa Paphnouti, the steward of all the monasteries and the brother of Apa Theodore, was also ill. In the evening of the Saturday of the Lord's Feast, he died. At once our father Pachomius remembered what the angel had said to
29 March 346. him, '[The Lord] will take a great offering from your house on the day of the Feast.'

So many of the brothers died from that epidemic that one of them was dying every day, indeed some days two died, and other days three or four. That visitation had occurred in all the communities of brothers by order of the Lord. Many of the leaders of the monasteries had also died in that epidemic. When the fever seized them, suddenly their color changed, their eyes became bloodshot, and they became like men being choked until they gave up their spirit.[1] Apa Paphnouti, the steward of the Great Monastery of Phbow, the brother of Apa Theodore, had died in that epidemic, as well as Apa Sourous, the leader of the monastery of Phnoum, and Apa Cornelios, the leader of the monastery of Thmoušons. The number of all those who had died in this epidemic at Phbow was about one hundred thirty.

G[1] 115.

Pachomius refuses a special treatment again

120. Theodore waited on our father Pachomius while he remained ill. He had been lying for forty days in the infirmary where all the sick brothers were. He received the same care as all the other brothers in every respect. There was no difference at all between him and them, in accordance with the instruction which he had given them earlier. Although his body had become very weak because of the prolonged illness, nevertheless his heart and his eyes were like a flaming light. He said to Theodore, 'Please bring a mantle which has been worn thin and spread it over me, because this one is too heavy.[1] I will not be able to bear it, since I have been sick for forty days now. Yet I give thanks to the Lord.' Theodore went at once and got a good light mantle from the steward. He brought it and spread it over him. When our father Pachomius saw the difference in the mantle,[2] he became angry at Theodore and said to him, 'What a great

injustice you have done, Theodore! Do you wish me to give scandal to the brothers? Then later on when they say, "Apa Pachomius had an easier life than the rest of the brothers," I shall become liable to judgement before the Lord. Now, take it off from me; I will manage somehow until I go to the Lord.' Theodore then took it off him. He brought another one, more worn and worse than those of all the other sick brothers and spread it over him.

G[1] 114b.

Pachomius appoints Petronios as his successor

121. He remained ill during the days of the Fifty Days [of Eastertide]. Three days before he died, he sent for and gathered around him all the great ones among the brothers. He spoke to them, saying, 'You see that I am about to go to the Lord who created us and gathered us together that we might do his will. Now then decide together who you wish to become father to you.' But they went on weeping, and because of their grief no one answered him, for they were thinking how miserable they would be after his departure from their midst, like sheep whose shepherd has been taken

Cf. Mt 9:36.

from them. After that he asked Apa Horsiesios a second time, 'Speak to them and find out who they wish to become their father.' They answered him together, 'If this is how it must be, we do not know anyone except the Lord and you. Whatever you determine, we will do.' He answered them, 'The man among you who the Lord has revealed to me might build up your souls in the fear of the Lord is Petronios, father of the monastery of Tsmine.' (Indeed, because of his purity of heart, he used to have revelations often and was qualified in every respect.) 'I think that he too is ill, but if he lives, he is your father.' Then while he was still alive, he called some of the ancients and sent them after [Petronios]. Actually even before[1] he had assembled the brothers and said to them, 'You see now, I am about *to go the way of all the earth,'* they had all gone together to the *synaxis*. They spent three days praying and weeping before the Lord that He might leave him to them a little longer on earth. After three days, our father Pachomius sent Theodore to them, saying, 'Enough of your weeping, for the order concerning me, that I am to go the way of all my fathers, has come from the Lord.' The brothers returned to the place where he was lying and continued to weep over him with profound sorrow.

1 K 2:2.

G[1] 116a.

Pachomius' last recommendations to Theodore

122. Then he turned to Theodore and spoke to him, 'If the Lord visits me, do not leave my body in the place it will be buried in.' Grief-stricken, he answered him, 'I will do what you say.' Then he grabbed his beard, struck him on the breast, and said a second time, 'Theodore, pay attention. Do not leave my body in the place where it will be buried.' Again he answered him, 'My Lord and father, I will do gratefully whatever you command me.' Theodore thought to himself that he was saying this so insistently out of fear some people would steal his body and build a *martyrion* for it as they do for the holy martyrs. For many times he had heard him criticize those who did such things, ‹saying, 'The saints have not been pleased with those who do such things,›[1] because everyone who does this is commercializing the bodies of the saints.' Then he seized him again by the beard and said to him a third time, 'Theodore, take care to do quickly what I have told you. Likewise, if the brothers become negligent, you are to stir them up in the law of God.' Theodore thought to himself, 'What does he mean by this, "If the brothers become negligent, you are to stir them up in the

law of God"? Is he saying that after a time the brothers will be entrusted to me? I do not know.' And while he was reflecting on these things in his heart, our father Pachomius answered him, 'Do not be hesitant. Do not waver. I am referring not only to what I am saying to you but to what you are thinking in your heart.' Weeping, Theodore answered him, 'It is well.'

G[1] 116b.

Pachomius' death

123. When he had said these things, he fell unconscious for a little while and did not say anything more to any of them. Then he made the sign of the cross with his hand three times. Suddenly he opened his mouth and gave up his spirit, on the fourteenth of the month of Pašons at the tenth

9 May 346.

hour of the day.[1] Such great fear [overcame them] at that moment that the place trembled three times. And many of the ancients who often had visions said, 'We saw throngs of angels ranked above each other contemplating him. They preceded him singing very joyfully till he was received into his resting place.' The result was that the place where he rested gave off a fragrant odor for many days. Theodore placed his hands on his eyes and closed them as Joseph [had done].[2] Of him the Lord has said to Jacob, *Do not be afraid of going down to Egypt, for I will make of you a great nation there. I myself will go down to Egypt with you; I will bring you out of it, and Joseph will place his hand upon*

Gn 46:3-4.

your eyes. Weeping, all the brothers rushed to him. They kissed his mouth and all his holy body.

The rest of that day and the whole night they spent around him before the altar, reading [lessons from Scripture]. When they had finished the morning *synaxis*, they prepared his holy body for burial just as they did all the other brothers, and they offered the Eucharist for him. Then they preceded him singing psalms as he was taken to the mountain and buried on the fifteenth of that same month of Pašons. While the brothers were returning to the monastery in a very subdued and humble manner, many of them said to their neighbors, 'We have indeed been orphaned today'.

After they had come down from the mountain, Theodore that night took three other brothers with him, removed him from the place where he had been buried, and put him with Apa Paphnouti, the brother of Apa Theodore and accountant of the *Koinonia*. *No one knows to this day where he lies.* Dt 34:6.

All the days of his life numbered sixty years. He became a monk when he was twenty-one years old and the other thirty-nine years he spent as a monk.[4] Actually, when the Lord saw that he had crucified his flesh in everything so as to do His will, he wished to give him rest. Cf. Ga 5:24. He took him to himself and did not allow him to reach such a great age that he would suffer the weakness of the body more than he wanted.[5]

G[1] 117a.

Petronios sends Theodore to Alexandria with a letter for Athanasius

124. ⟨Our father Apa Petronios was lying ill⟩[1] and, in accordance with their rules, he was giving directions to the brothers on every subject about which they questioned him. When he learned that the brothers were going to Alexandria that year to visit the archbishop and [to procure] the things needed for the sick brothers, he called Theodore. He sent him for the service of the monastery with the other brothers, having first written for him a letter to the archbishop concerning the death of our father.[2] Then he embraced Theodore and those with him. He said to him, 'Greet the father of the faith warmly. I also bid you farewell because very likely we shall see one another [the next time] in the presence of our

father and those [already] with him.' The brothers departed and went on board their boat sadly because he had said, 'You will not see me again'.

The brothers' boat is impounded at Antinoe

125. They sailed north in their boat until they reached the city of Antinoe. There their boat was impounded. The brothers wept and became very depressed. They said, 'This is really a sign that God has forgotten us since our father died. While he was still in the body with us, such a thing never happened to us.' Apa Theodore responded by encouraging them. He said, 'Do not be afraid, my brothers, for the Lord God, who is with all the saints and with our father, is also with us. Consider the case of a man who at present is a friend of the king of this world. Even though he may be far away from him, he is not afraid of anyone because he is a friend of the king. And not only does nobody do him any harm, but many even ally themselves with him so that he may obtain favors for them, for they know that the king loves him. Then later on, when he leaves his own city and goes to the king's city, will he not enjoy even more confidence because he is closer to the king, though he is only a king of this world? If then when our father was with us on the earth, the King of kings, the Lord of the universe, used to show wonderful goodness to us because of the entreaties and prayers he offered for us in all respects, then now that he has drawn closer to God, will he not be heard all the more when he is in the tents of the just appealing for us? Even if he tests us and does not help us, we do not have a very strong faith if we say, "The Lord has forsaken us", because our boat was impounded. What could we say if the earthly authorities were to exile us, reducing us to slavery like Daniel and

his companions? Of them it was written to us,
they were in the court of the lawless king Nebu-
chadnezzar as his slaves. For they were subject to Dn 2:49.
him in everthing except that which would have
been a sin against God. Then, when he set up a
golden image and said to them, *If you do not*
worship it, I will punish you, they chose to *hand* Dn 3:14.
over their bodies to the fire rather than to deny Dn 3:28.
the God of their fathers.[1] Also to the point is what
the blessed apostle Peter wrote for us, *Humble*
yourselves before every human being for the sake
of God, whether it is the case of the king as being
sovereign or of the governors as sent by him to
punish evildoers and to honor those who do good.
One must obey such persons for the sake of the 1 P 2:13-14.
Lord. On the other hand, so that these may fear
him, one may not deny Him or sin against Him
because of men who are today in power according
to the flesh. In the words of the blessed Paul, *If*
possible, try to make peace with every man. However, by saying, *If possible,* he makes the matter Rm 12:18.
clear to us, "If you will not be sinning against God
in the peace you make, then make peace with
everyone". If, however, it is a question of a heretic
or another such person, and if you sin against God
in making peace with him, then flee far from him
like someone fleeing from a serpent, that you may
not die from the poison of his wickedness.'

When the brothers heard these words from Apa Theodore, they were much encouraged. And when evening came that day, he said to the brothers, 'Let us rise and pray to the Lord that he may deliver us from those who do evil to us'. So they rose and prayed to the Lord with such great pleading that their prayer was prolonged into the middle of the night.

The next morning the duke assembled all his officers and spoke to them as follows: 'Last night I saw such distressing things that it almost seemed my soul would be taken. Now it occurred to me that perhaps these things came over me because you have seized the boat of the Tabennesiots. Go quickly and return it to them, for they are servants of God.' At once the duke's servants went out, running beside each other. They saluted them and returned their boat. Apa Theodore turned and said to the brothers, 'You see the goodness of God, how he has provided this great benefit for us. Actually it is not because of our righteousness that he has done this for us but because of our righteous father, who has entered God's presence, and because of the prayers of our holy father who is among us today, Apa Petronios, the man *in whom there really is no deceit*.'[2] The brothers were in fact amazed at the faith our father Theodore had in God and at his perfect confidence in every good work.

Jn 1:47.

Then they sailed north in their boat.

G[1] 120a.

Visit of Theodore and Zacchaeus to Antony

126. When they reached the mountain of Tiloč, they asked after the blessed Apa Antony, the anchorite. They were informed that he was lying ill in his monastery on the outer mountain.[1] At once they tied up their boat on the shore and they went up to meet and visit with him. When he was informed, 'There are brothers here from the *Koinonia* of Tabennesi who wish to visit you', on hearing their name, he had one of those around him give him his hand to raise him up, since for a long time he had been weak because of advanced age. The brothers gathered about him were surprised and took hold of him. He walked out to

meet them at the door of his monastery where he embraced them with a holy kiss.

Then Apa Theodore took his right hand and Apa Zacchaeus his left hand. They walked with him, and all the other brothers followed behind until they came to the place where he lay. Then they prayed and sat down. All the brothers were seated around him. There was great joy on his face like that of an angel of God. Then he began to speak these words of exhortation to them: 'Do not be grieved, brothers, because the righteous man, Apa Pachomius, has died. For actually you have become his body and you have received his spirit. Indeed, I longed very much to see him while he was still in the body, but perhaps I was not worthy. For the fact that he gathered souls about himself in order to present them holy to the Lord reveals that he is superior to us and that it is the path of the apostles he took, that is, the *Koinonia.*' Apa Theodore answered very politely, 'You are more praiseworthy than we, for you are the last of the prophets'. But Apa Zacchaeus could not restrain himself and answered thoughtlessly, 'Surely you are deceiving us. If the *Koinonia* in which our father walked is the superior path of the apostles, then why did not you also live in a *Koinonia* and nurture a multitude of souls as you have said? For we all know that you are a righteous man, accomplished in every good way of life. The Lord knows that our father never stopped speaking to us constantly about you, holding up your life for us to emulate in the days when he was in the body with us.'

127. Apa Antony replied, 'I will convince you, *G[1] 120b.*
little Zacchaeus—for he was short of stature—in

Antony praises Pachomius and the *Koinonia*

the question you pose to me. Actually, when I became a monk, there was as yet no *Koinonia* on earth to make it possible for me to live in a *Koinonia*. There were only a few people who used to withdraw a little way outside their village and live alone.[1] This is why I too became an anchorite. Then the path of the apostles was revealed on earth. This is the work our able Apa Pachomius undertook. He became the refuge for everyone in danger from the one who has done evil from the beginning. Now then, if I too wanted to assemble a *Koinonia*, I would not be able to do it, for I did not grow up in this kind of work from the beginning so that I acquired [those skills] necessary for dealing correctly with each one. Likewise, if I wanted to join some brothers already gathered for this kind of life and stay with them, so I would be a subject like one of the young ones, I would not be able to do it because of my advanced age. Therefore I have chosen to continue as I am.

Cf. Jn 8:44; 1 Jn 3:8.

'Actually, every time I have come from the mountain to visit the brothers, my whole aim has been this: to speak with one of the brothers, fortifying him with the word of God that I might obtain a reward for this from the Lord. I tell you this, I am filled with great zeal in the Lord that a single soul may be healed in the Lord through me. Beyond that I am not allowed to do as I wish. When they heard that I had come to the outer mountain, many groups and crowds, besieging one another with importune requests, would come running to us and persist in demanding that I write the authorities and the judges concerning their requests. But I saw that there was no profit in this as far as our vocation[2] is concerned.

So I would rise quickly and withdraw to the mountain and live by myself.'[3]

128. While the blessed Apa Antony was talking to them and praising the way of life of the holy brothers of the *Koinonia*, a large crowd of clerics and dignitaries, who had come to visit him and receive his blessing, was milling about. But he who knew their thoughts, that they were murmuring about the way he praised the brothers of the *Koinonia*, addressed them all, 'I tell you, you have got very angry in your hearts because I have praised the way of life of the brothers'. The clerics answered him, 'Have we become angry without reason? Certainly not! We have become angry in our hearts because for a long time you have been so weak that you were simply unable to get up to embrace any of us who came to visit you, whether he was a bishop or a tribune or a count or an official; instead we had to bend over you and kiss your head or your mouth or your breast as if receiving a favor. On the other hand, as soon as the news about the brothers of Tabennesi was brought to you, suddenly you went away and, leaving us all where we were sitting, you walked out to embrace them with great joy and warmth.'

Discontent of the clerics who were with Antony

Apa Antony answered them, 'I will convince you in this matter and tell you exactly what happened. As the Lord knows, it was not only because of them that I came out to meet them, but a glorious angel of the Lord had preceded them and, before the news was brought to me, informed me that "the sons of Pachomius of Tabennesi have come to you". And while the angel was still speaking with me, the news about the brothers was brought to me, "The brothers of the *Koinonia* have come to visit us". Suddenly the Lord's power came upon me. I got up and ran out to embrace them. And in fact they really are blessed if they accomplish what their father, Apa Pachomius, the perfect man in every respect, commanded them.'

G[1] 120c.

Discontent of Antony's own monks

129. The brothers in his own monastery reproached him similarly. 'If the brothers of the *Koinonia* are worthy of all the praises you have spoken of them, then how is it that when we need to stay in their monasteries,[1] they give us a hard time, asking, "Are you Meletians?" We are tired of declaring that we belong to Apa Antony. They say, "Many come here and assert, 'We belong to him', and we receive them according to the precept of the Gospel. Then when they have left us, if we inquire about them, we discover that they were Meletians." Nevertheless we are upset because even though we belong to you, they do not believe us.'[2]

Apa Antony replied. He said to them, 'O you naïve people who do not know how to apply the Scriptures and who receive everyone without testing! Do you want the brothers of the holy *Koinonia* to act as you do and not test anyone? In fact, they remember the saying written in the Gospel. They are all on guard as our Lord said to be: *Beware of false prophets who come to you in sheep's clothing, but within are plundering wolves.* And also, *Test everything; retain what is good.*[3] Because there is a love which men think to be good but which ends up in hell.' The brothers and the clerics became convinced of all the complimentary things which Apa Antony said to

Mt 7:15.
1 Th 5:21.
Cf. Pr 14:12.

them about the brothers of the *Koinonia.* Then he got up and prayed with them and they departed in peace for their boat. He sent a letter by them to the blessed Apa Athanasius, the archbishop.

130. While the brothers were still in Alexandria, Apa Petronios became seriously ill at Phbow. He said to the brothers gathered about him, 'You see it is decreed that, as the Scriptures put it, *I am to go the way of all the earth.* Now then, decide whom you wish to be father to you and to nourish you with the Lord's commandment.' They answered him together tearfully, 'After God and our father, we do not know of anyone but you. You are in fact the one to whom our father entrusted us when he was about to die.' He answered them, 'As for me, it has already been decided that I am to leave the body like everyone else. Now then, it has been revealed to me many times that Horsiesios is the person to edify your souls in the fear of the Lord.' [Horsiesios], who was sitting nearby weeping, said, 'I do not have the strength for this'. Apa Petronios answered him, 'It is not I who am appointing you to this task nor is it man, but it is God and our father.' After a little while, the righteous man Apa Petronios opened his mouth and gave up his spirit on the twenty-fifth of the month of Epip.[1]

G[1] 117b.

Petronios' death

1 K 2:2.

19 July 346.

Apa Horsiesios and the brothers spent the whole night reading and praying around him. In the morning at the time of the *synaxis*, he had them prepare him well for burial and they offered the Eucharist for him. They went before him singing psalms as he was taken to the mountain and buried beside our father.

Horsiesios takes charge of the *Koinonia*

131. The ancients among the brothers conversed with one another, saying sorrowfully, 'Would it not be fitting for us to go on grieving over the one who has died, whom our righteous father appointed to nourish us as a nurse warms

Cf. 1 Th 2:7.

up her little ones? Indeed, if we were to say, "Perhaps the Lord is angry with us", it would be senseless. Now then, blessed is the one who has been given to us! May he be with us a long time! Actually he too, Apa Horsiesios, is a close associate of those who have died. We often used to hear our father speak favorably of him. Also, Apa Petronios said before he died, "It is not I who am appointing you to this task but God and our father." And we know very well that no lie came forth from his mouth.'

Apa Horsiesios courageously took charge of the holy *Koinonia*. All the brothers obeyed him very humbly and submissively. Some time later he sat and spoke to the brothers, 'The Lord knows that I have not been convinced for a single day that I am the right one for this task. It is you who are worthy of this rank because you are senior to me. Actually the one who is really worthy of this task is Apa Theodore, because he is the one who truly imitated our father in every respect. Nevertheless if this is the will of God, then no one can oppose

Cf. Rm 9:19.

God's decision. I urge you out of your love for God to pray for me that the Lord may support me in every good work. Also, if God and you are will-

Cf. Rm 1:19.

ing, as the blessed Paul says, I would like to go to visit all the brothers.' The ancients among them answered, 'May the Lord support you in everything and grant you the spirit he gave our father. May he let his peace rest on you forever.' Then he got up and prayed. Each one went back to his cell much encouraged. The next morning he took two brothers with him and went to all the monasteries to visit the brothers and to strengthen them in the fear of the Lord and in the rules set up by our father.

Theodore, while in Alexandria, receives the news of Petronios' death

132. When the news reached the brothers in Alexandria that Apa Petronios had gone to his rest, they sat down and wept. At the moment they received the news in their boat, Apa Theodore was visiting in the city with two other brothers. When he returned and found them weeping, he said to them, 'Why are you weeping today?' They said to him, 'We are weeping because we are overcome with grief. It is said that Apa Petronios has died. And it is said that he has established Apa Horsiesios of Šeneset in his place.' Then Apa Theodore wept as well because of the death of Apa Petronios. After a little while, he said to the brothers, 'Brothers, let us not weep. Let us say rather, "Let the will of the Lord be done." If the Lord has taken from us a good father who nourished our souls, you see that in his abundant mercy he has remembered the sufferings of our father and his tears. He has also raised up for us another capable father filled with the power of the Holy Spirit. This man is *really the Israelite in whom*
there is no deceit. This man is really Joshua, son Jn 1:47.
of Nun, whom God gave as a lieutenant to Moses. Cf. Nb 27:18ff.
He is also one of *the three champions.* It is said 2 S 23:16,23.
also, *There were three behaving properly.* It is 1 S 10:3.
said also, *No one takes the honor on himself but*
receives it from God. And likewise, *It has passed* Heb 5:4.
by, it has come to my brother from God. Actual- 1 K 2:15.
ly, brothers, I would not praise our holy father Apa Horsiesios on my own initiative alone. Rather

it is the Lord who praises him and commands him through the mouth of our righteous father. The Lord knows that I once, in fact often, heard our righteous father. . .'.[1]

G[1] 120d.

Antony's letter to the brothers

133. . . .consoling the brothers about him by saying,[1] 'Devoted brothers, I want to tell you this. When I heard that the holy Apa Petronios, whom our father Pachomius had appointed over the *Koinonia* to succeed him, had died, I was very saddened indeed about him and apprehensive that the holy brothers might become orphans. While I was still overcome with sorrow, a soft voice reached my ears, "The Lord has raised up over the holy *Koinonia* another capable father, Apa Horsiesios." Thanks to the spirit of God which is in him, he will be able to care for your souls and bodies. For, because of your devotion, this saying of the Lord has been fulfilled: *I will*
Jn 14:18. *not leave you orphans; I will come back to you.* Now then, holy brothers, we should not call him
Jn 1:47. Horsiesios, but rather the "Israelite", that is, the one who sees God with interior as well as exterior eyes. You, brothers, are blessed because God has made you worthy of a father strengthened with the Spirit of God. Pray then to the Lord, the God of our father Pachomius, that he may confirm you in his peace and that, like all the saints, you may always submit to him. Greetings to those who are with you!'

Then he also wrote a letter to the athlete of Christ, Apa Athanasius the archbishop, asking him too to console the brothers with encouraging words because both their father and the one whom he appointed to succeed him, Apa Petronios, had died. He actually said it this way: 'Even though it is not necessary to write to you concerning the brothers who are with you, the sons of Pachomius of the holy *Koinonia*, since God has given rest to both their father and the one he appointed to succeed him, having received them into his glorious dwelling, nevertheless we were very worried that the *Koinonia* might be dispersed or that the holy brothers might become orphans. But then, thanks to the raising of your holy hands, it was not long before we also heard that the blessed Apa Petronios, the successor of the blessed and holy Apa Pachomius, had installed another in his place, Apa Horsiesios. We believe that he will become a great light for the *Koinonia* and that many will receive comfort, strength, and edification when he speaks words prompted by the grace God will bestow on him. We are convinced therefore that this man should be called the "Israelite". We urge Your High-priesthood now to encourage those with you, to instill loyalty to him in them, and to take care of their every need. Pray for us, O unquenchable light, source of intelligence, boast of the saints! Greetings!' Jn 1:47.

G[1] 136,120e.

Praises of Antony, Athanasius and the *Koinonia*

134. When the letter Apa Antony wrote to encourage them reached Apa Theodore and Apa Zacchaeus and the other brothers with them in Alexandria, they were very much cheered, and all the more so because he had written to the archbishop, the father of the faith about them, commending them to him as sons of the Israelite so he would treat them with great kindness. And the brothers said to Apa Theodore, 'We are certainly fortunate to be worthy of having these great luminaries take an interest in us. They are looking after our souls because of their great de-

votion to our father.' Apa Theodore answered them, 'It is the labors of our father, his tears, and those of the holy Apa Petronios which intercede for us everywhere. Moreover, our father Horsiesios will also become a source of life for our souls in every good work. I tell you this, my brothers, I heard our father say one day (and the ancients from that period also heard him say it): "In Egypt now in our generation, I see three principal things flourishing with the favor of God and man. The first is the blessed athlete, the holy Apa Athanasius, the archbishop of Alexandria who struggles for the faith even to the point of death. The second is our holy father Antony, who is the perfect model of the anchoritic life. The third is this *Koinonia*, which is the pattern for everyone who wants to gather souls together according to God in order to help them achieve perfection."'

G[1] 125.

Theodore's submissiveness toward Horsiesios

135. When the brothers heard these things from Apa Theodore, they admired his faith in God and his deep humility. He was like a simple sheep, having rooted out of himself every evil. For he was advanced not only in his visible practices but also in the fruits of the Holy Spirit, which are humility and submissiveness. Indeed, from the time when they heard that our father Apa Horsiesios had taken over as father of the *Koinonia*, whenever he was asked to explain to them a saying in Scripture, he would answer them humbly, 'We must be patient, for we will not discover the explanation of the passage until we reach the south and our father Apa Horsiesios explains it to us'. Those who asked him would be surprised at his deep humility in answering them this way because formerly when he used to teach them

Cf. Ga 5:22.

from the Holy Scriptures, no saying in Scripture had been too obscure for him. Actually he often acted this way, putting himself in the background without gaining confidence so that the brothers' hearts would be attached not to him but to our father Apa Horsiesios of whom he said, 'This man is capable in word and deed'. Cf. Lk 24:19; Ac 7:22.

Theodore's return to Phbow

136. After a few days, they finished their slight business in the city of Alexandria. They received from the archbishop a letter to Apa Horsiesios and took leave of him, saying, 'Pray for us, athlete of our Lord Jesus Christ'. Then they departed from him in peace. When they came to Apa Antony's place, they tried to visit him but were informed that he had gone to the interior mountain.[1] Then they sailed on south.

Whenever one of the brothers asked Apa Theodore for the explanation of a saying or brought him a problem, he would try to calm them by saying, 'Let us practise patience until we reach the south and tell our father of our problem. The Lord will give us rest through him.'

When they arrived south at Phbow, Apa Theodore, Apa Horsiesios, and all the brothers embraced one another with a holy kiss. Apa Theodore gave him the writings of the holy archbishop at once and when he read them to the brothers they were much comforted by the words of life written in them. Then he also gave him the letter which Apa Antony had written to them in Alexandria. When he also read that to the brothers, they blessed God, saying, 'Blessed are you in all your deeds for because of the prayers of our righteous father, you have given us such confidence in the presence of your holy servants.' Cf. Ps 145(144): 13,17.

G¹ 121a.

Horsiesios sends Theodore to Phnoum

137. When Apa Theodore saw how the brothers were having recourse to him more and more, he got very upset about it. He wanted to withdraw for a while to [another] monastery until Apa Horsiesios was securely and peacefully in charge. He prayed constantly and tearfully to the Lord about this matter both night and day. While he was still upset and saddened by this problem, Apa Macarios, the leader of the Phnoum, came north to visit Apa Horsiesios. Apa Theodore went to him and spoke to him privately, telling him the whole problem. He said, 'I want you to ask Apa Horsiesios to send me south with you to spend a few days with you, for you have seen everything that is happening in this holy place'. Apa Macarios obeyed him as he had asked him. He went to our father Horsiesios and made the request, saying, 'I would like you to send Theodore south with me so that we can make our little [supply of] bread, since he knows all about baking, and also so that the brothers can receive some encouragement from him.' When [Horsiesios] ascertained that this was Apa Theodore's wish, he sent him with [Macarios].[1]

G¹ 121b.

Theodore humbly listens to recommendations from a young brother

138. While they were still in the boat before they had reached the monastery, a brother who had not met him before that day came up to him. He thought that he had recently joined the brothers, having already been a skilled baker. And so he said to him, 'How many years has it been since you joined the brothers?' Apa Theodore answered him, 'I've been around for a little while.' Then he said to him, 'Was your occupation baking when you were in the world?' He answered him, 'Yes'. He went on, speaking to him

a third time, 'If you go to the bakery to make bread and you see one of the brothers joking or playing around, do not be scandalized because it is inevitable that you will find all sorts of people in such a group'. He answered him, 'It is good you warned me'. A while later they disembarked at the monastery. All the brothers came out and embraced him joyfully. When the brother who had warned him in the boat realized that he was Apa Theodore, he went aside and hid himself out of shame. And [Theodore] went along, doing recitations with the brothers until they reached the monastery. He stayed with them, and all the brothers were edified by his profound humility toward each of them.[1]

c. AD 347.

G[1] 127,128,129a.

Revolt of Apollonios of Thmoušons; Horsiesios' resignation and Theodore's appointment

139. When our father Apa Horsiesios saw that certain monasteries had begun to separate from the *Koinonia*, that they were continually causing him sorrow, and that they disobeyed the guidance he gave in accordance with the strength given him by God, he became very grieved indeed. He was afraid that the result would be the dispersion of the souls the Lord had gathered together by means of his servant.

There was a certain Apollonios, leader of Thmoušons, who had provoked numerous disturbances with the result that all the other monasteries were following his words. They were saying, 'We will have nothing to do with Horsiesios nor will we have anything to do with the rules which he lays down'.[1] When [Horsiesios] became aware of the great tribulation in the monasteries, he was very worried that he himself might be the cause of the dissolution of the *Koinonia*. One day, as he remained afflicted over this, he stood praying in

c. AD 350.

the evening. He begged God repeatedly to instruct him how to act so that he would not be in jeopardy in the Lord's eyes because of this. Then he had a vision: He saw two beds in front of him, one of them was old and patched,[2] the other new and quite strong. As he continued to gaze at the vision, he saw a man like our father Pachomius who spoke to him in confidence, 'Do not be afraid, Horsiesios. Just let the old bed rest upon the new and you will be unburdened.' Suddenly there leapt into his mind the thought that in this ecstasy he was the old bed and the new was Theodore.

When morning came, he assembled all the ancients in the monastery with the sole exception of Theodore and held a great council. He said to them, 'Look, you are aware of the affliction and trouble which the brothers have caused with the result that they are dispersing the community which God gathered together by means of our righteous father. Now then, choose for yourselves a man with the power to guide you according to God. As for me, my weakness is apparent to all of you.' But the brothers raised their voices and wept. He said to them, 'Do not weep, brothers, for you need not think that I am being constrained. Not at all. On the contrary, I am doing this for my relief as well as for your salvation.' The brothers answered, 'We do not know anyone but Your Holiness. You act now as it pleases you.' He answered them then, 'If you consent to what I decide, the one revealed to me by God as having the ability to shepherd you in all affairs, before God and men, is Theodore. Indeed, you know that he was formerly a father to us after our father Pachomius.' When he had said these things he got up and went to the monastery of Šeneset where he kept to himself.

140. Apa Horsiesios had not called Theodore to the council saying, 'It should not happen that, hearing us pronounce his name, he refuse because of his deep humility.' When Apa Horsiesios had named him and had left, the brothers went to the place where he was, took hold of him, and all embraced him very gladly and joyfully. They all said, 'Our father Pachomius is indeed living again for us'. When he heard these things he wept, for he would not agree to such an appointment. For he remembered the bondage he had endured when he had listened to other brothers who had once spoken to him about becoming superior.[1] He had begged the Lord to take such thoughts away from him altogether so that the seven years' time he had spent [since then] might not be wasted.[2] Thoughts of this sort no longer entered his heart at all. And so he spent three days neither eating nor drinking but constantly weeping. He said to the brothers, 'I will not consent to this until I first meet with the man who named me previously.' In four days they arrived at the monastery. . .[3].

G[1] 129b.

Theodore's reaction to his appointment

141. . . . [Theodore] sat and spoke sorrowfully to the brothers. He said, 'You are aware that our father Horsiesios has given himself for us all. He has neglected his own exercises for the sake of our formation so that our communities,[1] which the Lord assembled through the tears and labors of our father, might not be dissolved. Now then, brothers, let us all maintain a single community and proper discipline. Let us correct the negligence and contempt into which we have fallen.

G[1] 131a.

First instruction of Theodore as father of the *Koinonia*

For, once the Lord visited our father, it was not long until we had nullified his rules. Indeed, because of this the devil has troubled the souls of many of us. For it is written thus in Ecclesiastes: *Him that overturns a wall, the serpent shall bite.*[2]
Qo 10:8. We are not indeed ignorant of all the labors and pains which our father endured, whether
Cf. 2 Co 11:27. through hunger, thirst, or many vigils, that he
Col 1:22. might present us pure to the Lord.[3] But we, following our own will, have given ourselves over to the devil to let him swallow us up, with the result that we lose the benefit of the labors our father suffered for us.'

While he was saying these things, the brothers wept loudly. Their weeping got so loud that those passing by on the road outside the community heard the sounds of the weeping. Whenever the sound of their weeping died down, then he himself wept loudly. When finally he paused from weeping with them, he suddenly wiped away his tears in order to restrain his weeping. Then he struck them with the goat-skin he wore, saying, 'Control yourselves and pay attention to my words'. Then he began to address them again, saying, 'As long as you have enough feeling left to weep, it is a sign that your spirit of repentance has not yet vanished. For when someone tries to cut a dead man, he does not feel anything because he is dead. If his breath is still in him and you only move him, he feels it at once. So if the Lord wills it, it is likewise possible to make you live again.'

When they heard these words, they cried out and wept still more loudly because of the contrition stirred up in their hearts by the Spirit of the Lord through his words. He continued, 'Will the brothers of the holy *Koinonia* of Tabennesi again be sons of that righteous man, our father Pachomius? Or will there be anyone who asks his neighbor again, "What does this saying mean?" Or, indeed, shall we again see one another, whether working or in a wagon or on the road, reciting the word of the Lord as our righteous father instructed us? Now then, brothers, let us strive against ourselves and walk in the fear of the Lord. Let us not violate a single commandment from the rules laid down for us. Let none of us act according to his own will but, on the contrary, let us act in accordance with what pleases the Lord who has called us to that great purity.' When our father Theodore observed their humility as they went on weeping over the contempt and negligence into which they had fallen,[4] he stopped speaking. They got up and prayed all together. Each went off to his own cell praying constantly to God.

Cf. Jn 16:17.

G[1] 131b.

Theodore's discourse to the leaders of the monasteries

142. When the leaders of the monasteries heard that Apa Theodore had been installed in place of Apa Horsiesios,[1] they arose and went quite cheerfully to visit him. They were thinking to themselves that, when they met him, his heart would be relieved because they had come to visit him. But as soon as he saw them, he became very angry and they almost had to force him to embrace them. When they saw the expression on his face, they were seized by great fear. Then he sat down and spoke sorrowfully to them, saying, 'Is God going to put up with us? Is he not going to bring down his anger upon us because you have risen up against our blessed and holy father, Apa Horsiesios? You have removed from his position

the truly good man of whom we are not worthy, whom God and our father installed in his holy place, the one who took the place of our other fathers who have died. Is any man going to contend successfully with the decree of the Lord,* in whose presence every breath is like nothing?† I am astounded that your mouth stretched open to say, *We do not want this man to rule over us.*‡ We should be aware that if we speak this way, he on his part will answer us,[2] *My people, what have I done to you or how have I offended you? Answer me!*[3] Has our righteous father not seen us from his place among the saints and been astounded? Has he not sat down sorrowfully and said in distress, *Was it not good seed that you sowed in your field? Where does the darnel come from?*[4]

*Cf. Gn 50:19; Est 4:17b(13:9).
†Cf. Is 40:17; Dn 4:32.
‡Lk 19:14.
Mi 6:3.
Mt 13:27.

'Now then, brothers, if we have sinned, let us repent. You see, I am going to make a covenant with you today before the Lord concerning the granting of forgiveness for the contempt into which some of you have fallen. For you have raised your hands to tear apart the holy place which the Lord bestowed on our holy father Pachomius because of the prayers and tears which he had offered Him on our behalf. You remember how, while he was with us, the Lord revealed to him all those things which have come about[5] among us today, before they had yet come about. When the Lord opened his eyes in a vision, he saw the greater part of the brothers—some in the mouths of crocodiles, others in a fire, and some in the mouths of wild beasts. Others, about to be drowned in the middle of the river, were crying out seeking help. At once he stood praying for the salvation of those he saw endangered.

'Now then, I am making this agreement with

you, that from this day forward everyone who keeps such guard over his soul as not to sin against the Lord until the day of his visitation will have forgiveness for all the wicked deeds into which he has fallen until now. He will be like one newly born into the world, to whom neither sin nor righteousness are ascribed, but he will be in a new state of life from this day on. But let us strive to *produce fruit worthy of repentance*, in accord Mt 3:8.
with the word spoken in Isaiah, *If you make an offering for your sins, your souls will see the descendants of a long life.*[6] Is 53:10.

'Indeed, if we[7] conduct ourselves well, with humility of heart and effort, after the contempt into which we have fallen, our souls shall become worthy to see the holy ones who are in the long life, that is, in the age without end. If by your free choice you prepare yourselves to act in accord with the covenant I am making with you today, not only will the merciful and compassionate Lord, who bears our sins and our infirmities at all Cf. Is 53:4.
times, rejoice over our conversion and help us, but even the angels who are said in Scripture to be *flames of fire* who are unable to endure evil Ps 104(103):4; Heb 1:7.
will turn toward us in compassion. They will watch over us, as it is written, *The angel of the Lord visits those who fear him and he preserves them*. By saying of them that they watch over Ps 34(33):7.
those who fear the Lord, it is made clear that they are unable to endure those men whom they observe to be knowingly contemptuous. But he who created the universe as well as the angels, and to whom all power belongs, is better able to bear Ps 62(61):13.
our folly and our weakness, for he is well-disposed toward our nature. He endures them in order to

make us repent so that we will not become altogether worthless. Therefore he also invites his disciples to be compassionate and sons of God, saying, *Be compassionate, for your father in*
Lk 6:36. *heaven is compassionate.*[8] And also, Be...'[9]
Mt 5:48 (?).

'...he will derive no benefit, for not everyone is able to tolerate these words, but only the perfect men in whom the Spirit of God resides. For it is written, *You give thanks very well but the other is*
1 Co 14:17. *not edified*. In order then that we may be certain that it is right for the repentant man to confess his sins to such worthy persons as those of whom we are speaking, he says this, *Reveal your sins to one*
Jm 5:16. *another*, and also, *The prayer of the just man is very powerful and effective. In fact, Elijah was a man like us and in a prayer he prayed for the heavens not to rain and it did not rain upon the earth for three years and six months. Afterwards he prayed again and heaven gave its rain and the*
Jm 5:16-18. *earth put forth its fruit*.

'I am saying these things to you, brothers, so that, if it pleases the Lord, ⟨he⟩ may heal the wounds of ⟨those⟩ of you who have been wounded by the devil ⟨who reveals⟩[10] their evildoing. For it is written, *Whoever conceals his evildoing,*
Pr 28:13. *will not be upright*. Now then, my brothers, you who are leaders of the holy places of God which he gave to our righteous father, I hear perverted words issuing from your mouths. Some in fact are saying, "This monastery is mine", others, "This object is mine". Now things of this sort ought not to take place here. But if you really are prepared with all your heart to act in a spirit of renunciation like that of our righteous father, then let

each one of you confess to me, "I am not a leader of a community but we are prepared to submit to anything you impose on us."'

When they heard these things, they answered gratefully, saying, 'We are prepared to act as you direct us.[11] Only act quickly to reestablish our rules, which our righteous father Pachomius laid down for us, and the holy laws which he gave us for us to walk in. Indeed we heard him bless you one day with the blessings which Jacob spoke to his son Joseph as he was about to die and all his sons were gathered about him. For just as Joseph received great afflictions and many sufferings in the beginning—but in the end God gave him great glory and much honor and sovereign power so that in the time of the famine he fed his brothers together with his whole family and they became submissive and grateful to him in everything thoughout his life—so also it was with you in the beginning. You were in abasement and of less account than anyone because of your deep humility and the way in which you obeyed everyone.[12] And now in contrast the Lord has exalted you so that you might nourish all of us with the traditions which our righteous father Pachomius gave us to walk in and the commandments of our Lord Jesus which we have heard in the holy Scriptures.'

G[1] 131c.

Theodore makes a visitation of all the monasteries

143. After they had made this fine profession before him, 'We are prepared to submit to the discipline of the holy *Koinonia* of our righteous father', he left the eight leaders [of monasteries] in Phbow weaving mats like all the brothers. He himself went with two other brothers to visit all the monasteries, community by community. He fortified them with the word of God and the laws

of our righteous father Pachomius and the rules which he had established[1] for them to follow in order to save their souls. Then he returned again quickly to Phbow.

When the leaders of monasteries whom he had left in Phbow heard that our father Theodore was about to return to them, they got up and with all the brothers went to meet him joyfully, because of the abundance of God's grace in him. They used to do the same for our father Pachomius when he arrived from the monasteries he had visited. When he had embraced them, they walked together reciting [Scripture] until they entered the community. He was walking very humbly and with face downcast because he did not want to receive from men the empty glory of this world. He always sought only to do the will of God and to be humble toward all the brothers.

Theodore gives new assignments to all the superiors of the monasteries

144. Then he prayed again to the Lord about the leaders of the communities, asking him to inform him what he should do with them. The Lord listened to his request and made a revelation to him. An ecstasy and a vision came upon him. He saw the likeness of our father Pachomius clothed in a garment white as snow and two angels of the Lord shining brightly[1] were with him. When he saw them, he was afraid to approach him. But the angels made a sign to him to approach him. Then he drew near them, trembling violently. One of the angels took hold of the robe which clothed our father Pachomius and showed it off. When he had done this, he made a sign as if to say to him, 'You see what kind of garment he is wearing!' indicating by this that he is in glory like one of the saints, as it was said of Abraham that

Cf. Mt 28:3.

he was a king by God's act. For the garment which he wore at that moment in the vision was like royal purple, flashing as lightning. After he had shown him such glory, he told him how to assign the great ones[2] of the communities, naming by name each one and the community to which he was to be assigned. He was not to leave any of them in their former places but to place them in new ones so they might live in a spirit of renunciation. Cf. Gn 14:19.

After the vision, he assembled the leaders and the ancients who were at Phbow and held a council. He assigned them as the Lord had indicated to him. After he had assigned them, he testified, 'It is not I alone who have made these assignments but I have acted as the Lord and our father directed me.'

He used to do this twice a year for their own good and their salvation, changing many from one job to another and from one community to another. Likewise the brothers used to assemble with one another during the days of the Passover, as I have said previously, and also during the days at the end of the year, called the days of remission, during which they would read the records of their manual labor.[3]

Exhortation to renunciation

145. On one occasion they had assembled and he had made assignments again in this manner. Some of them had built new houses and *synaxes* to meet the brothers' needs. After he had made the assignments, he said to them, 'You see, I have assigned you—as you believe, by God's will—because this is for the salvation of our souls and of the brothers who are with us. If then we have named someone from a difficult community to

an easy one and he rejoices within himself on hearing it, I assure you that the Spirit of God is not in such a man. Or on the other hand, if someone in an easy community whom we have assigned to a difficult one is saddened over this, I tell you this man has neither the Spirit of the Lord nor humility in him.[1] For the man who truly loves God with his whole heart does not rejoice over anything except the idea that he is fulfilling a commandment of God or unless he sees his neighbor making progress in the law, as it is written, *If one member receives honor, all the members re-*
1 Co 12:26. *joice with him*. And sadness has no power over
such a person unless his heart reproaches him because he has neglected God or unless he sees someone behaving contemptuously, as it is writ-
2 Co 11:29. ten, *Who is scandalized and I am not indignant?*
Likewise you, O man of renunciation, who have no desire other than the Lord, if you are assigned to a monastery in difficult circumstances, are you not obliged to control yourself and say within yourself, "I give you thanks, my Lord, because I have in fact found a place that will make me stretch out my hands to you." Or again you may say, "Why am I not grateful and joyful since I have fulfilled a commandment by being submissive?" Or even if the tempter has cast into your heart a feeling of vain sadness, remember the blessed Job who though a king[2] had become perfect through evangelical renunciation before the coming of our Saviour. When he heard about the plundering of all his goods and the death of his sons and daughters, not only did he not falter over this, but even the little remaining to him, his garments, and the hair on his head,

he joyfully renounced, blessing the Lord who was his hope. He worshipped, saying, *I came forth from my mother naked; I will also return naked. It is the Lord who has given these things. It is the Lord who has taken them away. As it pleases the Lord, so let it happen. May the name of the Lord be blessed*! If the righteous man had not been practising renunciation daily in the decision of his heart, he would have been grieved and would have sinned against the Lord at the plundering of his goods. How would we know this if it were not for what he said while he was being tried? While he was still afflicted with sores, he informed everyone that he had not received these sufferings on account of sins which he had committed or because he had enjoyed his riches. Rather it was a test which had come to him from the Lord. He said, *If I have put my trust in jewels or if I have rejoiced when great wealth came to me*, because he wanted those who believe in the Lord to know that the wealth of the saints is not given them for the comforts of the flesh and for pleasure but only so that they may nourish the poor and the needy. The rich man is like an administrator whom a commander has installed over his property to feed his servants, as in the Gospel parable. For the righteous man said speaking like this, *I was an eye for the blind, a foot for the lame; I was a father to the weak*, etc., etc.

Jb 1:21.

Jb 31:24-25.

Mt 20:8.

Jb 29:15-16.

'The Apostle also stressed for us the renunciation of the lawgiver Moses, when *he refused to be called Pharaoh's son, having chosen to suffer with God's people rather than accept for a time the pleasure of sin.*[3] We know also that the patriarch Abraham was a wealthy may with

Heb 11:24-25.

gold, silver, and numerous slaves. Why then have we not been told about all the donations he made to the poor? Surely, this is so that the saying of the Apostle might be fulfilled, *Our elegant members*
1 Co 12:24. *need no honor*. Actually when it is written of them that they pleased the Lord, it is made clear that in their conduct they practised every good work and every charity. Indeed, we find it asserted of the saints that many of them[4] were rich but, because of renunciation of heart, they confessed with their mouth, "We are poor and we are wretched", just as David, although he was a king, said, *I am a poor man and wretched; the Lord is*
Ps 40(39):17. *my concern*.

'Paul the apostle also told us with regard to the patriarchs, *They welcomed* [them]; confessing
Heb 11:13. *we are strangers and nomads on earth*. So much then have we explained to you about these men. But in order that none of you may be scandalized in reading about the banquet of Solomon, we should reflect that it must be understood as a mystery, because Solomon prefigures our Saviour who came forth from his seed according to the flesh. It is he who has sent his servants to everyone as it is stated in a Gospel parable: *My young calves and the fattened cattle have been slaughtered and everything is ready. Come to the*
Mt 22:4. *wedding*. In fact, he is truly the wisdom of God, as it is written, *Wisdom has built herself a house. She has erected seven columns. She has slaughtered her sacrifices. She has mixed her wine in a bowl. She has laid her table and despatched her*
Pr 9:1-3. *servants* to invite everyone, whether good or evil. Now then, my brothers, you see we have spoken

about the poverty and renunciation of the saints. Let us also imitate their lives in order to become their sons.'

146. When Apa Theodore had said all these things, he got up and prayed. He let the leaders go to the monasteries to which he had assigned them. They left at once, saying to him gratefully, 'Pray for us, our father'. After Apa Theodore had dismissed them and they had gone, he arose and went to the monastery of Šeneset to visit our father Apa Horsiesios. He encouraged him by saying, 'Be confident, for we two are a single man as regards every good work. Actually it is you who appointed me, and we are sons of a single man.' For his part, when our father Apa Horsiesios saw his humility, he was relieved of his anxieties and he no longer worried about having laid aside his responsibility, but he would say to himself, 'Our father Pachomius did not die completely.' After Apa Theodore had visited him and had inquired about all the affairs of the monasteries, he got up and by order of Apa Horsiesios returned to Phbow.

Theodore visits Horsiesios in Šeneset

147. When the bonds of unity in the *Koinonia* had been reestablished, Apa Theodore sat and spoke to all the brothers together. He said, 'I am going to tell you about something the Lord is going to do in your midst quite soon so that you may all know, especially those among you who are doubtful, that we have been assembled together not by man's design but by God's. Now then, my brothers, the thing I am going to tell you about is this: There is among you a brother whom God is going to visit soon. He is well-acquainted with the

Akulas' death

whole situation which we have experienced so that when his visitation comes, he will tell our father and those with him in the other age about the unity and the conversion in which we live by the Lord's grace. For the boast of men with God and their joy is this: that they cause their seed to grow and prosper on the earth, as the master, Paul, said to the servants of the Lord, *What is our hope or our joy or the crown of which we boast? Will it not be you, above all before our Lord Jesus*
1 Th 2:19. *Christ when he comes.*'

Five days later there occurred just what he had predicted. An ancient brother, ascetic and faithful, by the name of Akulas fell ill. He was the accountant who kept the books for the steward who was over all the communities of the *Koinonia*.[1] While he was still suffering from the illness, the news was brought to our father Thedore that another ancient brother, also a skilled scribe, had become ill in another community and was in danger of death. This man had been sent as a service to the brothers of the monastery in which he had become ill. When Apa Theodore heard that he was sick, he said to the brothers, 'I am really very saddened because of the two brothers who are ill. Of course, if the Lord visits them, they will have eternal rest. On the other hand, we need them for the service of this multitude of brothers assembled in the *Koinonia*.[2] But we believe that the Lord will not visit both.' It happened as he predicted. After a few days the Lord visited Akulas, and the brothers as well as our father Theodore were deeply saddened at his loss. While he was still grieving over Akulas, our father Theodore received the news that the other sick brother had recovered. And when he went south, he installed him in place of Akulas. The brothers, on their part, were surprised that what he had predicted had been fulfilled so quickly.

Story of a brother who refused to be corrected by Theodore

148. One day our father Theodore approached a brother who had fallen into sin in an effort to heal his soul secretly. In fact, no one knew of the things into which he had fallen. When he began to speak to him about his faults (since they had been revealed to him secretly) this man refused to admit it: 'I have done none of the things you say.' But that brother knew also that nothing was hidden from him just as it had not been from our father Pachomius.[1] When he saw that he would not confess his fault, he left him, saying, 'You are responsible'.

A few days later Apa Theodore called him and sent him with another brother to do a job in one of the monasteries. When they finished their work, they returned south. While they were on the road, this man got thirsty and went down to the river to drink water. Suddenly a crocodile lunged at him, but by the help of God he was saved. Then, when he arrived at Phbow, a scorpion bit him in the evening of that same day and he was in danger of death. Suddenly he burst into tears and sent for our father Theodore, begging him to come before he died. But he did not want to go. He said to the person who had been sent to him, 'On the day it was possible to help him, he refused and did not want to accept God's help. Now then, why should I go to him after the Spirit of God has left him? Furthermore, the confession which he wants to make now will be of no benefit to him at all because it is too late.' When this brother went and told him that [Theodore] would not come now, he kept on pleading with the brothers, 'Go and beg him and bring him to me before I die'. So they went and kept pleading with him until he got up and followed them. When that brother saw him, he said to the brothers, 'Please leave because I want to say something to our father'. When they had withdrawn, he said to our father Theodore, 'My father, forgive me for I have sinned because I did not confess the truth that day when you spoke to me about my salvation but refused to admit it to you. Pray for me now, my lord father, that I may receive mercy, for I am about to fall into the hands of God. I know that everything is possible for you.' Our father Theodore answered him, 'The Lord has power not only to forgive you but to forgive the entire world.' Then the brothers wept. Two days later he died.

After he had died, the brothers asked our father Theodore, 'What sort of person was this brother who died?' He answered them, 'I tried to speak with him so that he could receive the grace of repentance from the Lord. But he refused and was stubborn saying "I have not done the things". Now, I tell you, he will receive great blows.[2] And not only he but a great many of you will suffer severely when the Lord visits you.'

Theodore calls the brothers to repentance

149. In the midst of them all he had mentioned the names of some, saying to each of them, 'If you do not repent and do not do penance, you are also going to undergo sufferings and punishment'. And when he saw that many of them whom he had named did not repent of their negligence, he expelled them from the midst of the

holy brothers. After he had expelled them, he sat and spoke to the brothers, saying, 'You should not imagine that I have expelled our fellow members from our midst without adequate reason. Actually I tried to seek the salvation of their souls. But they did not want to obey the laws of God, who saves everyone. In fact, even while they heard me warning them, "You will receive great blows", they were sneering at my words and actually saying, "Such things don't happen". In point of fact, the seniors among you heard our father, when he was in the body, say on the occasion of the death of a certain brother whose actions had been less than honorable, "He is going to receive great blows from the Lord". Actually he even ordered the brothers not to inscribe his name among the deceased brothers. And when a great ancient brother answered him, "As far as blows are concerned, it is a matter of no consequence", did our father not answer him at once, "How lacking in discernment you are! Perhaps you even think that the blows of God are like the blows of man." Often, in fact it is a matter of those severe blows of which we are told in the Gospel, *He will be thrown into the fire* until the end of the age, or even worse than that.' Mt 13:42.

When the brothers heard this additional testimony from our father Theodore, namely, that of our father Pachomius, they were alarmed and took steps to make greater efforts to escape these painful blows.

Theodore's humility

150. In fact, they admired how humbly he behaved toward them all, how he sought to be of service and to be self-effacing among the brothers. Often, due to the fact that neither his habit

nor his entire bearing distinghished him from the brothers, he was found to be more shabby looking than they. Similarly, on some occasions people would come from quite a distance and bring with them painfully sick patients to get him to pray for them so they might obtain relief. They would encounter him as he was going into the monastery and not recognize him because his habit appeared so modest. Likewise he did not walk in front of the brothers like someone seeking human glory. These people would approach him and say to him, 'Brother, we beg you to call our father Theodore, the man of God, for us so that he can intercede with the Lord for our sick people and they may receive relief.' And after he had gone they would learn from the brothers that he was the one with whom they had spoken. Then they would run forward, observe and take the soil on which the soles of his feet had stood and rub it on the sick. The Lord would heal them because of their faith, thus honoring his servant, as it is written, *Him that honors me, I will honor* .[1]

1 S 2:30.

G[1] 133.

Theodore's reputation throughout Egypt

151. In fact, his reputation for piety had spread throughout Egypt. Many sick and possessed persons used to be brought to him that he might heal them through his gift of the grace of the Lord, who in former times had glorified his servant Elisha....[1]

Theodore heals a sick man

152. ... like someone who had never been sick. The bystanders and his relatives were astonished and glorified God. When one of the brothers standing by saw this great miracle, he prostrated himself in reverence at his feet.

153. One day as he was going with the brothers

into the monastery, a person who had been sick for three days was brought to him. His body had been weakened by fever and chills. They begged him to pray over him so that he might be relieved. Our father Theodore said to him, 'Go quickly and dive into water in the first place you find it and you will be restored in the name of the Lord'.

Another healing

154. Another day a prefect[1] was brought to him, carried in a chair. A spell had been cast on him so that he was like a dead person. When the man of God saw what was afflicting him, he had him taken into a room. There he washed him with his hands and he revived at once. He began to speak, thanking him. Then he had him taken to his relatives who took him away praising God.

Another healing

155. On another occasion when he was sitting by himself some place reading the book of the twelve prophets, he came to the prophet Micah. An angel of the Lord appeared to him and asked him about this verse from Micah; *Like water coming down from its source*. He said to him, 'What do you think this means?' While he was still puzzling over it, trying to understand, the angel answered, 'Theodore, why do you not perceive its meaning? Is it not obvious that it is the water of the river coming down from Paradise?' As soon as the angel had said this, he ceased to see him.

The need to understand the literal meaning of Scripture

Mi 1:4.

The same day he sat and spoke to the brothers about the word of God and he told them of the vision and of the verse which the angel had explained to him. He said to them, 'As for this obvious explanation which the angel gave me of the literal sense, he spoke it as a word of caution for us. Every verse of Scripture which we examine we should try to understand first of all on the literal level before we speak of its spiritual meaning, unless it is a saying which will not edify the person who hears it on the literal level at all, such as this verse of the psalmist, and those like it, *All my bones will say to the Lord, who is going to be like you?*[1] And. . .'.[2]

Ps 35(34):10.

G[1] 139.

Another outburst of plague

180. . . . to our father Theodore, saying, 'Father, are we all going to die from this mortal illness?'[1] He said to them, 'No, but as many as thirty men from among us whom I have seen lying down.' And indeed it happened just as he had said. This is how it occurred: a severe plague developed among them and the brothers said to him, 'Are we 〈all〉[2] going to die? What will become of us? You see the water has risen and has begun to reach the path going to the mountain.' He answered them, 'I believe that if the water covers the walkway going to the mountain, the Lord will then so order things that no one will die because of the distress [it would cause to] the brothers.'[3] But some of the brothers replied, 'Does the Lord take care of us even in such an insignificant matter?' Our father Theodore answered, 'I assure you that he takes care of us at all times. If he often afflicts us, even in this he is also caring for us, because it is he who knows what is good for us. Let us then thank him always and for everything. But what I have said will take place, for we are confident of the saying in the Gospel, *Ask and you will receive.*' It happened exactly as he had said. None of the brothers died from that very day until the water dried up on the

1 Th 5:18.

Jn 16:24.

ground. There were also thirty men whom God visited. The brothers marvelled at the Spirit of God in him because none of the words he had spoken went unfulfilled.[4] Cf. Lk 21:33.

181. Our father Theodore was working one day with the brothers somewhere outside the monastery. While they were working, they were overcome with fear. When he saw how fearful they were, our father Theodore signaled to them, 'Let us pray to the Lord'. When they had prayed, he looked up to heaven. He saw a soul before whom the angels of God were singing psalms as they brought it to its resting place. When he saw this, he turned to the brothers and was still speaking the Lord's word to them when the report was brought to him from the monastery that the young Paphnouti had died.[1] He went at once to the monastery with the brothers to see the one whom the Lord had visited, to prepare him for burial, and to inter him on the mountain alongside the other brothers who had died in the monastery.

Young Paphnouti's death

182. Again one day he passed by some animals and saw among them a bull whose handsome appearance was the boast of certain ignorant carnal men over whose hearts the fear of God did not yet rule. He then remembered how the Apostle urged the servants of the Lord to be *patient with the wicked and gently teach those who raise objections, in order that the Lord might give them repentance, that they might know the truth and keep themselves from the snares of the devil and his demons.*[1] Our father Theodore was in fact patient with them. 2 Tm 2:25-26.

Not to boast about material things

He did not rebuke them in an authoritarian

way by seizing abruptly the thing by which they were being led astray into evil. But he prayed, 'My Lord Jesus, you who are working for the salvation of our souls in all things, strike this animal now so that it dies, so that these wretched men may not be discovered to be [hardened] in idolatry after having renounced the world and its evil desires.' The following day the bull suddenly fell down and died.

Not to be attached to material possessions

183. Another time one of the brothers' boats, loaded with flax for their clothes[1], sank. When [Theodore] received the report that it had sunk the brothers were very upset about it. That day he was speaking to the brothers about the Scriptures as was his custom, and he said to them, 'Some of you are upset because they have heard that the boat loaded with flax sank. Did we not for the sake of the name of our Lord Jesus Christ joyfully abandon the property of our parents which belonged to us when we were still in ignorance? Are we then going to be upset over those things which have been withdrawn from us now that we have received the knowledge of the Lord's truth? We read from the Scriptures every day and we recite them. Yet we have not paid attention to what Job said: *It is the Lord who gave them; it is also the Lord who has taken them back; as it pleased the Lord, so has it happened. Blessed be the name of the Lord.*[2] (Jb 1:21.) Since the occasion has arisen for us to prove ourselves sons of the righteous Job by blessing the Lord in the trial we are undergoing, let us not, my brothers, be so faint-hearted then as to attribute ignorance to God, who has tried us. In fact, everything the *Koinonia* has belongs not to us or to our parents

according to the flesh, who are in the world, but to our Lord Jesus, who has gathered us together with one another. If he lets us have them for our needs, it is out of the compassion and mercy he shows us in his love. If he takes them away from us, let us thank him.[3] May his will be done to us, for we know with certainty that nothing will happen to us except what is to our advantage. So, my brothers, let us not be upset over any such thing which may come our way. Let us be distressed rather about the need of our souls and let us do the will of the Lord. Then he will take care of us in everything; as it is written, *Seek rather his kingdom and his justice, and all these things he will give you in addition*, and we shall not lack anything.' Indeed, what our Saviour said in the holy Gospel was carried out by our father Theodore as he kept the commandments which our Lord Jesus Christ gave to us. As he said to his disciples, *Anyone who has my commandments and observes them is the one who loves me and anyone who loves me my father will love; I also will love him and I will show myself to him.*[4]

Mt 6:33.
Cf. 1 Th 4:12.
Jn 14:21.

184. Another day, as our father Theodore was lying asleep, an angel roused him and said to him, '*Get up quickly*[1] and go to the church[2] for the Lord is there!' He got up as the voice had instructed him, for he always used to walk with great vigilance and with unshakable trust because his thoughts were always in heaven beholding the glory of God. As the psalmist David said, *I began by seeing the Lord before me at all times,*[3] *positioned at my right hand that I might not be shaken*. When he came to the doorway of the church, he looked in and saw an apparition.

Another vision of Theodore
Cf. Ac 12:7-8.
Ps 16(15):8.

Where His feet were, there appeared to him
Cf. Ez 1:26. something like a sparkling sapphire and he was unable to look at His face because of the great light which unceasingly flashed forth from Him.

One of the angels standing by the Lord said to Theodore, 'Why do you not frequently exhort the brothers not to neglect the *synaxis* at the hour of prayer and to offer their prayers to the Lord? Do you not realize that the Lord frequently comes
Cf. Mt 18:20. among them[4] then to restore those who are
Cf. Ez 24:16. broken down and to forgive those who have sinned?'
Cf. Mt 6:14. When our father Theodore heard this, he was troubled and overcome with fear. He said, 'Forgive me, my Lord, for if I have been negligent until today, I will not be forgetful in this matter from now on.' After having seen this vision, he continued to be fearful and troubled. He thought about all Israel long ago in the desert and how such great fear came upon them and their sons and their daughters and their wives when the Lord revealed himself to them, frightening them so that they would not sin against him. They all saw him on Mount Sinai; the whole mountain was so filled with fire, flashes of lightning, clouds and darkness, and trumpets blaring forth, that, suddenly overcome with fear, they cried out to Moses, 'May you—rather than God—speak to us, and then we will not all perish and be consumed
Cf. Ex 19. by fire.'

G[1] 137,138.

Artemios searching for Athanasius

185. Our father Theodore told us another day about a vision he had had concerning an imperial general who would be coming to the monastery of Phbow with his whole troop and creating a disturbance. After he had seen these things, he informed the brothers, saying, 'It is quite certain

that an imperial general is going to come to us with his troop to cause trouble among us and difficulties. But be strong, let your heart be firm and do not be afraid, for the Lord will certainly bring his plan to nothing. I have been assured that he will not cause any harm among us.'

That year he was going with some others in a boat to visit the brothers and, as he approached those monasteries he intended to visit in the diocese of Šmoun, the duke passed them, going south on his way to carry out certain orders. Our father Theodore said to the brothers with him, 'Let us return south, for this duke has to go to the monastery of Phbow, according to the vision I had. I told you some days ago this would happen to us.' But when they heard this, they did not agree that he should return. They said, 'After all the trouble we have taken to get here, now that we are so close to the brothers to whom we wanted to go, we are going to go back again without meeting them?' Since the brothers with him did not agree, he had them bring the boat to shore.[1] He went apart and prayed with some of the brothers. While praying, he was assured by the Lord that, although the duke would enter the monastery, he would also depart peacefully. Thus he and his companions went back to the brothers. AD 360.

The name of that duke was Artemios.[2] When he was about to arrive at the monastery, he ordered his troop to take up their weapons and mount their horses as if they were going somewhere. Then during the night he came surreptitiously and had his army surround the monastery securely. He gave these orders to his troops; 'If a monk comes to enter, do not prevent him, but if he wishes to leave, do not let him go. If some disobey these orders, kill them with the sword.' When he had gone into the midst of the monastery, he sat down with an axe in his hand, surrounded by prefects[3] and archers. He said to the brothers through the interpreter, 'Bring your father to me'. They replied, 'He is not here; he has gone to visit the brothers'. Then he said to them, 'Bring me his second in command'. They called the one named Apa Psahref, an ancient. The duke said, 'I have come here because I have to carry out a commission from the emperor. I have heard that there is an enemy of the emperor hiding among you. He is a Persian.[4] Now then, turn him over to me and I will not harm you. If you do not turn him over to me, I will loot all your monasteries and scatter you.' Apa Psahref answered him, 'We are men who have renounced [the world]. We are gathered together because of the name of the Lord and there is no enemy of the emperor hidden among us. You see that all our cells lie open before you. Send and have them all searched as you please.' Then the duke ordered all the brothers' cells to be searched.

After the whole monastery had been searched, a pious and ascetic brother named Domnius, an Armenian in origin, said to the duke in Greek, 'We pray you to trust three ancients among us. Have them swear to you before the Lord that the man whom you are seeking is not among us.' The duke replied, speaking to his retinue, 'This foreign monk has spoken to the point.' So the one who was the superior among the brothers,[5] Apa Psahref, got up at once with three other brothers and they went to the church to take this oath with him. When they got inside, he said to them, 'Athanasius, the archbishop, is the enemy of the emperor. He is the one for whom we are looking because the emperor has sent for him and we have not found him. But we have heard that he is hiding among you.' The old man answered the duke, 'Athanasius the archbishop is our father after God but we testify to you before God that not only is he not hiding among us, but I have never seen his face.' After the others had testified to him likewise, he said to them, 'Pray for me before I leave you.' But they said to him, 'Our father has commanded us, because of the Arians, not to pray with anyone until the Church is set right again.'[6] The duke said to them, 'Am I also an heretical bishop? Am I not a sinner? Why will you not pray for me, the sinner?' They said to him, 'We are not permitted to break the commandment our father gave us.' When he saw that they would not agree to pray with him, he told them to leave the church so that he might pray there with his retinue. When he had finished praying in the church, he came out and visited the brothers' refectory. He was surprised when he saw what the brothers used to eat. They usually ate very frugally for they were limited to essentials in everything.

The governor of the Thebaid with all his party was waiting at the riverside for him to return, for the two of them were making the trip together. When the duke rejoined him, he said to him, 'Truly, if there are any real ascetics on the earth, I have seen some. They are the monks of the community of Pachomius where I went. For I saw that they do not wear fitted garments nor do they wear shoes on their feet even on the days where there is heavy frost outside. Truly I felt so sorry for them that I would have gladly given them as alms the clothes I was wearing. When I visited the refectory, I saw no food except greens.' When the governor heard this, he also felt very sorry for them, all the more so since he had not gone to the monastery himself to pray and to see how the holy brothers of the *Koinonia* of our father Pachomius lived.

That same day when the general left Phbow our father Theodore was sitting speaking to the brothers in the diocese of Šmoun. He informed them about the imperial general, 'Through the goodness of God, the prayers of our righteous father who is with God and the intercession of our devout father Apa Horsiesios, all the malicious thoughts which were in the duke's heart regarding us have come to nothing. He has left Phbow without harming any of the brothers. Now it is written, *What shall I give the Lord in return for*
Ps 116(115):12. *everything he has given to me*? Let us then thank our gracious God, our benefactor.' The brothers were amazed at our father Theodore's enlightened understanding and at how he had had this clear perception of events at such a great distance.[7]

When he had visited the brothers in all the monasteries, he went quickly back south to Phbow.

G[1] 140b,141,142.

Thedore's teaching

186. Later on, he spoke the word of God to the brothers as follows: 'I assure you, my brothers, that if we do not keep watch at all times with the words of the holy Scriptures, the enemy will take

from us the fear of the Lord and make us fear him. Then we will do his evil works and provoke God, our creator. But I am going to tell you a parable so that you may learn to fear God always and not to sin against God, our creator. This [parable] is like a very narrow rock rising up to the clouds with a width of only four cubits[1]. On both sides there is a bottomless drop. The rock rises very sharply from east to west. When a man has been baptized and has committed himself to monastic life, he is sealed and walks toward the east. Now let us consider the drop and how narrow the path is. If someone deviates from it even a little he is obviously finished and no trace of him is going to be found. The person who strays off this path in the middle of the rock and walks to the left will then be in danger because on the left are the desires of the flesh. The person who wanders over to the right-hand side of the rock will also be in danger. There lurks pride of heart. This is what is signified by the sharp drops on both sides. The soul which wanders on to them is struck down into the Tartarus of hell and the unquenchable fire. [On the other hand], when the person who walks carefully reaches the east, he finds the Saviour seated on a high throne. A great army of angels stands with eternal crowns which they place on the one who walked with care and arrived joyfully.

Cf. Ba 4:7.

Cf. Ws 4:19.

Cf. 1 Jn 2:16.

Cf. Rv 4:2.

'But if someone says this, "What if ever a person is deceived or is seized by one of these, that is, lust or pride? Has he then perished for good? Is there no repentance for him from that time on?" On the contrary, I say that if a man is repentant, even though he comes close to falling through

negligence, the Lord will not let him perish completely. As it is written, *My feet were on the point*
Ps 73(72):2. *of stumbling*, and so forth. Then he will make
him appreciate the graces he has been given
through the scourge of sickness, or grief or shame
for the sins he committed. And may he thank the
Lord! [For it was done] so that he might understand and keep to the middle of the narrow path
all the way to the end and not wander off even a
foot, because the path is only four cubits wide.
The one who wanders off is like Judas for whom
God did many good things and who witnessed
many miracles including the raising of those
Jn 12:6. already dead, and who *held the purse* and ate
with the Lord. Yet despite all these things, he did
not understand the graces and honors and glories
which our Lord Jesus Christ had given him,
things of which he was not worthy. Finally, when
he had wandered off the straight path, he perish-
Jn 18:2-3. ed from greed and became a traitor.

'Those who are good, even though they be-
Ps 66(65):10. come a little negligent, *the Lord refines like silver*
and cleanses of their rust and they become clean.
Therefore blessed David said, *Because of the*
abundance of your mercy, I will go to your house
and I will worship before your holy temple in fear
Ps 5:7-8. *of you; Lord, lead me to your justice.* If this man,
who was just and a prophet, spoke this way, then
how much more so should we weak sinners!

'Let us also try to understand this matter which is useful for our souls. We heard it from our righteous father among the interpretations[2] of the holy Scriptures, for through the grace of God his mind shed light upon them. He said, "If a man who wishes to cleanse himself from a serious sin is struck once, let him say to himself, 'I have gained a *solidus*'. And if he is struck a second time, let him say again, 'I have gained another'. Thus, little by little, he will come into a great fortune." Indeed, if he does not maintain[3] this thought in himself, he will not be able to master the anger and all the other sins which the devil, wishing to make us commit them, sows in our hearts to make us like himself, strangers to God.

'On the other hand, if a person behaves as if he cannot endure it when he is offended the first time,[4] how is he going to act the second time? Indeed, if hard things are said to him often, what is he going to do? But the commandments of God really are *better than gold and silver and precious stones and they are sweeter than honey and the honeycomb,*[5] as it is written. Ps 19(18):10.

'What wise and prudent man would ever say to the man who sent him pure bread, "I will accept it from you this time but if you do this again, I will put out your eyes"? Will he not love him for the things he sent him? Devout men do not act this way. Not only are they patient with *those who persecute them**[6] but they *pray for them,*†[7] as our Lord Jesus Christ commanded. This is the person who will inherit his glory and his blessing and everlasting goods in his kingdom along with his saints. O man, what have you done worthy of making you become an heir of Christ?[8] Were you persecuted as he was? Or were you struck as he was? Or were you put to death as he was? And have you been grateful for all these things? At any rate, the glory and the comfort which you receive in this world are sufficient reward to you for the few pains you have endured in this world. But how

*Mt 5:11.
†Mt 5:44.
Cf. Rm 8:17.

great is God's goodness to us! God is like a man who says to us, "Give me all the earthenware vessels in your house so I can break them and I will give you in exchange one of gold and silver and precious stones." And if we do not understand these things now, this word of Scripture will also apply to us, *A man who is held in honor does not understand; he resembles animals without in-*
Ps 49(48):12. *telligence and is like them.* But the Lord through his grace is able to help us regain our senses so that we always do his will, keep his commandments, and obtain his everlasting goods.'

G[1] 140a.

Theodore's teaching

187. When our father Theodore had said all this, one of the ancient brothers spoke up, 'Holy father, why do I get angry as soon as a harsh word is spoken to me?' Our father Theodore said to him, 'This is not surprising. If someone strikes an acacia tree with an axe, it puts forth gum almost at once.' The brothers replied, 'What does that mean?' He told them, 'The man of God may be thought of as a vine. When someone picks its fruit and presses it, it yields nothing but sweet wine. That is, if one of the faithful is seized by a thought, he produces only the sweetness of the words of God written in the Scriptures. A carnal and angry man, on the other hand, produces only bitterness and words which are unprofitable for the faithful men who submit patiently to everything which comes upon them from God. I assure you, my brothers, that I who say such things am
Ga 5:4. also afraid of *falling away from the face of God* by becoming powerless in the face of the bold onslaughts of the enemy who is fighting against me. Indeed, it is said, *all day long they have*
Ps 56(55):1. *pressed me hard in battle.* If some of the angels

have fallen, as well as some of the prophets and even some of the apostles who followed our Lord Jesus, such as Judas, and those whom Paul set apart from the good, according to Acts, then we too, my brothers, should hasten to put into practice what Solomon said, *Do not let your heart be envious of sinners but increase in the love of God and spend the whole day in fear of the Lord.*'[1]

Ac 19:9.

Pr 23:17.

How the brothers listened to Theodore's teaching

188. Most of the brothers used often to speak up this way, asking him about the meaning of things he had said and they had not yet understood. When he sat to instruct the brothers, they would ask him about many things he had said to them since they did not understand the full depth of their significance. On the other hand, if he was standing, no one except the interpreter questioned him, according to the rule laid down from the beginning. But they would stand completely attentive, taking in everything he said. They would stand house by house, according to its rank and order, with each housemaster standing in front of his men. The seconds would also stand behind each of them, checking on the brothers to make sure no one was absent. This is how they stood, in order, listening to the words of God. It was really amazing to see how fervent they were about the words of God which he was expounding. (Indeed the brothers of the *Koinonia* are like an assembly of angels. As they stand alongside one another, each one listens for what cuts him to the quick as well as for what he has fulfilled. In fact, the eyes of some well up with tears because of the reproaches they feel directed to themselves, as they resolve to make themselves holy to God. For others, whose consciences are at rest because they have

Cf. Col 1:22.

done as well as they could, the words of God are a further incitement to their exercises and to doing what pleases God.) Then, when he had finished instructing them, most would prostrate themselves while the brothers prayed. They would weep profusely, saying in their hearts, 'We are not worthy to stand and to pray with the brothers'.

Cf. 2 Co 5:9.

(*Cf. G*[1] *99*).

About Athanasius' paschal letter

AD 367.

189. Later on he addressed them again. He said, 'Let us consider what firm guidelines our blessed father Apa Athanasius, the holy archbishop of Alexandria, has produced for us this year, writing them in his paschal letter[1]. He has established the canonical books of the holy Scriptures and their number, for he too is a son of the holy apostles and takes good care of the Lord's flock, *giving them food in due season.* Indeed, when I heard of it I rejoiced and marveled at it. I rejoiced because it will profit those who hear of it and observe it. [I also] truly marveled at the word which the Lord provided as a legacy for his apostles in former times. For he remains until today on the earth, as he said to them, *I am with you all days until the end of the age and forever.*[2] He raises up in each generation, and in ours as well, perfect teachers in whom he dwells, to preserve us from all the deceits of the devil. Now then, my brothers, there is great profit and healing for our souls in the letter which he has written us this year. Thus in it he has defined for us the wellsprings of the waters of life from which it is very necessary for us to drink to be made whole through the grace of God and the favors he gives us.

Ps 145(144):15.

Mt 28:20.

'For plentiful are the waters of deceit and wells filled with bitterness which some have dug to their own destruction and to that of those who drink from them. These are the ones about whom he has written as follows: "They have fabricated for themselves what are called apocryphal books, claiming for them antiquity and giving them the names of saints". In so acting, those who have dared to write these kinds of books have in fact made themselves doubly despicable, for with their false and contemptible knowledge they have blasphemed those who are filled with the true knowledge. Moreover, the less knowledgeable and guileless among the people have been led astray by their evil ravings from the orthodox faith which is supported by all truth and which is correct in God's eyes.

'Therefore, my beloved brothers, let us at all times thank God who cares for us now and always in his exceedingly abundant mercy. But let us be vigilant and take care not to read the books composed by these defiled heretics, atheists, and truly irreverent people, so that we ourselves may not become disobedient to the Lord, who is now saying to our father Athanasius and all those like him and also to those who will succeed him, *Anyone who receives you, has received me.*[3] And Mt 10:40. we must not lead others astray so that they read them and learn to be disobedient to the commands of the holy Scriptures which are founded on the orthodox faith our holy father taught us. Now then, my brothers, I assure you before God and his Christ that a single psalm is possibly enough to save us if we understand it well, act on it, and observe it. But, above all, we have always at hand the holy Gospels of our Lord Jesus Christ and all the rest of the holy Scriptures and their

thoughts. According to the parable which he himself told about the precious stone of great value, *the merchant sells everything he owns so*
Mt 13:46. *that he can buy it* because of its value.'

Our father Theodore helped them by explaining these things to them. He ordered them to translate the letter of the archbishop, Apa Athanasius, and they wrote it in Egyptian. He placed it in the monastery as a law for them. After he had risen and prayed for the brothers, each one returned to his cell marvelling at what they had heard from our father Theodore from the holy Scriptures of God.

Theodore's *ascesis* and prayer

190. They used to say to one another, 'Really, no other son among all the ancients except our father Theodore has arisen who has so attained to the works and practices of our father Pachomius'. Thus he walked very humbly throughout his life until the day when the Lord was pleased to visit him and remove him from the vain world. And he brought him into his tent of light, full of gladness and joy, and made him inherit the everlasting goods.

Often our father Theodore used to keep vigil, praying to God from evening until morning. Having become a son of our father Pachomius, he resembled him in every way. Every time he prayed, he would make a request of God. But first, in accordance with the instruction of the Gospel, he would ask in the name of Christ, as he had bidden his disciples, *Everything for which*
Jn 16:23. *you ask the Father in my name, he will give you.* This is what our father Theodore did in his prayers and supplications. After he had invoked the name of the Lord and all the saints together

he would also pray, 'Lord, remember your servant, our father who through his labors and his holy tears gathered us together here in your holy name'. He would name him often in his prayer, for he believed he would obtain mercy through the compassion of the Lord and the tears and righteousness of our father Pachomius, since he had come to know God through him. He remembered the saying of Scripture, *God remembered Abraham and rescued Lot out of destruction.*[1] Gn 19:29.

Whenever he spoke to the brothers from the holy Scriptures of the Lord, he would recite the passages for them and also explain their spiritual significance to them. He would say, 'This is how our father used to explain them to us in the days when he was still with us in the flesh'.

(*Cf. G^1 132.*)

Theodore's care for souls

191. Often, in fact, he used to call two faithful brothers and visit all the brothers' cells, keeping watch over them to make sure that none of the brothers was being negligent concerning sleep[1]—he vied with their housemasters or their seconds—and that none was suffering afflictions or trials because of the temptations of the demons. He would counsel them privately out of love of God. He would have the brothers accompanying him stay a little distance away so that they would not hear him speaking with any of the brothers whom he was urging to stand firm in the face of evil thoughts. And he would calm those in affliction by his compassionate spirit. They would carry out promptly whatever he bade them, whether it was prayer or *ascesis* or nights of vigil. He took care of their souls night and day, as it is written of our Lord as man, *For it was through*

Heb 2:18.

the sufferings he received that he was tempted so that ‹he is able›[2] *to aid those who are being tempted.* Still others, for whom he knew consoling words would not be profitable, he would rebuke skillfully and bring to their senses by recalling the right discernment toward God in order to make them keep his commandments and do his will always and in everything.

So also, if he saw that some were obstinate, he would expel them from the midst of the brothers that others might not perish because of them and that he might not be judged by the Lord because of them. This is how he always behaved, cleansing the dirt from his people, as it is written in Isaiah the prophet, who says, *The Lord will cleanse the dirt from his people.*[3]

He was also very diligent in frequently making the rounds of all the monasteries. He would visit them, encourage them, and teach them to keep the commandments of the Lord in purity and peace. He used to speak individually with all those whom the housemasters brought to him out of concern that the enemy, wishing to destroy their souls, might secretly have sown evil thoughts in them and also in order that he might instruct them by means of the Scriptures to despise their evil and empty thoughts. Then he would depart and they would accompany him as one would an angel of God.

Theodore's admonition to the brothers

192. On another occasion when one of the boats which had got old fell into disrepair, our father Theodore rebuilt it by order of our father Apa Horsiesios. When it came time to launch it in the water, the brothers started shouting loudly, like chariot drivers in a hotly disputed race—

some shout, 'We will be ready before you'; others reply, 'No, we will'. — When our father Theodore saw the wrangling and the great commotion among them, the man of God cried out, ordering them not to quarrel over a matter in which there was no profit for their souls. But they paid no attention to him and our father Theodore, very much distressed, fell silent and cast all his care on the Lord.[1] He went a little way apart and sat down in a depressed state until they finished launching the boat into the water with great hilarity. Cf. Ps 55(54):22.

Then he sat down and spoke the word of God to them until evening time. He addressed them in their midst in the following way. 'When you were engaging in all the loud shouting, I ceased then to see anyone, especially because of the seculars who were watching us and listening to your shouting. Now then, if you continue to behave this way, you are going to weep and be afflicted and groan because of the pleasures in which you are indulging. But let no one who hears me speaking misunderstand my language and say in his stupidity, "If you die, will the world really become deserted because of you?" We all know this, that God will not desert his whole creation which he made. But the Lord knows that if you continue to behave so stupidly, you are going to weep and weep and weep again with groans. Where now is the fear of God which has vanished from the hearts of some of you? Did you not hear me when my throat was growing hoarse from crying out to you? Now, my brothers, what have we to do with a boat or a chariot or any of the things of this world which contain no profit for the soul but are

ephemeral and passing? If our souls perish from having become drunk on these vanities, how then are we different from those who played before the
Ex 32:1-6. bull at Horeb, who ate and drank and worshipped it, having abandoned the God who created them? But if you will not obey me and will not accept my teaching, then may God be responsible for you.
Jb 6:11. *As for me, what is my power?*'

When he had said these things, most of the brothers wept, understanding the pains which he took for their salvation and the safety of everyone's soul. Then he got up and prayed sorrowfully for those among them who neglected the salvation of their own souls. Each one withdrew to his cell having derived much profit from it.

Theodore's illness

193. But our father Theodore lay down ill because of the greatly increased anxiety in his soul. He was worrying himself sick over all the rules from which the brothers were deriving no benefit. They had so altered[1] because of their negligence and disregard for them that he found it impossible to restore them to their former order because of the laxity into which they had fallen. He saw that the majority of the brothers had grown cold in their desire to put into practice the commandments which the perfect man, our father Pachomius, had laid down for them to practise with all diligence. When all the leaders of the monasteries heard that our father Theodore was ill, they all came to visit him. Moreover, the days of the holy Passover were approaching. All the brothers used to assemble at Phbow for the baptism of the catechumens and to set all their affairs in order according to the rules which had been laid down. When they all came to him and saw

how altered his face was, they were very disturbed and were afraid to approach him. He, on his part, was grieving over what had occurred.

After a few days, God gave him relief and cured him of his illness. When he was well, he sat and spoke the word of God from the holy Scriptures to them. He would sit daily and encourage them from early in the morning until the time for the assembly. He would do this during the whole Passover as they blessed and thanked our Lord Jesus Christ.

Theodore tells the brothers about Pachomius' life

194. Then he began to tell them of the life of our father Pachomius from his childhood on and of all the labors he underwent from the beginning when he established the holy *Koinonia*. [He told them of] the temptations of demons and how he snatched away from them the souls which the Lord gave him and of the revelations which the Lord disclosed to him. [And he told them] everything he had heard from that saint's mouth as well as those things he had seen with his own eyes.

He spoke to them as follows: 'Listen to me, my brothers, and understand well the things I am telling you. For the man whom we are exalting is truly the father of us all after God. God established a covenant with him to save a great many souls by means of him. And us also the Lord has saved through his holy prayers. For he—I am speaking of our righteous father Pachomius—is also one of the holy men of God and one who did his will always and everywhere. I am fearful that we may forget his labors and actually be unmindful of who it was who made this multitude one spirit.[1] and one body. It was accomplished by means of

Cf. Ac 4:32; Eph 4:4.

him and of our other holy fathers who aided him in the establishment of this holy institution. Consider how the Lord blessed the house of Jonadab, the son of Rechab, through Jeremiah, saying, *The sons of Jonadab will not cease to stand before me all the days of the earth because they have kept the commandments of their father.* We also believe that the blessing of our father will remain with us and with those who come after us before God forever. Now then, let us not be negligent and forget his laws and his commandments, which he gave us while he was still with us in the body.

Jr 35:19,18.

'What indeed is the advantage which we have over other men? Does our advantage consist really in this, that we wear a special habit? Or that we wear a belt around our loins? Or that we are gathered with one another in a single *Koinonia*? Indeed there are many who are gathered together in many places also wearing our habit. For the glory of the Lord our God and his grace have filled the whole world. But actually the advantage which the Lord has given us is what our righteous father gave us. He pursued in its entirety the way of life of the prophets and the way of service in which, according to the Gospel, our Lord walked. He was without blame before all, as you yourselves bear witness. You are also not unaware how he used to teach us frequently with tears, as Paul said in the book of the Acts of those whom he was teaching. [You know] how he used to gather us together daily and speak to us about the holy commandments so that we might observe each of the commandments in the holy Scriptures of Christ, and how he used first to put them into

Cf. Ps 72(71):19; 33(32):5.

Cf. 1 Co 10:32.

Ac 20:20-21.

practice before giving them to us. It is through our contact with such a righteous man that we have learned the will of God even in such details as the manner of stretching our hands upward to the Lord and how one should pray to God. It is he who taught it to us. Is it not right for us to bless him next after the Lord who created us? Indeed, did God not say to Abraham, who had done his will, *I will bless him who blesses you and I will curse him who curses you*? Now then, my brothers, let us all say, "Blessed be God and our righteous father Pachomius who through the labors of his prayers has become for us a guide to eternal life"'. Gn 12:3.

Then all the brothers replied with a single mouth and a single voice, 'Blessed be our holy and righteous father, our father Pachomius, in everything and in all his works'. When they all, joyfully and with great confidence in him, had made this proclamation, he spoke to them again, 'Perhaps some of you may think that they are giving glory to flesh. Not at all! Or on the other hand that our hope is placed in a man. By no means! Rather we glorify and we bless the Spirit of God which is in him. And indeed, if we also bless the flesh it is truly worthy of it, for it became a temple of the Lord. Not only is it fitting to act this way, Cf. 1 Co 3:16; 2 Co 6:16.
but, we know besides, and we believe that his name is *written in the book of life*[2] with all the saints. Ph 4:3.
Now then, my brothers, I tell you that it is necessary and right for us to write of his labors from the beginning, of the perfection he achieved, of his way of life, and of all the ascetic practices he performed, so that his memory may remain on earth as also it remains forever in heaven. As the

blessed Job also said, *If only my words were writ-*
Jb 19:23-24. *ten down and left in a book for ever!* But let no
one say out of ignorance, "It is also written,
Jr 17:5. *Cursed is a man whose hope is in a man.*" For you
were told often that whoever is joined to the Lord
is not called man, but spirit, as it is written,
Anyone who is joined to the Lord is one spirit
1 Co 6:17. *with him.*[3] It is said also, *You are not in the flesh,*
Rm 8:9. *but in the spirit.*[4] Therefore, according to this
saying, the man who is joined to the Lord and
serves him has ceased to be man because of the
Rm 8:6. mind of the Holy Spirit in him. Indeed it is like
the case of a sword in its scabbard. One does not
say "sword and scabbard" as if they were separated from one another, and use two names for
them, but one calls it simply "the sword". It is
also like wine in a jug which has been mixed with
water. It is not called "wine and water" but simply "wine" by those who drink it. So it is with a
man who becomes a temple of God through the
1 Th 5:23. purification of his soul, his body and his spirit.

'Let us consider those saints mentioned in the Scriptures, how each of them exalts the one before him who guided him to the life, that he might know God. This they did by the command of the Lord according to His will. Therefore it is fitting for us also without hesitation to bless our righteous father who has led us to the knowledge of God. When God spoke to the patriarch Isaac, he blessed him, saying, *Do not go down to Egypt but stay in the land I shall tell you of. I will be with you and I will bless you and I will make your offspring increase in number like the stars of heaven. I will give this whole land to your offspring and all the nations of the earth shall be*

blessed through your offspring because Abraham your father listened to my voice and kept my commands, my ordinances and my laws. If Isaac Gn 26:2-5.
had not pleased the Lord, he would not have spoken to him this way and he would not have called him "son of Abraham" when he said, *Because of Abraham your father, I will bless you, for you have done my will.* By this he taught his *Ibid.*
servant and held up to him unlimited uprightness so that he might exalt the one who had begotten him either by the flesh or by the spirit. Likewise, the just man Lot also practised the hospitality and righteousness in which he had been instructed by Abraham while he was with him, before they separated from one another. When he was living in Sodom, he continued to practise them and always did good to everyone who came to him. Indeed it is also written of him, *God remembered Abraham and rescued Lot out of destruction.* He has become an object of admira- Gn 19:29.
tion and is blessed in many places in the holy Scriptures because he obeyed the teaching of Abraham. We also find Jacob, when blessing the sons of Joseph, likewise exalting his fathers when he said, *May God in whose eyes my fathers Abraham and Isaac were pleasing, bless these chil-* Gn 48:15.
dren! And also, *May my name and the names of my fathers Abraham and Isaac be invoked on them.* Likewise Joseph, when he was about to die, Gn 48:16.
spoke to his brothers, saying, *God will bring you up from this land to the land which he promised to my fathers Abraham, Isaac, and Jacob* and to Gn 50:24.
their offspring.

'You see then, we have recounted for you from this multitude of witnesses from the holy Scriptures how all these saints exalt and glorify their fathers before them. Is it not right for us also to exalt and honor a just man[5] and a prophet whom the Lord gave us, in order that through his holiness, we might come to know Him?'

Theodore's care for souls

195. Our father Theodore had great concern in his heart day and night for the souls which the Lord had entrusted to him. He guarded them very firmly in accordance with all the precepts and rules which our righteous father laid down for us as law in the *Koinonia* of the brothers. Those among them who were upset he would comfort. Others he would reprimand as they deserved, for the restoration of their souls in the eyes of our Lord Jesus. Still others he would transfer from one community to another or from one house to another, doing his utmost for them and seeking the salvation of their souls. But others again he would urge to *ascesis* and mortification for the sanctification of their flesh. Still others he would oblige to fast so that they might be able to conquer those fighting against them. In short, he would speak with each of them privately, discerning their thoughts and their actions by means of the Spirit of God that was in him. If he perceived that someone was negligent in his heart about his own salvation, he would pray to God for him or expel him from the community of the brothers out of fear that some others might perish because of him. [Otherwise] he would be subject to a judgement from God because he had been so negligent that some souls perished because he did not reprimand them. He also took care of all the material needs of the community—of the large number of brothers at

Cf. Mt 5:21-22.

Phbow and of the others in all the monasteries. The other sex who are gathered together for the sake of God, that is, the nuns, he also used to administer with regulations and speech by means of a righteous father whom he appointed as father to them. He would guard them in all holiness according to the rules of our righteous father Pachomius.

196. This is how our father Theodore used to attend to their strengthening by means of the word and perfect teaching of the righteous man, our father Pachomius. While they celebrated the holy Passover of the Lord, he would dispose of all their affairs according to the traditions of our father Pachomius and they would celebrate the holy Resurrection of our Lord Jesus Christ. Then he would pray over them all and dismiss them in peace after having transferred many of them from one community to another for the sake of their salvation.

Theodore's teaching during the Passover

The brothers who acted as his interpreters into Greek for those who did not understand Egyptian—because they were foreigners or Alexandrians[1]—heard him speak many times about the way of life of our father Pachomius. Since they had paid full and precise attention to what he said concerning him, they wrote these things down for [the brothers]. For after our father Theodore finished speaking to them about him and praising him and all his labors, he used to sigh, saying to the brothers, 'Pay attention to the words I am speaking to you, because a time is coming when you will not be able to find anyone able to recount them for you'.[2]

197. Our father Theodore was always in distress *G¹ 146a.*

Theodore is distressed because of the *Koinonia's* possessions

before the Lord out of fear that one of the souls entrusted to him by the Lord might perish. He taught them to abandon their evil deeds and to do what is good in the Lord's eyes. When he observed that, owing to the excuse of needing food and other bodily needs, the monasteries had acquired numerous fields, animals, and boats—in a word, numerous possessions—he was deeply distressed. He felt certain that the feet of many had slipped from the right path because of material concerns and the empty cares of this world. He longed to go to Šeneset to our father Horsiesios to consult him about this problem.[1] Suddenly he got up with a burning heart and walked at night—he and two other brothers with him—until they came to him at Šeneset. When he arrived and embraced him once again, he suddenly burst into abundant tears and Apa Horsiesios also wept. After they had wept together a long while, Apa Theodore, with tears streaming from his eyes, took the hand of Apa Horsiesios and led him aside to speak to him alone. He said to him, 'My lord and holy father, you are the one who, by the Lord's direction, placed this burden on me and you know that up until now I have done all that was in my strength. You know also that I have not done anything without your knowledge since we are a single body, a single soul, and a single spirit in every matter, according to God. Now then I ask you, my lord and father, what am I to do with this great wealth and these numerous material possessions which have increased so, for we know that there is no profit in them?' As he said this, he was pained because he desired to make the material goods decrease by far. Our father Apa

Cf. Jb 31:7.

Horsiesios said to him, 'It is the Lord who has blessed the *Koinonia* and has expanded it. He also has the power to constrict it again in accordance with his good ordinances and according to his just and right judgement.' Apa Theodore said to Apa Horsiesios, 'Well said indeed! Everything you tell me, I will do and observe as if it was the Lord who had spoken to me.' And when he had risen, he prayed over him and he departed sadly.[2] He went south to Phbow to the brothers who were in that monastery.

G[1] 146b.

He prays to God about this

198. But then he continued to be so distressed that he often cried out to the Lord, entreating him tearfully, 'I beg you, my Lord Jesus Christ, to take from me my soul, that I may no longer see the continuing dissolution of the souls which are going to perish on account of the material goods and empty cares of this world'. In fact, he often used to put on hair garments and go up to the mountain by himself. He would spend the whole night praying tearfully to the Lord and he would come down to the monastery in the morning.

Then one evening one of the senior brothers followed him at a short distance. When he reached the tomb of our father Pachomius on the mountain, Apa Theodore stood over it and, weeping profusely, he prayed to Christ, saying, 'Lord God, merciful and alone tender-hearted* judge of the living and the dead,† you O Lord who know my heart,‡ my thoughts, my conscience, and my goal, may your mercy and your goodness rest on us*[1] in the whole sorry state in which we find ourselves. For we have turned from the paths of life† and from your laws and your commandments‡ which you gave to our righteous father,

*Ps 86(85):15.
†Cf. Ac 10:42.
‡Cf. Ac 1:24.
*Ps 33(32):22.
†Cf. Pr 2:19.
‡Cf. Dn 9:5.

over whose holy body I am now standing. Indeed, we are like those at sea in the time of a storm because we pay no attention to the proper behavior which your servant, our holy father, enjoined upon us. Pay heed to my grief and do not treat us as strangers to you because of our sins, that we may not become despicable in the eyes of our father and all the righteous ones with him whom we have seen with our eyes and who, with him,
Cf. Ga 2:19. have hung from the cross in all innocence according to the Gospel of your blessed son Jesus Christ. Now then, I beg you to spare us for the sake of the tears of our righteous father with whom you established a covenant. Do not pour forth your
Cf. Ps 69(68):24; 146(145):4. anger upon us because of the evil deeds we have committed and the errors into which our negligence has led us. Otherwise we may remain hardened in our evil hearts and nullify the works our father performed night and day, with fasts, prayers and abundant tears. Finally, you gathered around him this multitude of souls from every place that they might be saved and bless your holy name at all times, for you are our
Cf. Ps 62(61):8. helper and our hope. Now then, my Lord Jesus Christ, it would be better for me if you were to visit me quickly and take my soul from me rather than let me see the devil gloating over the works of our father. Do not let me be in danger because of your creatures whose souls you have entrusted to me that I might give them back stainless into your hands.'

Our father Theodore remained standing the whole night in prayer to God with these words until the time of the morning *synaxis*. The brother who had followed him was ⟨watching⟩ [2] him. He did not know that that brother was standing a little way off listening to him utter all these words with bitter weeping and groaning. After he had gone down from the mountain, that brother secretly told all the brothers all the words which our father Theodore had spoken tearfully before the Lord.

199. Often afterwards when he was sitting speaking to the assembled brothers, he would indicate to them that his visitation would be soon. But they did not understand what he was saying. Sometimes he even said to them, 'There is among us a brother whom the Lord is going to visit this year. He is outside and inside, exalted and humbled.' Sometimes [he said] also, 'They have been brought to the wine press to be squeezed so that we may draw off their juice'. Often he used also to say only to certain ones, 'I am about to go to the feet of my Lord Jesus'. Sometimes he also used to say openly, 'I think that God will visit me in the course of this year'. It was not because he saw old age coming or his strength decreasing that he perceived that he was approaching death, but it was because he had been informed by the Lord that the time had come for him to rest and to be with his fathers who had gone before him and whose many virtues he also had practised.

G[1] 119.

Theodore speaks of his death

Cf. Mk 9:32.

Again one day he was sitting speaking to the brothers about the word of God with tears streaming down his cheeks. The brothers too were weeping. Then he said to them, 'Listen to me, my brothers! Jacob spent seventeen years feeding Joseph. Joseph also spent seventeen years feeding his father Jacob and all his brothers. I too spent eighteen years while our father fed me with

Gn 37:2.

Gn 47:28.

the commandments of God. I, in my turn, have passed eighteen years in your midst to the best of my ability by the command of God and our father Apa Horsiesios. For he is really the father of us all and we believe that if we obey him and carry out the commandments he has given us, then God is with us and will be with us forever. But if we were also to begin to speak the praise of the other mighty men who came after our father Pachomius, above all about our holy father, Apa Horsiesios, the perfect man, this speech would get very long indeed. Most of you heard our righteous father pronounce great blessings on him and praise him highly at the time he made him father of Šeneset. Then he compared him to
Ws 7:48-49. a *golden lamp shining in the house of the Lord.* And he said, "A bride of Christ has been received today." For he knew him to be a man of good will toward all and without guile like a sheep. He obeyed him and devoted himself to the affairs of the brothers wholeheartedly as if he were two men. I tell you these things often because our father loved him.'

Our father Theodore used to speak with each of the brothers, eagerly encouraging them in everything, as if he was preparing himself to go to the Lord. He was persuaded that then he would be irreproachable with regard to them all, since he had taught each of them to save his own soul. Then he arose and prayed with the brothers. Each one went back to his cell saddened because he had told them that he was going away to the Lord and would leave them orphans.

G^1 143a. 200. Somewhat later in that year, during the holy Forty Days when our Lord Jesus fasted for

our salvation, [Apa Horsiesios] heard in Šeneset that the blessed Apa Athanasius, the archbishop of Alexandria, was on his way south to the Thebaid for the purpose of strengthening all the Churches in the faith of Christ. He sent south to Phbow immediately for our father Theodore to come to meet him. At once he arose and took five other brothers with him. They boarded the little boat and went north to Šeneset. When he met our father Apa Horsiesios, he begged him to come along himself to meet the archbishop—but he did not want to—especially since they had often heard our father Pachomius praise and call him constantly, 'the father of the orthodox faith in Christ'. Apa Theodore saw that Apa Horsiesios would not be persuaded to come because of great humility. Instead he urged him to go to the archbishop, saying to him, 'If you go, it is also I who have gone, because we two are like a single man, a single soul, and a single spirit'. Apa Theodore then said to Apa Horsiesios, 'Remember us in your holy prayers until God brings us back to you safely and peacefully'. Then he departed with the brothers. Apa Horsiesios and some other brothers went to accompany him to the boat saying to him, 'Greet the archbishop and father of the faith'.

Athanasius' visit to the Thebaid

201. Apa Thedodore and the brothers went north. They found the archbishop in the northern part of the diocese of Šmoun.[1] He was mounted on a donkey and countless people were following him, including bishops, innumerable clerics with lamps and candles, and also monks from various places who were preceding him chanting psalms and canticles. Apa Theodore quickly put

G[1] 143b,144a.

Theodore comes to meet Athanasius

into shore in front of the monasteries of the diocese of Šmoun.[2] He took with him, too, all the brothers of those monasteries and, reciting all together from the words of the holy Scriptures and the Gospels of our Lord Jesus Christ, they went north on foot to meet him. When the archbishop saw them at a distance, he knew that they were the sons of Pachomius, to whom God had given the grace to assemble the holy *Koinonia*. At once, while they were still at a distance from him, he spoke of them in the following way, '*Who are these flying toward me like the clouds and like the*
Is 60:8. *doves with their lovely young ones*?' As they approached him, Apa Theodore put some ancient brothers in front of himself so that they might embrace the archbishop first, for he was trying to flee from vainglory. But the archbishop recognized him in the midst of all the brothers by means of the Spirit which was in him; it was he whom he embraced first and after him the brothers. When he had prayed over them, they sat down and he spoke to them: 'How is the *true Israelite in whom there is no deceit,* our father
Jn 1:47. [3]Apa Horsiesios, and all the other holy brothers?' Apa Theodore answered and said to him, 'By the help of God and your holy prayers, we are all well. Our holy father and all those with him greet you.' He took hold of the bridle of the archbishop's donkey to walk with it but the bishop ordered him not to do this. Apa Theodore said to the archbishop, 'Allow me, my holy father; is it not a favor for us to humble ourselves to the one who has often died for us for the sake of maintaining the faith of Christ?' So he permitted him to take it. Then the brothers, a hundred men strong, preceded him singing psalms.

The archbishop observed our father Theodore bubbling over with the Holy Spirit within him, walking very briskly and resolutely, without concern for the crowd which pressed against him or for the flames of the numerous glowing and burning lamps in front of him. And the archbishop said to the bishops walking with him, 'Are we worthy to say of ourselves, "We are the fathers of the world"? Not really! Truly our fathers are these who have humility and submission to God. Truly happy and blessed are those who bear the cross at all times,[4] whose greatness is due to their humility and who will have rest after their labors, when they receive the imperishable crown.'[5] They preceded him singing psalms until they brought him into the church of the city of Šmoun. After he had prayed for the crowd accompanying him, each one went to his own lodging. Apa Theodore and the brothers with him received the archbishop's blessing and withdrew to the monasteries located there. They rested there for a few days.

Cf. Mt 10:38; Lk 9:23; 14:27.

Cf. 1 Co 9:25.

G[1] 144b.

Athanasius visits the monasteries of Nouoi and Kahior

202. When the archbishop had spent a few days in those cities, encouraging them with the word of God, he arose and with the brothers accompanying him went up to the monasteries of Nouoi and Kahior[1] in order to see the brothers' accommodations.[2] When he entered, he saw their discretion, their mildness, their perfection, and the seclusion in which they lived. He was very much moved and praised the Lord. Preceded by [the brothers] singing psalms, he went into the church and prayed. Then they took him into their refectory and their houses and their cells and he prayed in all of them. When he saw their buildings and how they slept on the ground, he marvelled and blessed God, glorifying him for

the brothers' way of life and their practices. Then the archbishop said to our father Theodore, 'You have indeed established in the world something great and splendid, which gives rest to every soul who comes to you.' Apa Theodore said to the archbishop, 'This great gift of God has come to us through our righteous father and especially, our lord and father, through your holy prayers. Indeed the Lord knows that when we saw Your Holiness, it was as if we had seen our Lord Jesus Christ in the heavenly Jerusalem, because of our great trust in you, for you are our father.'

When [Athanasius] had spent a few days in that[3] monastery, ministering to them with the word of God, he said to Apa Theodore, 'If it is the Lord's will, we wish to spend some days here because the days of the holy Passover of our salvation are approaching. But as for you, take a letter from us to Apa Horsiesios and let him also come to us that we may receive his holy blessing. You go and take care of your monasteries as you know how to do.'

G[1] 144c.

Theodore bids the archbishop farewell

203. When evening came, our father Theodore sat and spoke the word of God to the brothers. Then he said to the brothers who were with the boat, 'Since the archbishop has informed us that he will spend some days here before he comes south to visit us, I am therefore directing you to wait for him with the boat in case he has need of it, for he is our father after God. Not only does he have power over our little boat but he also has authority over our bodies as well. Serve God and him. As for us, we are going south because the days of the holy Passover of our salvation are approaching, when Christ suffered for us that he

might save us from the devil's grip.' When morning came, he took the brothers and went into the city to the archbishop, embraced him, and received from him the letter to our father Apa Horsiesios. When he had received the archbishop's blessing, he said to him, 'Our lord and father, remember us in your holy prayers.' And the archbishop said to him, '*If I forget Jerusalem, may I forget my right hand,* which is you.' So [Theodore] departed in peace and left the boat with the brothers for [Athanasius]. Ps 137(136):5.

204. Apa Theodore himself went on foot until he arrived in the south. He did not want to go in one of the boats which the monasteries had acquired because he did not want them to produce things of this sort in the monasteries. When he reached Šeneset, he met with Apa Horsiesios and embraced him and all the brothers. Then he gave him the archbishop's letter. When [Horsiesios] received it, he kissed it before he read it to the brothers. This is what was written in that letter: 'Athanasius, the archbishop of Alexandria, is writing to greet his beloved brother Apa Horsiesios and all the brothers with him whom I love in the Lord. Greetings! Truly, when I saw your fellow-worker in the Lord, Theodore, who is filled with every divine virtue and radiates light among you, I also saw through his shining face the Lord of our father Pachomius within him, strengthening him in everything he does. And I rejoiced very much to see the sons of the Church; they made us glad by their gratifying presence. May our Lord Jesus Christ reward them in the land of his saints. May God our hope make us abound in his peace, in his love, and in perseverance forever and ever.

G[1] 145a.

Theodore brings Horsiesios back to Phbow

Amen. We pray always that we may see you.' When they finished reading this letter, they got up and prayed with the brothers and each one withdrew to his cell giving thanks to God and blessing the holy archbishop, Apa Athanasius.

Then Apa Theodore spoke with Apa Horsiesios alone. He comforted him because of the tribulation which had occurred earlier because of Apollonios, the head of Thmoušons, when the latter had sent to Alexandria to buy supplies for those who were sick. Apa Horsiesios had not consented that he should keep them in a place under his own authority because he knew that our father Pachomius did not wish it so.[1]

[Theodore], knowing that the days had drawn near for him like all his fathers, to go to the Lord, also urged him to come south to Phbow with him that the brothers might be encouraged by him. Because of his insistent urging, Apa Horsiesios consented. He arose and travelled with Apa Theodore and the brothers to the south. As they approached the monastery, our father Theodore sent on ahead one of the brothers travelling with him. 'Go quickly and have the brothers gather and come out to meet our holy father.' He went at once and had the weekly server assemble the brothers. They all came out to meet him singing psalms and they embraced him with a holy kiss. Then they also sang psalms as they walked with them in an orderly fashion, with humility, discipline, and decorum, until they entered the monastery. And in this manner they prayed in the monastery church with the brothers.

c. AD 367

Rm 16:16.

Then our father Theodore persuaded Apa

Horsiesios to sit and speak to the brothers from the word of God as [he had done] formerly. He obeyed him with great humility and sat and held long discourses from the holy Scriptures. Apa Theodore also sat listening like all the brothers, with his face cast down and weeping because of the penetrating words he heard from Apa Horsiesios. And he said with his mouth and with all his heart, 'I am the son of Apa Horsiesios and his assistant'.

The two of them were like a single man. And everyone admired them and praised them because of the sweetness of their love for one another. They *loved God with their whole soul and their whole heart*[2] as our perfect father Pachomius had commanded them. And Apa Theodore was like his second. In his great humility he did nothing without his counsel, even in the smallest matter. Often he used to be heard weeping, saying, 'The time has drawn near for me to be separated from my father Horsiesios and to go the way of all my fathers'. After he had spoken at length to them, urging them to imitate the life of our father Theodore, his steadfastness and humility according to God, our father Horsiesios got up and prayed with all the brothers. Each of them withdrew to his cell reciting the word of God and practising many virtues intensely. Cf. Mt 22:37.

G[1] *145b,147.*

Eron's death during the Passover

AD 368.

205. Four days later it was the Passover, and all the brothers assembled at Phbow to celebrate the Passover with one another in accordance with the rules of our father Pachomius. Apa Theodore entreated Apa Horsiesios to address the word of God daily to the brothers during the celebration of the Passover. But because of his humility, he

would not consent to do it continually. Sometimes our father Apa Horsiesios would give the instruction to the brothers. Other times Apa Theodore would do it too, for the two of them were like one man. This was what they did until the Closing of the Passover.

On the evening of the Closing of the holy Passover, all the brothers were gathered in church to receive in the holy mysteries the body and blood of our Lord Jesus Christ. One of the ancient brothers, Apa Eron, was lying ill in the place of the monastery where all the sick brothers lay. He was the second of Apa Theodore the City-man, the housemaster of the Greeks. The brother who ministered to the sick brothers came and informed Apa Theodore that the ancient brother was approaching his death. Apa Theodore left the church at once and went to the infirmary. He saw that the brother was about to give up his spirit and immediately he bent over him and spoke to him intensely while all the brothers listened. A short while later, when the brother gave up his spirit, they were suddenly overwhelmed by a great fear. Actually none of the brothers understood the words which Apa Theodore had spoken to him, but what we imagine he said to him is this: 'When you arrive in the presence of our righteous and perfect father Pachomius plead with him for me, saying, "Theodore your child begs his holy father to ask the Lord to permit him to follow you."' We imagine this because we observed him to be more distressed in spirit than we knew was normal for him and we were acquainted with his daily pattern of walking and speaking.

Apa Theodore sat and wept intensely a long time in great distress, as did Apa Horsiesios and the brothers of the monasteries gathered around him. And Apa Theodore said to them, 'This brother who has died today is like a sign and points to another who will die after him, one whom you do not expect to die at present.' All the brothers spent the whole night in vigil around him, reciting until the first light appeared. Very early, at dawn of the holy Sunday which is the Resurrection of our Lord Jesus Christ, they prepared his holy body for burial. Then Apa Theodore sat and, by order of the just man, Apa Horsiesios, gave directions to all of them, the housemasters as well as the seconds, in accordance with the tradition they had received from our righteous father Pachomius. Then, when he had disposed of all their business, as was fitting, they preceded Apa Eron singing psalms. All the leaders of the monasteries and all the brothers followed him. They brought him to the mountain and buried him with great honor beside all the brothers. When they had come down from the mountain and [Theodore] had prayed over them, he escorted them as each of the leaders departed to go to the brothers of his own monastery. Our father Apa Horsiesios was also going with them to depart for Šeneset, saying to the brothers, 'Remember me'. Our father Apa Theodore said to our father Apa Horsiesios, 'Do not go far because there is another brother among us, one exalted and humbled, who is approaching his death.'[1] When he had said this, each of the brothers departed for his own monastery, while he and his companions returned to his monastery.

G[1] 148.

Theodore's death

206. Three days later he fell sick and he sent some brothers to bring Apa Horsiesios to him. The brothers of the monasteries in the area around Phbow also came. When Apa Horsiesios saw that the fever of the illness was overpowering him, he became very distressed. He took all the brothers and went into the church. They prostrated themselves before the altar, weeping and begging our Lord Jesus Christ to give him the grace of healing through the prayers of our father Pachomius. Our father Apa Horsiesios cried out to the Lord, saying, 'Lord of the universe and God of our father Pachomius, if you take Theodore from us now, we shall be miserable. It would be better for me to die first, for I am old, and to leave him behind so that all the brothers might be strengthened through him.' Then all the brothers lifted up their voices, weeping very bitterly and saying, 'Lord have mercy on us. Pity us and accept our pleading. Leave us the righteous man, our father Theodore, for it would be better if you were to take most of us and leave behind for us the one who nourishes our souls with your law and your life-giving commandments.'

After they had spent many days grieving for him and pleading with the Lord to give him the grace of healing that he might guide them a little while longer to the salvation of their souls, Apa Theodore sent to the church and called for our father Apa Horsiesios. He said to him, 'Do not trouble yourselves, you and the brothers, pleading to the Lord on my account for it has in fact been decided that I am to go to the Lord like my holy fathers before me.'[1] But Apa Horsiesios went on weeping in great distress, with tears streaming down his cheeks.

Apa Theodore turned to Apa Pšentaesi, Pachomius, and all the other ancients who were gathered around his bed and said to them, 'You see that I am about to go to the Lord and to my righteous father Pachomius, as everyone must do. Now then, you must assist our father Apa Horsiesios in all obedience, in all humility, and without any murmuring at all. For the inheritance is his; I am only his assistant. The Lord knows that it was not my wish to do this work, for I am more of a sinner than all other men on the earth. Nevertheless, lest I perish, the grace of God was always with me so that I was never disobedient in anything the Lord made come my way. Now then, pay attention! I testify to you, *and my testimony is in the heavens,* that I have Jb 16:20.
not forgotten the sins of my soul for a single day during the whole time I have been living in this world. Also, I do not think that I have done anything ‹without the permission of Apa Horsiesios or›[2] without his blessed directions and by his very good counsels, for his soul has now been troubled on our account for eighteen years. Now then, my devout and beloved brothers, I request that, when the Lord visits me, you remove my body from the place where it is first placed and put my bones alongside those of my father.' When our father Theodore had said these things, the man of God opened his mouth and gave up his spirit very quietly and calmly on the second of the month of Pašons.[3] [May he rest] in peace! 27 April 368.

207. At that moment a great fear and a sweet G^1 *149a.*
fragrance came over them. All the brothers prostrated themselves and, weeping bitterly, they cried out, 'Woe to us, for we have been orphaned

Theodore's burial

today. Indeed it was really our righteous father Pachomius who died today. We have become miserable and wretched today as we recall his virtuous conduct, his mild speech, his great humility, and his constant and gentle love toward each of us.' Then our father Apa Horsiesios and all the brothers spent the whole night reciting around his venerable body. When morning came, at the time of the *synaxis*, they prepared his body carefully for burial with fine linens and offered for him the holy liturgy, the body and the blood of our Lord Jesus Christ. Then they went before him singing psalms until they reached the mountain where they buried him solemnly and with veneration. Then they returned to the monastery in deep sorrow with much weeping. That night our father Apa Horsiesios took with him three brothers and went to the mountain to the grave of our father Theodore.[1] He removed him from that site and took him and buried him alongside the bones of our righteous father Pachomius, the father of the holy *Koinonia*, in the place where [Theodore] also had buried his brother Paphnouti. They returned to the monastery quietly and no one noticed them.

G[1] 149b.

Horsiesios becomes the father of the *Koinonia* again

208. Three days after our father Theodore died, when all the brothers were in deep mourning, our father Horsiesios became ill from grief over the death of our father Theodore of happy memory. Then some of the ancient brothers, including Apa [Pšentaesi][1] and Apa Pachomius,[2] strongly urged Apa Horsiesios to go and speak some words of comfort to the brothers. He consented, arose, and went out weeping. He sat in the midst of the brothers, who were all gathered

together weeping and grieving over our father Theodore. He began to speak to them sorrowfully and tearfully, saying, 'God has certainly taken from us in Apa Theodore a righteous father who encouraged us with the word of the Lord. And this great grief of ours is all the greater because it is we who have grieved him so much that he asked the Lord to take him from us quickly and we have been orphaned. Indeed, you all know his great love for us and how he always interceded with God on our behalf to save us from the hands of the devil who is envious of us. Now then, my beloved brothers, let us always remember his labors, his ascetic practices, and the tears which he shed in the Lord's presence day and night on our behalf, that this word of Scripture may not apply to us: *They quickly forgot his deeds and did not keep his counsels,* and that we may not come Ps 106(105):13. under judgement. For this I truly believe: that if we walk in accordance with the directions he gave us, he will be an ambassador for us in the presence of God and of our father Pachomius. It is, in fact, just as our Lord Jesus told his holy disciples and his holy apostles: *I am going before you to prepare a place for you.* He also said, *We have* Jn 14:2. *one who intercedes for us in the presence of the Father, Jesus Christ our Lord, who loved us and gave himself as a ransom for our sins.*[3] *It was not on account of ours alone but on account of those of the whole world that he suffered for us.* In- 1 Jn 2:1-2. deed, during all the days he was with us in the body, our righteous father Pachomius prayed to the Lord day and night for the salvation of our souls and those of the whole world. This is also what our holy fathers did who came after him,

Apa Petronios and Apa Theodore, who became
his sons by emulating his life with a great [love of
the] Cross. Now then, my brothers and leaders of
the monasteries who are the members of our
father, let us observe the laws which our fathers
laid down for us and the commandments which
they gave us to carry out so that as a result their
hearts may be at peace about us where they are
now resting. As Christ said to his father about his
apostles, *Those things which you gave to me, I
also have given to them; they in their turn have*
Jn 17:8. *received them and have kept your word.* May our
turn come for them to say of us, "Welcome are
the sons who obeyed their father and kept the
commandments which he gave them. Come, inherit
eternal life with your fathers because you
walked in their footsteps and in the commandments
which they gave you." The bones of our
righteous father actually remain in our midst today:
these are the laws he gave us that through
them we might be victorious over the evil one.
Then the hearts of our fathers may be at peace
about us, when they see their offspring producing
spiritual fruit for God their creator, *like trees*
Ps 1:3. *growing on the edge of the water,* as it is written.
Now then, my brothers, let us not be negligent,
that the work of our fathers may not have been in
vain and may not be dissipated and that we ourselves
may not be in danger of God's judgement
when we arrive in the presence of our fathers. For
this reason the Lord has appointed me together
with our fathers to be your servant, even as the
Lord said in the Gospels, *I have been in your*
Lk 22:27. *midst as one who serves.* Abigail likewise said to
the blessed David, *I will be your slave and wash*

the feet of your servants. Because of her humility she saved all those who belonged to her.' 1 S 25:41.

When our father Apa Horsiesios had said these things to the leaders of the monasteries and all the assembled brothers, he rose and prayed over them, and they embraced him very joyfully as if they were seeing our father Pachomius and Theodore in their midst. When they had received the Eucharist of the third day for Apa Theodore,[4] [Horsiesios] walked with the brothers of the monasteries, escorting them all as each one departed for his monastery in peace. He also often used to go and visit the monasteries and strengthen them in the law of the Lord and the commandments of our father.

G[1] 118.

Horsiesios' teaching

209. One day as he was sitting speaking with the brothers about the word of God, he said to them, 'Our father strengthened us with the holy Scriptures and the perfect knowledge of the Lord. I think that if a man does not guard his heart well he will forget all those things he has heard. Then, because of his negligence, the enemy will overpower him and cast him down. I will tell you a parable which may surprise you. It is in fact like the case of a burning lamp which produces a strong light. If we neglect it, its light diminishes little by little and it gets dark in that house. Then the mice come around it. If they see that there is no light or heat in it, they pull down its wick and eat it. They hit the lamp and knock it down. However, if that lamp is made of bronze, then the master of the house will take it and fix it up again. Then once again it will make light in the house. But if it is made of earthenware, then it has been broken and it is thrown out. This is

how it is with a soul. If it is a little negligent, then the Holy Spirit withdraws from it until it is completely dark and deprived of his light. Then the enemy eats up the zeal of that soul and also corrupts the body through wickedness, uncleanness, and the pollution of evil desires, because it was not vigilant and did not struggle against its enemy. Instead it neglected its own salvation, so that it became a stranger to the kingdom of God and his eternal goods. If in fact that person was of good character before God and had simply been trapped by negligence, God, who is also compassionate, will put into him his fervor[1] and remind him of the punishments in order to make him recover his senses and get a firm hold on himself from then on until the day of his visitation.' When he had profited them with the explanation of the parable which he had told them, he got up and prayed over them all. Each one then withdrew to his cell, reciting the word of God.[2]

G[1] 150.

Athanasius' letter to the brothers about Theodore's death

210. When Apa Athanasius, the archbishop of Alexandria, who was in the diocese of Šmoun, heard that Apa Theodore had died, he quickly wrote a letter to Apa Horsiesios comforting him and the other brothers with him.[1] He said this: 'Athanasius, the archbishop of Alexandria, writes, greeting his beloved son Horsiesios and all the brothers with him who are firm in the faith of our Lord Jesus Christ. Greetings! When I heard that the blessed Theodore had died, I was deeply affected by what I heard, for I knew how valuable he always was to you because of his great zeal. And so, if Theodore, who is our beloved Horsiesios, were no longer, I would have written to you many

very tearful words about what would happen after his death, but Theodore, whom we know as Horsiesios, is still in your midst, because the two of them are one.[2] Indeed if one went on a journey, the tasks of both were fulfilled at home. Blessed is Theodore *who did not walk according to the counsels of the wicked*, who are the devil Ps 1:1.
and his wicked demons. Now then, let us not weep over one who has gone to that place from which weeping, mourning, and groaning have fled, who is resting with his fathers, and who said, *I will dwell in that place because I have chosen it.* Ps 132(131):14.
Let us not grieve over one who has tied up his boat in that fair haven which offers full security, complete relief and all joy. Would that each of us might exert himself until he brings his boat into that haven. For indeed, Theodore *is not dead but asleep* in a good repose in the presence of the Mt 9:24.
Lord.[3] I am writing this to all of you in common, and especially to you, my dear and beloved Apa Horsiesios, so that ‹now that he is dead, you may accept the whole care and›[4] take his place among the beloved [brothers]. For when Theodore was alive, you two were as one man. When one went away, the duties of the two were fulfilled at home; and when the two of you were at home, you were as one man for the beloved [brothers], speaking with them about what is useful.[5] Do the same. And so doing, write to us and tell us about your health and that of the brothers. And I exhort you all to pray in common that the Lord may more and more *bestow peace* on the Church. In Col 3:15.
fact, we have celebrated the Passover and the Fifty Days [of Eastertide] and we have rejoiced in the Lord's kindness. We have written to you. I greet

all those who fear the Lord. Those who are with us greet you. I pray that you may have health in the Lord, dear and beloved brothers.'

Notes to the Bohairic Life

SBo 1. [1]The first two pages of the Bohairic manuscript are missing and no Sahidic fragment gives us the beginning of this Coptic Life. The first folios of the Vatican Arabic Life (Av) are also missing. Fortunately the Arabic Life published by Amélineau (Am) follows a Coptic text very similar to SBo in this section. We therefore translate the first ¶ of SBo from Am 337-339.

[2]It is very interesting to see how the appearance of monasticism is presented here as a fruit of the increased faith of Christians after the time of the martyrs. This goes against the commonly held opinion that monasticism was a reaction to diminishing fervor in the Church after the persecution era.

[3]This vivid description of the sufferings of the saints taken from Heb 11:37-38 is quoted twice by Pachomius (Instr. 1:13 and 18) and twice by Theodore (Instr. 3:5 and 30). The text is used again below, ¶ 16 (= G[1] 13).

SBo 2. [1]The Bohairic text begins here. The title 'Apa' given here to Antony is the normal Coptic form, while 'Abba' is the normal Greek form. Although we often find 'Abba' in Coptic texts and occasionally 'Apa' in Greek documents, we shall always use 'Apa' in our translation of the Coptic Life and 'Abba' in the translation of the Greek documents.

[2]The story of Amoun of Nitria, with Antony and Pachomius, the third great founder of Egyptian monasticism, is told by Palladius, H.L. 8. Born c. 295, an orphan from a prominent family, he married at the insistence of his uncle. He and his wife lived a life of virginity for eighteen years. Then in 315, he retired to the mountain of Pernouč in the Nitrian desert, where he became the first monk. Disciples joined him and he became their father. He died in 337, having visited his wife twice annually. By the end of the fourth century the desert of Nitria held five thousand disciples of Amoun. Both Amoun and Theodore, his faithful disciple, are mentioned in Am. Letter 30 and 34 as well as in *Vit. Ant.* 60 and H.M.A. 29.

[3]In SBo 194 Theodore applies the same text, Ph 4:3, to Pachomius.

SBo 3. [1]The Coptic word *thoš* is used to designate a *nome* (administrative subdivision of Egypt) as well as a *diocese*. The boundaries of the dioceses usually—but not always—corresponded with those of the nomes. We shall translate *thoš* by diocese except in the few instances where another translation is required by the context.

[2]Šeneset, called Χηνοβόσκιον by the Greeks, is now Kasr-es-Sayad. It was in the diocese of *Diospolis parva*, Hew in Coptic.

SBo 4. [1]Latopolis (Coptic Sne, modern Isnâ) draws its name from a kind of fish called λάτος which was worshipped there. 'Those [creatures] that are in the waters' are evidently the idol fish.

SBo 5. The Coptic sentence is obscure. It reads: 'when he was sent where he was going.' There seems to be an inversion of the two verbs. We follow the correction proposed by Lefort, VC 81, n. 2.

[2]This story is not found in G[1]. In SBo it looks like an interruption between ¶¶ 4 and 6. At the beginning of ¶ 6, the expression 'concerning the interpretation of this story' clearly refers to ¶ 4 and not to ¶ 5.

SBo 6. [1]That God created man upright and man has turned aside toward sin of his own free will was a conviction of the Pachomians. Qo 7:29(30) is quoted by Pachomius in SBo 107.

[2]The image of the 'darnel', taken from the parable of the darnel sowed in a field of good wheat (Mt 13:24-30. 36-43) is often used, v.g. in SBo 106, 142; G[1] 38; Hors. Letter 4:4.

SBo 7. [1]The mention of the 'Persians' is a mistake, since there was no war between Constantine and the Persians. Absent from the Greek Lives, this reference is proper to SBo. We find it in Bo and Am, but it is absent from S[4] where, however, the fact that the word 'tyrant' is the last word of the page can explain the omission of the Persians. Moreover, the mention of Constantine, found in G[1] as well as in SBo, is also erroneous, since Constantine was not in control of Egypt until 324. It has been generally admitted since Ladeuze that Pachomius was conscripted in 312 for Maximinus Daia's campaign against Licinius, who then dominated the eastern part of the Empire and was an ally of Constantine. In fact, the MS B of G[2] gives the name of Maximinus. Pachomius was therefore released in 313, when Maximinus was defeated and killed.

[2]This is evidently the clumsy interpolation of a copist, since Pachomius does not know Jesus yet. But as soon as he is converted, this prayer will be constantly on his lips; see SBo 145. It was a prayer familiar to Palamon also (SBo 12 and 17).

[3]The Bohairic text has *Sne* (Latopolis), which is obviously a mistake of the Bohairic translator or of a copist, since Sne was never the capital of the ancient Empire. The mistake is repeated by Am, but S[4] has Ne, which is the Coptic name of Thebes. G[1] also has Thebes.

[4]Lit. 'for the needs of the body.'

SBo 8. [1]*Pmampiserapis* means 'the place of Serapis'. The same place is later (SBo 51) called *Pmampesterposen*, that is, 'the place of the baking of bricks'. This last name is the good one, the first being one of several blunders of the Bohairic translator. See Lefort, 'Les premiers monastères. . .', 397-399. All the theories about the origins of pachomian monasticism being linked with the cult of Serapis are founded on this error of translation.

[2]His catechumenate must have lasted more than 'some days' in conformity with the general custom of the time and what would later be the custom in the pachomian monasteries themselves. He was probably baptized at Easter.

SBo 9. [1]This biblical expression is quoted again in SBo 105 concerning scandal.

[2]This quotation of Jm 1:27 does not hang together with what follows. This whole ¶ 9, which does not have a parallel in G[1], could express preoccupations of a later time with what is befitting a monk.

SBo 10. [1]There is no reason to doubt the accuracy of this mention of a period of three years in Šeneset, although G[1] is silent about it. The letter of Ammon (¶ 12) seems to confirm it, since it implies an interval between Pachomius' baptism and the time he became a monk under Palamon.

[2]'Until you get to know yourself' is a beautiful expression of the aim of monastic *ascesis.*

[3]This shows that there was already a monastic *tradition.*

[4]The meaning is obviously that during the summer they fasted one day at a time, eating only once and in the evening, while during the winter they 'joined' two or three days of fast together, eating only every other or every third day. Lefort's translation in VC, p. 85 ('En tout temps nous jeûnons jusqu'au soir, quotidiennement pendant les jours d'été, tandis qu'aux jours d'hiver tous les deux ou tous les trois jours. . .') is misleading. On the meaning of 'joining' the days of fast, see note SBo 35,1 below.

[5]The word *synaxis* here has the meaning it had in anchoritic circles, where it was used to designate the number of prayers as anchorite had determined in his way of life (his πολῖτεία). In general in the apophthegmatic literature, for a monk to make his prayers is either βαλεῖν τοὺς ψαλμοὺς or βαλεῖν τὴν σύναξιν (see v.g. *Apoph. Patr.*, Theodora 3; PG 65:201). The mention of 'sixty prayers' in Coptic means literally 'sixty times of prayer' or 'sixty sections of prayer'. On the meaning of the Coptic expression *nsop nšlêl,* see Veilleux, *La liturgie*. . ., pp. 309-312. The *unceasing prayer,* with reference to 1 Th 5:17, will be one of the foundations of Pachomius' teaching. He will remind Theodore one day that it is one of the things that the Scriptures command us to do and that are therefore more important than supererogatory fasting. See also Pach. Instr. 2:2

[6]Lit. 'liars'.

[7]Two pages of the Bohairic manuscript are missing, and there is no corresponding Sahidic text extant. We translate the next few ¶¶ from Am 348-349

[8]We return to the Bohairic text.

[9]About the meaning of vigils in ancient, and especially pachomian, monasticism, see H. Bacht, 'Agrypnia. Die Motive des Schlafentzugs im frühen Mönchtum'.

SBo 11. [1]In pachomian terminology, the *Passover* corresponds to our Holy Week; it is ended by the *Closing of the Passover* which corresponds to our Easter Vigil, and is followed by the *Sunday of the Resurrection,* called also the day of Joy (see G[1] 7). The *Passover* was preceded by the *Forty Days* (of Lent), and the *Sunday of the Resurrection* was followed by the *Fifty Days* (of Eastertide).

[2]A gesture of annoyance. Cf. Paral. 10. Lefort (VC, p. 86, n. 2) gives the following references; Aristoph., *Vesp.* 584; *Plut.* 612.

[3]The negation was omitted by haplography; cf. Am 351.

[4]Palamon's justification for the presence of oil in his cell has all the signs of a later addition. He certainly did not have a sanctuary lamp in his cell. Lefort, VC, p. 86, n. 4, and Festugière, *La première Vie grecque*. . ., p. 17, after him, say that the same curious mention of oil for the sanctuary lamp is also found in G[4]. In fact, G[4] 10 (Halkin, p. 415, 1.2) simply says, at the beginning of this story, that Pachomius took some of the oil prepared for the *lamps*! ἔλαιον ἀπὸ τοῦ ταῖς λαμπάσιν ἡτοιμασμένου λαβων. . . .

SBo 12. [1]What is called here a 'vision' (*orama*) was called a 'dream' (*rasoui*) in ¶ 8.

[2]According to Am this vision happened after *three* years, and not *four*. The reiteration of this vision is proper to SBo. The stories of SBo 12 and 13 are absent from G[1], but G[1] 16 speaks of Pachomius' abundant sweating during his nightly prayers (cf. beginning of SBo 12).

SBo 14. [1]The Lord's Prayer.

[2]Eph 6:16 is often explicitly or implicitly quoted in pachomian literature. See Theod. Instr. 3:4 and 30; Hors. Test. 19.

[3]There are similar stories in Fragm. Draguet 2 and in H.M.A. 14.

[4]Šmin, called Panopolis by the Greeks, is the modern Akmim. It was about fifty miles from Palamon's desert.

SBo 15. [1]*Exercises*: this is our translation of *nipoliteia*, the Coptic plural form of πολῖτεία which in the singular designates the ascetic way of life proper to a monk.

[2]Šeneset means 'the acacias of Set'. On Palamon's desert and the acacia forest, see Lefort, 'Les premiers monastères...', pp. 383-387. On the significance of the Cross in pachomian spirituality, see H. Bacht, '... Vexillum Crucis sequi...'.

SBo 17. [1]The theme of conversion, with reference to putting off the old self and putting on the new (Col 3:10.12), is central in pachomian spirituality. For example, in G[1] 65 Theodore is said to have refused to treat his own brother Paphnouti as a brother according to the flesh, because 'he had already *put off the old man*'. Cf. also Pach. Instr. 1:30 and Theod. Instr. 3:10.

[2]Tabennesi is a compound word, the first part of which means either *palm grove* or *sanctuary*, and the second the name of the goddess Isis. One of the several Greek forms of the name being Ταβεννῆσος, a copist of Sozomen's *Ecclesiastical History* erroneously wrote ἐν Ταβέννῃ νήσῳ instead of ἐν Ταβεννήσῳ. Hence the mistaken assumption for centuries that Tabennesi was an island. In fact, Tabennesi (modern Nag'-el-Sabrîyât, half way between Faw and Dechna) is well on solid ground on the north-east bank of the Nile, ten miles upstream from Šeneset. See Lefort, 'Les premiers monastères...', pp. 393-397.

[3]Palamon is referring not to the vision of Tabennesi (recounted in this ¶) but to the dream Pachomius had during the night of his baptism and which was repeated three years later, according to SBo 12. According to Bo and S[3] Pachomius spent seven years with Palamon. G[1] says nothing about the length of his stay. Am's mention of seventeen years is evidently a mistake.

SBo 18. [1]Four pages of the Bohairic manuscript are missing. We translate from S[3], complemented from Am, in the following order:

S[3]: VS, p. 102,A,36-B,32
S[3]: VS, p. 104,A,26-105,B,25
Am, 361, 1-17
S[3]: VS, p. 109,B,2-36.

[2]Lit. the *Prosphora*, which is the name usually given the Eucharist in our Coptic sources.

[3]The Coptic word *toou* means 'mountain' as well as 'desert' (hence, also a community of solitaries). It often means 'cemetery', since according to a millenial tradition, the dead were buried in the desert.

SBo 19. [1]The tunic (Coptic: *cacitôn*; Greek: λεβίτων or κολόβιον; Latin: *tunica, lebitonarium,* or *colobium*) was the characteristic garment of monks, which was generally called in Coptic as well as in Greek the σχῆμα. It was a long sleeveless linen robe. The hood (Coptic: *klapht, klbt,* etc. or *kouble, koukli,* etc.; Greek: κουκούλλιον; Latin: *cucullus*) covered the head and the neck only, according to the description of that monastic garment given by Cassian, Inst. I, 3: 'Cucullis namque perparuis usque ad ceruicis umerorumque demissis confinia, qui capita tantum contegant, indesinenter diebus utuntur ac noctibus.' It was therefore very different from our modern 'cowls'; but it is possible that the hood was generally attached to the mantle; see R. Draguet, 'Le chapitre de HL...', 1944, p. 105-106. The mantle (Coptic: *prês*; Greek: μαφόριον; Latin: *pallium, palliolum, sabanum, amictus, mafors*) was used during the night and for a few other occasions. For a more detailed study of the pachomian monastic clothes in general, see Jerome's Preface to his translation of the Rules of Pachomius and Pr. 81.

[2]The same quotation occurs in Hors. Test. 27.

[3]In G[1] 15, it is John who tells Pachomius to 'stop being conceited', and Pachomius who gets angry about it.

[4]The Arabic text simply has 'went down', and Amélineau suggests in a note that the meaning is 'went down [from the wall they were building].' But the general context as well as a comparison with G[1] shows clearly that the meaning is 'went down [to an underground place].'

[5]This idea is frequently expressed by Pachomius. See SBo 67c (= G[1] 75).

[6]There is another, more vivid, description of this incident in S[1] 7-9.

SBo 20. [1]We return to the Bohairic text.

[2]Cubit: a measure of length corresponding to the length of the arm from the end of the middle finger to the elbow (about 18-22 inches).

SBo 21. [1]Cf. a similar story in H.M.A. 2, 52ff.

SBo 22. [1]Bo (followed by Am) read *ma* (a place, somewhere) in the Sahidic original; but S[3] and Av read *moue* (island). That this is the good reading is confirmed by its correspondence with G[1]: ἐν νήσῳ.

[2]Both in Coptic and in Greek (G[1] 23) this is a general, absolute, statement about what is the will of God. In their translations, both Lefort and Festugière limit the significance of this statement by restricting it to Pachomius: 'the will of God is for you to...'

[3]S[1]8 places this vision before the wrangle between Pachomius and John and gives a better description of the event. The compilation S[3], which combines elements from S[1] and SBo duplicates this vision artificially by inserting both the story of S[1] before the wrangle, and the story of SBo after it. See the translation in Lefort, VC, p. 60,21-61,19 (= S[1]) and 64,19-23 (= SBo).

SBo 23. [1]See correction of the Bohairic text indicated by Lefort, VC, p. 94, n. 2.

[2]Bo has *iohi* (field), but it is certainly a mistake. The Sahidic original had *hoi* (water wheel), which is confirmed by Av and Am as well as by G[1] (εἰς μηχανήν). See Lefort, VC, p. 95, n. 5.

[3]If fact, some disciples had come before, but Pachomius, unable to discipline them even after years of patient efforts, had expelled them. See below, note SBo 24,2.

[4]Instead of these simple regulations, G[2] and G[3] (and its Arabic translation in Am) introduce here the too-famous Rule of the Angel taken from Palladius' *Historia Lausiaca*.

SBo 24. [1]Pecoš is the normal form of this noun. The Bohairic text here has Piethoš (= the Ethiopian) which according to Lefort is a clumsy attempt of the Bohairic translator to interpret the etymology of the Sahidic noun. The Pachomius mentioned here is evidently Pachomius *the younger*.

[2]S[1] describes how people from the surrounding villages came to live around Pachomius (S[1] 10), how he organized them into a community (¶ 11) and made himself their servant (¶ 12), and how after suffering their contempt for five years (¶¶ 13-14) he spent a long night in prayer (¶¶ 15-16). Then he imposed on them a few very clear rules which they refused to obey (¶ 17) and he finally expelled them (¶ 18). They went to the bishop who sided with Pachomius (¶ 19). It is this long, vivid and moving, story of failure that is summed up here in two sentences. See a similar edulcoration in G[1] 38.

SBo 25. [1]Tabennesi.

[2]The offering of bread and wine for the celebration of the Eucharist.

[3]The same text is applied to Theodore the City-man when he was a lector in the Church of Alexandria; see below, ¶ 89.

[4]The celebration of the Eucharist twice a week, Saturday evening and Sunday morning, was the common practice in Egypt as well as in Palestine at that time. For Egypt, see J. Muyser, 'Le Samedi et le Dimanche dans l'Eglise et la littérature Copte', in T. Mina, *Le Martyre d'Apa Epima* (Cairo, 1937) pp. 89-111. For Palestine, see some examples in the Life of Saint Georges of Chozibam published in *AnBoll* 7 (1888)c. 3, p. 190 and c. 15, p. 115. See also Cassian, Inst., 3,2(ed. Guy, p. 93); Saint Jerome, Ep. 108(PL 22: 896); Nil, *Narrationes* 3(PG 79:619-622); Cyrille of Scythopolis, *Vita S. Euthymii*, 89-90(PG 114:672); Socrates, *Historia Ecclesiastica* 3(PG 67:6-66).

SBo 26. [1]See Hors. Reg. 23; cf. Pr. 33, 35.

[2]Concerning the care of the sick brothers and their food, see Pr. 40-47; Hor. Reg. 24 and Jerome's Pref. 5.

[3]Cf. Pr.1, 49-54.

[4]Cf. Paral. 22-23.

[5]These classes (*tagma*) of monks seem to correspond to the tribes mentioned by Jerome in Pref. 2 and by Palladius in H.L. 34, 4. G[1] 28 (= SBo 26) has this mention of the classes also, but this is its only use of τάγμα. In the Rules of Pachomius, they are mentioned in Pr. 15 (Latin text only) and Pr. 115, where the Coptic text has *phulê* instead of *tagma*. In all the other instances where *tagma* is used in the Coptic Lives (VB, p. 26,6; 43,11; 125,24-25; 126,14; 144,23; and VS, p. 138,27; 168,19; 221,8) it has the general meaning of 'group', 'category'.

[6]See Jer. Pref. 6.

[7]See Pr. 20-22; Inst. 15; Leg. 12. We will study more in detail the number and nature of these instructions (κατήχησες) in the notes to our translation of the Rules.

SBo 27. [1]This theme of the reward according to each one's works, with reference to Rm 2:6-7, is frequent. See Inst. 18; Pach. Letter 5: 12; Pach. Fragm 2: 3; Hors. Test. 27, 33.

[2]Lit. 'a place of worship' (*maneršôouši*). Mention of this oratory is absent from Av and Am. It could be a late addition.

[3]Here the author applies to Pachomius' sister the word *chellô* (or *hellô*) which we usually translate by 'old man'. It is a technical monastic term which expresses someone's experience of monastic life rather than his/her age.

[4]This shows that there was already a set of rules at this early period.

[5]See Pr. 143.

[6]Titoue is listed in G[1] 79 among the prominent ancient brothers. In SBo 94 he is described as one of those who came to encourage Theodore during his great penance. In G[1] 123 he is called 'great' (ὁ μέγας) and is mentioned as one of the ancient brothers still alive during Horsiesios' first period as the superior of the *Koinonia*.

SBo 28. [1]The internal order of this sentence is disturbed in the Bohairic translation. With Lefort, VC, p. 99, n. 2, we re-establish the order as in S[5] and Av.

[2]ἀρχή, i.e. ecclesiastical rank.

SBo 29. [1]Nothing can be concluded from the use of the Coptic word *alou* concerning the age of Theodore. *Alou* is used in Coptic, according to different contexts, of any young person, from a baby to a young man of twenty-five. See Crum, *Coptic Dictionary*, p. 5a.

[2]We follow the correction of the Coptic text indicated by Lefort, VC, p. 101, n. 5: *pichrôm eth⟨ouôm⟩ ouônh*.

SBo 30. [1]Another version of this story appears in Am. Letter 9.

[2]Unquestioning obedience: the Coptic expression means literally: 'without a double heart.' It corresponds to the Greek ἀδιάκριτος (G[1] 36)

SBo 31. [1]The sequence of the narrative is better in Am and G[1] than in Bo. As P. Peeters ('Le dossier copte...', p. 268) has already noted, we have here two different versions of the same story put together in a clumsy manner.

[2]The Coptic expression *sek* (like *hôtp*) corresponds to the Greek ὑπερτίθεσθαι and to the Latin *superponere*. It is a technical term for an absolute fast during which two or more days are 'joined' without any meal. See A. Veilleux, *La liturgie*..., pp. 253-256.

[3]There is a considerable discrepancy among the various documents concerning the chronology of Theodore's life, and especially his age at the time he came to Tabennesi. According to Bo, he began to fast in his parents' house at the age of twelve and he left the house two years later to go and live for six years with a group of anchorites. He arrived at Tabennesi at the age of twenty or, more precisely, in his twentieth year. Moreover, in SBo 199 Theodore states that he was eighteen years under Pachomius, which means that he was about thirty when he became Pachomius' assistant and that he arrived at Tabennesi in 328. The small fragment S[14], which gives the same text as Bo, also mentions twenty as Theodore's age when he came to Pachomius. But all the other sources are silent about a period of six years with a community of anchorites in Latopolis, and they give fourteen (G[1] and Av) or thirteen (Am. Letter) as his age at that time. Am adds that it

was the fifth year since the foundation of the monastery. That gives us a date of 329. According to G^1 78, Theodore was about thirty years old when he was appointed by Pachomius as steward of Tabennesi, around 337, which would give the impossible date of 321 (two years before the foundation of the monastery) for his coming to Tabennesi. Ammon, according to whom Theodore was thirteen when he came to Pachomius, also states that he was twenty-two when he witnessed a vision of Pachomius that must be identified with the one described in SBo 73(= G^1 88). He was then recently appointed steward of Tabennesi, and it was about the year 337—which gives us 328 again as the date of his arrival, as in SBo. The year 328 (allowing for a certain vagueness in numbers, the difference of one year in Am is insignificant) can therefore be accepted as the date of Theodore's coming to Tabennesi. The convergence of three independent sources (G^1, Am. Letter, Am) in giving thirteen or fourteen as his age at that time militates against Bo's figure (twenty) and against the authenticity of Theodore's six-year period as an anchorite in Latopolis prior to his coming to Tabennesi.

SBo 32. [1]SBo and G^1 have been pretty much parallel up to this point. The next three ¶¶ of SBo (33-34-35) are absent in G^1. They have their correspondent in the section of Am-Ag parallel to S^{10-20}, and as in the other ¶¶ that SBo took from that source and that are absent from G^1, the compiler of SBo follows very closely the S^{10} version.

SBo 33. [1]During the period of solitude at the beginning of his monastic life, Pachomius paid great attention to that beatitude (see G^1 18) and, therefore, 'he was, as it were, seeing the invisible God as in a mirror' (G^1 22). And when Theodore expressed to Pachomius his desire to see God, Pachomius advised him to practise this same beatitude; see SBo 33 (= S^{10} 4).

SBo 34. [1]About keys given to Pachomius, see above, SBo 12.

SBo 35. [1]During the early centuries, at least in the Eastern Churches, the fast of the Forty Days (Lent) and the fast of the six days of Passover (Holy Week) were two distinct things. They are clearly distinguished v.g. in the fifth book of the Apostolic Constitutions (ed. Funk, T. I, pp. 269-271). We find the same distinction in the festal letters of Athanasius of Alexandria. (See L.-T. Lefort, *S. Athanase. Lettres festales et pastorales en copte*, CSCO 150 [text] and 151 [translation], Louvain, 1955: text: p. 41,24ff, translation: p. 13,25ff). Also *ibidem*, letter no. 42, of 370 (text: p. 66,30ff, translation: p. 47,36ff). See V. Peri, 'La cronologia delle lettere festali di sant Atanasio e la quaresima', in *Aevum* 35(1961) 28-86. An important detail to remember is that Athanasius' letters from 329 to 336 mention only the date of the fast of the Passover, i.e. from Monday to Saturday. It is only from the year 337 on that the fast of the Forty Days before the fast of the Passover is also mentioned. (The festal letter of 337 is lost, but we have the accompanying letter addressed to Sarapion of Thmuis.) We know that the pachomian monks received those letters (see below, ¶ 189). Theodore's question to Pachomius in this present ¶ concerns only the six days of Passover. It is therefore surprising that the story begins with the words: 'During the Forty Days. . .', especially since this seems to have happened during the first years of Theodore at Tabennesi, well before 337. Fortunately the first few lines of this story has been kept in a fragment of S^{20}, where we read simply: 'During the days of the Passover...' (Coptic text in *Muséon* 1941, p. 138). We may conclude that 'During the Forty Days' is an interpretation of the Bohairic translator at a later date, when the two fasts tended to be united into one. Concerning the story of Lent and especially the time when the forty-day fast ended in the early Church, see the studies by C. Callewaert assembled in *Sacris Erudiri, Fragmenta liturgica* (Steenbrugge, 1940) pp. 449-560. Callewaert's positions, commonly accepted by liturgists, have been challenged by H. Frank, first in 'Das mailändische Kirchenjahr in den Werken des hl. Ambrosius', *Pastor Bonus* 51 (1940) 85ff, and more recently in 'Die Paschavigil als Ende der Quadragesima und ihr Festinhalt bei Augustinus', *Archiv für Liturgiewissenschaft* 9 (1965) 1-27. About the expression 'to join together' two or more days of fast, see above, note SBo 31, 2.

[2]In Am. Letter 21, Theodore gives the brothers a lesson similar to the one he has received from Pachomius here.

SBo 37. [1]See SBo 27 on how Pachomius received his own sister.

[2]The sequence of the sentence in Coptic is different. The clause 'so that she may be satisfied' comes after 'because...the Bishop has written to us about that'. Moreover, a letter is missing in the MS; and if we read *ñtepe[f]hêt* instead of *ñtepe[s]hêt* (VB, p. 39,12), the translation could be 'so that he [= the Bishop] may be satisfied'.

[3]Lit. 'according to their habit (*schêma*).' See Pr 52: 'If seculars, or infirm people or *weaker vessels*—that is women—come to the door, they shall be received in different places according to their calling and their sex.'

[4]This story is found in the collections of *Apophthegmata: Verba Seniorum* n. 34b.

SBo 38. [1]The conclusion of this account is less distressing and more 'edifying' in G^1 37: Theodore's mother remained in the sisters' monastery. But according to that Greek Life, she had come alone; Paphnouti came later (G^1 65).

SBo 39. [1]In Theod. Instr. 3:2 this incident is mentioned as one of the trials Pachomius and the early brothers had to undergo.

[2]The Greek word πολιτευόμενος used here in Coptic can mean either a 'councillor' (see Lefort, VC, p. 108, n. 1, with reference to Preisigke, *Fachwörter...*) or a 'dweller', an 'inhabitant' (see Festugière, *La première vie grecque...* p. 25).

[3]Bo has 'our father'; but S^5 has 'your father', which is more consistent with the context.

[4]*Eulogies* were small gifts, usually food, that monks would give to each other or to visitors as a sign of brotherly love.

SBo 40. [1]See Pr. 51-52; cf. H.L.c. 32,5.

[2]This is a combination of Mt 25:40 and 18:6. G^1 has the same combination not only in ¶ 40 (= SBo 40), but also in ¶ 125. Mt 25:40 is quoted in Paral. 41 as well.

SBo 41. [1]See above, note SBo 39,2.

[2]The whole story is clearly inspired by the account of the cure of a woman with a haemorrhage in Mt 9:18-22.

SBo 42. [1]A fragment of this story which has been kept in S^2 (VS 24-25), seems more original. The brother had committed a secret fault, which explains that recourse to Pachomius' gift of clairvoyance was necessary. See P. Peeters, 'A propos de la Vie sahidique...', pp. 300-302.

SBo 45. [1]Cf. S^2 13 and *Verba Seniorum* n. 34c.

SBo 47. [1]Bo has 'somewhere'; but S^4 and S^5 as well as Am and Av have 'on an island', which corresponds to G^1 51. The Bohairic translator made the same mistake in Bo 22; see above, note SBo 22,1.

[2]Concerning uniformity, see Pr. 39. There are many other instances in the Life when Pachomius refuses special treatment for himself, even on his deathbed; see SBo 117 and 120. We also see from this story that the brothers lived in huts when they were working far away from the monastery.

SBo 48. [1]The special food prepared for the sick brothers had to be eaten in the infirmary; see Pr. 43.

[2]This text, so consonant with the spirituality of the *Koinonia*, is often quoted; see G^1 38; Paral. 39; Theod. Fragm. 4.

SBo 49. [1]This prophecy is not found in G^1 54. But there is a similar promise made by Christ in an apparition to Pachomius in Paral. 18.

[2]Lit. 'the little place [where] to make the festival'.

[3]Phbow, the modern Faw-el-Kebli (Southern Faw), was only two miles downstream from Tabennesi. Pachomius could therefore easily remain in charge of the two monasteries. SBo does not mention the appointment of a local superior at this stage. If Phbow was in the diocese of Diospolis parva (Hew), it appears that the boundaries of the diocese did not always correspond exactly with those of the 'nomes'. See above, note SBo 3,1 and Lefort, VC, p. 116, n. 3. About the geographical location of Phbow, see Lefort, 'Les premiers monastères...', pp. 387-393.

SBo 50. [1]The expression 'ancient old man' is certainly redundant in English, but in pachomian terminology 'old man' (*chello*) means a man of experience in the monastic life, or a spiritual father, while the adjective 'ancient' (*archaios*) can mean both his great age and the fact that he was one of the early monks. This Apa Ebonh ('Επώνυχος) is probably the one mentioned in the title of Pach. Instr 1. But it is not sure that he is also the same as the 'Επωνύχος (same name?) mentioned in G^1 134 as Peter's successor as the father of the monastery of virgins. About Šeneset, see above, note SBo 3,2.

[2]The Coptic text has *m̄piêi* (the house) instead of the plural *n̄niêi*; it is evidently a mistake.

SBo 51. [1]According to Lefort, VC, p. 116, n. 1, this Jonas of Thmoušons could be the same as the gardener of Thmoušons, also called Jonas, in Paral. 28-30. This is possible, although not totally certain. While the first three foundations were close to one another on the north-east bank of the Nile, Thmoušons was on the other bank, somewhere in the plain of Nag' Hammadi, at about a six-hour journey from Phbow. See Lefort, 'Les premiers monastères...', pp. 399-401. The first four foundations were in the diocese of Diospolis parva (except Tabennesi in the diocese of Nitentori); the last five will be more distant. The accounts of the first foundations in SBo and

G[1] have been parallel up to this point. Now, while SBo continues with the story of the remaining foundations, G[1] reserves the second group for much later.

[2]Four pages of Bo are missing. The gap can be filled with S[5] (VS, p. 145,4-146,23), complemented with Am 569-571.

[3]The Sahidic text reads: 'he organized *him*'; but the context calls for '*them*', unless 'him' stands for 'monastery', which is masculine in Coptic.

[4]It is difficult to explain this account of the annexation of Pmampesterposen. The Greek Life is silent about it, and the number of nine monasteries stated by Pachomius himself at the Latopolis Synod (G[1] 112) is complete without it. (See Chitty, 'A Note on the Chronology...' pp. 383-384). The description of the annexation is also different from the descriptions of the other foundations, with no mention of the establishment of housemasters and seconds, etc. It must have been a loose affiliation distinct from the others, or the story is a late interpolation. On the name of the place, see above, note SBo 8,1.

SBo 52. [1]'the monastery and the cells'. Lefort, VC, p. 247, 8-9, inadvertently translates: 'le monastère et la salle de réunion'. The Coptic *m̄ma n̄nouôh* corresponds to the more usual *m̄ma šôpe*, which means 'dwelling place' in general but has become the technical name of the cell (along with *ri*) and which, in any case, is a plural. See Crum, *Coptic Dictionary*..., p. 508a-b.

SBo 53. [1]*Kos* is the *Apollonopolis* of the Greeks and the modern *Kous*.

[2]This story, which interrupts the list of foundations in SBo, is absent from G[1]. Is it a kind of justification for the possession of boats by the *Koinonia*, something that will create problems later on?

SBo 54. [1]Latopolis of the Greeks. The expression 'an orthodox bishop of the city of Šmin' (ἐπίσκοπος τίς in G[1] 81) is a bit vague. In fact, bishop Arios was only a coadjutor appointed to assist bishop Artemidoros, at the latter's request, owing to his great age and infirmity. Arios' appointment must have been between 339 and 343, which gives some indication of the date of the second group of foundations.

[2]The fragment of S[5] ends here and we must rely on Am for the next page or so.

[3]The monastery of Šmin (Panopolis) and that of Tse (¶ 52) in the same region are really two different foundations. (See the argumentation of Chitty, 'A Note on the Chronology...', p. 383, against Lefort.)

SBo 55. [1]We return to the Bohairic text.

[2]Taking olives to Šmin was like carrying coals to Newcastle.

[3]Enoch's ascension to heaven is also mentioned in Paral. 37 and Pach. Instr. 1:25.

SBo 56. [1]Diospolis parva. The monastery of Thbew was therefore in the same diocese as the first three foundations after Tabennesi. It was on the west bank of the Nile, but much farther north than Thmoušons. It was on the site of the modern Abou-Choûche, twelve miles downstream from Farchout and five miles upstream from Beliâna. See Lefort, 'Les premiers monastères...', p. 402-403.

[2]'and they made a beautiful death' is the most obvious translation of *ouoh aučôk ebol kalôs.* The translation proposed by P.Peeters, 'A propos de la Vie sahidique...', p. 300: 'il les fit moines *et ils le furent en perfection*' is hardly acceptable.

SBo 57. [1]This is the third monastery in the region of Šmin.
[2]Petronios is transferred from Thbew to Tsime, in the vicinity of Šmin, and is entrusted with the care of the other two monasteries of the area. Chitty ('A Note on the Chronology...', p. 384) rightly stresses the significance of this appointment. Petronios, a relative newcomer, is given an authority over the group of monasteries comparable to that of Pachomius over the first group in the diocese of Diospolis parva. He was already singled out as a probable successor to Pachomius. The intervention of the ancient brothers asking Theodore to become their father if Pachomius dies (see SBo 94; G[1] 106) appears in a new light if we remember this.

SBo 58. [1]Phnoum is the last foundation, and was made before the autumn of 345, the date of the Synod of Latopolis. It was far away from the other monasteries, in the mountain (desert) of Sne, the Latopolis of the Greeks (modern Isnâ), in the region where Pachomius was born. See Lefort, 'Les premiers monastères...', pp. 404-407.
[2]For the Pachomians, this text from 1 Th expressed very well the attitude a superior must have toward the monks entrusted to him. It is quoted again about Pachomius in the account of his death (SBo 118), and Horsiesios uses it about Petronios. The same text is also quoted in SBo 89 (the attitude of Pachomius toward Theodore the City-man) and SBo 91 (the attitude of Theodore the City-man toward the brothers of his house).

SBo 59. [1]Egyptian bread was very hard and had to be soaked a long time before it could be eaten. We are told in SBo 77 that a whole year's supply of loaves was baked at a time. See also SBo 81, where Pachomius and Theodore placed their loaves in water and began to pray while they waited for them to soften.
[2]See above, SBo 10.

SBo 60. [1]This ¶, absent from G[1], does not seem at the right chronological order here, since it is only later, in ¶ 70, that Pachomius, after appointing Theodore superior of Tabennesi, will establish his headquarters at Phbow. But it is not impossible that the material administration of the whole *Koinonia* had been established there even earlier.

SBo 62. [1]Omitted by haplography; see Lefort, VC, p. 123, n. 1.

SBo 63. [1]Cf. Pr. 56.
[2]This text is also quoted in S[1] 2.

SBo 64. [1]Although the indications in the Life and the Rules are not absolutely clear and perhaps not entirely consistent, it seems that two meals were served every day in pachomian communities, one at noon and one in the evening, after a *synaxis* that may have been held at the ninth hour. Everybody had to go to the noon meal, but after the *synaxis* in the evening, each monk could go either to the refectory or to his cell; see Jer. Pref. 5; Pr. 103, etc.

[2]It is not always clear, in the Life, whether the verb ψάλλειν has the general meaning of 'to sing' or the more specific meaning of 'to sing psalms'.

SBo 65. [1]Cf. Theod. Instr. 3:2, where Theodore recalls that during a famine which was probably that described in SBo 39 (= G[1] 39) the 'great ones' among the brothers said to Pachomius: 'You are murdering the children of men'.

[2]The same story is found in S[10].

SBo 66. [1]This sentence, omitted by Bo, is found in S[4] and Av, and corresponds to G[1] 71.

[2]This vision of Pachomius (also found in S[10]) concerns the difficulties that will shake the *Koinonia* during Horsiesios' first tenure as superior of the *Koinonia*; see SBo 139 (= G[1] 127-128-129).

SBo 67. [1]This story also is found in S[10], although very fragmentarily.

SBo 68. [1]'An ancient old man': see above, note SBo 50,1.

[2]Mention of the huts means that the brothers were working far away from the monastery and did not return to the monastery for the night.

[3]This is another story found very fragmentarily in S[10], where the teaching of Pachomius that upset Mauo concerned a case of pederasty. The common source of SBo-G[1] has edulcorated the story, as in many similar instances. See S[10], VS, p. 66-71; VC, pp. 33-34.

SBo 69 [1]Bo gives Theodore's age as thirty-three, which could be due to a dittography. Both Av and S[4] give thirty, which is more consistent with the chronology of SBo. See above, note SBo 31,3.

[2]We find the same quotation in S[10] 2.

[3]Pr 25:25 is quoted also in Pach. Letter 9b.

SBo 70. [1]The Bohairic translator has inadvertently replaced *oikonomia* (administration) by *koinonia*, and has forgotten the word *ke* (other). The two corrections can safely be made from S[4].

[2]Here Pachomius is said to have been *proven through fire* by the word of God. In G[1] 123, shortly before Theodore assumes the superiorship of the *Koinonia*, he is said to have been *tested through fire* by our father Pachomius.

[3]We find the same quotation in Pach. Letter 3: 3 and in Hors. Letter 4: 3.

[4]The same text is applied to Theodore and Horsiesios in SBo 204.

SBo 71. [1]Cf. Jer. Pref. 7.

[2]Lit. '*till* the twentieth of *Mesore*.' But the real meaning of the preposition *ša* in this context is not clear. The same problem is found in Theod. Letter 2: 3, and H. Quecke who has carefully analyzed the problem could not arrive at a perfectly certain answer. See H. Quecke, 'Eine Brief...', p. 428; *Idem*. 'Eine Handvoll...', pp. 323-324. If we maintain the normal meaning of the preposition *ša* (till), it is not clear whether this means that the brothers had until the twentieth of Mesore to assemble or that the meeting lasted until the twentieth of Mesore. H. Quecke suggests that *ša*

has perhaps another meaning in the pachomian terminology and could perhaps mean '*on* the twentieth of *Mesore*'. We adopt that translation, which remains conjectural. There is yet another problem concerning the date of that annual meeting of the brothers. SBo 71 (Bo and S[4]) speak of the twentieth of Mesore, and Jerome's title to Pach. Letter 7 gives the same date; but Theod. Letter 2 gives the first of Mesore as the date of the meeting; and since the date is indicated twice, it cannot be a copist's mistake. SBo 144 simply mentions 'the end of the year' (Mesore is the last month of the year in the Coptic calendar—it corresponds to the period from the twenty-seventh of July to the twenty-fourth of August in our calendar), and G[1] 122 (= S[3b]) does not mention any date. It is possible that there has been an evolution concerning the date of that meeting as well as its nature.

[3]These two annual meetings were very important in the life of the *Koinonia*. H. Bacht, *Das Vermächtnis*. . ., p. 23, n. 74, suggests that they may have had a direct or indirect connection with the two annual synods of bishops that were held twice a year according to the fifth Canon of Nicea, the first one before Lent and the other in autumn. The only reason given here and elsewhere in the Life for the second annual meeting of the *Koinonia* concerns administration: to render accounts to the Great Steward and to receive appointments. It seems that at a later period it also became a celebration of a mutual forgiving of offences. During Theodore's tenure as head of the *Koinonia* all the local superiors seem to have been changed or moved from one place to another at each one of these two meetings. See below, ¶ 144.

SBo 72. [1]I.e. that they may give a good sound when struck with the hand, which showed that they were well made.

[2]Omitted by Bo; restored from S[5].

SBo 73. [1]The distance between the two monasteries was only two miles. Another version of the story that follows is found in Am. Letter 10. According to Ammon, Theodore was then twenty-two years old, and it had been nine years after his arrival at Tabennesi.

[2]This assembly room is what is called elsewhere the *synaxis*. S[5] uses the word *synaxis* both for the assembly of the brothers, and for the place where they assemble. The Bohairic translator, without always being consistent, tends to reserve the word *synaxis* for the meeting itself and used the expression *pimanthoouti* (the place of the assembly) for the room where it is held. We have tried to respect this distinction in our translation of Bo.

[3]The expression 'the fruits of the Holy Spirit' was very often used by the Pachomians. It means not only the fruits of the Spirit listed by Paul in Ga. 5:22-23, but also the virtues of the Beatitudes and all the christian virtues in general. See A. Veilleux, *La liturgie*. . ., pp. 345-347.

SBo 74. [1]See Pr. 116; Hors. Reg. 39-40.

SBo 77. [1]See Pr. 116; Hors. Reg. 45.

[2]Word omitted by Bo; restored from Av; see Lefort, VC, p. 138, n. 2.

[3]Lit. 'He fasted the two [days]', which means that he joined two days of fast together (see above, note SBo 31,2), i.e. he ate every other day. Lefort's translation 'Il jeûnait un jour sur deux' says just the opposite! (See Lefort, VC, p. 139, 1.8).

[4]This story (¶ 77), as well as ¶ 78, follow very closely the text of Ag (see Am 446-449), and is absent from G[1]. But a summary of SBo 77-78 is found in SBo 74, with its correspondent in G[1], and is absent from Ag-Am of course. The explanation is that the common source of SBo-G[1] has made a short summary of the story of Am 446-449. Both G[1] and SBo have this short summary, but SBo also re-introduces the long story from Ag-Am afterwards. There is another case absolutely similar in SBo 92 and 102. See A. Veilleux, *La liturgie...*, p. 91.

SBo 78. [1]We follow the spelling of the Jerusalem Bible. In our pachomian texts, *Joshua, son of Nun* is always called *Jesus, son of Nave*. The same image of Joshua as Moses' helper is applied to Theodore in Hors. Letter 4: 5 and to Horsiesios in SBo 132 (= S[5] 126).

SBo 79. [1]About that expression, see above, note SBo 31,2.

SBo 80. [1]In Coptic: *pi ništi*, i.e. *the great one*, which corresponds to *major* in Jerome's translation of the Rules. But it is rare that this name is used of an individual superior in the Lives. Usually the plural ('the great ones') means the ancient brothers in opposition to the newcomers or novices, who are called 'the little ones'.

[2]The last sentence is an adaptation made by the Bohairic translator. The text of S[4] is a little more elaborate: 'having heard these words, Theodore took them to heart as God's law, and said, "This is a small thing, but it is written in the Gospel..."'. The text of S[4] is fragmentary, but we know from Av that the quotation introduced here was Lk 6:10.

SBo 81. [1]Omitted by Bo; restored from S[4].

[2]To reach Thmoušons they had to cross the Nile at Šeneset and to walk about ten miles on each bank of the Nile.

SBo 82. [1]Omitted by Bo; restored from S[4].

[2]Here again the Bohairic text has to be corrected from S[4]; read *nemtoumethêki* instead of *n̄tetoumethêki*.

[3]Other correction from S[4] and S[5]; instead of *erof*, read *e⟨chrêi e⟩rof*.

[4]Omitted by Bo; restored from S[4] and S[5].

[5]*Idem*.

[6]This title of God, taken from 2 Tm 4:8, is often used in our sources; see G[1] 49; Pach. Fragm 3: 3; Hors. Test. 56.

[7]Is 26:2 is used in the same manner in Hors. Test. 4.

[8]This belief in the intervention of the angels at the time of death should not be attributed only to the naivety of uneducated Coptic monks. It was a common theme throughout pagan and christian antiquity; see F. Cumont, *Les Vents et les Anges psychopompes*, in *Pisciculi. Studien zur Religion und Kultur des Altertums* (*Franz Dölger dargeboten*) (Münster i. W., 1939) 70-75.

SBo 83. [1]Same story in Paral. 13.

[2]One instance when this happened to Pachomius is described in a homily in Coptic attributed to Athanasius. See Lefort, VS, pp. 347-348 (Translation in VC 383-384). On the role of the angels in the liturgy according to the Fathers of the Church and the early monks, see E. Peterson, *Le livre des*

Anges (Paris, 1954) 45-82; *ET, The Angels and the Liturgy* (London, 1964); J. Daniélou, *Le Mystère de l'Avent*, pp. 94-116; *Idem, Les Anges et leur Mission d'après les Pères de l'Eglise* (Chevetogne, 1953[2]) G. Colombás, *Paraiso y Vida Angélica. Sentido escatológico de la vocación cristiana, Biblioteca Vida Cristiana* 3 (Montserrat, 1958) 215-241.

SBo 84. [1]The Coptic word (*schêma*) is the one normally used for the monastic habit.

[2]Both the *sticharion*, a variegated tunic, and the *chlamys*, a cloak for infantrymen, were military clothes.

SBo 85. [1]We do not know for sure the exact measure of a *schbo*; but we know that the distance between Phbow and the monastery of Tse at Tkahšmin was a little more than sixty miles.

[2]Here again the Bohairic text is faulty; we follow S[5].

SBo 87. [1]This is the correct form of the name, although Bo mistakenly writes *Pataoli*.

[2]Omitted by Bo; restored from S[5].

[3]Patlole is one of the monks corrected in public by Theodore in Am. Letter 3. There he is called in Greek Πατελλολὶ.

SBo 88. [1]The same quotation from 2 Co 12:2-3 is applied again to Pachomius in SBo 114, in a similar context. Cf. also S[2] 6.

[2]Lit. 'soft' (μαλακοὶ). Homosexuality seems to have been a vice Pachomius was particularly anxious to extirpate from his monasteries.

SBo 89. [1]Bo is alone in giving his age as twenty-seven. The figure seventeen given by S[5], S[4] and Av is more reliable. Am, for his part, gives twelve, which is certainly erroneous.

[2]This detail is probably borrowed from the story of the vocation of the other Theodore. See above, ¶ 30.

[3]This text is applied to Pachomius in the account of his death; see SBo 123. It is also quoted in Hors. Instr. 5.

[4]In the Coptic Life we see that Pachomius 'made efforts' to learn Greek, but he does not seem ever to have become fluent in it. It is Theodore, on the contrary, who mastered Coptic and became not only the housemaster of the Alexandrian and other foreign monks, but also Pachomius' interpreter. This is very different from the account in Paral. 27 of Pachomius miraculously receiving the gift of tongues in order to comfort a Roman brother.

SBo 91. [1]Sahidic, the Coptic dialect of Upper Egypt.

[2]In the Bohairic text, read *efibi* instead of *efiri*; see Lefort, VC, p. 156, n. 1.

[3]Lit. 'the first fruits of the fructification of his house. . .'.

[4]The Bohairic text has *three* years; but since both Av and G[1], which are certainly independent, have *thirteen*, Bo must probably be corrected. Nevertheless, this creates some difficulties. It means that Theodore was already housemaster in 333 and, therefore, had come to Pachomius a few years earlier. In that case he could not have been twelve years lector in Alexandria under Athanasius, who became archbishop only in 328. If this

figure twelve is maintained, then three years must be correct as the length of Theodore's tenure of office during Pachomius' life.

SBo 93. [1]See a much longer version of this story—or of a similar one—in Paral. 5-6. Bo and Av have omitted another story we find partly in S[5], S[13], S[3], that has its correspondent in G[1] 104-105 and in Am. In the synoptic table of SBo-G[1] we give it the no. SBo 93bis.

SBo 94. [1]There is an inversion of the words in the Bohairic text.
[2]Bo has mistakenly: 'they got up, they prayed...'.

SBo 95 [1] *Westward*: because the Nile generally flows from south to north. But Phbow, Tabennesi and Šeneset are along the portion of the Nile that flows from east to west. When someone takes the ferry at Šeneset he actually crosses the Nile southward.
[2]The exact meaning of the word μαργώνιον is not clear, and long, erudite, discussions have been made to decide whether its origin is Arabic or Syriac. See Lefort, VC, p. XLVIII-L; P. Peeters, 'Le dossier copte...', pp. 272-276; D.J. Chitty, 'Pachomian Sources Reconsidered', pp. 73-74. But whatever the form of the basket in question or the origin of its name, it does not change the general meaning of our story.
[3]The Bohairic text is obscure; see the correction made by Lefort, VC, p. 162, n. 3.
[4]The same text is quoted in H.L. 34, 1 about the sister who pretended to be a fool.
[5]To put the head on or between, the knees is a typically Egyptian attitude, as Lefort notes in VC, p. 47, n. 15, with reference to Maspéro. But see also the similar attitude of Elijah on the top of Mount Carmel in 1 K 18:42.

SBo 96. [1]The order of the sentences has been disturbed in Bo. We follow Lefort's correction; see VC, p. 164, n. 1.
[2]Omitted in Bo by homoeoteleuton; restored from Av.
[3]This trip was made during 345, probably in September or October, which seems to have been the usual time of the brothers' trip to Alexandria (see G[1]113 n. 1). At that time Gregory, who had taken possession of Athanasius' archiepiscopal seat in March 339, was still occupying it and Athanasius was still in exile. He came back to Alexandria only on the twentieth of October 346. Therefore the mention of Pachomius' letter to Athanasius at the beginning of this ¶ is false. It is during this trip that the Synod of Latopolis took place. The account of this Synod (see G[1] 112) is not found in SBo, but is in Ag (fol. 30ff; = Am 591-595). It must have been in the souce common to SBo-G[1]but left aside by the SBo group. It is the only story from Ag absent from SBo which we find in G[1] (although G[1] 59 and 84-85, absent from SBo, have some vague contacts with stories of Ag; cf. Am 435-440 and 504).

SBo 97. [1]Words omitted by haplography; restored from Av.
[2]This text is quoted also in Pach. Instr. 1: 17.
[3]Theodore's rehabilitation took place at the end of 345 or at the beginning of 346, only a few months before Pachomius' death. But although Pachomius sent him to visit the brothers as before, it is not clear whether he

really treated him as his assistant, as in the past. Note that the end of this ¶ practically repeats the end of ¶ 74.

SBo 98. [1]The use of a personal pronoun in Coptic leaves some doubt whether this ¶ is about Pachomius or about Theodore. But the parallel text in Am 485 is about Pachomius.

[2]Words omitted by haplography.

[3]Cf. G[1] 21.

[4]Words omitted in Bo; restored from Av.

[5]1 Th 5:18 is quoted again in SBo 180 and Pach. Instr 1: 14.

[6]Lefort, VC, p. 167-168, n. 8, thought that this story, as well as the one in the next ¶ (99), were the source of two stories that we read in the *De oratione*, formerly attributed to St Nilus, which I. Hausherr has restored with great probability to Evagrius. But D.J. Chitty, 'Pachomian Sources Reconsidered', pp. 39-41, established that Evagrius' two stories are based on Am. Letter 19.

SBo 99 [1]'. . . assembled *for the synaxis*,' according to G[1] 101.

[2]Lefort, in his French translation (VC, p. 168, n. 2), modifies the order of the sentences in this ¶. But we find the order of Bo quite satisfactory and follow it in our translation.

SBo 100 [1]The same text is quoted below, ¶ 145, to stress the need to be concerned about our neighbor's progress in the law.

[2]This prayer seems to be based on a liturgical model, perhaps an anaphora.

SBo 101 [1]1 Tm 2:2 is quoted in Pach. Letter 7: 1 also.

[2]Our documents contain many direct or indirect quotations of this text; see Am. Letter 23; Pach. Instr. 1: 45; Hors. Test. 19 and 53.

[3]A part of the sentence in Coptic has been shifted and written twice. We could not ascertain whether the mistake was in the manuscript or is a misprint in Lefort's edition.

[4]This text is quoted also in Theo. Instr. 3: 5 and Hors. Test. 43. In both places, the beginning ('*The Lord is our God*'), which actually is not in Is 33:22, is replaced by '*The Lord is our father*' which is from Is 64:8.

SBo 102. [1]See a different application of this text below, ¶ 108.

[2]Omitted by haplography; restored from S^{3a}.

[3]Or 'to the household' (Av and Am).

[4]'. . . because you have accomplished his whole will' is the text from S^{3a}(= Av); it hangs together with the context better than 'by reason of the exercises you practise', which we read in Bo.

[5]This is another case of duplication of the same story. Bo 102, with its exact correspondent in Ag-Am, is absent in G[1], but Bo 92 and G[1] 100 have the shortened version of the same story, made by the common source of SBo-G[1]. See a similar case above, in SBo 74 and 77-78.

SBo 103 [1]This plural is surprising since the account has mentioned only one pillar up to this point. But G[1] 102 speaks of 'pillars' right from the start of the story.

[2]This text is quoted again below, ¶ 105.

[3]This passage was omitted by Bo. Fragments of it are found in S^{3a}, which can be complemented by Av (see Lefort, VC, p. 174).

[4]There is an account of the same vision in Am. Letter 12, and something similar in Paral. 17-18. Ammon states that this vision happened at the beginning of Pachomius' monastic life, just before he joined Palamon, and that it was during the time of archbishop Alexander. Since Alexander was archbishop from 313 to 328, this is consistent with our dating Pachomius' baptism in 313.

SBo 104. [1]Omitted by Bo; restored from S^{3a}.

[2]The pachomian *Koinonia* is called the vineyard of the Lord by Horsiesios, who uses this text of Is 5:7 in conjunction with Sg 8:11 in Hors. Test. 28. See also Hors. Test. 47; Hors. Instr. 3: 2. The image of the vine and the branches, from Jn 15, is used also in Pach. Instr. 1: 37 and Hors. Reg. 4.

SBo 105. [1]This text was quoted above, ¶ 9.

[2]Omitted by Bo; restored from S^{3a}.

[3]Omitted by haplography.

[4]In Coptic there seems to be a play on words: 'are you going to bring on their ruin (areten-*šeršôr*ou) by your scurrilous (*šerši*) words?'

[5]Ga 6:2 is often quoted; see Am. Letter 3; Pach. Letter 5: 11; Hors. Test. 11.

[6]See a similar combination of Ga 5:13 and Eph 4:2 in ¶ 107. Note the modification at the beginning of the quotation here: 'By the love of the Spirit' instead of 'in works of love' (NT) Ga 5:13 is quoted also in Pach. Letter 7: 1; Hors. Test. 26; Hors. Letter 3: 1.

SBo 106. [1]On the use of this image of the 'darnel', see above note SBo 6,2.

[2]The 'image of God' means a fellow-man. See Pach. Instr. 1: 22 and 36.

[3]Cf. the reflection of the author in G^1 after the departure of the first group of disciples (G^1 38). The similarity is all the more striking since in both cases it goes against the Gospel text (Mt 13:29-30) where the owner of the field orders his servants *not* to weed out the darnel but to let it grow till the harvest.

[4]Omitted by haplography; restored from Av. The order of the sentences in this ¶ is upset; we re-establish it as did Lefort: VC, p. 179, n. 6.

SBo 107 [1]Lit. 'the great one'; i.e. the elder of the group that went to Alexandria.

[2]Omitted in Bo.

[3]Bo says 'three hundred and sixty'; Av and Am say 'three hundred'. We are far from the large figures given by Jerome and Palladius. But this incident may have happened shortly after the foundation of Phbow or after the first group of foundations. Note that the Bohairic text speaks of 'the whole community (*ti thôouts têrs*) of the *Koinonia*; Lefort has inadvertently translated: 'toutes les communautés formant la Congrégation.'

[4]Although this is introduced as a scriptural quotation, we have been unable to find it in any canonical book of the Scriptures.

[5]Modern women will be right in seeing in this text a good example of the traditional male, chauvinistic, way of looking at the distinction between the sexes!

[6]This text, found again below in the same ¶, is quoted also above in ¶ 6 (= G^1 3).

[7]With Lefort, VC, p. 181, n. 10, and following Av and Am, we reestablish the right order of the sentences, upset in Bo.

[8]This text is applied to Theodore's spiritual progress in G^1 36.

[9]Pachomius uses the same expression when he warns some monks against reading Origen, in Paral. 7.

[10]The Bohairic text is corrupted; we follow S^5.

[11]Pachomius himself did not easily believe that he was sick; see ¶ 117; cf. G^1 52.

[12]We find the same scriptural reminiscence in G^1 96 and Theod. Instr. 3: 10.

[12]This part of the sentence, which does not hang together with the rest, is absent from the other witnesses of SBo (S^5, Av, Am).

[14]This text is quoted by Pachomius in G^1 85 to the brother who had sacrificed to the idols; see also Pach. Instr. 1: 59.

[15]This recommendation to accept either praises or insults with the same indifference is a theme familiar to Pachomius. We find it, v.g. in Pach. Instr. 1: 24.

SBo 108. [1]The same conception of the *Koinonia* as 'the life of the apostles' is found in Theodore: 'It is by a favor from God... that the holy *Koinonia* appeared upon earth, by which he made known the life of the apostles to men who desire to follow their model...' (Theod. Instr. 2: 1); 'that [Koinonia] has for its author after the apostles Apa Pachomius...' (Theod. Instr. 3: 5).

[2]There is some inconsistency in the Bohairic text: Pachomius saw that *one* brother had sinned and he prayed for *him*; then the angel told him to expel *them* and he expelled *them* the next morning. The Arabic version has the plural throughout the story. The inconsistency must therefore be attributed to the Bohairic translator or to a copist.

[3]The same text is quoted in Hors. Test. 28.

SBo 109 [1]In the rest of the Life the adjective δίκαιος is very often applied to Pachomius. Lefort translates it by 'feu' (our 'late' father Pachomius) in most of the cases, although not consistently. It is obviously a type of honorific title, and we prefer to translate it simply by 'righteous', which is the normal meaning of the word δίκαιος.

SBo 111 [1]Eight pages of the Bohairic manuscript are missing. The text can be reconstructed from fragments of S^2 complemented by Av, in the following order:

Av 87r–88r (cf. Am 562–564)
VS, p. 15,B,3–17,A,1
VS, p. 17,A,16–23,A,26.

SBo 112 [1]Here we abandon Av to translate from S^2 which, in this section, follows the group SBo.

SBo 113 [1]Pachomius recognizes that this apparition is from the demon by the fact that he is still thinking, since he stops thinking at all when he has an apparition from good spirits. The text is clearer in G^1 87. Cf. Also S^2 3.

[2]The short reflection of S^2 in VS, p. 17,A,2–16 (= VC p. 8, 29–32) does not belong to SBo (see Av and Am).

SBo 114. [1]In the Sahidic text, read *r*[*ô*]*me* instead of *ro*[*o*]*u*; see L. Lefort, VC, p. 9, note 16.

[2]This text is quoted also in Hors. Reg. 5 and 53.

[3]This text is quoted also in Hors. Test. 14 and Hors. Instr 4:2.

SBo 115. [1]Here we return to the Bohairic text.

[2]The Bohairic text is interrupted again by a long *lacuna* of 104 pages. The missing part has been reconstructed with texts from Av, S^2, S^5, S^6 and S^7. See explanations in the *Introduction*. The next few pages are taken from S^2 (Sahidic text in *Muséon* 1936, p. 223,A,1-B,14). A few gaps in the Sahidic text are filled with borrowings from Av 91, indicated by angular brackets (〈 〉).

SBo 116. [1]From this point to the end of ¶ 123, we translate from S^7 (Sahidic text in Lefort, VS, p. 86-96).

[2]See above, ¶ 88.

SBo 117. [1]Cf. G^1 52; see above, note SBo 107, 11.

[2]At the beginning of this sentence in Sahidic, there is a *hôsde* (so that...) which has no antecedent. Something seems to be missing.

SBo 118. [1]'He spent the four days of the Passover...' i.e. the *last* four days, since the Passover counted six days. Cf. Theodore's question to Pachomius in SBo 35: 'Since the Passover numbers six days...' On the question of 'joining' together days of fast, see above, SBo 31,2; on the terminology of the Passover, see note SBo 35, 1. The present ¶ seems to have been written at a later period, when the fast of the Forty Days and the fast of the Passover had become one.

[2]Pachomius will repeat this sentence again in ¶ 121, and Petronios will use it also on his deathbed. Cf. also *Vit. Ant.* 90: 'I am going the way of my fathers, as Scripture says'.

[3]This sentence is omitted by haplography in S^7. We take it from S^3 (VS, p. 124,A,16-18).

[4]Lefort, VC, p. 44, n. 14, establishes a parallel between this long negative confession and the one found in The Book of the Dead of ancient Egypt.

[5]See above, note SBo 95, 5.

[6]See above, note SBo 58, 2.

SBo 119. [1]Symptoms of the plague. G^1 114 says this explicitly: 'The disease was the plague....'

SBo 120. [1]The word *prêš* can mean a mantle or, in general, a blanket or any type of covering. G^1 understood 'covering', since it used the Greek στρῶμα, but we prefer to translate by 'mantle', which is the meansing that *prêš* usually has in our pachomian texts. That piece of clothing, called *palliolum* by Jerome (see above, note SBo 19, 1) was used during the night and especially by the sick; see Pr. 42, 61, 102, 105; and R. Draguet, 'Le chapitre de HL...', pp. 104-108.

[2]I.e. he saw that the mantle was different from the ones used by the rest of the brothers. Cf. Pr. 81.

SBo 121. [1]Av, like S^7, has 'before'; but S^3 has 'after'.

SBo 122. [1]Omitted by haplography; restored from Av; see Lefort, VC, p. 50, n. 28.

SBo 123. [1]Pachomius died on the fourteenth of Pašons, that is, the ninth of May on our calendar. He had been sick for a little more than forty days, for he told Theodore a few days before his death: 'I have been sick for forty days now', and his illness had started during the Passover. All this clearly indicates 346 as the year of his death. In that year Easter fell on the thirtieth of March (see Athanasius' *Festal Letters*, Index XVIII). The only other early dates of Easter during that period were 343 (27 March) and 349 (26 March).

[2]This parallel between Theodore and Joseph will be drawn again by the brothers in SBo 165, and by Theodore himself in SBo 199.

[3]Paphnouti is usually given the title of 'Great Steward' (οἰκονόμος); here he is called *prefčiêpe* (the accountant).

[4]According to these indications, Pachomius, if he really died in 346, would have been born in 286 and would have become monk in 307; which goes against a great number of clear chronological indications of the Lives and of Ammon's Letter. These figures must therefore, be considered as an awkward attempt by a late compiler or scribe to enlighten his readers.

[5]The codex S^7 and the Vatican Arabic version (Av) end the Life of Pachomius at this point. For what follows and can be considered an *Appendix* to the Life, covering the period of the superiorships of Horsiesios and Theodore till the death of the latter, we must rely on three fragmentary documents: Bo, S^5 and S^6. From S^{3b}, which contains sections of the *Appendix* amalgamated with long homilitic developments, we will borrow only the last few lines of this long Life. On the manner in which we have reorganized these documents into a continuous text, see the *Introduction*. Note that our numbering of paragraphs differs at times from that of Lefort's French translation. Our ¶¶ 124-138 (taken from S^5; Sahidic text in Lefort, VS, pp. 174-187) correspond to S^5 118-132 in Lefort's translation (VC, pp. 264-278).

SBo 124. [1]The first few words of this ¶ are borrowed from the parallel text in S^6 (Text in Lefort, VS, p. 265, B, 21-25).

[2]Here again the chronological indications of the Coptic Life are incompatible with history. Theodore and other brothers are supposed to have left for Alexandria sometime between 9 May 346 (the date of Pachomius' death) and 19 July of the same year (the date of Petronios' death). They are going to visit the patriarch Athanasius, and Petronios gives them a letter to take to Athanasius. This is impossible, because Athanasius was still in exile at the time and would return to Alexandria only on 21 October 346. (See Ath. *Festal Letters*, Index XVIII). The story of the letter and the visit to Athanasius must be an invention of a late compiler ignorant of Athanasius' movements.

SBo 125. [1]The figure of Daniel's faithfulness and his delivery from the fiery furnace are evoked in Pach. Instr. 1: 15 and 25, as well as in Hors. Letter 4: 4.

[2]The expression applied to Petronios here will be applied to Horsiesios hereafter: see ¶¶ 132, 133, and 201.

SBo 126. [1]We know from Palladius (H.L. 21) that after Maximinus Daia's persecution Antony abandoned his Outer Mountain, called Pispir (or

Tiloč), near the Nile, and withdrew to the Inner Mountain, Mount Kolzim, toward the Red Sea. But, according to a pact made with his disciples of Pispir, he would come from time to time to the Outer Mountain. The trip of the pachomian monks happened to be during one of these visits.

SBo 127. [1]We read practically the same sentence in *Vit Ant.* 3. This shows a literary dependence of at least this *Appendix* of the Life of Pachomius on the *Vita Antonii.*

[2]Lit. 'our habit' (*schêma*).

[3]This praise of the cenobitic life by Antony is probably an artifice of pachomian biographers using Antony's authority to bolster their own way of life.

SBo 129. [1]S[5] normally uses the word *heneete* as the name for the monastery, while Bo usually translates it by the Greek word μοναστήριον. It is interesting to note here that S[5], while reserving *heneete* for the pachomian monasteries, uses μοναστήριον when he speaks of Antony's monastery.

[2]These Meletians were the followers of Meletios, bishop of Lycopolis in Egypt, not to be confused with the other Meletians, followers of Meletios of Antioch, a half century later. This early Meletian schism seems to have originated with Meletios' disagreement with Peter, archbishop of Alexandria († 311), over the treatment of the *lapsi* during the Decian persecution. In Am. Letter 12, Pachomius relates that he was bothered by them during his first years as a Christian, in the time of the patriarch Alexander. Later on, the Meletians went into the camp of the Arians and were bitter enemies of Athanasius.

[3]This text is quoted also in Pach. Instr. 1:33.

SBo 130. [1]According to G[1] 117, Petronios died the twenty-seventh of Epip, that is the twenty-first of July. Lefort suggests the possibility of an error in Greek. But the MS. Ath. 1015 (fol. 61^r,) has ἑβδόμῃ καὶ εἰκάδι written out in full, as does Halkin's edition. This divergence of two days remains unexplained.

SBo 132 [1]Two pages of the manuscript of S[5] are missing, without any parallel text to allow us to fill the gap.

SBo 133. [1]Here begins the text of a letter written by Antony to the brothers to console them for Petronios' death, which he has heard of in the two missing pages. . .

SBo 136. [1]See note SBo 126, 1.

SBo 137. [1]G[1] 121 tells us before this that Horsiesios appointed Theodore housemaster of the builders in Phbow, and says it is Macarios who asked Horsiesios to send Theodore to Phnoum to work at the bakery. The text of S[5] makes much more sense.

SBo 138. [1]Our ¶ 138 corresponds to S[5] 132 and the beginning of S[5] 133 in Lefort's numbering. The end of this last ¶ is missing. It is difficult to evaluate the length of the *lacuna* between that ¶ and the section of S[6] that we will use in the next few ¶¶ (Sahidic text in Lefort, VS, p. 268-280).

SBo 139. [1]There is a clear allusion to this crisis in Theod. Instr. 3:46.
[2]The meaning of *efcoole*, which we translate by 'patched', is uncertain.

SBo 140. [1]See above ¶ 94 (= G[1] 106-107).
[2]These seven years comprise the two years of Theodore's great penance and the five years that followed. According to G[1] 131, Horsiesios' resignation took place less than five years after Pachomius' death. This permits us to place the beginning of Theodore's penance a little more than two years before Pachomius' death and his rehabilitation shortly before the founder's death.
[3]Two pages of the manuscript of S[6] are missing. The content of this *lacuna* can easily be inferred from G[1] 130, 11-21.

SBo 141. [1]This is the only case where the word *Koinonia* is used in the plural form to designate the local communities. *Koinonia* usually means the whole assembly of the brothers from all nine monasteries.
[2]This text is quoted again, in a similar context, in Hors. Letter 4: 4.
[3]Compare to this the vision Pachomius had at the beginning of his monastic life, when he was told that his mission was to 'fashion souls so as to present them pure to God' (S[1] 7).
[4]We continue to follow S[6] although a fragment of S[5] begins here.

SBo 142. [1]This expression, as well as many others of this ¶ suggests clearly that Theodore did not only become the coadjutor of Horsiesios, but that Horsiesios was effectively 'removed from his position' and that Theodore was 'installed in his place'. The biographers seem to have been embarrassed by the situation, and there may be something suspicious in their eagerness to show Theodore's reluctance to accept the office and his deference to Hosiesios.
[2]For this sentence we follow S[5], which gives a better meaning than S[6].
[3]Cf. Pach. Instr. 1: 42.
[4]See above, note SBo 6, 2. Also, compare this passage with Hors. Test. 47.
[5]End of the parallel S[5] fragment.
[6]Pachomius uses Is 53:10 in a similar call to repentance, in Pach. Instr. 1: 31.
[7]In the Sahidic text, read *enšan-* (if we) instead of *eušan-* (if they). See Lefort, VC, p. 329, n. 30.
[8]Lk 6:36 is quoted also in Theod. Instr. 3: 15, where we read 'Be compassionate, *for*. . .', as here, instead of 'Be compassionate *as*. . .', as in the N.T.
[9]Four pages of the S[6] manuscript are missing.
[10]The Sahidic text seems faulty; correction *ad sensum* by Lefort, VC, p. 330, n. 41-42-43.
[11]The end of ¶ 142, the whole of ¶ 143, and the beginning of ¶ 144 are translated from a Bohairic fragment, parallel to S[6] (Text in Lefort, VB, p. 155-158). In Lefort's translation (VC, p. 191-193), these ¶¶ are numbered Bo 165-166-167.
[12]Allusion to Theodore's great penance; see SBo 94-95.

SBo 143. [1]Correct *n̄tafsemnêtou* by *etaf-*. See Lefort, VC, p. 192, n. 1.

SBo 144. [1]The next page of the Bohairic fragment being in a very poor state, we return to S[6] (Text in Lefort, VS, p. 278, 33-280,5).

[2]Here the context shows clearly that *noc* (= Boh. *ništi*) is the equivalent of ἡγούμενος, and designates the father of the monastery.

[3]About the two annual meetings of all the brothers, see above, notes SBo 71, 2-3. Although these two meetings were the normal time for appointments already in Pachomius' time, the systematic transfer of the local superiors from one place to another on these occasions seems to have been initiated by Theodore. Cf. G[1] 122.

SBo 145. [1]Here begins a long section of S[5] (Text in Lefort, VS, p. 189-197).

[2]The patience of 'the righteous Job' is often given as an example, but we find no explanation for this isolated mention of him as a *king*. See SBo 82 and Theod. Instr. 3: 2, where he is named along with David.

[3]Moses is one of the saints of the O.T. who are often given as models to monks. Heb 11:25 is quoted in a similar context also in Pach. Instr. 1: 32.

[4]In the Sahidic text, read *n̄hê[tou č]ehen* (see Lefort, VC, p. 281, n. 11).

SBo 147. [1]Nothing else is known of this Akulas or of his office as bookkeeper for the Great Steward.

[2]Although all the monks had to learn how to read (see Pr. 139-140), those who could write must have been very few.

SBo 148. [1]'But that brother knew also...'; one would expect a negative sentence, and, in fact, Lefort translates 'en fait ce frère aussi *ignorait*...' But the Coptic sentence is positive.

[2]This is a frequent and very concrete expression of eternal punishment.

SBo 150. [1]This text of 1 S is often quoted. See G[1] 99; Hors. Reg. 52; Pach. Instr. 1: 22.

SBo 151. [1]Two pages of the manuscript are missing. No other Coptic text is extant, but G[1] 133 is a good parallel.

SBo 154. [1]The meaning of *apopraipositos* is obscure; perhaps 'ex-prefect'? Lefort understands 'sous-préposé', which supposes *upopraipositos* instead of *apo-*. We prudently ignore the prefix and translate it 'prefect'.

SBo 155. [1]This verse is actually understood in a spiritural meaning in Hors. Letter 3: 2.

[2]This ends the S[5] fragment and we return to the Bohairic manuscript for the rest of the Life. We shall follow Lefort's numbering of the ¶¶, but we must note that the *lacuna* between our ¶ 155 and ¶ 180 is probably much shorter than the numbering seems to indicate.

SBo 180. [1]The fact that the beginning of this ¶ is missing makes it difficult for us to determine the exact date of this outburst of plague.

[2]This word is absent from the Bohairic text, but it is required by the context.

[3]The mountain (or desert) was traditionally the burial place for the Copts (see above, note SBo 18, 3). The brothers were distressed because if the water of the Nile continued to rise they would no longer be able to carry the bodies of the deceased brothers to the mountain on foot. On the other hand, the parallel text in G[1] 139 explains that there was not enough water yet to use the boat for that purpose.

[4]Lit. '. . . none of the words . . . passed away.'

SBo 181. [1]This seems to be another Paphnouti than Theodore's brother. The latter died during the outburst of the plague during which Pachomius and many other ancient brothers passed away. See above, ¶ 119 (= G[1] 114). There was probably a third Paphnouti, who was for a time superior of Phbow; see G[1] 124, note 1.

SBo 182. [1]The same text is quoted in S[1] 13 (in the story of Pachomius putting up with the ill conduct of his first disciples); and again in S[1] 25.

SBo 183. [1]Pachomian monks did not use wool for their clothes. Except for the hood, about which they give no detail, Jerome and the Rules say explicitly of all the clothes that they were of linen. See Jer. Pref. 4 (mantle and belt); Pr. 2 (tunic); Pr. 61, 102, 128 (mantle); Hors. Test. 22 (belt). Woolen garments are explicitly excluded by Pr. 81.

[2]This text is quoted by Pachomius in G[1] 90, to exhort Theodore to be patient in trials, and here by Theodore himself (¶ 145), to invite the brothers to detachment.

[3]In the Bohairic text, read ⟨*n̄*⟩*tenšephmot* (see Lefort, VC, p. 195, n.2.)

[4]This text is quoted again in Hors. Test. 44.

SBo 184. [1]There is a reminiscence of this text, in a similar context, in Am. Letter 14.

[2]This is one of the very rare cases, in either our Coptic or Greek texts, where the word ἐκκλησία is used of the oratory of the monastery. The oratory is usually called *synaxis*, or 'assembly room'. G[1] and Paral. never use ἐκκλησία in this sense, but Am. Letter does four times. See Am. Letter, 12, n.1.

[3]In G[1] 48 this text is applied to the unintermittent clairvoyance by which the saints see God constantly.

[4]This text is used again in G[1] 94 to express the faith in the Lord's presence in the midst of the praying community; it is quoted in Hors. Reg. 2 also.

SBo 185. [1]In G[1] 137, it is the brothers who want to return to Phbow right away in order to arrive there before the duke, lest he should trouble the community.

[2]In conformity with the system of administration set up for Egypt by Diocletian in 297, each of the three 'epistragies' or provinces (the Delta or Egypt proper, the Etanomidis, and the Thebaid) was administered by a governor (ἡγεμών) under the authority of a civilian 'prefect' and a military 'general' called 'duke', residing in Alexandria. (See M. Gelzer, *Studien zur byzantinischen Verwaltung Aegyptens* [Leipzig, 1909] p. 5; J.G. Milne, *A History of Egypt under Roman Rule* [London, 1924] pp. 1-24.) Artemios succeeded Sebastianos as duke of Egypt. We know from the Index to the

Festal Letters that he instituted a search for the fugitive Athanasius in 360. G^1 137 adds that this happened during the persecution of the emperor Constantius (353-361) against Athanasius. Artemios was put to death by Julian the Apostate in 362 and he was therefore venerated as a martyr throughout the Church in spite of his Arian past. This may explain why he does not come out as a persecutor in the present story. Lefort, VC, p. 199, n. 7, mistakenly identifies this search for Athanasius by Artemios with bishop Ammon's report of Athanasius' flight to the Thebaid at the time of Julian's death in 363 (Am. Letter 34). See D.J. Chitty, 'Pachomian Sources Reconsidered', p. 42.

[3] *Praipositai* (without prefix); see above, note SBo 154, 1.

[4] This curious mention of 'a Persian' is not found in G^1 138; but it can be explained by the fact that Constantius was at war with the Persians.

[5] Lit. 'the one who was the great one among the brothers', i.e. the father of the monastery.

[6] In G^1 138, they do not want to pray with the duke because there is an Arian bishop in his retinue.

[7] Am. Letter 31 mentions briefly the role of Artemios in the persecution of the orthodox bishops under Constantius. Athanasius was driven out of Alexandria on 8 February 356. It is during that exile that Athanasius, who hid in the desert with the monks, wrote the *Life of Antony*. He came back to Alexandria in 361, only to be driven into exile again in 362, until Julian's death in 363.

SBo 186. [1] A cubit is a measure of length corresponding to the length of the arm from the end of the middle finger to the elbow; about 18-22 inches.

[2] G^1 99 and 142 refer to what seems to have been very early collections of homilies or instructions of Pachomius, his νοήματα τῶν Γραφῶν. What follows may be the teaching of Pachomius related by Theodore rather than Theodore's teaching. See D.J. Chitty, 'Pachomian Sources Reconsidered', pp. 51-52.

[3] In the Bohairic text, read *af‹šan›štem*; see Lefort, VC, p. 202, n. 13.

[4] The Bohairic text is obscure and probably corrupt; we follow the correction proposed by Lefort, VC, p. 202, n. 14.

[5] This text is quoted also in G^1 131

[6] This text is quoted also in Pach. Instr. 1: 23 and Theod. Instr. 3: 32.

[7] This text is quoted also in Pach. Instr. 1: 37 and Pach. Letter 7: 3.

[8] A similar allusion to Rm 8:17 occurs in Hors. Test. 18.

SBo 187. [1] This text is quoted also in Hors. Test. 20, in a similar context.

SBo 189. [1] On this festal letter and its mention by Theodore, see L.-T. Lefort, 'Théodore de Tabennèse et la lettre festale de S. Athanase sur le canon de la Bible', in *Muséon* 29 (1910) 205-216. The Egyptian monks received the annual festal letters of the Patriarch of Alexandria, and we know that it was Theophilos' festal letter of 398 that started the Origenist controversy.

[2] We find the same interpretation of this text in G^1 135; see also Paral. 18 (twice) and Theod. Instr. 3: 32.

[3] This text, applied here to Athanasius, is applied to Pachomius in G^1 41.

SBo 190. [1] This text is quoted again below, ¶ 194.

SBo 191. [1]S^{3b} adds: 'and neglected to sleep on their [reclining] seats in conformity with the rule.' About these reclining seats for sleeping, see Pr. 87 with note 2 *ibidem*.

[2]Words omitted by haplography.

[3]This text is not from Isaiah. Lefort thinks it could be an allusion to Nb 33:52-53.

SBo 192. [1]Ps 55(54):22 is quoted in Pach. Instr. 1: 34.

SBo 193. [1]The meaning of the Coptic word *ouôt* in this context is uncertain. See Crum, *Coptic Dictionary*, p. 493 B.

SBo 194. [1]Ac 4:32 is fully quoted in S^1 11 as the model for the way of life of the *Koinonia*. There is another shorter quotation in Theod. Instr. 3: 23.

[2]The same expression is applied to the early monks in SBo 2 (= G^1 2).

[3]This text is also quoted in S^1 18.

[4]This text is also quoted in Hors. Test. 20.

[5]Pachomius is constantly called 'a just (or righteous) man.' In the *Appendix* to the Life, it has become his normal honorific title.

SBo 196. [1]Under the Roman rule Egypt remained very 'Coptic' and the Greek language and culture penetrated very little except in the province of the Delta. But Alexandria was a Greek-speaking metropolis, and many of its inhabitants would not have known Coptic at all.

[2]It is generally admitted that the core of Pachomius' Life was first written by Theodore's disciples after they had listened to what he told them about the father of the *Koinonia*. It is not surprising therefore that the biographers have given such a prominent place to their father Theodore in that Life, which often has the appearance of an *apologia pro Theodoro*.

SBo 197. [1]In ¶ 204, below, Theodore refuses to use a boat in protest against the multiplication of boats in the monasteries. The material growth of the community is once more causing a crisis, and after seventeen years of superiorship Theodore is facing the same situation that brought him to power after Horsiesios' resignation (¶ 139). G^1 does not mention the visit of Theodore to Horsiesios related here.

[2]We have left this typically Coptic sentence in its original form, with its ambivalent use of personal pronouns. Who is who is any translator's guess!

SBo 198. [1]See another allusion to Ps 33(32):22 in Theod. Instr. 2: 3.

[2]The Bohairic text seems corrupt; see the correction made by Lefort, VC, p. 219, n. 11.

SBo 201. [1]Athanasius' trip to Upper Egypt took place in 363. He was then in flight from Julian the Apostate, having left Alexandria on 24 October 362.

[2]These two monasteries were founded by Theodore; see G^1 134.

[3]See above, note SBo 125, 2.

[4]The carrying of the cross is one of the central themes of pachomian spirituality. See, v.g. G^1 7, 74, 108; Pach. Instr. 1: 19, 32, etc. On this theme in Horsiesios, see H. Bacht, '. . . Vexillum crucis sequi . . .'

[5]There is a similar allusion to 1 Co 9:25 in Pach. Instr. 1:50.

SBo 202. [1]The Bohairic text has: 'to the *monastery* of Nouoi and Kahior', which is certainly a mistake, since they were two distinct monasteries. These two monasteries were founded by Theodore 'with our father Horsiesios' approval'; see G^1 134.

[2]This is the first and normal meaning of διάθεσις: disposition, arrangement, etc. although it can be understood (as G^1 did) of the spiritual dispositions of the brothers toward Athanasius.

[3]The Bohairic translator is consistent with his using of the singular (see above, note SBo 202, 1). G^1 134 has simply ἐκεῖ, in Halkin's edition following the Ms. F; but in the *Ambrosianus* and the *Atheniensis* (fol. 77v) manuscripts, we read ἐν τοῖς μοναστηρίοις.

SBo 204. [1]Above, ¶ 139 (= G^1 127).

[2]This text is applied to Theodore in G^1 78.

SBo 205. [1]See the beginning of ¶ 199.

SBo 206. [1]These words are very similar to those of Pachomius in ¶ 121 (end).

[2]Words omitted by Bo; restored from S^5.

[3]Theodore presented to the brothers the festal letter of Athanasius on the Canon of the Scriptures (above, ¶ 189), which was the letter of 367; therefore he certainly died after that date. In ¶ 199, he says that he has served as the superior of the *Koinonia* for eighteen years. Horsiesios having resigned in 350 (less than five years after his appointment in 346), we are left with 368 as the year for Theodore's death. The date of Easter that year fits very well with the details given in the present ¶. In 368 Easter fell on the twentieth of April. Theodore fell ill three days after he had seen the brothers on their way and died some days later, on the twenty-seventh of April. The year 369, in which Easter fell on the twelfth of April would be another possibility, but 368 is generally accepted with very good reason as the most probable date.

SBo 207. [1]In G^1 149 this is done by Naphersaes, the second of Phbow.

SBo 208. [1]The scribe of Bo has written 'Apa Šeneset', which is an obvious mistake, since Šeneset has never been a person's name. Lefort (VC, p. 230, n. 1) has corrected it in Apa Pšentaesi. Pšentaesi belonged to the group of the three first disciples of Pachomius (see SBo 23).

[2]This is Pachomius *the younger* of course. He belonged to the second group of five brothers who came to Pachomius at the very beginning of the *Koinonia* (SBo 24).

[3]This text, rather paraphrased here, is also quoted in Theod. Letter 2: 4.

[4]This is the only mention in the Life of Pachomius of a celebration of the Eucharist on the third day after the death of a monk. But we know from other sources that it was a custom in the early Church to celebrate the Eucharist for a deceased person on the third, the ninth (or the seventh) and the fortieth (or thirtieth) days, as well as on the anniversary. See E. Freistedt, *Altchristliche Totengedächtnistage und ihre Beziehung zum Jenseitsglauben und Totenkultus des Antike, Liturgiegeschichtliche Quellen und Forschungen* 24 (Münster i. W., 1928); about Egypt, see pp. 16-26; on the importance of the three days following death, see pp. 73-89.

SBo 209. [1]Lit. 'his warmth'. S^{3b} and G^1 118 have 'his fear'.

[2]In G^1 118 this instruction is placed at the beginning of Horsiesios' first tenure of office as superior of the *Koinonia*. This parable of the lamp is found in the *Apophthegmata* collections (PG 65:316; PL 73:938).

SBo 210. [1]Neither S^{3b} nor G^1 mentions the presence of Athanasius at Šmoun at that time.

[2]The meaning is that Theodore is still alive in the person of Horsiesios. Cf. G^1 150.

[3]The last pages (probably only two) of Bo are missing. But S^{3b} gives us the end of Athanasius' letter. (Sahidic text in Lefort, VS, p. 302,B,25-303,B,14).

[4]A short *lacuna* in the text of S^{3b} is restored from G^1 150.

[5]Cf. SBo 97 where Theodore is said to have carried out the same ministry together with Pachomius and in the same spirit.

THE FIRST GREEK LIFE

(G[1])

THE WORD OF GOD, who made all things, is truth. That Word came to our father Abraham at the end of what had been well-pleasing to him, the sacrifice of his only son as a whole-burnt offering. The Lord said, *I will shower blessings on you, I will make your descendants as many as the stars of heaven*, and again, *All the nations of the earth shall bless themselves in you by your seed*. Speaking after Moses his servant and the other prophets, the same Word appeared as man and as the seed of Abraham and he fulfilled the promise of blessing to all nations, saying to his disciples, *Go and make disciples of all the nations, baptizing them in the name of the Father and of the Son and of the Holy Spirit.*

SBo 1. **Prologue**

Gn 22:17.

Gn 22:18.

Mt 28:19.

Then as the Gospel spread throughout the whole world, by permission of God and to put faith in Him to the test, pagan emperors stirred up a great persecution against Christians everywhere. And when many martyrs, including Peter the archbishop of Alexandria, after many various tortures unto death had received their crowns, faith in Christ increased greatly in

† 24 Nov. 311.

strength throughout the Churches in every country and island. From that time on there began to
appear monasteries and places of ascetics hon-
ored for their chastity and renunciation of possessions. When those who from being pagans had
become monks had seen the struggles and patient endurance of the martyrs, they began to
renew their life. Of them it was said, *They were*
destitute, afflicted, maltreated; they wandered
over deserts and mountains, in dens and caves of
Heb 11:37-38. *the earth*. Thus they raised themselves by a
stricter *ascesis* and a befitting reverence, to keep
their eyes by both night and day, looking not only
to Christ crucified but also to the martyrs whom
they had seen take up the struggle as they had.

SBo 2, 3. 2. The life of our most ascetic and truly vir-
Beginning of monasticism tuous father Antony was like that of the great
Elijah, of Elisha, and of John the Baptist, as the
most holy archbishop Athanasius attests in
writing.[1] For he wrote about him after his death,
revealing at the same time the same conduct of
our holy father Amoun, arch-monk of the brothers on the mountain of Nitria, and of Theodore, his companion. We know that because *in-*
*Is 35:10; 50:11. *stead of sorrow and lamentation* grace has*
†Ps 45(44):2. *poured forth from the lips of*† the blessed one
‡Cf. Eph 1:3. who blesses all‡—for *he visited the earth** and
*Ps 65(64):9. made it drunk—[2] wonderful fathers were given
to the monks in every land, as we have said
earlier, and their *names are written in the book*
Ph 4:3 *of the living*.

In Egypt and the Thebaid there had not been
many of them. But after the persecution of
AD 284-305 Diocletian and Maximian, the conversion of
305-306. pagans increased throughout the Church—the

bishops leading them to God according to the Apostles' teaching—and began to bear much fruit. And there was a man called Pachomius, who was also born of pagan parents in the Thebaid.[3] He received the great mercy of becoming a Christian and, making progress, he became a perfect monk. We ought to recount his life from childhood, to the glory of God who from all sides *calls* all men *into his wonderful light*.

c. AD 292.

1 P 2:9.

3. As a child he went one day with his parents to an idol's temple to sacrifice to the phantoms of demons in the river.[1] When the priest in charge of the sacrifice saw him, he had him chased out of the place, shouting angrily, 'Chase the enemy of the gods out of here.' On hearing this, his parents became very grieved about him, that he should be an enemy of the so-called gods—who are not gods at all—all the more so because on yet another occasion they had given him wine to drink from the libations there, and immediately the child had vomited what he had drunk.

SBo 4, 6.

Pachomius' childhood

After he became a monk, as he was telling the monks around him about his childhood, he told them about this. 'Do not think,' he said, 'that the demons, who know nothing good, had me driven out on that occasion because they knew beforehand that I was later going to receive mercy through the true faith. Rather, they saw I hated evil even then—for *God made man upright*—and it was for this reason that they thought to themselves, "Will he not really be a fearer of God later on?", and so their servants chased me out.'

Qo 7:29(30).

SBo 7a.
Pachomius is conscripted

4. After the persecution, the great Constantine, the first-fruit of the Christian emperors of the Romans, ruled. Making war against some tyrant, he ordered many conscripts to be impressed.[1] Pachomius himself, who was then about twenty years old, was impressed. As the conscripts were sailing downstream, the soldiers who were keeping them put in at the city of Thebes and held them in prison there. In the evening some merciful Christians, hearing about them, brought them something to eat and drink and other necessities, because they were in distress. When the young man asked about this, he was told that Christians were merciful to everyone, including strangers. Again he asked what a Christian was. They told him, 'They are men who bear the name of Christ, the only begotten Son of God, and they do good to everyone, putting their hope in Him who made heaven and earth and us men.'

SBo 7b, 8.
Pachomius' conversion

*1 S 1:11; cf. Lk 1:48.
†Jn 17:3.

Cf. Lk 22:26.

5. Hearing of this great grace, his heart was set on fire with the fear of God and with joy. Withdrawing alone in the prison, he raised his hands to heaven in prayer and said, 'O God, maker of heaven and earth, *if you will look upon me in my lowliness,** because I do not *know you, the only true God,*†[1] and if you will deliver me from this affliction, I will serve your will all the days of my life and, loving all men, I will be their servant according to your command.' After saying this prayer he set sail with them. Although he was often importuned in the cities by his companions to worldly pleasures and other disorderly affairs, he avoided them, remembering the grace of God which had come to him. For he had loved chastity even from his childhood.

Constantine defeated his adversaries and the conscripts were then discharged by an imperial edict. Pachomius went to the Upper Thebaid, and came to the church of a village called Chenoboskion. There he was instructed and baptized. The night he was made worthy of the mystery, he had a dream. He saw the dew of heaven descend upon him. When the dew had collected in his right hand and turned into solid honey and the honey had dropped onto the ground, he heard someone say to him, 'Understand what is happening, for it will happen to you later.'

AD 313.

6. Then, moved by the love of God, he sought to become a monk.[1] When he was told of an anchorite called Palamon, he went to him to share his anchoritic life. When he arrived, he knocked on the door. The old man looked down from above and said, 'What do you want?'—for he was abrupt in speech. He replied, 'I ask you, father, make me a monk.' He said to him, 'You cannot. This work of God is not so simple; for many have come but have not persevered.' Pachomius said, 'Put me to the test at it and see'. The old man spoke again, 'First try yourself out for a while, then come here again. For I have a hard *ascesis*. In summer I fast daily and in winter I eat every other day. By the grace of God I eat nothing but bread and salt. I am not in the habit of [using] oil and wine. I keep vigil as I was taught, always spending half the night and often the whole night in prayer and reciting of the words of God.' When the youth heard the old man say this, he was still more strengthened in spirit to endure every hardship with him. 'I believe,' he said to him, 'that with the help of God and your prayers,

SBo 10.

Pachomius coming to Palamon
c. AD 316.

I will endure all you have told me.' Then opening the door, [the old man] let him in and clothed him in the monk's habit.

They practised the *ascesis* together and gave time to prayers. Their work consisted of spinning and weaving hair sacks. In their work they toiled not for themselves but they *remembered the*

Ga 2:10.

poor, as the Apostle says. If when the old man was keeping vigil, he saw that sleep was weighing them down, they both went out to the sand [field] of the mountain. Then they carried [sand] in baskets from one place to another, giving the body labor in order to stay awake for prayer. The old man would say, 'Stay awake, Pachomius, lest

Cf. Mt 26:41; 1 Co 7:5.

Satan tempt and harm you.' Seeing his obedience in everything and his progress in endurance, the old man rejoiced at his salvation.

SBo 11.

Palamon's fasting

7. On the Day of Joy after the Passover,[1] he said to him, 'Since today is the christian feast, rise up, prepare lunch for us.' In preparing it, he put some oil into the crushed salt, which was, as was said above, what they eat—sometimes [they eat] also charlock without oil or vinegar, and they often mix ashes into the salt[2]—then he invited [the old man] to eat. Having come to what had been laid out, he saw the oil in the salt. He struck his face and began to weep and said, 'The Lord was crucified and am I to eat oil?' Even when the saucer was emptied out and he was asked with respect, he barely agreed to sit down and eat as was their custom. Such was Palamon the saint,

*Cf. Mt 10:38; Lk 9:23; 14:27. †Ibid.

always *carrying the cross,*[3]* according to the word of our Saviour, and *following Him*† with humble heart.

SBo 14.

8. Once as they kept vigil there was a fire in

front of them. Another brother who by that time had come to stay with them got up and said to the old man, 'Whichever of you has faith, let him stand on these charcoals and pray the prayer of the Gospel.' The old man, realizing that this was a word of pride, rebuked him saying, 'Stop talking like that, for you are deceived.' Not taking any note of what [the old man] said, he stepped onto the charcoals and said the prayer. When he got off, he saw the activity of the demons [realized] by divine permission: his feet were not burnt. His heart was kindled yet more, as it is written, *To the devious God sends devious ways.*

Story of a boastful monk

Cf. Mt 6:9.

Cf. Pr 6:28-29.

Pr 21:8.

So he withdrew from them and retired alone far away. The demon who had deceived him in this, seeing he had him in hand, took the form of a beautiful, exquisitely adorned woman and came knocking on the door where he was. When he opened it, she said to him, 'I am troubled by creditors pursuing me for repayment when I have not got the means. I beg you, take me into your cell till they have passed.' In the clouding of his conscience he did not discern what this might be and he let her in. As the demon spurred him on to evil desire, he inclined to sin. As he drew near to do this, the demon struck him down in a fit and he lay on the ground as one dead.

After some days he came to his senses a little. He went weeping to them[1] and said trembling, 'I am the cause of my own ruin. You warned me many times and I did not listen. Help me nevertheless in my wretchedness. For I am in danger of being destroyed by the demon.' As he was saying this, and the others were weeping for him, suddenly the demon overpowered him in a similar way and he leapt outside. Running a long way up the mountain, he came to a city called Panopolis.[2] A little while later, when he was beside himself, the demon threw him into the furnace of the bathhouse and he was burnt.

SBo 15a.
Pachomius' virtues
Pr 4:23.

9. Seeing this as an invitation to fear the offence,[1] Pachomius cared still more *to guard his heart* in every way, as it is written. So much so that the good old man was amazed at him, because he not only eagerly endured the open intensive *ascesis* but applied himself to cleanse his conscience perfectly to fulfil the law of God, looking to the greater *hope in heaven.*[2] When he began to read or to write by heart the words of God, he did not do this in a loose way or as many do, but worked over each thing to assimilate it all with a humble mind in gentleness and in truth, as the Lord says, *Learn from me, for I am gentle and humble of heart.*[3]

Col 1:5.

Mt 11:29.

Sources of this Life

10. We learned about these things from the fathers of old who lived a long time with him. For he would often recount these things to them after explaining the words of the holy Scriptures. But we would not be able to put down most of what we heard, but only part.[1]

SBo 15b.
Pachomius' mortifications

11. Around that mountain was a desert full of thorns where he was frequently sent to gather and carry wood. And since he was barefoot, he was sorely troubled for some time by the thorns which fixed themselves in his feet.[1] But he endured them, remembering the nails in the hands and feet of the Saviour on the Cross. He used to stand especially in the desert for prayer, asking God to deliver him and all men from the deceitfulness of the enemy. And so was he greatly beloved of God.

12. Once, journeying through that desert a considerable distance, he came to a deserted village called Tabennesi. There he prayed to express his love of God. And as he protracted his prayer a voice came to him—until that time he had not yet had a vision—and the voice said to him, 'Stay here and build a monastery; for many will come to you to become monks'. When he heard this and in purity of heart discerned according to the Scriptures that the voice was holy, he returned to his father and told him about it. He had to use great persuasion, for his father was greatly grieved, because he held him as his true son. Then they both made their way to the place and they built a cabin or a small cell. Then the old man said, 'Since I believe this has come to you from God, let us make a covenant between us, that we shall visit each other in turn, you and I, so as not to be separated from each other from now on.' This they did as long as Palamon, the true athlete of Christ, lived.

SBo 17.

Pachomius' vocation to build a monastery

c. AD 323.

13. After this the holy Palamon suffered in his spleen from ascetic practices which were beyond his capacity. His body was weak all over. For often he ate without drinking water and at other times he drank without eating anything. Having been counselled and persuaded by some brothers and a doctor to take care of himself so that he might be healed, for a few days he ate what was appropriate to his sickness. Then, having realized that the trouble was still continuing, he put those foods aside, saying, 'If the martyrs of Christ, having their limbs cut off and being beheaded or burnt, persevered to death in their faith in God, shall I be a coward in a very minor

SBo 16, 18.

Palamon's illness and death

Cf. Heb 11:33-37.

trouble and must I give in? Although I was persuaded to eat the foods thought capable of giving comfort, there has been no improvement. So if I return to the rigorous *ascesis* in which is all comfort I will be healed, for I do it not according to men but according to God.' So courageously giving himself to *ascesis,* he fell ill after a month. Pachomius was visiting him from Tabennesi. Sitting at his side, he tended his father as was appropriate until God visited him. Our father Pachomius buried him and returned to his own place of *ascesis.*

c. AD 323.

SBo 19a.

The coming of John, Pachomius' brother
c. AD 323.

14. His brother according to the flesh, who was called John, heard [about him] and came to him. Pachomius rejoiced greatly when he saw him, for he had never visited his relatives since coming back after his discharge. John, choosing the same life, remained with him. And there they both were, having nothing save the law of God. For if they obtained anything from their labors, they gave the surplus to those in need, keeping for themselves what was necessary to live. In clothing, too, they were exceedingly poor, so [poor] that they did not soon have a second tunic to wear while they washed the one they wore. Our father Pachomius often put on a hair garment to humble the flesh. And for a long time whenever he wanted to refresh his body with sleep after growing weary in keeping awake for prayer, he would simply sit on something in the middle of the place without leaning his back against the wall. This he did for about fifteen years. Many of the ancient fathers, hearing or rather seeing this, tried also to humble the flesh by this and similar practices to enhance the salvation of their souls.

They contended mightily to accomplish the will of God. Later on they made reclining seats for themselves. For each of them practised *ascesis* with faith according to his capacity.

15. Remembering the promise he had made to God, Pachomius began with his brother to build a larger monastery, to receive those who would come to this life. As they were building, Pachomius was extending the place with this aim in view while his brother, thinking of withdrawal apart, was making it smaller. And once John, who was older according to the flesh, was vexed and said to him, 'Stop being conceited!' When Pachomius heard this he became angry as if for a good cause, but did not say anything in reply to him. As he kept control of his heart, he went down to a little cavern[2] during the following night and began to weep in sorrow. He prayed, 'O God, the mind of the flesh is still in me. I still live according to the flesh; alas for me, I am *going to die,* as it is written. Practising such *ascesis* and having such a preparation of heart, I am again caught up in anger, although for a good cause. Have mercy on me, O Lord, lest I be destroyed. If the enemy finds a place in me, I will fall under his hand unless you strengthen me.[3] For *if a man keeps the whole of your law but fails in one point, he is guilty of breaking it all.* But I believe that if your many mercies help me I will be taught henceforth to walk in the way of the saints, *stretching out towards what lies ahead.* For with your help they put the enemy to shame as they ought. And how will I teach those whom you call to choose this life with me, O Lord, if I have not first conquered myself?'[4]

SBo 19b.

Wrangle between Pachomius and John

Cf. Rm 8:6,13.

Jm 2:10.

Ph 3:13.

Pachomius' prayer

16. Having said this prayer, he spent the whole night weeping and repeating it until dawn. From his sweat the ground under his feet became like mud, for it was summer and the place was very warm. He also had the habit when he extended his hands in prayer, of not right away drawing them a little to himself for rest. Rather, by extending them as if on a cross he would wear down the body to stay awake for prayers.[1]

Pachomius tempted by the demons

17. Instructed by the holy Scriptures and especially by the Gospel, he endured many temptations from the demons. The holy Scriptures did not mention in detail the saints' struggle, since they used concise language in showing us the way to eternal life. Thus, for example, the law given to our father Abraham was complete in one saying, *Be well-pleasing before me and be blameless.*[1] But since we are like *infants,* when our *fathers break the bread* for us, we need to be given as well the true *water,* as it is written. Therefore, *what we have heard and known and our fathers have told us should not be hidden from the next generation.* For, as we have been taught, we know that these words of the psalm are about the signs and portents accomplished by God for Moses and those after him. And after the model of the benefit given by them, we have also recognized in the fathers of our time their children and imitators, so that to us and to *the rising generation,* until the end of the world, it might be made known that *Jesus Christ is the same yesterday, today and for ever.*

Gn 17:1.
Lm 4:4; Is 33:16
Ps 78(77):3.
Ps 71(70):18.
Heb 13:8.
SBo 21a.

More temptations

18. If he had to endure many temptations this was by God's permission for his own testing as well as for the benefit of others. In his period of

withdrawal before the Community was formed, he paid great attention to the Beatitudes, striving especially to be found *pure in heart.*[1] In his strug- Mt 5:8.
gle he did not allow a foul thought to settle in his heart. He was always meditating on the fear of God, the thought of the judgement, and the torments of everlasting fire. His heart was as vigilant as a bronze door secured against robbers. And the Lord, seeing him exceedingly eager to fear Him, granted him the request of his fathers, who said to Him in the words of one of them, *May my heart be blameless in your statutes, that I be not put to shame.* When the demons saw this they Ps 119(118):80.
envied him and sought to cast him down. They began to attack him openly.[2] Sometimes, when he was going to bend his knees during his prayer, they made an apparent pit in front of him, so that fear would prevent him from kneeling down. But understanding the wiles of the tempters, he knelt with faith, putting them to shame and blessing God. At other times they came to march in front of him on both sides, as people do in escorting a commander, saying to each other, 'Make way to the man of God'. But by his hope in the Lord, he mocked them as helpless creatures.

19. They also tried to shake his cell[1] to make *SBo 21b.* **More temptations**
him afraid that it should collapse upon him. Then against them he would recite the psalm, *God is our shelter, our strength, a help in the afflictions that try us exceedingly. So we shall not be afraid when the earth is shaken.* Another time, Ps 46(45):1-2.
when he sat down to work, [a demon] came to tempt him in another way; taking the form of a cock he crowed in his face. Or again they would bring into the middle of the place a tree leaf and

tie it securely with thick ropes. Then they would stand on each side as though they were about to drag a big stone, shouting to each other, so that he would laugh with a relaxed heart and they would overcome him. When he saw it, he sighed at them, and since he paid no attention [to them], they withdrew. When he sat to eat, they would come in the form of naked women to sit with him to eat. But he closed the eye of his mind to them and the enemies disappeared without accomplishing anything against him. He was indeed preserved by the Lord who says to all the
Gn 26:24. upright, *Do not be afraid, for I am with you.*

20. He was tempted in many other cruel ways.
Hieracapollon's visit His body was beaten and he suffered visibly from evening till morning, without any consolation except the remembrance of God who was chastening him. As he was enduring these afflictions with perseverance, an ancient monk called Hieracapollon came to visit him. After embracing him, [Pachomius] began to tell him about his struggle. The other replied, 'Be valiant. The devil knows that if carelessness overtakes you, he will also dominate us, for you are our model. Therefore endure, lest you have to answer for
Cf. Lk 11:50. our blood if you are defeated.' He was greatly strengthened by these words. They prayed not to be separated from each other for ever. A while later Hieracapollon made a beautiful death in the *Koinonia,* as the Lord knows.[1]

(*Cf. SBo 98*). 21. And even before he had received perfect
Pachomius' faith knowledge from the Lord, [Pachomius] manifested such perfect faith as to *tread under-*
Lk 10:19. *foot serpents and scorpions* openly, and to stand on crocodiles in the water and to brave wild

beasts fearlessly and daringly without being harmed by them.[1] Since he was doing these things then through the uprightness of his heart and not yet through perfect knowledge, he was being preserved by the Lord who intended to teach him later how to act. For Moses, when he saw his own staff turned into a serpent, was frightened by it until the Lord ordered him to take hold of it. Then the serpent turned into a staff again in his hand. Before [God] gives power to the saints, fearful things are fearful and impossible things *are impossible to men*. Since Pachomius knew this, he wept over his ignorance and said in his prayer, 'O Lord, *guide of the blind*, I thank you that in this also you have not allowed me to be led astray, condescending to my ignorance until you teach me *your whole will*.'[2]

Ex 4:3-5.
Lk 18:27.
Rm 2:19.
Rm 12:2.

SBo 21c.

Pachomius does without sleep

22. Because he had spent a good deal of time wrestling with the demons as an athlete of the truth, like the most holy Antony, he asked the Lord to keep sleep away from him, that being awake night and day alike he might put to rout the adversaries, as it is written, *I will not turn away till they have vanished*. They are powerless indeed against faith in the Lord. And God granted him the request for a long time. And because of the purity of his heart he was, as it were, seeing the invisible God as in a mirror.*

Ps 18(17):37.
*Cf. Heb 11:27; Mt 5:8; 2 Co 3:18.

SBo 22.

Pachomius' vocation made clear by an angel

23. After this, he went with ⟨his brother⟩ [1] to an island to cut rushes for mats. And as he was keeping vigil alone, praying to be taught *the whole will of God*,* an angel appeared to him from the Lord, just as one appeared to Manoah and his wife about the birth of Samson. The angel said to him, 'The will of God is to minister to

*Rm 12:2.
Jg 13:3-21.

the race of men in order to reconcile them to himself.' He said this three times and went away.[2]

SBo 23b.

Coming of the first disciples

24. He thought about the voice which he had heard and was reassured. Then he began to receive those who came to him. After appropriately testing them and their parents, he clothed them in the monks' habit. He introduced them to the life gradually. First, they had to renounce all the world, their parents, and themselves, and follow the Saviour who taught doing so,* for this is *to carry the Cross.*† Being well taught by him according to the Scriptures, they bore fruits *worthy of their vocation.*

*Lk 14:26-27,33.
†Lk 14:27.
Eph 4:1.

They marvelled greatly when they saw that not only was his body broken by mortifications, but he also had nearly all the care of the monastery. He prepared the table for them for mealtime; he sowed the vegetables and watered them; and he also answered the door when anyone knocked. If any of them was sick, he eagerly took care of him and ministered to him at night. For the neophytes had not yet attained to such a disposition as to serve each other. Therefore he set them entirely free from care, saying, 'Strive, brothers, to attain to that to which *you have been called*: to recite psalms and teachings from other parts of the Scriptures, especially the Gospel. As for me, it is by serving God and you according to God's commandment that I find rest.'

I Tm 6:12.

SBo 23a, 23c.
c. AD 324.
*Ac 16:32.

Pachomius makes himself the servant of his disciples

25. The name of the first to come was Pšentaesi; then there were Sourous and Pšoi. And so, *speaking the word of God** to them, he edified them and led them to the zeal of good works. And even when he kept silent, they saw his conduct and it was for them a word. They marvelled and

said to each other, 'We used to think that all the saints were made holy and unswerving by God without regard to their free will, from their mothers' womb, and that sinners were not able to have life because they had been created that way. But now we see the goodness of God manifested in our father who, although born from pagan parents, has become so dear to God and has clothed himself with all God's commandments! Then we, too, and all men can follow him, for he follows the saints. So is realized what is written, *Come to me all you who labour and are overburdened and I will give you rest.*[1] Let us die with this man and we shall also live with him, for he guides us straight to God.' Mt 11:28.

They also said to him, 'Why do you toil alone in all the works of the monastery, Father?' He replied, 'Who yokes his beast to a water wheel and without caring lets it toil until it falls? So the merciful Lord himself, looking upon my poverty, will strengthen you or will bring others able to assist me in caring for the monastery.'

They lived a cenobitic life. So he established for them in a rule an irreproachable life-style and traditions profitable for their souls. These he took from the holy Scriptures: proper measure in clothing, equality in food, and decent sleeping arrangements.

SBo 24, 25b.

Names of the disciples

26. And so, as God called and increased them others came to practise *ascesis* with him: Pecoč, Cornelios, Paul, another Pachomius, and John, who had heard about his sound faith. And after a few days there came a certain Theodore, a boy of about fourteen years,[1] who became for Pachomius a true child after his likeness. Then

for the first time he assigned to those who were able the material cares of the monastery. The brothers multiplied and reached the number of one hundred.

SBo 25c.

Monks and priesthood

27. When there was need for the Eucharist, he called in from the nearest churches a priest who made the celebration for them. For among them there was no one invested with the clerical office. He had deliberated on the subject and often told them that it was good not to ask for rank and honor, especially in a community, for fear this should be an occasion for strife, envy, jealousy, and then schisms to arise in a large community of monks. He told them, 'In the same way as a spark of fire, however small at the beginning, if cast into a threshing-floor and not quickly quenched, destroys the year's labor, so the clerical dignity is the beginning of a temptation to love of power. It is better to be subject modestly to the Church of God and to consider as minister of this sacred rite the one we find at any time and who has been established by our fathers the bishops. In the past also not all the people were Levites. But if a monk from another place is ordained a cleric, we must not—heaven forbid!—vilify him as someone who loves power, but rather consider him as someone who has been ordained unwillingly. We reckon him an obedient father and an imitator of the saints, if only he performs the service blamelessly. And likewise if someone, being human, is found blameworthy, we do not judge him. God is the judge, and in each case he has as judges under himself the successors of the Apostles, able in Spirit to *judge according to what is right*. As for us among the flock, we must be compassionate

Jn 7:24.

and merciful to each other.' When someone from the clergy came to him and wanted to become a monk, he submitted himself to the law of God normally, according to his rank, but he would willingly be as all of them in regard to the rules of the community of the brothers.[1]

Cf. I Tm 1:8.

SBo 26.

First organization of the Community

28. He was full of mercy for the old men or the sick or for the younger ones, and he cared for their souls in every thing. And he rejoiced at those who made progress in virtues and increased in faith, for they pursued what was good with great zeal. Then he appointed some of them as his assistants to take care of the brothers' souls. He established one as steward of all the bodily needs of the monastery, and a second under him to help him.[1] And he appointed a housemaster in each house, with a second as helper. The first house is the one of the lesser stewards who prepare the table for the brothers and cook foods according to their needs. For among the great number of the brothers, there were diverse dispositions. And anyone who wanted to return to abstinence did so eagerly and unhindered.[2] After that, he appointed another house of stewards to give comfort to all the sick brothers with attentive care according to their rules, and over them a housemaster and a second in the same way. And at the doors he appointed religious, strict, hospitable brothers to receive visitors according to each one's rank. These porters also kept with themselves those who were going to become monks, teaching them the way to salvation until he clothed them in the habit. Similarly he appointed other faithful brothers noted for their devotion to sell the monks' handi-

work and to buy what they needed. Apart from this service, each one of the three housemasters had to replace every three weeks with a new class those who served the brothers. Then these had to do the manual work that was determined for them by the housemaster according to the direction of the Great Steward, that is, the father of the monastery.[3] He established as well other houses[4] with their housemasters and seconds to work at the crafts and at the mat-making and to be ready for every obedience without any personal wish in their hearts, so that they might *bear*
Rm. 7:4. *fruit to God*. When the father of the monastery is absent, the second has full authority until his return, without any pride or boasting but in
Eph 4:2. *humility and meekness*, for the edification of the brothers. The same applies to the housemaster and his second. The father of the monastery should give three instructions a week, one on Saturday and two on Sunday, while the housemaster does it on the two fastdays.[5]

SBo 25a.

Pachomius builds a church in the village

29. Our great father Pachomius also took great care to build a church in the deserted village[1] for the shepherds of the surrounding region, who were common folk, so that they might assemble on Sunday and Saturday to hear the word of God. This he did not on his own accord, but on the advice of Sarapion, the bishop of the Church of Nitentori.[2] He would go there with the brothers and would do the reading for them at the time of the *synaxis*, since there was no lector. He took care of the expenses [of the offering] for them and for the strangers who came, until a priest was appointed there.[3] Thus he would do the reading for them, with the understanding and reverence

that he had, guarding his eyes as is befitting, and also his mind and his mouth.

When the men of the world saw a man of God in their midst, they were very eager to become Christians and faithful. For he was full of mercy and a lover of souls. And many times when he saw men who did not recognize God their maker, he wept copiously by himself, desiring to save all men if he could.

SBo 28.

Athanasius' visit to the Thebaid

AD 329-330.

30. At that time, Athanasius, the most holy archbishop of Alexandria, was beginning his episcopate[1] and he wanted to go to the Upper Thebaid, up to Aswan, to give comfort to the Church of God. And as he sailed through Tabennesi, Pachomius and the brothers came out before him with joy and psalm-singing. There was a great crowd about [Athanasius], glorifying God for his coming. Now the aforesaid bishop of Nitentori had already made this request to pope Athanasius; 'I have a father of monks in my place and since he is a man of God, I want you to set him over all the monks in my diocese as father and priest.' Pachomius who had heard about this hid from the pope among the brothers until he had passed by. But he gazed at [Athanasius] on the boat, and recognized him as a holy servant of God, all the more as he had heard of the trials which Athanasius had endured for the sake of the Gospel and of his right faith for the sake of which he was also going to suffer later on.[2]

Pachomius' hatred for Origen

31. [Pachomius] also hated the man called Origen, first of all because he was cast out of the Church by Heraclas, the archbishop of Alexandria, before Arius and Melitius, who had uttered blasphemy against Christ.[1] He hated him also

because he recognized him as a blasphemer, having heard that there were dreadful things in his writings, and because he had acted rashly against his own life. [Origen] had mingled things he thought plausible with the true words of divine Scripture, to the ruination of the ignorant,[2] just as a poisonous drug is mingled with honey. Therefore the great Pachomius emphatically ordered the brothers not only not to dare to read that man's writings but not even to listen to his sayings. One day, having found a book of Origen, he threw it into the water and destroyed it, saying, 'If the name of the Lord were not written in it, I would have burnt his blasphemies and nonsenses.'

The Holy Man gave to the orthodox bishops and successors of the apostles and of Christ himself the heed of one who sees the Lord ever presiding upon the episcopal throne in the church and teaching through it.[3] If he heard anyone speaking against them in any way at all, he would not allow it, estranging himself from

Si 21:2.

such people *as from a snake* even if they were men of repute. He would say, 'No good man utters an

Cf. Lk 6:45.

evil word, especially against the holy fathers.' He remembered Miriam,[4] the sister of Moses, and

Nb 12:1-16.

her murmuring against him. So exceedingly forthright was he and profitable to those who met with him!

SBo 27.

Pachomius' sister founds a monastery for women

32. The Great Man's sister heard [about him] and came to see him.[1] He sent the brother attending the gate to tell her, 'Behold, you have heard that I am alive. Do not be distressed because you have not seen me. But if you too wish to share in this holy life, so that we may find mercy

before God, examine [yourself].[2] The brothers
will make a monastery for you to live in quietly
there,[3] and perhaps the Lord will call others as
well to be with you. For man has no other hope in
the world than to do good for himself and for his
neighbor before he departs from his body to the
place where he shall be judged and rewarded according to his works.' Hearing this she wept, and Rm. 2:6-7.
touched by compassion she inclined her heart to
salvation. So a monastery of women was built in
the village, a short distance from the brothers.
And as they grew in number little by little, she
became their mother.

He appointed a certain Peter, a man very
religious and advanced in age, to visit them. *His
speech was seasoned with salt*, and his eyes as well Col 4:6.
as his mind were full of dignity. He would often
stand to preach to them the words of salvation
from the divine Scriptures. Pachomius wrote
down for them the rules of the brothers and sent
them by the old man Peter, that they might
govern themselves by keeping them.

If ever any of the brothers who had not yet attained to perfection wished to visit a relative Cf. Heb 6:1.
[among the sisters], he would send him through
the housemaster's [direction] to the old man
Peter, and so information was imparted either to
his mother or sister. In the presence of another
sister capable in the Lord he would visit his
relative with great discretion, forgetting at the
same time their kinship according to the flesh. He
would bring her nothing—for he owned nothing—and would not receive anything either, for
sufficient to them both was the hope and the
remembrance of eternal goods.

When there was some building or other kind of work that needed to be done there, he would choose out an intelligent and discreet brother and would send him there with others like him to do it. They would work until meal-time and they would return to the monastery at the time of eating.

When one of the virgins there died, those advanced in age among them would first order a shroud to be cast over the body of the deceased. Then the brothers sent and appointed for this would stand with dignity under the portico there in the *synaxis*, and they would sing psalms decently until she was prepared for burial. The virgins would stand at a distance in the other part. After this the men would lead the way to the mountain singing psalms with great dignity, while the virgins followed behind the bier. Their father Peter would not leave them at all until, in the fear of God, they had entered their own monastery.[4]

SBo 31.

Theodore's childhood

33. We ought—for indeed it is profitable to all—to tell also about his true child Theodore, mentioned above. He was a Christian from his earliest age and from parents who held the faith. But it seems he stood out above the others yet more by greater progress. For he was not obscure from boyhood, but from a great home thriving according to the world. On a feast-day of the Christians, the eleventh of the month of Tobi, seeing the table abounding, he considered to himself that, 'If you enjoy these foods, you will not find the eternal ones[1] and the true life,' and his heart was pierced with divine perception.[2] He sighed and went at once into a quiet place in his house.

Epiphany 6 January

Falling on his face, he began to weep and say, 'O God, I do not want the things of this world. I want you alone and your mercy.' When his mother found him, after a long search, she saw from his eyes that he had been weeping and she asked him, 'Who has vexed you, my child, and where have you been? I and your brothers were waiting for you to eat.' He answered, 'You go and eat, for I do not want to eat.' Thus keeping this way of life, he used to fast until evening and often eat only every other day, abstaining from expensive meats and foods like a monk for two years. After that he was permitted to withdraw to the pious monks who lived in a monastery in the region of the Nome of Latopolis. He was then about fourteen years of age.[3]

34. Once the monks were sitting in the evening, as was their custom, to speak the word of God, and he heard one of them telling about the Tabernacle. He explained the Holy Place and the Holy of Holies, applying the explanation to the two peoples, 'For the first people,' he said, 'is the outer Tabernacle, whose service consisted in animal sacrifices, visible loaves, the lampstand and the lamps, and some other things. But the calling of the Gentiles is the Holy of Holies, that is, the *fulfilment of the Law*. And everything in the Holy of Holies is more glorious than the outer Tabernacle. For instead of animal sacrifices it has a censer of incense; instead of a table, the Ark of the Covenant with the spiritual loaves, the book of the Law and all that is to be found there, and instead of the light of the lampstand, the Mercy-Seat where God appears as *a consuming fire*, that is, God the incarnate Word who was

SBo 29.

Theodore hears about Pachomius

Cf. Heb 9:1-5.

Rm 13:10.

Cf. Lv 16:12.

Dt. 4:24; Heb 12:29.

I Tm 3:16; I Jn 4:2, 10.

made propitiation for us by *appearing in the flesh.*'

And after giving this interpretation, the brother said, 'I heard this saying and the explanation from the holy man, our father Pachomius, who has assembled in Tabennesi many brothers progressing in Christ. And I am confident that the Lord will forgive some of my sins because I have just now brought to mind a righteous man.' When Theodore heard this, his heart was kindled and he prayed, 'Lord, if there is a saint upon earth, allow me to see him and become his disciple, that through him you may save my soul.' And he spent most of the night praying this way.

SBo 30a.

Theodore's coming to Pachomius

c. AD 328

35. A few days later, Pecoš, himself a pious old man, came south for some need of the brothers. Theodore asked him to take him to the monastery, to the great Pachomius; and he took him.[1] Reaching the place, he adored the Lord, saying, 'Blessed are you, O Lord, for you have heard my request'. And when he met our father Pachomius, he began to weep at the door. Pachomius said to him, 'Do not weep; I am a servant of your Father.' He meant God.

SBo 30b, 32.

Theodore's progress in virtue

36. He was introduced into the monastery. Then, hearing and seeing the brothers walking in uprightness, he emulated them in pursuit of the good. Taught by Pachomius, who was an imitator of the saints, he progressed, found comfort, and was strengthened in the commandments. He was a wise boy and he kept for himself these three things; purity of heart, a measured and graceful speech, and an unquestioning obedience unto death. He was second to none in *as-*

cesis and prayer vigils, but he *strove to acquire*
the highest gifts,[1] so that he became a comforter I Co 12:31.
to many who were grieved and a corrector to his
seniors. For *the spirit blows wherever it pleases*. Jn 3:8.
Seeing his remarkable progress, our father
Pachomius realized in his heart that God would
entrust him with souls after himself.

37. His mother heard of him and she came *SBo 37*.
with letters from bishops ordering the boy to be **Visit of**
given back to her. Being given hospitality at the **Theodore's mother**
monastery of virgins, she sent the letters so she
might at least see himn. The father said to him, I
hear that your mother has come for you and has
brought letters from bishops. Because of these
letters, go to meet her and persuade her.' The
boy replied, 'Tell me; if I go to see her as my
mother, after [being given] such great knowledge, will the Lord not blame me in the day of
judgment? For instead of becoming enough of a
man to reform others, I will set up a stumbling
block in the way of so many. The sons of Levi
killed their own parents and brothers to please
the Lord and escape the danger of his wrath. I Cf. Ex 32:27-28.
too, I have no mother, nor anything of the world,
for it passes.' Pachomius said to him, 'If you love
God more than your mother, shall I prevent you?
I shall rather encourage you. For, *he who loves*
his father or his mother more than me is not worthy of me. This is perfection. And certainly our Mt 10:37.
fathers the bishops will not be vexed when they
hear about this, but will rather rejoice at your
progress. But if someone meets his relatives not as
his relatives but as *members of Christ* whom he Ep 5:30.
loves as he loves all the faithful, he does not sin.
For *the flesh is of no avail*.' And so the boy did not Jn 6:63.

want to meet his mother. But, because of her great love for him, she did not want to return home and she remained with the virgins, saying to herself, 'Not only will I see him some day among the brothers, but I too shall gain my soul.'[2]

(*Cf. SBo 24*).

Expulsion of bad monks

38. Before the community increased to great numbers, there were some with our father Pachomius who had a carnal mind, for not everyone chooses the fear of God. He admonished them often, but they did not obey and did not follow the straight path, but instead caused him grief. [One day] he went far away and falling upon his face he prayed, 'God, you commanded us to love our neighbor as ourselves. Look then upon these souls, have mercy on them, and spur them to fear you and to know what the life of monks is, so that, like the other brothers, they may hope in you.' But after this prayer, he saw that they did not want to follow him, but persisted in their opposition. Therefore he imposed on them the rules of the *synaxis* and the other rules. Recognizing that he would not allow them to walk according to their own will, they withdrew in fear. And so, after their withdrawal, the rest grew as wheat does when the darnel is rooted up.[1]

Cf. Lv 19:18; Mt 19:19.

SBo 39.

Gift of wheat to the Community

39. Since they used to give away in alms whatever they had, it happened once that they ran short of bread. The divine Pachomius wanted to sell two blankets which one of the monks had brought with him when he renounced [the world], to buy wheat. But at dawn that same night someone knocked at the door. When he came in, the father asked him what he wanted. He answered, 'I had promised for my salvation to

give wheat to those working in the mines; but I was instructed in my sleep that you need it and to bring it to you, since you are men of God.' Pachomius answered, 'We do need the wheat, but give us a fixed date to return it.' The wheat was then taken from the boat and the brothers marvelled at how, all of a sudden, God had helped them because of his servant.

40. There was a certain confessor after [the time ofı the martyrs, a devout man whose name was Dionysios. He was the steward of the Church of Nitentori and one of the closest friends of Pachomius. And because he was his friend, he was grieved when he learned that Pachomius did not allow visiting monks from other places to stay inside the monastery with the brothers, but had them stay apart in a place by the gates. He came to him at Tabennesi and began to censure him about this. Pachomius answered with great patience, 'God knows my intention. And indeed your fatherly love knows that I simply never wanted to harm a soul. How would I have dared to grieve the Lord who said, *Inasmuch as you have done it to one of those who believe in me, you have done it to me*. And how would I have segregated my brothers so unreasonably, as if I had contempt for them? Heaven forbid! But since I have often seen that the community has many neophytes who do not yet know what a monk is, and boys *who cannot tell their right hand from their left*,[1] I thought it good and more respectful to the fathers and brothers who visit us for them to come together with us only at the hour of the *synaxis*. After the prayer, they retire to rest and eat in an appropriate and quiet place, where I

SBo 40.

Reception of visiting monks

Mt 25:40; 18:6.

Jon 4:11.

wait on them myself as Abraham waited on the
Gn 18:1-8. Lord alone under the oak tree.' When he heard these explanations, Dionysios the priest was convinced, recognizing that [Pachomius] did everything according to God.

SBo 41.

Healing of a sick woman by Pachomius

41. The wife of one of those dwelling in that place[1] was suffering from a flow of blood. She heard about the great Pachomius and asked the same Dionysios, as a friend of him, to send for him on the pretext of talking with him about a pressing matter. Pachomius came and as he was sitting in the church conversing with Dionysios, she came near him and touched the hood on his head, believing in the words of the incarnate God to his disciples, *Anyone who receives you receives*
Mt 10:40. *me.*[2] And she was healed immediately.

SBo 42.

Story of a monk who wanted a charge

42. The father of a nearby monastery used to visit the holy father. One of his monks was asking for the rank of steward, but he did not consider him worthy of that task. Not being able to persuade him, he told him guilefully, 'Our father Pachomius warned me not to do this, knowing well that you are not yet worthy of your request.' When he heard this, the brother dragged him along angrily, saying, 'Come, let us go to him, and he shall have to prove what he says against me!' The other followed him in fear and sorrow, wondering what the result of that affair would be.

When they arrived, they found Pachomius with the brothers, building a wall for the monastery. That brother approached Pachomius and told him very angrily, 'Come down, liar, and give me a proof of my sin!' As [Pachomius] kept silent,
Ps 63(62):11. he said to him again, *'Is your mouth silenced,*

finding nothing in your defence? Who compels you to lie, you who call yourself clairvoyant, when you are stone-blind?' When he had said this, the Great Man answered, knowing nothing of what the other was talking about, 'I have sinned against you; forgive me. Have you never transgressed?' When he heard this his anger calmed down. Cf. Mt 6:23.

The Old Man came down from his work and sought the father of the other monastery. He found him weeping and heart-broken, and he asked him,'What is going on?' He answered, 'This brother has asked us for a ministry beyond his worth. I knew I could not make him give up his claim, for he does not listen to me. So I used your name to quiet him down. For we know that the Lord has granted you the gift of discovering guile swiftly. And behold this fool has added to his evil deeds reviling a righteous man.' Pachomius said to him, 'Have you not come to seek from me the will of God? Listen to me. Grant him his request that by this means we may snatch his soul away from the enemy. For it happens when good is done to a bad man that he may come to some perception of the good. This is God's love, to have compassion for each other.' Eph 4:2.

When that brother had got what he wanted, he returned immediately to the great Pachomius, greatly sobered. He embraced him and confessed, 'O Man of God, you are much greater than we had heard. We have seen how you have *conquered evil with good*[1] by sparing a foolish sinner like me. If you had not been truly patient and had said something against me, I would have rejected the monastic life and become estranged Rm 12:21.

from God. Blessed are you, for thanks to you I live.'

SBo 43.

Healing of a possessed girl

43. A man came to the monastery and asked the Great One to heal his daughter, who was possessed. Since it was not his custom to speak with women, he had the porter tell the man: 'Send here a piece of her clothing which has been washed.' It was brought [to him], and when, as he was going to bless it, he looked at it, he said, 'This garment is not hers', And as the man persisted in affirming that it was hers, [Pachomius] sent him this message, 'It is hers, but she does not keep her chastity, although she has promised virginity. Just looking at it I understood she was not chaste. This is why I said, "It is not hers". Let her then promise God in your presence that from now on she will keep herself chaste, and he will heal her in his mercy.' When her father questioned her with anger and sorrow, she confessed and promised by an oath no longer to do evil. Then he sent him some oil over which he had prayed. He anointed her in faith, and she was healed.

SBo 44.

Healing of a possessed boy

44. Another man brought him his son, possessed by a stubborn demon. And the porter received from [Pachomius] a loaf of bread and gave it to the [father] to give a portion of it to his son according to [Pachomius'] instruction, that he might be healed. When the sufferer was hungry, his father brought him the loaf of bread. He did not touch it, but ate from the others. Another time the father opened dates and green cheeses and put little fragments of the bread inside them, so that he might eat them without realizing it. But when he began to eat, he opened them, threw

out the fragments and did not eat them. Then his father left him two days without food, until he became weak. Then he made some porridge in which he mixed the bread, and he gave it to him after anointing him with holy oil. And after eating he immediately fell asleep. The father came to the monastery praising God, and told [Pachomius] about the healing of the boy.

SBo 45.

Pachomius' attitude toward miracles

45. The Lord, who always provides for the salvation of souls through the saints, did many other healings through him, both among the worldlings and among the brothers. But if he prayed about someone's health and was not granted his request by the Lord, he was not surprised or afflicted at not being heard, for he knew the purpose toward which the saints tended. And he said in his prayer, *May your will be done, not mine.*[1] For he who is one with the Father in all things taught us that it ought to be so.

Lk 22:42; Cf. Mt 6:10; 26:42.

Sources of this Life

46. Perhaps the person who will read the words of his prayers on each occasion will say, 'Where have you received knowledge of the things you have written down?' First let him remember that it has been said before that inquiring of them with exactness, we heard these things from the ancient fathers. And sometimes too, when the Holy Man sat for the instruction, he would reveal to them even his personal thoughts. He also taught them how to pray about each request and how to have faith and hope in the Lord and a sincere love toward their neighbor.[1]

SBo 46.

Pachomius' teaching on spiritual healings

47. He also taught that besides visible physical healings there were also spiritual ones. 'For if a man is blind in his mind,' he said, 'because he does not see the light of God on account of his

idolatry, but is subsequently guided by faith in the Lord and receives sight to recognize *the only true God*,[1] is this not healing and salvation? And if another person is dumb from lying, *not speaking the truth*, but is instructed by men of God to speak what is true, has he not also been spiritually healed? And if another's hands are maimed because of his idleness in following God's commandments, but through God's mercy he ceases to be indolent and *does some good*, is this not also a healing? Finally, if someone is a fornicator or proud, but repents in the fear of God through the help of some servant of God, is this not also a miracle?

Jn 17:3.
Eph 4:25.
Eph 4:28.

Attitude toward visions

48. 'One of the brothers asked me, "Tell us about one of your visions," and I said to him, "A sinner like me does not ask God to see visions.[1] It is against God's will, and a mistake. But in everything he does by God's will, even if he should raise a dead man, the servant of God remains unhurt by pride or boasting. For, without God's permission, he would not even see that Providence governs all things. But all the same, hear about a great vision. For what is greater than such a vision, *to see the invisible* God in a visible man, his temple?[2] And likewise let us understand the clairvoyance of the saints who see the thoughts of souls, as in the case of Elisha and Gehazi.[3] When the Lord who dwells in the saints and searches all things gives them a revelation, they are clairvoyant; but when he does not, they are like all [other] men. But yet they have another unintermittent clairvoyance, which is to see the Lord. Thus one of them declared unto us, *I saw the Lord always before me*.[4] And a man is

Heb 11:27.
2 K 4:27.
Ps 16(15):8.

not judged for not seeing the hidden things, but he is judged if he is like those whom the Spirit condemns by the words of the psalm, *They have not set God before them.*" Ps 54(53):3.

49. 'It is easier for children to reach this degree, that, being obedient from their earliest age, they may eagerly *strain ahead to the things that are before,** until they *reach perfection,*† like Samuel[1] in the Temple.‡ For ground that has been cleared is ready to be planted with vines step by step, but fallow land can scarcely be planted with good seed after it has been cleaned with great toil. But we know that even clean ground, if it is neglected, will become fallow, as it is written,[2] even if it was planted with good seed. Just as with fallow land then, purity is attained by care and proper zeal. So let us watch over the children as God wills, so that He who watches over the little ones, as it is written, may keep watch over our souls *like the apple of his eye*. Let no one dare to harm a soul, even if [only] in thought, lest he tear out the apple of an eye which sees God *the righteous judge.*[3] As for the manner of keeping [the children], there is no need to say many words; one word is sufficient. The man who *cleanses his own conscience* to perfection, in the fear of God and in truth, he it is who can keep the little ones with the Lord's help—for he needs his help.'

Spiritual care of children

*Ph 3:13.
†Eph 4:13.
‡1 S 2:18, 26.

Pr 24:31.

Ps 116(114):6.

Ps 17(16):8.

2 Tm 4:8.

Heb 9:14; Cf. 2 Co 7:1.

50. As Theodore, of whom we spoke before, was young, he fed eagerly on the true words of God and was strengthened in the Spirit. In all things he looked to the father, who was guiding him and was blameless, and he was obedient to him as to God. And if it happened that Pacho-

Theodore's obedience

mius ordered him to do something, and later changed the order and blamed him, saying, 'Why did you do this?', he was not surprised and did not excuse himself to defend his actions but he kept silent and trusted the one who was reprimanding him, saying to himself, 'A man of God does not change his word. But perhaps he gave me that order, according to my will,[1] being moved by the Holy Spirit in ecstasy, because I was not right. If it were not so, how would he blame me after that command? I find indeed a similar thing in Jeremiah, when the Lord blamed the people about sacrifices which they did not accomplish in truth. [He said], *I did not give that*
Jr 7:22. *precept to your fathers*, and yet he had given it through Moses. I ought therefore to weep until
Cf. 2 Th 3:5. the Lord straightens my heart and I am worthy to obey his saints.'

SBo 47a.

Pachomius refuses privileges

51. Once the brothers were on an island to reap rushes and Theodore was with them, preparing the tables. One evening our father Pachomius came back from work sick. As he lay shivering, Theodore threw a hair blanket over him. When he saw it he refused it. 'Take it away', he said, 'and cast over me a mat like all the brothers [use].' [Theodore] also held out to him a handful of dates for him to take. He refused them, saying with tears, 'Because we have to administer the labor and the needs of the brothers, do we have the right to go to expenses for ourselves? Where is the fear of God? Have you visited all the huts of the brothers and made sure that none of them is sick at this very hour? For God judges us even in these matters.'[1]

SBo 47b.

52. Through the discernment of the spirit, he

also tested the nature of the different states of health,[1] because the demons try to impede the faithful in every way. Once he was seized by a fever in the monastery and he lay without food for two days. On his third day without eating, he got up a little for prayer, in his great desire for God, and he felt relief from the disease. And when the steward gave the signal for eating, as was the custom, he girded up his loins and went to eat at the table of the healthy brothers, realizing that the disease was not physical. And he gave thanks to God who had strengthened him. And so, when he saw another [in the same situation] he straightened him out so that he would not be mocked by the enemy.

Pachomius' discernment of various kinds of illness

53. At another time, holy though he was, he got physically sick. And he was bearing the sickness because God tries his servants in various ways.[1] Another brother, sick to death, was lying in another cell nearby. He had been ill so long that his body was mere bones. He had asked the father of the monastery to be given a little meat, and it had not yet been given to him. Then he said to one of the brothers, 'Take me and lead me to our father Pachomius'. And when he arrived he threw himself upon his face, relating the matter. Pachomius, understanding that he deserved what he had asked for, sighed. And when at the hour of the brothers' meal they brought him to eat exactly what all the others had, he did not eat but said, 'Respecters of persons, where is [the precept of] the Scripture, *You shall love your neighbor as yourself*? Do you not see that this man is a corpse? Why did you not take good care of him before he made his request? And why did

SBo 48.

Pachomius' compassion for a sick brother

Lv 19:18; Mt 19:19.

you overlook him after he made it? But you will say, "We neglected his request because this sort of food is not customary among us". Are there no differences among sick persons? Are not *all things*
Tit 1:15.
pure to the pure? And if you were unable to discern by your own judgement[2] that this was good, why did you not tell me?' And saying this he wept—tears are always a mark of emotion. And even if someone does not weep although he is moved at the time the event happens, there is also the inner weeping.[3]—When they heard these things, they hastened to buy the article and give it to the sick brother to eat. Then [Pachomius] himself ate the cooked vegetables as was everyone's custom.

SBo 49,50,51.

Foundations of Phbow, Chenoboskion, and Thmoušons.

c. AD 329.

54. As the number of the brothers increased, Pachomius saw that the monastery was overcrowded. He transferred some of them to another deserted village called Phbow.[1] And with them he built a large monastery, seeing that many were called by the Lord. And he appointed a steward with some seconds[2] to minister to the brothers, as well as housemasters and seconds, according to the rules of the first monastery at Tabennesi. And he enjoined them in writing, as a form of memorial, that no one should hurt his neighbor, but each should keep to his rule of conduct, for order is a good thing, although the perfect man is irreproachable even amidst disorder, as it is written, *And even in the day of famine they will be*
Ps 37(36):19.
filled. And he used to visit the two monasteries day and night, as a servant of the *Good*
Jn 10:11.
Shepherd.[3]

After a while, the number of the brothers also increased in the monastery called Phbow. Then came an old ascetic named Ebonh,[4] father of another monastery of ancient brothers. He asked Pachomius to receive his monastery into the brothers' Community.[5] The name of the monastery was Chenoboskion.[6] So, taking other brothers along, he led them there. After praying in that place he entrusted them to God, having them remain there with the original brothers, conforming to the same rules. There also he appointed a steward of the monastery with his second, and housemasters with their seconds.[7]

Fourthly, he brought the brothers to the monastery called Thmoušons,[8] which also existed of old, and at the request of the great monks of that monastery, he established them according to the rule of the *Koinonia*. And he gave them their constitutions. There was there a certain early and holy monk named ⟨Jonas⟩, who was a perfect ascetic.[9]

So he used to visit the brothers with great zeal. And he took spiritually capable brothers and appointed them in each monastery to govern the brothers, as though he were present, until he should come.[10]

SBo 59a.

Pachomius' abstinence

55. Once he was sailing with two other brothers in a boat to Thmoušons, and at evening, at meal time, they prepared it. As they sat down to eat, he saw the great variety of food on the table: cheeses, figs, olives, and many other things, and he began to eat only bread. But they indiscriminately laid hands on everything there. One [brother] looked up and saw him weeping. After they got up they queried him on the meaning of this; but he said nothing. As they asked him a second time, he said, 'It is because of you that I am

grieved, because you are not abstinent. For he
Col 3:2. who *has his mind in heaven*[1] ought to practice a worthy abstinence, and not to have a desire for foods. For surely it is not a sin to eat, especially the cheap things; but it is good *not to be dominated by anything*, as the Apostle says. As for me,
1 Co 6:12.
a sinner, finding the bread good, I was satisfied with it. Another time I will eat according to the Lord's gift.' Hearing this, they were eager to become abstinent in foods.

Pachomius' spiritual teachings

56. He would often sit to instruct the brothers, teaching them first of all to know blamelessly and without any ignorance the craftiness of the enemies, and to oppose them with the Lord's power.
Ps 60(59):12. For it is written, *In God we shall have strength.* Then he would interpret for them the words of the divine Scriptures, especially the deep and not easily comprehensible ones, and those about the Lord's incarnation, the cross, and the resurrection.

'Concerning the Word of God becoming man,' he said, 'among many other things in the Old [Testament] this [word] of Isaiah is sufficient: *I*
Is 66:18. *am coming to gather all the nations.*[1] And in the Gospel [we read], *The Word was made flesh and*
Jn 1:14. *he lived among us*.

'And about the Cross, it is explained well enough by the *ram caught by his horns in the plant sabek*—which is a wood—*and offered as a whole-*
Gn 22:13. *burnt offering instead of Isaac*, especially since Abraham says about it that, *The Lord was seen on*
Gn 22:14. *the mountain*, signifying the Cross of God's only-begotten Son. And in the Gospel the creation bears witness about the Cross by its portents that
Mt 27:51-53. the crucified Christ Jesus is the Lord of all.

'About the resurrection of his body it is said in Isaiah that after his death, *The Lord desires to cleanse him from the stroke,*[2] that is, to raise him Is 53:10.
up because he did not deserve death, for he died for us. And in the Gospel, when he touches the crucified and risen flesh in which the Word was as in a temple, Thomas says, *My Lord and my* *Jn 20:28.
*God.** He, too, is a *faithful witness.*† †Rv 1:5.

'Concerning the resurrection of all flesh, as the Lord rose so we also shall rise—and we have already risen with him—since his crucified body is Cf. 1 Th 4:14-16.
like ours. For not only God the Word rose but we also rose because he himself raised us with his own body. And this we do not say of ourselves, Cf. 2 Co 4:14.
but because we heard it from him, when he said, *The hour is coming when all those who are in the tombs will hear the voice of the Son of Man and will come forth.* Paul also said things concerning Jn 5:28-29.
the resurrection that we need to understand with true knowledge. Let one word of his suffice, *If the dead are not raised, neither has Christ been raised.* 1 Co 15:16.

Pachomius' spiritual teachings

57. 'Brothers, believing in the resurrection to come, we ought also to know about the spiritual resurrection, since the Lord says, *He who believes in me, even though he dies he will live.* For indeed Jn 11:25.
the word of the Lord is true; *Every sinner who believes and obeys his commandments shall live,* Cf. Ez 18:21.
and as David says, *My soul shall live and praise you.* Let us also find strength, brothers, in the Ps 119(118):175.
commandments that the Lord gave us through his own conduct. When *he was insulted** with *1 P 2:23.
these words, *You have a demon,*† he *did not* †Jn 7:20.
retaliate with insults‡.[1] And at another time, ‡I P 2:23.
refuting the Pharisees and the Scribes, he said,

*Mt 23:16.
†Ibid
‡Mt 23:27.

*Woe unto you,** calling them *blind guides,*† *white-washed tombs*‡ and the like. Just as someone seeing a pit grabs the blind lest they fall into its deadly depth, so too the Lord revealed their evil conduct to the believers, lest they become *like them* (Mt 6:8) and die with them. By the fact that *he was insulted and did not retaliate with insults,* (1 P 2:23) he taught us not to retaliate and to persevere in virtue. And when he said to Peter, *Get behind me, Satan!* (Mt 16:23) he did not mean Peter but Satan who had suggested he should *think* and speak *the things that are of men.* (Ibid.)[2]

(*Cf. SBo 104.*)

The brothers reflect together on the teachings

58. After these words our father Pachomius rose and prayed with the brothers so that they should always remember God's salutary words. Then each one withdrew to his own house, reciting the texts learned by heart.[1] And after making the Six Prayers they sat to talk together and to recall each one of the things they had heard.[2] For they cannot utter *idle* worldly *words,* (Mt 12:36) but can talk only about what they have learned or the interpretation of a saying, or about an action conformed to God's will.

(*Cf. SBo 104.*)

Regulations concerning material possessions

59. No one would do anything in the house without permission from those in charge, not even visit a brother in his cell. In each house, the housemaster or the second keeps all the surplus clothes locked in a cell until the brothers need them to wash and put on again those they are using. The books, which were in an alcove, were also under the care of these two. The brothers have no money, still less anything of gold; some of them died having never known such things. Only those entrusted with a ministry used money; and when they returned to the monastery they kept nothing

with themselves for a single day but gave everything to the steward until they might go out again. And all that government is written in detail in the book of the stewards.[1]

SBo 59b.

Pachomius gives a lesson to two brothers about vigils

60. One day our father was going again to visit the monasteries by boat. When evening came he said to [the brothers], 'Do you want us to keep vigil tonight?' They said, 'Yes'. Then he said to them, 'I learned three ways of praying from our holy father Palamon. Either let us pray till midnight and then sleep till morning; or let us sleep till midnight and then pray till morning; or let us sleep a little and then ‹wake up and pray and keep doing that› till morning.' They chose this last type, and [Pachomius] who had the experience of keeping vigil kept awake, arranging equally the hours of sleep and of prayer. One of the brothers, overcome by drowsiness, went off to sleep, but the other stayed till morning. At dawn he called the first one to make the *synaxis*, after which the other one went off to the hold to sleep. [Pachomius] himself, together with the one who had slept the whole night, rowed until they came to the monastery, a long distance.[2]

SBo 59c.

Same lesson given by Pachomius to Cornelios

61. Cornelios, whom we have mentioned before, was the steward of that monastery. When he heard [about Pachomius' arrival] he called the brothers together and went out to meet him. And when they saw him, they embraced him and the brothers. As one of them came in Cornelios asked him in a low voice, 'What is our father doing these days?' He answered, 'All this night he taught us a lesson'. And when he had told everything that had happened, Cornelios said, 'What weakness! You, a young man, you let a feeble old

man outdo you?' Abba Pachomius heard him say this, but he kept silent as though he had not heard.

And in the evening, about the time of fire-lighting, he said to Cornelios, 'Do you want us to pray?' He answered, 'As you wish.' They rose to pray and he lingered in his prayer. As he dragged on praying, in order to test Cornelios, the two brothers (having learned from the experience of the night in the boat) left the place and went off elsewhere to sleep. But Cornelios endured with him. And as the father was protracting his prayer exceedingly, Cornelios was reciting by himself the texts he knew by heart. When the signal was given for the *synaxis* in the morning, he told Pachomius, 'Father, what have I done to you? I have not even tasted water since yesterday's evening meal.' And he said to him, 'Cornelios, are you letting an old man outdo you in prayer?' Then, knowing that he had heard him say the same thing to the brother the night before, [Cornelios] said, 'I have sinned. Forgive me for I did not
Dn 4:15. speak correctly. *The Spirit that is in you is holy*; it is the power of God.'

62. Once, as he was passing by some tombs, he
Meaning of tears heard people weeping and he said to Theodore who was walking with him, 'They are weeping for the dead whom they cannot raise up. But let us weep first for ourselves and then for our neighbor. Perhaps through our *weeping with*
Rm 12:15. *those who weep*, the Lord will raise them up, for he says, *Wake up, you who sleep, rise from the*
Eph 5:14. *dead, and Christ will shine on you.*[1] And if we often hear [the brothers] weeping, let us not be surprised, because all the saints have been *in the*

valley of weeping, like Joseph[2] who wept more than once about his brothers' salvation and Jeremiah who wept for the Captivity. So these, who are the children of the saints, also weep.' Ps 84(83):6. Gn 43:30; 45:2, 13; 46:29; 50:17. Lm 1:1ff.

63. He also used to teach the brothers not to give heed to the splendor and the beauty of this world in things like good food, clothing, a cell, or a book outwardly pleasing to the eye. 'For the beauty of the faithful,' he said, 'lies in the commandments of God; as the psalmist says, *Lord, in your will grant strength to my beauty*.*.[1] Although Joseph *was extremely handsome*† and came to rule over Egypt,‡ he paid no attention to these perishable things, having chastity for splendor and prudence for power.* But others who took their delight in these things perished by an evil death, like Amnon† and Absalom.'‡

Contempt for material beauty

*Ps 30(29):7. †Gn 39:7. ‡Gn 41:40-44. Cf. Gn 39:7-15. *Cf. Gn 41:39-42. †2 S 13:28-29. ‡2 S 18:14-15.

64. Once he was sick, and when he was eating, some broth carefully prepared with oil was brought to him.[1] When he saw it, he remembered the salt with ashes of the past,[2] and he said to [the brother] who had brought it, 'Bring me a jug of water.' And when it was brought he poured it until the oil on top was emptied out. Then he gave the jug to Theodore saying, 'Pour water on my hands, that I may wash.' And as he was washing [his hands], he cast the water upon Theodore's feet, as if to wash them also. [Theodore] said, 'Father, why do you do this and what you did to the food?' He answered, 'I did that to the food so I may not have pleasure in eating. And when I washed my hands, I poured the water on your feet to wash them, so that I might not be judged in my conscience for being served by you instead of serving everyone myself.'

SBo 61.

Pachomius' abstinence

SBo 38.

Theodore's severity toward his own brother

Col 3:9.

65. Some time later, Paphnouti, Theodore's brother, came to become a monk.[1] Theodore refused to treat him as a brother, for he had already *put off the old man*. As Paphnouti wept because of this, Abba Pachomius told Theodore, 'Condescension is good with such a neophyte at the beginning, until he is rooted in the faith, as we do with a newly planted tree, tending it carefully and watering it.' Theodore listened and acted accordingly.

Cf. Col 2:7.

SBo 62.

Theodore comforting a brother

66. There was a brother in the monastery who was dejected because [our father Pachomius] had reprimanded him for the sake of his salvation. Theodore realized that this brother had estranged himself in his heart to the point of leaving the brothers because of this, and with his prudence and wisdom he told him, 'You certainly know that this old man's speech is abrupt beyond measure; and I do not know if I can stay here.' The brother answered, unburdening himself to him, 'Do you also experience this?' He answered, 'Even more so do I. But let us comfort each other until we test him once more. If he is good to us, let us stay; but if not, let us withdraw on our own to some other place[1] and get relief.' And hearing this, the weak brother was strengthened. Theodore went secretly to our father Pachomius and gave him an account of the matter. Pachomius replied, 'Very well! Bring him here and both of you reprove me for this, and according to God's inspiration I will persuade him.' So they came and Theodore pretended to reproach Pachomius, who replied to them, 'Forgive me. I have sinned. Should you, as sons, not bear with your father?' Theodore began to reproach him again

but the brother nodded to him, 'Stop. It is well; for I have been greatly comforted.' And so through his good artifice he benefited the brother.

SBo 63a.

Theodore accompanying a brother to his family

67. Seeing that [Theodore] was wise and obedient to the truth, our father Pachomius sent him once to accompany another brother who had asked to visit his family and was going home.[1] When they arrived there, the brother's parents at meal time prepared a meal for them in a quiet part of the house. The brother said to Theodore, 'Get up, let us go and eat.' But it was not the custom to eat in a secular house. Theodore realized that unless he gave in to him he would not return to the monastery, for he was going to eat even if Theodore refused to. So he ate a little, though with a tormented mind. And when they returned to the monastery, he reported what had happened to Abba Pachomius who did not blame him since he knew that he had done this against his will.

SBo 63b.

Theodore correcting a brother

68. After this Theodore asked an ancient brother,[1] 'How do you understand this saying of the Gospel, *If any man comes to me without hating his father and mother*, etc. . . ?' The other answered, 'Scripture has put its words high that we might attain to part [of them]. For how can we hate our parents?' He said this because he often used to visit his relatives and was unable, even after that great teaching, to renounce the *mind of the flesh*. Then Theodore replied to him with artifice, 'Is this truly your faith at Tabennesi? The Gospel says one thing, and you say something else? I am leaving; I won't stay here. I was well where I was before; the fathers there never denied the Gospel.' And he made a pre-

Lk 14:26.

Rm 8:6.

tence of withdrawing and hid somewhere[2] for a while. The other brother came to Abba Pachomius and informed him. Pachomius answered, 'Do you not know that he is a neophyte? Hurry up and search for him. If he leaves here, we will not have a good reputation for it.'[3] The brother found him and as he was exhorting him insistently, Theodore answered him, 'If you want me to stay and see that what you say is true, promise before the Lord and the brothers that you will conform to the Gospel.' He did this, and from that time on he never went away to visit his parents.

SBo 64.

Obedience superior to fasting and psalmody

69. There was a brother who used to practise *ascesis*, but was not doing it for God. Pachomius, who had often seen him, took him aside and told him, 'Brother, the Lord says, *I have come down from heaven, not to do my own will, but to do the will of the one who sent me*. Therefore listen also

Jn 6:38.

to him who says this through me. For I see that the enemy so envies you to destroy all your labor. So now, when the signal is given by day to call the brothers to eat, do not wait till evening. Go, eat about five pieces of bread as well as the cooked food which is served to the brothers. But on the other hand, do not eat your fill, in order to be master of your body, since you are vigorous. And outside the *synaxis* of the brothers, do not pray much until you master the demon of boasting, because he is plotting against you.'

The brother kept to this for a while; but later he went astray again, saying to himself. 'Where is it written, "Fast not; pray not"?' And as he was disobeying and was about to be possessed by the demon, Abba Pachomius called Theodore and said to him, 'You know that I am greatly grieved for this brother, because he does not listen to me. Go then and visit him, and find out what he is doing.' He went and found him continually praying. He came back and reported it to [Pachomius], who said, 'Go, stop him from praying. And as soon as you stop him, the demon will manifest himself in him. And if you see it, watch over him until I come.' And when Theodore kept him from praying, the brother cried out to him, 'Impious fellow, do you stop me from praying?' And as Theodore sat to watch him, he rose up with a big club, wanting to strike him on the head. Theodore protected himself and reprimanded him in the name of the Lord. Then he stopped, and the possessed brother said, 'Do you want to know that[1] I am the one who is at work in those who sing for pleasure? Pay attention to the one you hear presently and he will say the same verse nine times.' Now, there was someone in a cell singing the beginning of the Canticle of Moses, *Let us sing to the Lord, for he has triumphed gloriously*. Theodore checked and he heard as [the demon had said]; he marvelled and was afraid, considering the great vigilance man needs to escape the wiles of the demons. But Abba Pachomius prayed many times for the sick man and the merciful Lord healed him. And so sobered for the future, he guarded himself. Ex 15:1.

70. In one monastery there was a cistern needing to be cleaned. [Pachomius] took some brothers and went down to clean it. A certain old man who had come to the monastery after lingering in the world a long time saw him going down along with the brothers into the cistern. And because he did not yet know the courage of those who are faith- *SBo 65.*

About a murmuring old monk

ful in all things he began to murmur saying, 'This man is merciless, taking the children of men down into a cistern at night to die'. That very night he had a dream. He saw himself over that cistern and he saw those who were working below. And in their midst was a man shining with extraordinary glory who said to them, 'Receive a spirit of obedience and strength'. And to him he said, 'And you receive, as you deserve, a spirit of faithlessness.' And troubled by this nightly dream, he came in the midst of the brothers in the *synaxis* and falling on his face he confessed this.

SBo 66.

Pachomius' vision concerning the future of the *Koinonia*

71. Another time the brothers were with him cutting rushes. And as they were transporting the rushes to the boat, Pachomius suddenly fell into ecstasy. He saw some of the brothers surrounded by a fiery circle with flames licking them, and they were unable to pass over it. Others were barefoot on top of thorny pieces of woods, pierced by splinters, and they had no way out. And others were standing half-way up a steep precipice, unable either to climb up or to throw themselves into the river, for there were crocodiles below, watching them and leaping up at them. As he was still standing there, taken by his vision, the brothers passing by saw him. They cast their burdens down and they stood by him in prayer.

When he returned to himself after a long hour, he ordered food to be given to the brothers, for it was already evening. Then he told them to gather around him. He told them about his vision and they all wept with great fear. And as they asked him what this meant, he said, 'I perceive that after my death this will happen to the brothers, who will not find anyone capable of comforting them rightly in the Lord from their afflictions.'

72. An anchorite brother came to see him. And as they sat to talk about suitable matters, he said to Theodore, 'Prepare some food for the brother'. [Theodore] went outside and sat down, thinking that he had told him, 'Let me speak to the brother'. Since he did not prepare anything [Pachomius] asked another steward who was passing by. But he too withdrew, not knowing what he was saying. With his vigilant spirit [Pachomius] understood that this was a temptation. He himself rose and prepared food for the brother; he ate with him and dismissed him. Then he called Theodore and said to him, 'If your father according to the flesh told you something, would you ignore him? Why did you not prepare food for the brother?' He answered, 'Father, I thought that you were telling me, "Leave, that I may speak to the man." ' He also called the other one, who said the same thing. Then he sighed and said, 'An evil spirit caused this hindrance that we might be vexed. But blessed be the Lord who *grants patience* and prudence. As for you, learn patience from what has happened.

SBo 67a.

Theodore does not understand an order from Pachomius

Is 57:15.

73. 'For often I have heard the evil spirits speaking of their wiles against men in this manner. One would say, "I am assigned to a hard man. When I suggest an evil thought to him, he immediately stands to pray, and I go out ablaze." And another demon says, "Mine is easy. He listens to me and does what I suggest to him; and I love him very much." Therefore watch yourselves always, and sign yourselves in the name of Christ.

SBo 67b.

The wiles of the demons

And if you practise *ascesis* against them, they will have no power over you.'

A brother who did not come to the instruction

74. One day, as he was again explaining beneficial matters to the brothers, his heart was suddenly so seized that he could no longer speak. Understanding in his spirit why this happened, he called the steward of the monastery and said to him in a low voice, 'Go to such and such a cell and see who it is who is neglecting his own soul. Be yourself the witness of how this man has caused his own loss: First, he did not come to hear the word of God in order to be strengthened against the demon who afflicts him and drags him around. Secondly, having not come to hear [the word], why is he there sleeping instead of praying? I do not know if this man [can] become a monk.' In fact the man, who had not given himself up *to carry the cross*[1] according to his capacity, left the brothers and went back to his parents.

Mt 10:38; Lk 9:23; 14:27.

SBo 67c.

Pachomius' teachings

75. And he began to tell them a parable. '[Imagine] a house in which there are a hundred rooms or cells. If a stranger buys one cell from the master of the house, can he be prevented from entering his cell, even though it is the one furthest inside the house? So, too, the faithful man; if he has all the *fruits of the Spirit*, but by his negligence and the enemy's plot he is estranged from one of them, he will lack strength in the face of the enemy concerning that fruit. And perhaps, if he is not vigilant, the enemy will defeat him also in another, and so will get mastery of the whole man, leaving him destitute of anything good. But if on the other hand he pulls himself together again, he will not only gain possession ofthe one

Ga 5:22-23.

fruit from which he was estranged, but will also make great progress.

'For there is not just one measure of piety, but many. There are rich commanders in the spirit; there are, as it were, captains of tens, of fifties, of hundreds, and of thousands, and supreme kings,
even as Abraham was called *a king from God*. In- Gn 23:6.
deed he was not simply a king himself, but in him
the King of kings was seated as upon a throne.' 1 Tm 6:15.

76. A bishop once sent him a man for him to *SBo 68.*
judge. This man was a monk wearing a hair gar- **Story of Mauo**
ment and he was accused of stealing for a second time. Now, one of the brothers, a guileless and very good old man called Mauo, who was one of the ancient housemasters, had not gone out with the brothers at that time to reap rushes, for he was sick and grieved. His grief came from the evening instruction when he had heard our father speaking about the great safeguard to salvation. He was shocked by these words; not knowing the enemy's cunning against souls, and seeing himself firmly set, he said, 'Why does the Old Man teach us so great a safeguard? Are we good only to fall every hour?' Thus grieved, he was lying inside the huts and so he saw this man coming. And he said to the steward Theodore,[1] 'Take care of the man until our father comes in. For I see that he is great and pious.'

When Pachomius came in with the brothers, this man and the others who were with him went to meet him. He confessed his fault and Pachomius corrected him according to his spiritual discernment, quoting the Scripture, '*We all err
in many things*; but let us pray to the merciful Jm 3:2.
God, and he will heal us. And let us watch our-

selves in the future.' When the old man Mauo heard these things he marveled at Pachomius' spiritual discernment. He was now persuaded of what he had said in the evening, and he glorified God.[2]

SBo 69a.

Theodore's first instruction

77. Some days later [Pachomius] called Theodore and said to him, 'When the brothers come out from table[1] in the evening, give your ministry to someone else and come to where we gather for the instruction on Sunday.' And when Theodore came to the instruction, he told him, 'Stand here in the midst of the brothers and speak the word of God to us'—as he used to do himself. He obeyed him and stood up, though unwillingly; and he began to speak what the Lord gave him. All stood, including Abba Pachomius who listened as one of them. But some, out of pride, were vexed and they returned to their tents[2] so as not to listen to him. The one who stood [to speak] was younger in human age.[3]

After the instruction and the prayer Pachomius sat down as was his custom and he began saying, 'You have heard what was said. Whose was it? The speaker's or the Lord's? And those who were vexed, for what reason were they vexed? Because he is younger? But we find that the Lord said about a child, *Anyone who receives a child like this in my name receives me*. Was I not standing and listening as one of you? And I tell you that I did not only pretend but I was listening with all my heart, as one thirsty for water. For worthy indeed of all acceptance is the word of the Lord, as it is written.* Wretched are those who went away;† they have estranged themselves from God's mercies. And if they do not repent of their

Mt 18:5.

Cf. Pr 25:25.

*Cf. 1 Tm 1:15; 4:9.
†Jn 6:67; Ps 44(43):18.

pride, it will be difficult for them to have Life. For *he is near to those contrite in heart, and will save the humble of spirit.*' Ps 34(33):18.

SBo 69b, 70.

Theodore becomes steward of Tabennesi

78. After that he appointed [Theodore] as steward of the monastery at Tabennesi, considering him capable in spirit. He was then about thirty.[1] Abba Pachomius himself stayed in the Great Monastery called Phbow, where the administration of all the monasteries lay. (AD 336-337.) Although Theodore had been appointed there, it was as if he had not been appointed; for he had no will of his own. For *the word of God had proved him through fire* and strengthened him to *mind the things which are above*. (Ps 105(104):19. Col 3:2.) And all his zeal was devoted to *love God with all his heart* according to the commandment. (Mt 22:37.) And as he progressed he profited the brothers, for his word was full of grace.

Appointment of the ancient brothers

79. Cornelios, Pšentaesi, Sourous, Pšoi, Pecoš, another Pachomius, Paul, John, Paphnouti, and many others whom it is superfluous to name individually were all strong in spirit and true athletes of Christ. Pachomius saw the life of each and he appointed most of them as leaders and fathers of the monasteries.[1] Among those who were in second rank after them and who loved God was Abba Titoue, who was father of the virgins, holy, and fattened like suet on the mercies of God, and virtuous, as we have said before of father ⟨Jonas⟩.[2] Some of them were ascetics who, at the age of about seventy, had never tasted wine, either in health or in sickness. Others, when they were sick, did not yield to the request of those who asked to carry them from their reclining seat[3] and lay them down on a bed at the hour

of death, so that they might at least be fairly prepared for burial. They would rather stay and die crouched upon their reclining seat. But for the fact that it would be too long a story, it would do no harm to make memory of them also.

SBo 56.

Story of Petronios and foundation of Thbew

80. There was a certain Petronios who not only left his parents' house never to return there until he commended his soul to the Lord, but also while he was alive persuaded his whole household, father, brothers, sisters, relatives, and slaves to come to the brothers. They did come and they made a beautiful death. And his father, called Pšenthbo—we do not know how we shall praise him also—brought with him everything he had: cattle, sheep, and all sorts of gear, and he donated it to the community through our father Pachomius. And he gave him also a monastery called Thbew, and there the brothers lived according to the rule of the other monasteries.[1]

SBo 54,58b,55b.

Foundation of Panopolis

81. And before this monastery was founded—for the monasteries are ranked in order[1]—a certain bishop of Panopolis called Arios (but orthodox in faith, an ascetic and a servant of Christ) smelled the fragrance of the brothers' *Koinonia*. He summoned Abba Pachomius and asked him to build a monastery[2] near his city according to God's plans. Pachomius came with the brothers; the bishop gave them a place, and they built the wall. But some people who did not know *God's designs* and were moved by envy, kept throwing down by night what was being built. But by the patience of our holy father, [the brothers] were instructed by an angel from the Lord who stood and, as it were, demarcated with

1 Tm 1:4.

his finger the circuit of the wall with fire. And the monastery was built.

He appointed there as steward a certain Samuel, a man cheerful in spirit and abstinent, along with other capable men, for they were near a city. And he stayed with them some time until they were well established.

82. A philosopher from the city came to the monastery to test them and to see what kind of men they were. He said, 'Call your father to me. I want to speak to him.' Pachomius sent Cornelios to answer him. And the philosopher said to him, 'You have the reputation of being monks who are intelligent and speak wisdom. But who would ever bring olives fron elsewhere to sell them in Panopolis, since the city has an abundance of them?' Cornelios answered, 'Was it ever heard that the olives of Panopolis make oil? No! instead they are salted.[1] We are the salt; we have come to salt you.' Hearing that, the philosopher returned to report it to his friends. Another said to him, 'You have not questioned them more than that? I will go and test their understanding of the Scriptures.'

SBo 55a.

Visit of a philosopher from Panopolis

Cf. Mt 5:13.

Abba Pachomius called Theodore and sent him to this one when he came. Theodore himself told us, 'When I was sent out I was afraid, not knowing how to answer a philosopher; for Cornelios is wiser than I am.' And [the philosopher] put a question to him, though not a difficult one; 'Who was not born and died? And who was born but did not die? And who died but did not stink?' Theodore answered, 'He who died not having been born was Adam; he who did not die having been born was Enoch; and it was Lot's

Cf. Gn 5:24.

Gn 19:26. wife who did not stink, being *a pillar of salt*.' The other accepted this answer and departed.

There was in that monastery a holy man called Talmas. He was strong in the spirit but his body was consumed with a fever like Job's. And he persevered until death in the *ascesis* and the vigils.[2]

Jb 2:7b.

SBo 57,58a, 71,58c.

Foundations of Tse, Tsmine, and Phnoum

83. [Pachomius] received other monasteries. Before this one at Panopolis, he received the one called Tse, and after it those of Panopolis, Thbew, Tsmine, and later on the other one called Phnoum near Latopolis.[1] These the blessed Pachomius founded. And the brothers dwelt there according to the same rules, with fathers likewise appointed for them. And he provided them with their bodily needs. For Phbow is the Great Monastery where the steward ministers to all the monks. He ministers to them by the Providence of God according to circumstances and he receives the fruit of their work.

Twice a year they would come to the Great Monastery. At Passover those in charge would gather around our father Pachomius and they would celebrate the Passover together with the words of God and with love. And again in the month of Mesore it was their custom to come again to render account of their works to the Great Steward, writing it out in detail. And if the father of each monastery desired some disposition, he would tell him, and he would appoint a housemaster or another officer.[2]

Above all, the Man of God himself took care to go round the monasteries, strengthening those afflicted with various temptations. He taught them to repel them by the remembrance of God, and ordered everything profitable to their souls.

SBo 99b.
Heb 12:4.
Story of Titoue

84. There was another athlete who *fought even to blood against sin*. His name was Titoue and he was the housemaster of the stewards assigned in Phbow to feeding the sick brothers. One day as he was preparing [the food] an evil spirit came to tempt him and to trick him into the sin of eating first from the food of the sick. For through the struggle[1] the faithful are more tested for the glory of God. And so he did not go that evening to the refectory to eat; and wanting to continue his fast also the next day, he stood to pray and said with tears, 'Lord, I am prepared not only to fast until I win your love, but truly even if they subject me to martyrdom and *burn me*, I will not forsake temperance, in which all the saints are glorified. I pray you, make me perfect in your fear.' And so he died, a pure and genuine monk.[2]

1 Co 13:3.

A monk who offered a libation to idols

85. Once the barbarians were making war and a monk from another place was found and taken captive. As some of them were going to eat, they said to him, 'Get up, serve us; and first pour wine in libation to the gods before we drink.' As he refused, they drew near to kill him. Frightened, he poured the libation.[1]

Later he escaped from them and came to the monastery, to Abba Pachomius himself, and told him about it. Pachomius was pained when he heard this, and he told him, 'The crown was brought to you and you did not take it. Why did you not die courageously for the name of him who died for us? You have suffered a great loss. Yet, that you may not despair completely of yourself—for the Lord *desires not our death but our repentance*—do penance as much as you can, not only *in a contrite and humble spirit* but also

Ez 18:23,32; 33:11.
Ps 51(50):17.

through bodily toil, so that the word of Scripture may be fulfilled also for you: *See my abasement and my pain, and forgive all my sins.*'[2] And so he withdrew, rejoicing in hope.

Ps 25(24):18.

SBo 72b.

Pachomius accepts a lesson from a boy

86. One day [Pachomius] was weaving a mat in Tabennesi. A boy who was doing the weekly service in the monastery came by, and seeing him weaving said, 'Not so, father. Do not turn the thread this way, for Abba Theodore has taught us another way of weaving.' He got up at once and said, 'Yes, teach me the way.' After the boy had taught him, he sat down to work with joy, having forestalled the spirit of pride in this, too. For if he happened to have a carnal thought, he did not pay attention to it. And he did ⟨not⟩[1] rebuke the boy for speaking unduly.

SBo 113.

Discernment of apparitions

87. Another time as he was again weaving a mat, a demon appeared to him showing off and saying that he was Christ. Now without God's permission [demons] cannot appear to anyone or suggest an evil thought. And since the Holy Man had the discernment of spirits so as to discern the evil spirits from the holy ones, as it is written, he immediately thought, 'When the apparition is of spirits that are holy, the thoughts of the man who sees it vanish completely, and they[1] consider nothing but the sanctity of the apparition. Now here I am, seeing this and conscious and reasoning. It is clear that he deceives me; he is not among the spirits that are holy.' When the demon saw that he was so thinking, he began to deprive him of his thoughts. [Pachomius] rose with the faith of Christ and stretched his hand out as if to grasp the demon, while breathing into his face. And he vanished.

Cf. 1 Co 12:10.

88. Theodore had the habit of coming to Phbow every evening after his work at Tabennesi in order to listen to the words of the Scriptures from Abba Pachomius. He would then return to tell them to the brothers before they slept. And he did this for a long time. Once he came and as he did not find him, he went up on the roof of the *synaxis* to recite the parts of the Scriptures he knew by heart. And as he recited, the place where he was shook. Wondering what this might be, he came down into the *synaxis* to pray. He entered but could not stay because of the fear that filled the place. His body shuddered. And as the fear still rushed against him, he leapt outside the doors, not knowing what it was.[1]

SBo 73.

Pachomius has a terrible apparition

The next morning after the *synaxis*, he found Abba Pachomius relating this in private to some ancient fathers: 'I nearly gave up my soul this night. Indeed as I was praying in the *synaxis*, I saw some terrible apparitions; and I was so afraid that it was as if I were no more. And I prayed to the Lord that this fear might remain in me and in the brothers until the end, remembering the fathers who were with Moses at the foot of Mount Sinai where the fire was and the other fearful things. And as I was still distressed, a bold man came in, but by God's mercy he went out immediately.' Theodore said, 'I am the man. As I did not find you in the evening, I went to recite on the roof. But it started to shake and I came down to pray. And since I was unable to do so, I fled outside.' Those who heard him marvelled, all the more since he was not used to revealing to them the hidden things he happened to see by the Lord's will, unless it could foster faith and

Cf. Ex 19:16; 20:18.

edification. Indeed the holy men are always as if in heaven by their thoughts.[2]

SBo 74a.

Breach of silence in the bakery

89. After [Pachomius] had given his instructions for the constitution of the *Koinonia*, it happened once at the bakery in Tabennesi that some brothers who were kneading and working talked at a time when they should have been not talking but reciting, according to his binding commandment. Although he was far away, he realized in the spirit that they had transgressed his precept. So he called Theodore, who was at the time the father of the monastery, and he told him, 'Go and search properly to see if some brothers did not talk in the bakery during the evening, contrary to the precept.' He inquired and found that many had talked and he reported it to him. And Abba Pachomius said, 'They consider that these [commandments] are human; but even if a [commandment] is about a very small matter it is important. That great multitude that encircled Jericho obeyed the commandment by a silence of seven days; and when they received the commandment to shout, again they fulfilled the will of God by obeying the man who was commanding
Jos 6:10,16. them. Likewise, let these brothers be careful in the future and they will be forgiven for what has happened. If that commandment were not profitable for their souls we would not have given it.'

SBo 36.

Theodore's headache

90. Theodore asked him one day about a headache he had, and he replied, 'Do you think that a pain or any thing like it comes without God's permission? Bear it therefore. When he wills he will heal you. And if he tests you for a while thank him like the perfect man Job, who endured everything that came upon him and blessed the Lord

saying, *Blessed be the name of the Lord.*[1] Indeed although the one who bears the cross may not be suffering for anything in particular, the cross and the *ascesis* suffice for him. But the one who lies sick can be struggling far more than the one in good health in strength of soul and patience. Then such a man has a double crown. It is good for the one who suffers to bear his pain about ten years before speaking of it.' And Theodore was comforted by these words.

Jb 1:21.

91. [Pachomius] would send him often to make the rounds of the monasteries to visit them. And speaking once in the midst of the [the brothers], he told them, 'Theodore and I fulfil the same service for God; and he also has the authority to give orders as father.'

SBo 74b.

Theodore's kindliness and Pachomius' austerity

And whenever Theodore came to the monasteries, the brothers seeing him rejoiced. For as we have already said, he had great grace from the Lord. Our Father Pachomius was perfect in everything, but fearful and always mournful, remembering the souls in torment, as we have heard about the rich man.[1] Often after he had been very thirsty in the burning heat, he would take a pitcher of water to drink, but would not drink enough to quench his thirst.[2]

Lk 16:23.

92. Once while Theodore was in a monastery, they brought him a brother whom they accused of having stolen something and whom they wanted him to expel. He was not the culprit, however, but another brother, unsuspected and faithful in the eyes of men, was. But they had suspected the former because he was a little vulgar. When the thief realized that he had not only committed the first fault but that someone

SBo 75.

A brother falsely accused of stealing

else was also endangered on his account, he took Theodore aside and said to him, 'I am the one who did it'. He replied, 'You have committed a fault, but you have redeemed it by clearing the innocent for us.'[1] Then he called the other and said to him, 'I have learned that it is not you who did this. But even if the brothers afflicted you despite your innocence, you are indebted to the Lord in other things. Therefore give him thanks with fear.' And he said to the brothers about him, 'Did you not bring this matter for me to judge? Well, I have learned that God's will is to forgive him and ignore the matter for ever. Indeed we are all in need of mercy.'

SBo 83,82.

Vision of a soul escorted by angels to heaven

93. One day Theodore heard in the air voices singing a melody very delightful and pleasing to the ear, and he asked Abba Pachomius, 'Abba, do you hear?' He answered, 'Yes'. 'What is it?' said [Theodore]. He answered, 'A beautiful soul being taken to heaven has passed above us, and grace has been granted to us to hear for an instant the voice of those who sing and praise God in his presence.'

And another time, when they were both sitting near a brother in the pains of death, the Lord revealed to them the manner in which the soul leaves the body. They did not willingly tell anybody these things as long as they lived; they are mysteries. But the great brothers who were with them saw them gazing in quiet wonder at some holy men present at the time the sick man gave up his soul. And sometimes they would also tell a part of what they had seen by the will of the Lord, for the sake of edification. Abba Pachomius used to teach that the thought of desiring to see some of the invisible things should not be accepted at all, for they are full of wonder and frighten those who seek and hear them.

94. Another Theodore, lector of the Church of Alexandria and an ascetic, heard about Abba Pachomius and the brothers, and he came up to the Thebaid by boat. He was also pious and obedient as one of the Lord's sheep. [Pachomius] received him and for his encouragement placed him in a house with an ancient brother who knew the Greek language, until he could understand also the Thebaic language.[1] And he progressed greatly in the *ascesis*.

SBo 89a.

Vocation of Theodore the Alexandrian

Cf. Jn 10:27.

His orthodoxy is manifest, for he was near the *spring welling up to eternal life*, drinking from it so as to bear fruits. We mean the archbishop, not only the most holy Athanasius who was then sitting on the archbishop's throne but whoever sat on it.[2] Whoever sits on that throne is not just sitting there alone, but He who said that *where two or three are gathered in his name, he is in their midst*,*[3] *Christ, the son of the living God*,†the Church's *foundation*‡ and its founder, God and man.

Jn 4:14.

*Mt 18:20.
†Mt 16:16.
‡1 Co 3:11.

95. Abba Pachomius loved this [Theodore], because he bore the life well. And with God's grace he made every effort to learn Greek, to discover how to encourage him frequently. Then he appointed him housemaster of the Alexandrians and foreigners who came after him. And his house was full of piety.

SBo 89b,90,91b.

Pachomius' advice to Theodore the Alexandrian

AD 333 (or 343?)

The holy Pachomius did many things with him, instructing him how to govern men. He would say, 'It is a great thing! If you see someone of the house negligent of his salvation, admonish

him privately with patience. If he once gets angry, leave him until God moves him to repentance. It is just like when someone wants to extract a thorn from somebody's foot. He digs around it, and if it bleeds and is painful, it is better to leave it and to put on it a softening plaster or something similar. Then after a few days it comes out by itself and easily. A man who is angry even against someone who does not argue with him will gain more after this from the one who is teaching him according to the Law. But if the offence is serious, report it to us and we will do as the merciful Lord wants. Care also for the sick as for yourself. Practice continence and bear the
Cf. Mt 10:38. cross more than they do, since you hold the rank of father. And be the first to keep the rules of the brothers so that they also may keep them. And if after this there is anything else you want to decide and you do not know how, by the grace of God tell me about it. Together we shall try to find the ex-
Cf. Dt 1:18. act answer to each one of the problems.'

When Pachomius gave instructions to the brothers, Theodore would interpret for the sake of those who did not understand Egyptian.

He was housemaster for thirteen years before the blessed Pachomius' death.[1] The first spiritual fruits of that house among the Alexandrians were Ausonius the great and [another] Ausonius, and a boy called Neon. Among the Romans there were the God-bearers Firmus and Romulus, Domninus the Armenian and the other holy men. Some of them knew the Great Man in the body; others did not.

SBo 72a. 96. Once our father went to Tabennesi on an urgent matter concerning a soul. After embracing

Pachomius' teaching

the brothers he sat down as was his custom to instruct them on every measure of vigilance against what is opposed to salvation. He spoke about the chastity of the body, but also about various thoughts: lust for power, slothfulness, hatred of a brother, or love of money. He said, 'Just as fire cleanses all rust and burnishes the objects, so the fear of God consumes every evil in man and burnishes him into *a vessel for special occasions, sanctified, well pleasing to God and ready for any good work*. As for the temptation of blasphemy suggested by the enemies, if it finds a man who is not vigilant even though he may love God, and if [this man] does not keep awake as he ought or does not consult a man of experience on how to overcome that guileful suggestion, it will wreck him. And many have killed themselves either by throwing themselves off a cliff while being out of their mind or by opening up their belly with a sword or in some other way. It is a great evil not to confess one's temptation quickly to someone who has knowledge, before the evil has matured. Here is the therapy through discernment of spirits that the Lord has taught us: "If I grieve my neighbor with a word, my heart becomes contrite when conviced by the word of God; and if I do not persuade him quickly I have no rest. Unclean demons! How shall I join you apostates in a thought of blasphemy against the God who created me? I will not give in even if you should pull me to pieces in suggesting these things to me. These thoughts are not mine but yours who are going to be chastised *in unquenchable fire* for ever and ever. As for me I shall not cease blessing, praising, and thanking the One who created me

2 Tm 2:21; Ph 4:18.

Is 66:24; Mk 9:44.

when I did not exist, and cursing you, for cursed indeed are you apart from the Lord." When one says these things with faith, the demon vanishes like smoke.

SBo 72c.

Story of Elias

97. 'Concerning the cause for which I came to you today, what is sought is found in an earthenware jar.' By that figure he meant the spiritual offence of a man. And when Abba Pachomius spoke, there was present a brother named Elias, a man of simple heart. He had gathered five figs before time and had hidden them in an earthenware jar to eat them after the fast. As soon as he heard about the jar he went and brought his jar and said to him in the midst of the brothers, 'I tell you, Abba, I took only these.' Both [Pachomius] and the brothers marvelled. For it was not about him that he had spoken. Then he told them, 'You must realize that it is not when we want it that we see hidden things for the sake of salvation; it is when God's providence wishes.[1] Concerning this little matter, I assure you that I knew nothing and had not heard about it from anybody. But the Lord, willing that this brother no longer be mastered by food, showed us how to correct him.' Then he rose, prayed with the brothers and left without eating, for he was in a hurry to return to Phbow.

Sources of this Life

98. We write these things although we have not seen him in the flesh, as we have said before. But we have seen those who were with him and of the same age. They knew these things accurately and they have recounted them to us in detail. Should anybody say, 'Why did they not write his life?' our answer is that we did not hear them speak often about writing, although they had been with him

and were of the same age and he was their father. But perhaps it was not yet the time. And when we saw that it was necessary to do so, that we might not forget altogether what we had heard about this perfect monk who is our father after all the saints, we wrote down a few out of many things.

Our purpose was not to praise him, for he does not want human praise, being with his fathers where true praise is to be found. We have learned indeed that when he was living in the flesh he did not consider himself worthy to intercede even for himself in his frequent prayers. He would take the saints for intercessors, saying, 'You who are worthy of God, pray for me, the sinner.' He was not one of the prophets or the patriarchs or the apostles, but he is their true child, as also are all those who are like him in various places. For the *blood of our Lord Jesus Christ has purified** all the earth and continues to purify it, and instead of *thorns and thistles*† he has *loaded it with the riches*‡ of his divine knowledge.

*1 Jn 1:7; cf. Heb. 9:14.
†Gn 3:18; Heb 6:8.
‡Ps 65(64):9.

(*Cf. SBo 189.*)

Sources of this Life

99. Abba Pachomius often used to *speak the word of God* to them. Some who loved him dearly wrote down many interpretations of the Scriptures they had heard from him. And if he ever had a vision or an apparition by the permission of God, he would tell it privately to the great [brothers][1] for the sake of the faith and profit of the hearers.[2] For God always glorifies his own servants, as he says to Moses, *that they may believe you forever*. But we have learned in time that *it does belong not to all to believe*, especially in a monk. Yet he walked in the ways of the saints, according to what Scripture says, *Be my imitators.* For the way is open for everyone.

Heb 13:7.
Ex 19:9.
2 Th 3:2.
1 Co 4:16.

This is why we have put together these things in
writing, that we may gather without any loss the
fruit of the things we say. Let us be convinced
that God says even now, *Those who honor me I*
1 S 2:30. *will honor*. We know that one psalm is sufficient
for us, especially since the Lord says, *I will give*
Mt 11:28. *you rest*.[3] Even now in the Church of God there
are many ranks among the fathers. First are the
bishops, then the priests, deacons and others in
order, including monks; and *blessed are all they*
Ps 128(127):1. *who fear the Lord*. And although the life of each
perfect man has not been written among men, it
has been written with the Lord.

This text we have just written, we have not written for the sake of writing but as a memorial, as is the case with the letters that holy bishops and fathers have written for edification, as with the *Life of the Blessed Antony to the Monks and Brothers in Foreign Parts*[4] who had asked the most holy father Athanasius for it. In fact, it was after consulting well-informed monks that he wrote accurately about him. We who are sinners, we do not compare ourselves with that most holy man who also held such a high rank, but we have been writing as children eagerly desiring to recall the memory of the fathers who brought us up.

While he was still alive moreover, the father himself dictated not only talks and ordinances about the edification of the community, but also many letters to the fathers of the monasteries. He used in them the names of characters from A to Ω, expressing to those fathers of the monasteries in a secret spiritual language things for the governance of souls, when he had no leisure to come to them. And since they were spiritual men, they would answer him in the same manner. They understood so well that he would lead them to perfection, guiding them in detail with characters and a language that he was asked to make a book of those spiritual writings.[5]

SBo 92.

Story of ten ancient brothers who indulged in murmuring

100. In the monastery of Phbow there were ten ancient brothers who, although they were chaste in body, often used to murmur and would not listen to the Man of God with faith. Since he was patient and loved the souls, especially the ones for whom he had been toiling for a long time, admonishing and exhorting them, he did not want to neglect them. He mourned for them before the Lord, *humbling his soul with fasting*, spending six days without food and up to forty nights without sleep. And his body became extremely lean and feeble. Then the Lord heard him and each one of them received the understanding to be healed from his error as much as possible. And this is how they died.

Ps 35(34):13.

SBo 99a.

A brother stung by a scorpion

101. There was a brother strong in spirit emulating [Pachomius'] endurance.[1] One day a scorpion bit his foot as he was praying. Placing the bitten foot upon the scorpion he prayed saying, 'If God does not heal me, who will?' At the beginning, as he tested himself to see if he could endure it, the pain caused by the poision began to torment his heart, and he almost gave up the spirit. But forcing himself to endurance he conquered the torment until the hour of the *synaxis*.

SBo 103.

Other vision of Pachomius

102. One day Abba Pachomius himself told the brothers about this, which is a kind of vision: 'I once saw a large place with many pillars in it. And there were in the place many men unable to see where to go, some of them going around the

the pillars, thinking they had travelled a long distance toward the light. And a voice [resounded] from all directions, "Behold! Here is the light!" They would turn back to find it, only to hear the voice again and turn back another time. There was great wretchedness. Afterwards I saw a lamp moving, followed by many men. Four of them saw it and the others followed them, each holding his neighbor's shoulder lest he go astray in the dark. And if anyone let go of the man in front of him, he would go astray with those following him. Recognizing two of them who had let go of their neighbor, I shouted to them, "Hold on, lest you lose yourselves and the others." And guided by the lamp, those who followed it came up to this light through an opening.'

He told these things to some brothers in private. And we heard it from them much later, along with the following interpretation: 'This world is the dark ‹place, which is dark› [1] because of error, each heretic thinking to have the right path. The lamp is the faith in Christ, which saves those who believe aright and leads to the kingdom of God.'

SBo 93.

Burial of a bad monk

103. Once a brother died at the monastery. After the preparation of the body [Pachomius] did not let the brothers sing psalms in front of him while bringing him to the mountain according to custom. Nor was the Eucharist offered for him. He collected the man's clothes in the middle of the monastery and burnt them, putting fear into all that they neglect not their life. How he put up with him until he died we do not know. But this we know, that men of God do nothing hurtful; and their severity as well as their goodness are measured by their knowledge of God.

104. There was a boy called Silvanos.[1] Our father Pachomius had given him instructions before receiving him into the monastery, but afterwards he became negligent and laughed frequently. He called him and said to him, 'What were the instructions I gave you? Do you not know that it is a great thing to become a monk? I told you at the gates, "Examine yourself whether you are perhaps not able to become a monk". And you promised before God, "I will become one". Now, if you truly desire eternal life, why do you not pay attention to yourself and have you instead given free rein to your heart? But since you are yet unwilling to fear the judgement of God, get up, go to your parents. Do not stay here any longer.' When the boy heard this he wept copiously, for he did not want to go back to the world. And he promised with great supplication that he would be as a monk should be.

SBo 93(bis)a.
Story of young Silvanos

Then Pachomius was patient with him; he called a great monk named Psenamon and told him in the boy's absence, 'We know that you have labored in *ascesis* a long time. Now, for God's sake, take this boy and suffer with him in all things until he is saved. You know indeed how I am occupied with many affairs concerning the brothers.'

105. And so they worked together making mats, and they fulfilled the fast and the prayers properly. The boy obeyed Psenamon in everything, as he had been commanded. He would not eat even a vegetable leaf without asking. And so he was humble, great [in virtue] and meek, keeping his mouth closed; he was never quick to raise his eyes toward anyone and his *ascesis* was rigor-

SBo 93(bis)b.
Story of Silvanos (cont.)

ous. In private he applied himself to vigils in such a way that when he had prayed abundantly and grown weary, he would sit in the middle of his cell, weaving through the night, and in that position he would take the sleep he needed. And to say it in short, he became a living man.[1]

One day when the brothers were seated Abba Pachomius began to tell them, 'There is a man among us as I have not seen ever since I became a monk. And as a white wool [is] dipped in precious purple, and the dye never fades away, so that soul has been dipped in the Holy Spirit. If that man, hearing such testimony, realizes that we are speaking of him, he will not rejoice; and if he is blamed he will not be grieved; he remains the same, unchanged.' Theodore said, 'Father, show him to us. Is he greater than Petronios or Cornelios? Pachomius answered, 'Why do you name others? He is even greater than yourself. In age, *ascesis*, and knowledge, you are his fathers. But by his deep humility and the purity of his conscience, he is great. The beast that wars against you you have bound and put under your feet; and if you are negligent it will be set loose again and rise up against you. But Silvanos has slain it.' And after living in this way for seven years, he died and Pachomius rejoiced in him greatly.

The more they emulated each others' achievements, the more they progressed, especially seeing before them [a man] strong in the Spirit and in whom was Christ.

SBo 94a.

Theodore's great trial

106. As we have already said, Theodore was appointed to be, after [Pachomius], a comforter of souls for the brothers. After seven years he was subjected to a great trial by the Lord, [who

wanted] to test him. As Abba Pachomius was ill, some ancient fathers and heads of the monasteries gathered about him and said, 'Perhaps the Lord will visit our father suddenly and we will become wretched. Since none of us knows his whole manner of life as you do, be persuaded and promise us that should this happen you will not refuse to become his successor, so that the brothers will not be scattered.' After much asking to be excused from this and not getting their agreement, he gave them his word. AD 344.

Later, when Abba Pachomius heard this, it did not please him. He called all the leaders of the monasteries, Sourous, Pšentaesi, Paphnouti, Cornelios, and Theodore himself. And he said to them, 'Let each of you tell his shortcoming. I will tell mine first: I neglect to visit and to console the brothers because I am away working the fields on the island during the day to feed the brothers (for there was a famine at that time). And you, Theodore, tell yours!' And he said, 'For seven years now I have been sent by you to visit the monasteries and to settle everything as you do. And never did it come up to my heart that "after him, I will be in charge". But now I am plagued by this thought and I have not been able to conquer it yet.' Abba Pachomius told him, 'Very well! You no longer have authority over anything. Withdraw by yourself somewhere[1] and pray to the Lord that he may forgive you.'

So he rose up in very great grief and went to a quiet cell to mourn with weeping and great sorrow. He was afraid God had turned away his face from him because he had grieved his servant. Indeed he held [Pachomius] to be perfect and invincible. Cf. Ps 27(26):9.

SBo 94b,95a.

Theodore's great penance

107. He spent two years in that punishment. The great brothers encouraged him often, because in their eyes what had occurred was not a sin but only the thought, 'after him it will be me'. [Pachomius] had punished him because he wanted to make him perfect and completely free of ambition for power. And before withdrawing, Theodore said to him, 'I have some business to wind up in Thmoušons; send me, and I will come back quickly.' And he sent him alone. And he wept as he went, saying, 'Lord, do I still have repentance?'[1]

And when he reached the ferry at Chenoboskion, he boarded it. There were two old men in the boat. One of them started praising Theodore, saying to the other, 'Blessed is this monk'. The other replied, 'Why do you call the wretched man blessed? He has by no means reached the measure of the basket.' The first one said, 'What is its measure?' He began to say, 'There was a certain farmer who was so difficult that it was rare for anyone to be able to spend a whole year with him. But someone got up, came to him, and said, "I will work with you". He said to him, "Very well!" On watering day he said, "Let us draw water by night to irrigate the field, and not by day". The man replied, "This is wisdom. This way no one, either beast or man or any other creature, will drink from our ditch." And when he was going to plough, he said to him, "Let us sow our field in this fashion: one furrow of wheat, another of barley, another of lentils, another of chick-peas, and so on in this fashion." He replied, "This is intelligence greater than the first. For our sowing will be found lovely because of the variety of flowers." And when the green crop was come, yet without seed, [the farmer] said to him, "Let us go and reap!" The other replied, "Let us go. The profit from the chaff is great, for it is both green and good." And after threshing, he told him to bring the basket, "Let us transfer the chaff within with the measure." The other replied, "This shows more sense than the first decisions, because even the chaff is preserved." And after the farmer had tested the man in all these and found him obedient without questioning,[2] he told him, "You shall no longer be my hired servant, but my son and heir." Well then, if this one has also measured with the basket, he can deserve to be called blessed.'

SBo 95b. **Theodore's great penance (cont.)**

108. The other old man said to the first one, 'Since you told the parable, tell also its interpretation'. He said, 'The farmer is God; he is difficult since he commands us to *carry the cross** and not [to indulge] the will of our heart.† Now, Pachomius, this man's father, by obeying God in all things became well-pleasing‡ *in his sight.** And if this man too is steadfast after his likeness, then he will be his heir.'

*Cf. Mt 10:38; Lk 9:23; 14:27.
†Cf. Jr 23:26.
‡Cf. Heb 13:21.
*Gn 17:1.

Hearing this, Theodore was strengthened, marvelling at what was said and at those who said it. And stepping off the boat, he saw them no more, for they were angels from God who had appeared to him this way to correct and console him, as Abba Pachomius testified later. After he had come to the monastery and returned to Phbow, Theodore pondered by himself what he had heard, and was comforted.

He was grieved not because he had been punished, but because he had ever received such a thought; especially when he had heard Abba Pachomius saying, 'Just as a corpse does not say to other corpses, "I am your head", so too I never considered that I am the father of the brothers.

Cf. Mt 23:9.

God himself alone is their father.'

SBo 96a,97.

Trip of Theodore and Zacchaeus to Alexandria

109. After this a certain Zacchaeus, one of the ministers of the brothers and a man of God, asked Abba Pachomius for Theodore, saying, 'The eyes of Theodore have been harmed by weeping. Do you want me to take him with me on

AD 345.

the boat to Alexandria?'[1] He replied, 'Take him'. On the boat and everywhere he was as a neophyte having become a monk yesterday, adorned with

Eph 4:2.

much *humility and meekness*. And after this Abba Pachomius declared that God had granted him a sevenfold increase of his previous progress.[2]

Pachomius' obedience to the common rule

110. Even Abba Pachomius himself submitted to the housemaster, being more humble than all others, as it is written, *A land mountainous and*

Dt 11:11.

lowly. At the hour of the instruction, he stood listening with the brothers of the house. His tunics were in a cell under the authority of the housemaster. And he had simply no authority to take for himself anything for the body from the steward.[1] For more than the eternal tortures, he feared becoming estranged from the humility and the sweetness of the Son of God, our Lord

Cf. Mt 11:29.

Jesus Christ.

SBo 91a.

Question of Theodore the Alexandrian to Pachomius

111. One day when the brothers were coming out from eating and were receiving the so-called *korsenilion* in front of the doors, as was the custom there, [Pachomius] himself came to receive his portion.[1] And as he withdrew to his house, the aforementioned Theodore of Alexandria followed him after receiving his own portion. They came where he stayed and sat down; then [Theodore] asked him, 'I have heard about Cor-

nelios that he is extremely self-controlled and that during a whole *synaxis* he does not allow his mind to be distracted. Now in this very hour I too tried with great watchfulness, and could scarcely make three prayers while holding my thought. How can I hear the words of God then and pray without having my mind distracted?' [Pachomius] told him a parable, 'When a slave according to the flesh sees a free man—although he is a poor one—he desires freedom. When a poor man sees a commander he wants to be a commander. When a commander sees a king, he likewise greatly desires to become king. As for Cornelios, it is after struggling very hard that he has been granted this by the Lord's grace. And laboring also, you must likewise believe and you will receive according to your merit.'[2]

Synod of Latopolis

AD 345.

112. As Pachomius' fame spread far away and people talked about him, some would say balanced things, others would exaggerate. And once there arose a debate about his being called clairvoyant. He himself was summoned to answer this in the church of Latopolis in the presence of monks and bishops.[1] He came there with some ancient brothers, and seeing those who were contending against him, he kept silent. When he was asked by bishops Philo and Mouei[2] to answer the charge, he said to them, 'Were you not once monks with me in the monastery before you became bishops? Do you not know that by the grace of God I, just like you, love Him and care for the brothers? When Moses of Magdolon,[3] as he was called, was possessed and being snatched away by the demons into the caverns to be put to death, did you not know how the grace of God

through me helped him—to say nothing of the rest?' They answered him, 'We confess that you are a man of God and we know that you saw the demons, making war against them to ward them off souls. But since clairvoyance is a great thing, give some answer again about that, and we will persuade the murmurers.'

Then he told them, 'Have you not heard me frequently say that I was a child of pagan parents, not knowing what God is? Who then gave me the grace to become a Christian? Was it not the man-loving God himself? And after this, as there were few monks, one could scarcely find groups of two or five, or ten at the most, living on their own and governing each other in the fear of God with much toil. Now we are this great multitude—nine monasteries—striving night and day by God's mercy to keep our souls blameless. As you yourselves confess that we have knowledge concerning unclean spirits, so too the Lord has given us to recognize, when he wills, which of them is walking aright and which has only the appearances of a monk. But let the gift of God alone! When those who are wise and sensible according to the world spend a few days in the midst of men, do they not distinguish and recognize each one's disposition? And if the one
Heb 9:12. who shed *his own blood* for us, the *wisdom of the*
1 Co 1:24. *Father*, sees someone trembling with all his heart for the loss of his neighbor—especially of many—will he not give him the means to save them blamelessly, either by the discernment of the Holy Spirit, or by an apparition when the Lord wills? For I do not see the realities of our salvation when I wish, but when He who governs

everything shows us his confidence. For *man* in himself *is likened to vanity*. But when he truly submits to God he is no longer vain but is a *temple of God*, as God himself says, *I will dwell in them*.[4] He does not say in all, but only in the saints; in you and in all and also in Pachomius, if he does His will.'

Ps 144(143):4.
2 Co 6:16.
Jn 14:23.

When they heard these things, they marvelled at the confidence and the humility of the man. When he stopped speaking, a man possessed by the enemy came with a sword to slay him. But the Lord saved him through the brothers who were with him, while a tumult arose in the church. As some spoke this way and some that, the brothers made their escape and they came to their last monastery, called Phnoum, which is in the district of that same city of Latopolis.[5]

SBo 96b.

Theodore and Zacchaeus come back from Alexandria

113. When the boat returned from Alexandria—there were only two boats[1] for the whole Community, one to sell the mats to procure the food and other needs, the other for their tunics—Zacchaeus and Theodore came down and greeted [Pachomius] and the brothers. He said to them, 'How is the Church?' For he was grieved for it at that time because the blasphemous Arians, with a certain Gregory, had *risen up against it* with violence, like bandits. He prayed to God about this. His heart was deeply sad that the people of God were being so wronged and deprived of their archbishop, Athanasius the Christ-bearing.[2] He would say, 'We believe in the Lord; he has permitted this to happen in order to test the faithful, but *punishment* will come swiftly and *will not tarry*.' And after this he told them also about the affliction that had come upon him

Jb 30:5.
AD 339.
Si 7:16-17;
Cf. Lk 18:8.

in Latopolis, giving thanks and saying, 'We
Jm 1:12. ought *to endure* every *trial*[3], for it does not hurt. Those who inquire into our affairs are orthodox fathers and brothers; and though *the enemy has*
Ps 74(73):1. *wrought evil in* some who belonged to us but who were outside the wall—that is the law—for a little while, God has saved us and them. As for the most holy pope, against whom the enemies have been battling so long, he is truly blessed. They have no power against him for he has God to sustain his faith. The word of Scripture will be fulfilled in him: *Every voice that shall rise against*
Is 54:17. *you in judgement, you shall defeat them all.*' And so it did happen; he was restored to the Church
21 October 346. with honor.[4]

SBo 119,121.

Outbreak of plague in the monasteries

114. After the Passover a disease came from the Lord upon the brothers. In all the monasteries brothers died, about a hundred and more at a time. Pachomius himself was ill. The disease was the plague: when someone was seized by the fever, his color changed at once, his eyes became bloodshot, and he was as if suffocated until he gave up the spirit. Then Sourous, the father of the monastery of Phnoum died, and also Cornelios of the monastery of Thmoušons, and Paphnouti, the steward of all the monasteries, who lived in Phbow, and many other great brothers. Theodore ministered to Abba Pachomius whose body had become extremely thin from the duration of the diesease. His heart and his eyes were a burning fire.

Two days before his death he summoned the other fathers of the monasteries and the other leaders and said to them, 'Behold, you see that the Lord is visiting me. Choose for yourselves therefore the one who is able in the Lord to govern you.' And he called one of them, Horsiesios by name, from the monastery of Chenoboskion, a man mighty in faith, humble and good. He said to him, 'Go around and investigate whom they choose.' He went around, but they said with tears, 'Ever since the Lord delivered us into your hands we do not know anyone but you'. Then he said to them, 'Believe me in this; I think that Petronios, if he lives, is able to take care of you'—for he was also sick in his monastery, called Tsmine in the region of Panopolis.[1]

SBo 120.

Pachomius refuses special treatment in his illness

115. After they had prayed and withdrawn, Abba Pachomius said to a brother, 'Do me a charity, bring me a good blanket; this one is heavy and my body does not bear it. For I have now been ill for forty days, but I give thanks to God.' The brother went to the steward's quarters[1] and took a good light blanket and put it over him. But when he saw the difference of the blanket, [Pachomius] said to him, 'Take it away; I ought not to be different from the brothers in anything. I will manage somehow[2] or other until I depart from the body.'

SBo 122, 123.

Pachomius' death

116. And he was in pain, at the point of giving up the spirit. He grabbed Theodore entreatingly by the beard and said to him, 'If they hide my bones[1] take them away from there.' Theodore thought he was enjoining him not to leave his body in the place of its burial but to transfer it elsewhere secretly. So [Pachomius] told him, 'I say not only this to you but also this.'[2] And he enjoined him three times. What he also told him was not to neglect the negligent brothers, but to rouse them by God's law. And Theodore answered,

'Very well!' And so he gave up his holy soul on the
9 May 346. fourteenth of the month of Pašons.[3] All night long they kept vigil about him with reading and prayers. Then his body was prepared and carried away to the mountain in like manner with psalms and buried. When they had come down, Theodore and three other brothers transferred it to another place, where it is to this day.

SBo 124,130.
Petronios' death

117. Those who had been sent for Abba Petronios brought him back sick. Even in his illness he was extremely strict and vigilant. After governing the brothers for a few days in the word of God and the memory of their father, he died on the 27th of
21 July 346. the month of Epip. And as he was about to give up the spirit, he asked them about who should be father in his place. As they answered that this care was his, he appointed for them Abba Horsiesios, who was present and about whom we spoke above. When he heard this, Horsiesios wept, saying, 'This is beyond my power'. Then they prepared the body of the holy Petronios and they buried him on the mountain with prayers and psalms.[1]

SBo 209.
Horsiesios becomes the father of the *Koinonia*

118. Abba Horsiesios was very good and humble. He used to make the rounds of the monasteries to visit the brothers with vigilance, knowing how the holy Abba Pachomius, who was perfect, took care of them with zeal. And standing or sitting to speak the word of God to them, he profited them. He would often recall to them what Abba Pachomius had told him when he was head at Chenoboskion, 'Even if you have not received a great knowledge of God, tell them a parable, and God will make it work.' And so he would tell them parables and interpret them, and the brothers marvelled when they heard them.

One of these [parables] is this: 'We know that our father strengthened us from the Scriptures through his perfect knowledge. But I think, in my poverty, that if a man does not guard his heart well, he forgets and neglects all that he has heard. And so the enemy finds a place in him and casts him down. It is like a lamp made ready and shining. If one neglects to provide it with oil, it is quenched little by little and the darkness gains power against it. Not only this, but sometimes a mouse will come near it and try to gnaw the wick. It cannot do this before the lamp is completely quenched; but if it sees that the wick has not only no light but no heat of fire either, it snatches it out to eat it, knocks it down and causes the lamp to be shattered. If the lamp is earthenware, it is broken; but if it is brazen, it is found by the master of the house who fixes it up again. Likewise, when a soul is neglected, the Holy Spirit withdraws from it little by little until it is completely quenched of his heat. Then the enemy eats up the zeal of the soul and also destroys the body through wickedness. And if that man is well disposed toward God and has simply been overcome through negligence, the merciful God puts into him His fear and the memory of the punishments; then the man will be vigilant in the future, guarding himself with great caution until the day of his visitation.' After he spoke these words he rose to pray, having profited them by the parable.[1]

SBo 199.

How Pachomius had praised Horsiesios in the past

119. Abba Horsiesios, in the midst of the brothers, was emulating the life of Abba Pachomius, for he had known him a long time. And when Abba Pachomius had appointed him as father at Chenoboskion and had heard some who

murmured about his being too much of a neophyte for this rank, he had told this about him: 'Do not think that the kingdom of heavens belongs only to the ancients. An ancient who murmurs against his brother is not an ancient; he has not even made a beginning at being a monk. For
*Dt 10:12. *God wants* nothing from men but *fear and love**;
†Rm 13:10. and *love does not do harm to the neighbor.*† I tell
you, through his progress Horsiesios is a *golden*
Ws 7:48-49. *lamp in the house of the Lord.* And the word of
the Scripture shall apply to him, *I have betrothed you to one husband, so that I may present you as*
2 Co 11:2. *a chaste virgin to Christ.*'

SBo 126,127, 129,133, 134b.

Second trip of Zacchaeus and Theodore to Alexandria

21 October 346.

120. And it happened that when the archbishop, the holy Athanasius, returned with glory from the imperial court, the brothers who had come to Alexandria in the boat heard that our father, the blessed Antony, was in the Outer Mountain.[1] They moored and went up to see him and to receive his blessing, for he was a man of God. When he heard that the brothers had come, he forced himself to rise—he was very old indeed[2]—and came out to embrace them. Then he asked them, 'How is Abba Pachomius?' As they wept, he understood that he had died. And he told them, 'Do not weep; all of you have become as Abba Pachomius. I tell you, it was a great ministry he received, this gathering of so many brothers; and he walks the way of the apostles.' Abba Zacchaeus answered and said to him, 'It is rather
Mt 5:14. you, father, who are the *light of* all this *world*,
and your fame has reached the Emperors, and they glorify God on account of you.' And he said, 'I will persuade you by my answer, Zacchaeus.[3] In the beginning, when I became a monk, there

was no community to nurture other souls; each one of the ancient monks after the persecutions practised his *ascesis* alone. And then your father did that beautiful thing from the Lord. Another before him, called Aotas, wanted to obtain this ministry, but since he did not do it with whole-hearted zeal, he did not succeed.[4] Concerning your father, I often heard how *well he walked* according to the Scriptures. And truly, I too often desired to see him in the body. Perhaps I was not worthy of it. In the kingdom of heavens however, by God's grace, we shall see each other and all the holy fathers,[5] and especially our *Master and God, Jesus Christ*. Therefore take courage, and be strengthened and perfect. But tell me, whom did he appoint as his successor?' They said, 'A certain Abba Petronios; and at the moment of his death he appointed Abba Horsiesios'. Then he said, 'Do not call him Horsiesios but *Israelite*.[6] And if you go to the bishop Athanasius, who is truly worthy of the episcopate, tell him: "Here is what Antony says, 'Care for the children of the *Israelite*.'" And so, after praying and blessing them, he sent them with a letter written to Athanasius. When they arrived in Alexandria the holy pope welcomed them greatly, loving them especially because of the word of the blessed one, for he knew what kind of a man he was.

c. AD 271.

Heb 13:18.

Jude 4.

Jn 1:47.

121. After this, Abba Horsiesios appointed Theodore for a while as housemaster of the carpenters at Phbow.[1] And a certain Macarios, father of the monastery of Phnoum after Abba Sourous, asked Abba Horsiesios to send Theodore with him to his monastery to prepare their bread, for he knew that this would be a source of

SBo 137,138.

Theodore is sent to the bakery at Phnoum

encouragment. And after the Passover Theodore went with him to the monastery. As they were still on the boat a brother came to Theodore, who was sitting down. Seeing him humble and quiet as a neophyte, he asked him, 'How long have you been with the brothers?' He said, 'Not long'. The brother asked him, 'Did you know baking before you came?' He answered. 'Barely'. He told him again, 'When you come to the bakery, if you see someone laughing abundantly or another quarreling—for in a community also there are all kinds of people—do not be scandalized, but pay attention to yourself and to those who are vigilant.' Theodore answered, 'Very well!' After the boat had moored at the monastery all the brothers, having heard about him, came out with joy to meet him, for they knew him from before, when he was a comforter of souls together with our father. As for that brother who had spoken to him as to a neophyte on the boat, when he saw the brothers honoring him, he was ashamed and afraid for having dared to say such things to such a man.

c. AD 347.

122. Abba Horsiesios nurtured the brothers *according to the grace of God that was given* him. And the word was given him more and more so that he could speak for the exhortation of the brothers. He did not only speak to them in parable, but he also gave the interpretation of the sayings. And he enjoined them to keep the rules of the Community which Abba Pachomius had established for its constitution while he was still alive, as well as the decisions of the fathers, the housemasters, and the seconds of the monasteries. And these he appointed[1] at the two

1 Co 3:10.

Horsiesios watches over the observance of the traditions

moments of the year: at the Passover and at the time of the great remission of the accounts of their bodily needs and of their work and their expenditure, [which they do] so that the steward of the Great Monastery might know how to carry out his administration.

Example of the ancient brothers

123. And so the Lord kept them in concord and love, as they had been before. There were indeed many of the ancients who had not yet fallen asleep. These are Pšentaesi, Samuel, Paul, John, and Hieracapollon who had comforted in the Lord our father Pachomius in his trials, as we have said before, and also the great Titoue, and Jonas and many others, and Theodore the Cityman, and with them also Theodore whom the Lord had spiritually *tested through fire* by Abba Pachomius so that he would become *a vessel of election.*[1] Therefore, since there were so many lamps among the brothers, there was no darkness in sight; for *the commandment of the Lord shines afar, giving light to the eyes.*

Ps 105(104):19.
Ac 9:15.
Ps 19(18):8.

Psahref appointed Great Steward at Phbow

124. When Abba Paphnouti the great steward of the monastery of Phbow died,[1] Abba Horsiesios appointed someone else called Psahref to be steward in his place. He was a cheerful man and inured to toil, himself one of the ancients.

SBo 135.

Theodore listening to Horsiesios' instructions

125. As the brothers often asked Theodore to explain a spiritual saying to them or to tell them a vision of Abba Pachomius, he told them, 'Here is our father Horsiesios; let us ask him anything we want and he will tell us, for he is indeed our father'. And as Abba Horsiesios was sitting to speak to them—for it was their custom from the beginning to sit together every evening after work and meal to *search the Scriptures*;—because they

Jn 5:39.

were without concern other than the concern of
their salvation, and those who were able and ap-
pointed to have care did it as servants of God for,
In so far as you did this, says the Lord, *to one of*
Mt 25:40;18:6. *these who believe in me, you did it to me*—so, as
Abba Horsiesios was speaking to them, Theo-
dore himself sat and listened like a guileless
child, saying to himself, 'I know nothing because
I grieved God and our father by what I did then'.
He was so humble that Abba Pachomius testified
about him in his absence. 'By this punishment
Theodore has gained sevenfold beyond what he
was.'[1]

Horsiesios' teaching

126. Here is also what our father Horsiesios
used to say, 'I see some of you wanting to receive
titles and to rule, or to become housemaster or
something else. In the past, in the time of our
father, except in obedience nobody wanted to be
called great, fearing to be found *least in the*
Mt 5:19. *kingdom of heaven.*[1] And when Abba Petronios
appointed me, I wept copiously, in fear of the
danger to souls. Not only I, but the saints also.
Moses, being sent by God for the sake of the people, first declined in his humility, and then accepted that ministry only when God was angered
Ex 4:10,14. at him because of this. As for us, brothers, hearing what is written, *He who exalts himself will be*
Lk 18:14. *humbled,* let us watch ourselves. It does not
belong to all to govern souls, but only to perfect
men. Here is a parable: If an unbaked brick is set
in a foundation near a river, it does not last a
single day; but if it is baked, it endures like stone.
So if a man has a carnal mind and has not been
purified like Joseph through the fire of the word of
God, he is destroyed when he comes to a position

of authority. For many are the temptations of such men in the midst of men. And it is good for a man who knows his own limits to lay down the burden of authority after he is established, that he may not run into greater danger. Those who are *steadfast* in faith are *immovable.* Now if someone wanted to speak about the most holy Joseph, let him say that he was not of this earth. How many temptations did he endure, and in what country, where there was then no trace of the fear of God! But the *God of his fathers Abraham and Isaac and Jacob* was with him and delivered him from every affliction. And now he is with the fathers in the kingdom of heavens. Knowing our own limits, let us also strive; for even so we will scarcely *escape God's judgement.*' After saying many such things, he prayed, and the brothers withdrew to their tents.[2]

1 Co 15:58.

Ac 7:9-10.

Rm 2:3.

127. And it happened after this, as the brothers had greatly increased in numbers, that they began to expand in fields and many material things in order to feed the multitude. And each monastery began to be a little negligent as other preoccupations increased. A certain Apollonios, father of the monastery of Thmoušons, wanted—contrary to the rule of the *Koinonia*—to buy himself superfluous commodities. Questioned about this by Horsiesios and reprimanded by him, he was vexed. By the enemy's temptation, he wanted to separate his monastery from the Community and he persuaded many elders of the monastery to do so. Many other monasteries were harmed by him because he had seceded, saying, 'We no longer belong to the *Koinonia* of the brothers.' And because he would not listen to

SBo 139a.

Revolt of Apollonios of Thmoušons

Abba Horsiesios trying to persuade him, the temptation grew stronger.

SBo 139b.

Horsiesios' affliction and prayer

128. Seeing his great affliction, Abba Horsiesios, who had put up with him for some time and had considered persevering in this affliction until his death, later planned to have someone as collaborator in the discharge of his paternal office. He went into a quiet place at night and, as we heard from his own mouth, wept copiously saying, 'O God, Abba Petronios your servant gave me this office so that I might *win* more *and save* many. But now I see that not many listen to us for their salvation. Each one follows his own heart, except your faithful servants who *behave honorably* with our father, and the others who have your fear. I am afflicted at the sight of the whole monastery in a state of trouble that does not come from me. For as you know, I have not afflicted anyone. You know, Lord, that it is not only this monastery; I fear for the others as well, lest they take occasion for not wanting any more the early life of love in concord. Now therefore, Lord, I am no longer able [to go on] alone. Show me someone who is able and I will name him for them, lest I become responsible for [the loss of] souls.

1 Co 9:19,22. Heb 13:18.

SBo 139c,140.

Horsiesios resigns as father of the *Koinonia*

129. During that night he had a dream in which he saw two beds: one was beautiful but old; the other beautiful and firm. And he received this oracle: 'Rest on that firm one.' He understood in the spirit that that bed was Theodore, who had in the past been of one soul with the great Abba Pachomius. And when morning came, as one already relieved of his affliction—all the more since he loved [Theodore] very much for his humility and because he knew how

to *endure the opposition* of men—he gathered all the leaders [of the monasteries] without calling Theodore, and said, 'You are not ignorant of the enduring trial. I have remained for some time, thinking it would cease, but instead it is growing, as you see. Therefore I confess to you that I am no longer able to bear the care alone. I know that none of you forces me to resign, but I am perfectly aware that I am not able [to go on]. God and the fathers do not blame me, for they know my limits. The one I see capable of this in every respect is the same one who was in the past and is again our father Theodore.' After he said this he left again by night to go to the monastery of Chenoboskion and he remained there.[1] All the brothers, hearing it, took Theodore as their father with joy and exultation. And Theodore declared that he would not rise either to eat or to drink for three days, 'until I meet Abba Horsiesios'.[2]

Heb 12:3.

c. A.D. 350.

130. They sent for Abba Horsiesios and he came. Then they assembled again for him. And Abba Horsiesios said to [Theodore], 'Did we appoint you? It is our father who appointed you, signifying it ahead of time when he took hold of your beard and said three times, "Remember, Theodore, do not leave my bones where they are buried."'[1] When Abba Theodore heard this, he no longer objected. And having committed him to the brothers, [Horsiesios] departed again for Chenoboskion.

Theodore appointed by Horsiesios as his successor

Abba Theodore was established. When they heard it, the brothers of all the monasteries rejoiced, especially those who knew him from the beginning as a true child of Abba Pachomius, and knew that his word had the grace and *power*

Pr 16:24. *of healing for a soul* in affliction. And he was so wonderful a subordinate to Abba Horsiesios that the latter said, 'This man is truly a bed of all repose'. Even when he had received the rank and he toiled night and day that the brothers may be saved in the Lord, he never considered himself as father, remembering his punishment; but he called himself the deputy[2] and servant of Abba Horsiesios, even though he had withdrawn from administration. Thus when the man of God Theodore had to give an order, he would walk a long distance to come to him and ask, 'What do you want me to do?' Since he had perfectly eradicated from himself the lust for power, having been trained by God and brought to perfection through trial, he was, because of this and through his great bounty, a comfort not only to Abba Horsiesios, but to everyone; so that Abba Horsiesios said, 'I rule now more than when I was alone'.

SBo 141,142,143.

First instruction of Theodore as father of the *Koinonia*

131. When he assembled the brothers to give them his first instruction, he spoke as follows, 'Where are the ancient brothers?[1] Be strong in the Lord and let us be of one mind to suffer with each other, that the enemy may not scatter our father's labor. For you are not ignorant of his endurance in afflictions from demons all the time he was teaching us of our Lord Jesus Christ whose presence is fear and trembling. Now it is not yet five years since he passed away and we have forgotten that very great joy and peace which we then had with each other. For in the days of our father we did not have either in heart or in mouth anything but the word of God, which is *sweeter*

Ps 19(18):10. *than honey and the honeycomb.*[2] We were not conscious of living on earth but of feasting in heaven. A man who finds himself in the cold and deep frost runs somehow until he reaches the heat of the fire; then he is delighted and revives. So also was it with us then; the more we sought God, the more *his goodness manifested itself,* bringing sweetness to our souls. But how are we now? Let us, however, all return; we do believe that God will renew us in his mercy.' Tt 3:4.

As he said this he wept; and the cry of the brothers' weeping reached far from the *synaxis.* And so he prayed and dismissed the brothers. After this he boarded a boat with some brothers and went to visit and to strengthen the brothers of the monasteries. And after much struggle and spiritual understanding, he won over Apollonios, the father of that monastery, who made peace with the brothers. And the enemy who had tempted them was put to shame.

(Cf. SBo 191).

Theodore's care for souls

132. Abba Theodore was very vigilant over souls, encouraging each one privately and tending them as a doctor. Not one of the brothers refrained from privately confessing his mind to him, how he was fighting the enemy. Having himself the experience of victory in the Lord who says, *Be brave,*[1] he taught them to resist each one of the thoughts of the enemy, so that *competing according to the rules,* as Paul says, they might *be crowned.* If he saw someone unwilling to watch over his own life and disregarding it, he warned him with great patience of the dreadful judgements of God. For *it is a dreadful thing to fall into the hands of the living God.*[2] Even in punishing sinners God is beneficent and good, for *He wants everyone to be saved and to come to the* eternal Jn 16:33. 2 Tm 2:5. Heb 10:31. 1 Tm 2:4.

rest.[3] And he said again, 'If anyone is scandalized by the man who disregards [his life], because I am patient beyond measure, I am held responsible for this.' Because of this he would not rest, but with great zeal he would cast his care on the Lord, praying and saying, 'It is a great toil for a man to give account for himself; how much more for many? Therefore I know we are *like a shadow*; we are not keepers of souls. For we do not attain to such a measure. But you who know and *have moulded one by one the hearts of men,* guard us and the whole world from the envious demons, for no one can save us except you, Lord, Lord God of glory.'

Jb 8:9.

Ps 33(32):15.

SBo 151.

Theodore accomplishes healings

133. Whenever seculars came to him, either on the road or in the monastery, about someone possessed by the devil or otherwise suffering, he would tell them, 'Do not think that we can intercede with God on their behalf when we are sinners. If God in his mercy for his own creature wants to spare it, he has the power to do so, as he always shows his goodness to all.' And when they insisted very hard, asking him to pray, he would ask that the will of God and that which was expedient be done. And so the Lord would heal them. This he did remembering the father who had nurtured him, Abba Pachomius, for he always walked the way of the saints unswervingly.

Foundations made by Theodore

134. Then he himself also founded monasteries in addition to those which had existed from the beginning: two near Hermopolis called Kaior and Oui, with our father Horsiesios' approval. He likewise appointed there, according to the law of the *Koinonia,* vigilant and pious fathers with seconds of the monastery, and also housemasters

with seconds of the houses, after the manner of the other monasteries. He founded another monastery near Hermonthis, appointing there as well good leaders and brothers and the same rules. And he founded another monastery of virgins in the village called Bechne, about a mile from the monastery of Phbow.[1] At Tsmine Abba Pachomius in his life-time had also founded another one. These monasteries were able to do the weaving of the woolen garments,[2] the blankets, and other things, and also the spinning of raw flax for the tunics. The steward of the Great Monastery used to send them work through Eponyches, a holy and strict man who became their father after the death of Abba Peter, the ancient [father] in Tabennesi.

Theodore's teaching about visions

135. When Aba Theodore heard of the murmuring there had been in the past against Abba Pachomius concerning clairvoyance, and of his trial—Theodore was then in Alexandria on the boat—he began from that time on to hide the things he happened to see in vision by the will of God.[1] He understood indeed that it was better for him. And so he said to the brothers about this, 'What is greater than to *have the Holy Spirit*? If (1 Co 7:40.) the one who has an orthodox faith and keeps the commandments of God becomes worthy to be found a *temple of God,* it is obvious that where (2 Co 6:16.) God is, is all power and confidence. Even in a king's palace, what glorious thing is not there? Likewise the Tabernacle of old contained everything that contributed to the glory of God. Let no (Cf. Ex 25-27.) one therefore have doubts if he hears that a man of God has had a vision, for he who gives the visions *dwells in him.*[2] But here also there is need (1 Co 3:16.)

for prudence lest anyone, *thinking he is impor-*
Ga 6:3. *tant when he is nothing* and being deceived by
the enemy into a desire to see, be thrown down
and fall into folly as has happened to many.[3] Now
whether we have attained to this degree or not,
let us all alike have great humility, praying to
escape the eternal punishments. It is what the
saints prayed for, as one of them says, *Watch over*
Ps 25(24):20. *my soul and rescue it.* And again Paul, giving
thanks to the Lord for his own salvation, says, *I*
2 Tm 4:17; Cf. Ps 22(21):21. *was rescued from the lion's mouth,* meaning the
1 P 5:8. one who *roars to devour souls.* For he is full of
wiles and at times he makes a lie appear as truth.
And the man who is tempted is led astray unless
he is found to have a very keen discernment concerning [the enemy]. But the one who is not led
astray is the one who in everything obeys God and
his saints without questioning.

As for us, brothers, understanding these
things, let us keep each to his own measure, the
one who is considered a shepherd of souls as well
as the one who is considered a sheep. Yet let us all
pray to be sheep, for no one is the shepherd save
Jn 10:14. he who said, *I am the Good Shepherd.*[4] But when
he appeared—as David had foretold and signi-
fied, *God is the Lord and he has appeared to*
Ps 118(117):27. *us,*—God the Word appearing in human form
saved us, bestowing upon us knowledge of the
faith, and, before going up into heaven, he established the apostles as his successors, saying to
*Jn 21:15. Peter, *Feed my lambs** and, *Look after my*
†Jn 21:16. *sheep.*† For this reason there is need now too for
men who, generation after generation, feed the
Mt 28:20. souls in the Lord who says, *I am with you.*[5] For we
know that after the apostles it is the bishops who

are the fathers. But all those who listen to Christ who is in them are also their children, although they do not belong to the clergy and have no ecclesiastical rank.'[6]

136. Abba Theodore had been listening—for he was also present—[1]when blessed Antony received the brothers as his children, and the holy pope loved both of them greatly, as much as or even more than he loved Abba Pachomius. He remembered and he would say to the brothers, 'I heard, and you ancients were also present, when our father said, "In our generation in Egypt I see three important things that increase by God's grace for the benefit of all those who have understanding: the bishop Athanasius, the athlete of Christ contending for the faith unto death; the holy Abba Antony, the perfect model of anchoritic life; and this *Koinonia*, which is a model for all those who wish to assemble souls in God, to succour them until they be made perfect."'

SBo 134a.

Praise of Antony, Athanasius, and the *Koinonia*

137. And it happened after this, as the holy bishop Athanasius was being sought by the Emperor Constantius at the instigation of the enemies of Christ, the Arians, that a certain general by the name of Artemios received authority and was searching everywhere for him.[1] And as a rumor spread, 'Is he not hiding among the monks of Tabennesi, for he loves them?,' the duke sailed up for this purpose. As he was sailing up, it happened by chance that Theodore himself was sailing down to visit the monasteries of the brothers near Hermopolis. As he drew near the upper monastery called Kaior, he saw the duke sailing up; the Lord made him understand what was going to happen and he revealed it to the

SBo 185a.

Artemios searching for Athanasius

AD 360.

brothers. The brothers wanted to turn back and arrive before him lest he should trouble the brothers in Phbow, but Abba Theodore told them, 'He for whose sake we have come so long a way to visit His servants is able to take care of this affair without there being any grief.' Having said this, he went on to the monasteries.[2]

SBo 185b. 138. When Artemios came to the monastery he ordered the army to keep watch around the monastery by night, armed as during war. He himself sat with his lieutenants within the monastery, outside the *synaxis*, having archers standing by him on both sides. Seeing this, the brothers were afraid. But a holy man called Pecoš, whom we have mentioned above, exhorted the brothers to keep courage in the Lord. The duke asked through an interpreter, 'Where is your father?' Abba Pecoš answered, 'He has gone to the monasteries.' And he said, 'The one who comes after him, where is he?' They showed him Abba Psahref, the Great Steward. And [Artemios] told him privately, 'I have an imperial order against Athanasius the bishop, and he is said to be with you.' Abba Psahref replied, 'He is indeed our father, but I have never yet seen his face. Still, here is the monastery.' After he had searched and not found him, he said to those in the *synaxis*, 'Come, pray for me'. They said, 'We cannot, because we have a commandment from our father not to pray with anyone who follows the Arians'—for they saw with the duke one of the Arians who was acting as bishop—and they left. So he prayed alone. And as he fell asleep in the *synaxis* by day, he woke up with a bleeding nose and was troubled—we do not know for sure what happened to him—and full of fear, he said, 'When that happened to me in the vision, I hardly escaped death with God's mercy.'[1] Thus he withdrew. When Abba Theodore returned and heard these things, he gave praise to God.

139. Many of the brothers were dying, to the point that one or two passed away daily. And one day, as they were going to the mountain, they got very tired because the rising water had begun to fill the field. They told him, 'What are we going to do if someone else dies? For no boat can pass either, since there is not yet much water.' He told them, 'According to our faith, God will spare us also in this.' And no more died until the inundation was passed. And the brothers marvelled.[1]

SBo 180.

Another outburst of plague

140. One day as he was sitting and giving the instruction, a brother told him, 'Abba Theodore, how is it that as soon as the people say something hard to me I get angry?' He answered, 'This is not strange; the acacia also, when struck with an axe, secretes gum.' And the brothers asked him, 'What does that mean?' He said, 'The man of God is compared to a vine; if someone takes from its fruit a cluster of grapes and wants to squeeze it, it yields nothing but sweet wine. That is, if the faithful is afflicted in deed or word or thought, he cannot produce fruit other than the goodness of the words of God. Likewise, a carnal and irascible man produces unprofitable bitterness.

SBo 187,186a.

Theodore's teaching

'I tell you, I who say these things, I am afraid of *falling from God's grace* for being unable[1] to resist to the enemy's war against us. *All the day long*, it is said, *he has been fighting and afflicting me*. For if angels have fallen and others among the prophets and others among the apostles—I

Ga 5:4.

Ps 56(55):1.

do not mean only Judas, but also many of Paul's disciples from whom *he separated his true dis-*
Ac 19:9. *ciples,* in Acts—we, too, ought to fear.

'Do you want me to give you an example that we must fear God? Let us take a rock that reaches into the clouds, narrow and reduced to four cubits in breadth, with a bottomless abyss on either side reaching from west to east. When a man is baptized, if he makes profession of monastic life, he receives the seal of the Spirit and journeys toward the east. Now let us consider not only the abyss, but also the narrowness of the path. So narrow is it that if someone goes slightly
Cf. Ws 4:19. aside, he is lost and his memory is found no more.
Cf. 1 Jo 2:16. To the left of the path, the evil lust of the flesh; and to the right, pride of heart. These are the abysses. And if someone walks worthily, with fear, he reaches the east and finds the Saviour
Cf. Rv 4:2. upon a throne; on either of His sides are armies of angels with eternal crowns, crowning the man who walks aright to Him.

SBo 186b.

Theodore's teaching

141. 'If someone speaks like this: "If ever someone is deceived or snatched away in one of these [abysses], is he already lost and has he no longer repentance?", I will tell him that a man who has repentance and a true understanding regarding the faith and God's commandments, with a zeal for this, even if he comes close to falling through negligence, yet the Lord will not let him be lost altogether. As it is written, *My feet were on the*
Ps 73(72):2. *point of stumbling.* He shows him His grace through the scourge of a sickness or a grief or the shame of his offence, so that becoming conscious [of his negligence] he may walk in the middle of the narrow path until he arrives and may not wan-

der a single foot off, because the path is four cubits wide. He who wanders off is like Judas, who after receiving great benevolence from the Lord and seeing great signs—even the resurrection of the dead—*having the purse,* was not aware of grace. Because of this he was completely lost through love of money and betrayal. But the good, although as men with free will they may somehow have neglected what is fitting, are still *refined through fire like silver* casting away rust. This is why blessed David says, *I, in the abundance of your mercy will enter your house.* If he says this, how much more we wretches!

Jn 12:6.

Jn 18:2-3.

Ps 66(65):10.

Ps 5:7.

142. 'Let us also understand this profitable thing we heard from our father, from his interpretations of the holy Scriptures, about a man wishing to be purified from a sin such as anger.[1] Unless he says in himself when he is reviled the first time, "Behold, today I have gained a golden coin", and unless he considers it a further gain when he is reviled a second time, and so on until he has an abundance of gold, it is impossible for him not to get angry. For if he endures it as someone who is coerced when he is reviled once, what will he do when he is reviled a second time and especially if this happens often? For truly the commandments of God are *gold and precious stones, and sweeter than honey and the honeycomb,* as it is written. But we do not know or perceive things in this way, because of *the mind of the flesh.*

SBo 186c.

Theodore's teachings

Ps 19(18):10.

Rm 8:6.

'Who tells a man who has tossed him some pure bread, "I will bear with you this one time, but if you give me any more, I will gouge out the pupils of your eyes"? Does he not rather love the one who gives to him, even if this one does not wish to be

loved? Such are the men of God. Not only did
Mt 5:11. they bear *those who persecuted them* and did
Mt 5:44. them evil, but they even *prayed for them* according to the commandment of the Saviour, whose gold they were going to inherit according to the Scripture, *Heirs of God, and coheirs with Christ.*

Rm 8:17. 'What have you done so worthy, O man, that you should be God's heir? Were you persecuted? Were you put to death because of him? The glory of the world is quite sufficient to reward you for this. Who does not honor a man of God, especially a martyr of Christ? But yet, great is the goodness of God. God is like a man who tells us, "Give me all the earthenware vessels that are in your house and I will destroy them; and receive in their place vessels of gold and precious stones." But we do not know; as it is written, *Man having dignity has not understood; he has been ranked with the mindless beasts, and made like unto*
Ps 49(48):12. *them*. May it be given to us to be vigilant unto the end by His grace.'

SBo 200,201a.

Athanasius' visit to the monasteries in the region of Hermopolis

143. And saying this he dismissed them to go to meet bishop Athanasius, for he had heard that he had come up by boat to the Thebaid.[1] Abba Theodore took with him fathers of good conduct and brothers able to glorify God, and off he went. They found him when he had not yet reached the
AD 363. Hermopolite nome. The brothers saw him from a distance and went to him. There was a numberless crowd on both sides of the river, and many bishops and clerics and monks from the surrounding places. [Athanasius], seeing them at a distance and recognizing them, quoted this word about them, '*Who are these flying like clouds and like doves* with their young toward me?' When he

embraced them, although he did not yet know which was Abba Theodore—for Theodore did not embrace the pope first, but appointed respectable old men to greet him first—he recognized him and, taking him by the hand, said, 'How are the brothers?' He said to him, 'Thanks to your holy prayers, we are well, father.' And then the brothers began to sing psalms. There were there nearly a hundred persons, and among that great throng nobody knew his neighbor. And Abba Theodore was holding the pope's donkey, walking in front of him with the brothers who were singing psalms. And there were lamps and torches on every side.

144. Seeing that Abba Theodore was bubbling over with the Spirit and that not only did he not avoid being in the midst of the pressing crowd, but also that the torches were almost burning him and that he had such enthusiasm and strength, the pope said to the other bishops, 'Do you see how the father of so many brothers wearies himself running in front of us? It is not we who are fathers. Here are the fathers, those who have humility and obedience because of God. Happy and blessed are they who always, until they are crowned, carry the Cross of the Lord whose ignominy is glory and whose toil is refreshment.' And after he had spent a few days in the cities of Antinopolis and Hermopolis, benefitting them with divine words, he went up to the monasteries. Seeing the very sincere affection of the brothers toward him, he rejoiced and praised the Lord. Then visiting the monastery he marvelled at everything: the *synaxis*, the refectory, the cells of each house, even the reclining seats,[1] and he said, 'Theodore

SBo 201b,202, 203.

Athanasius' visit

Mt 10:38; Cf. Lk 9:23; 14:27.

you have done a great work procuring rest to souls. I have heard especially about your monastic rules. *Everything is very good.*' Theodore said to him, 'The grace of God is in us through our father. But to see you is like seeing Christ.'

Gn 1:31.

After he had spent a few days there, he said to Abba Theodore, 'Since the Passover is near, assemble the brothers according to your rule; and I shall do as the Lord will arrange for me.' Then he embraced him and dismissed him, after writing through him to Abba Horsiesios and the brothers a letter as follows: 'I have seen your assistant and the father of the brothers, Theodore, and [I have perceived] in him the Lord of your father Pachomius. I rejoiced at seeing the children of the Church;[2] and they delighted us with their presence. The Lord is the one *who will reward* them. As he was about to come to you, Theodore told me, "Remember me". And I told him "*If I forget you, Jerusalem, may my right hand be forgotten! Let my tongue cleave to the roof of my mouth, if I do not remember you.*"' And so Theodore left the boat with the brothers to the pope, and he said to them, 'Go with him wherever he wants; for he has authority even over our bodies.'

Heb 11:6.

Ps 137(136):5-6.

SBo 204,205a.

Theodore brings Horsiesios back to Phbow

c. AD 367.

145. Abba Theodore was consoling our father Horsiesios for his past affliction. And he began to move him little by little to come to the monastery of Phbow, first to make a visit to the brothers; for he was at Thmoušons.[1] With exhortations did he bring him. Arriving before him, he had the weekly server give the signal to call the brothers, and so they embraced him. Then at the hour of the instruction, he gave the instruction in their midst,

as he used to do in the past. Theodore, as his assistant, stood listening. After this, Abba Horsiesios did not want their mutual love to be shaken; and they two were as one man. Everyone marvelled at their life-giving goodness, for they had been trained by the Lord to be one. Then Theodore was as his second, for he asked him about everything. One time it was Abba Horsiesios who went to the monasteries to visit the brothers, another time it was father Theodore. Likewise he never took rest, on account of the care he had.[2]

SBo 197–198.

Theodore's sorrow for the monasteries becoming rich

146. As we have said before, they had acquired many fields, and again after some time many boats—each monastery built its own.[1] Because of this they had no leisure and were burdened with heavy cares. In the time of Abba Pachomius, as they were few, they were vigilant not to be burdened by worldly possessions, for *the yoke of the Lord is light.* Seeing that many of the brothers were beginning to alter the way of life of the ancient brothers, [Theodore] was very sad about them. He fasted, eating only every other day, kept vigil praying with tears, and wore a hair shirt under his tunic during the night; and many times when the brothers saw him, they understood he had something [on his mind]. He would often go quietly by night to the mountain at a distance of about three miles to pray where the tombs of the brothers were. One night a brother followed him and from afar saw him standing in prayer on the tomb of our father Pachomius. He heard the prayer and was afraid. Here is what he said in his prayer: 'Lord of your servant Abba Pachomius, upon whose tomb I am now standing, deign to visit me, if it is your will. For our

Mt 11:30.

negligence is multiplied and we are not doing what is right. Yet do not abandon your servants, Lord. If we are negligent, rouse us up! If we are contemptuous, instill fear into us, reminding us of the eternal torments. Grant they may walk
Ps 139(138):13. your good way, for *you have fashioned* us, O Lord, and *did not spare your Only-begotten Son,*
Rm 8:32. *but you gave him up for us all,* for our salvation.' He spent a very long time praying in this fashion, and then came down.[2]

SBo 205b.
Eron's death

147. Before Passover a young city-man called Eron had got sick.[1] He was the second of Abba Theodore the City-man. And in the midst of the Passover they were expecting him to die. The very
AD 368. Saturday evening when the brothers were in the *synaxis,* he was in the throes of death. So our father Theodore came out of the *synaxis* and found him breathing his last. He spoke to him and closed his eyes. And then he said, 'This brother who has just passed away is the sign that another is going to pass away unexpectedly.'So the brothers kept vigil, doing readings beside the body. Then on the morning of the Sunday of Joy, he prepared the body and, with the brothers singing psalms he buried him.

SBo 206.
Theodore's death

148. Theodore himself fell ill a few days later, having first with great consolation seen off the brothers of every monastery who had come for the Passover.[1] He had spoken to them with great zeal about useful things, *knowing that he had mi-*
Jn 13.1. *grated from the world* already. Abba Horsiesios and all the great ones and [other] brothers were at his sickbed. Seeing that he was inclining to leave this world, Abba Horsiesios called the brothers to the *synaxis* to pray to the Lord for him, that he

might let him live. Falling upon his face and weeping bitterly, he said with all the brothers, 'Lord, will you take away the one who gives rest to us all? To whom are you leaving us? Take me and let him live who is able to correct and to govern the brothers.' They did this for three days. The man drew near to giving up his soul and he said to Abba Horsiesios in the presence of the others, 'Have I ever grieved you by a word or a decision?' And he could not answer him, because of his weeping. [Theodore] said again, 'I am not conscious of having grieved you, and not only you but also any of the other brothers, for I never neglected the salvation of my own soul and of the brothers', so far as I was able. And this is not of my doing but comes from the merciful God. *Behold in heaven is my witness, and my confidant in the highest'.* With these words he gave up the spirit on the second of the month of Pašons.[2]

Jb 16:19.
27 April 368.
SBo 207,208.

Horsiesios becomes the father of the *Koinonia* again

149. The brothers' crying was heard by people on the other side of the river, for they were unable to control their weeping. And we cannot write all that happened. After keeping vigil as usual, they prepared the body in the morning. Then they carried it to the mountain singing psalms and they buried it. After they had come down, an ancient brother, the second of the monastery of Phbow, called Naphersaes, went with some others and transferred him near the remains of Abba Pachomius.[1]

The brothers spent days in great grief, saying, 'Because we grieved him so much he prayed the Lord continually [to take him]: and behold, now he has gone and left us!' Remembering his great goodness to all and his great fear of God, they were in very great sorrow, for he had spent a long time serving Him with all his heart.

Abba Horsiesios was again in possession of his own rank and he governed the brothers according to his capacity. He was very good and he loved to save the brothers' souls. God strengthened him and opened to him the meaning of Scriptures. Thus he governed the brothers in peace for a long time.

SBo 210.

Athanasius' letter to the brothers

150. When the most holy archbishop Athanasius heard about our father Theodore, he was grieved. He sent the following letter to Abba Horsiesios and to the brothers, consoling them for his death:

'Athanasius to Abba Horsiesios, father of monks, and to all those who practise with him the monastic life and are established in the faith of God; dearly beloved brothers, greetings in the Lord. I have heard about the death of blessed Theodore, and I have borne that news with very great care, knowing how useful he was to you. Now if Theodore were no longer, I would have written many words to you with tears, considering what [would happen] after [his] death. But since Theodore is alive—the one whom you and we know[1]—what need is there for me to write anything but, *Blessed is* Theodore *who did not*
Ps 1:1. *walk in the counsel of the wicked*? Moreover,
Ps 112(111):1. ever *blessed* is he since he also *feared the Lord*.
Now we can dare to call him blessed, and do it in all certitude, because he has reached, as it were, a haven, and has a life free from care. Would that this were true of each of us; would that each one of us in the race should reach the goal this way; would that everyone sailing might moor his

own boat in that distant haven free of storms, so that, resting with the fathers, he might say, *Here I will stay, for this is the house I have chosen.* Ps 132(131):14.
Therefore, dear and beloved brothers, do not weep for Theodore, for he *is not dead, but asleep.* Let no one cry remembering him, but em- Mt 9:24.
ulate his way of life. There is no point in grieving for someone who has gone to a place that is free from grief. I am writing this to all of you in common, but especially to you, very dear and beloved Horsiesios, so that now that he is dead you may accept the whole care and take his place among the brothers. When he was alive, you two were as one man. If one went on a journey, the duties of the two were fulfilled; and when both were present, you became as one, giving to the beloved useful instructions. Do the same then! So doing, write, and tell us about your health[2] and that of the brothers. Pray all in common, I beseech you, that the Lord may more and more *bestow peace* Col 3:15.
on the Churches. This year also we have indeed celebrated in joyfulness the Passover and the Fifty Days, and it is with rejoicing in the Lord's kindnesses that we have written to you. Greet all those who fear the Lord. Those who are with me greet you. I pray that you may have strength in the Lord, dear and beloved brothers.'

Notes to the First Greek Life

As a general rule we shall not repeat for G[1] the explanations that we have already given in the notes to SBo and that apply to both documents.

G[1] 2. [1]This is a clear reference to the *Life of Antony* which Athanasius wrote probably during his third exile (356-362), while he was hiding among the

Egyptian monks. In SBo 2 we find mention of Antony's virtuous life, but no reference to the biography by Athanasius.

[2]We correct the punctuation of Halkin's text according to Festugière's suggestion (Festugière, *La première Vie grecque*..., p. 15), replacing the dash after στεναγμῶν by one after αὐτήν.

[3]SBo 3 states that he was born in the diocese of Sne (Latopolis).

G[1] 3 [1]The sacrifices were offered to the fish called λάτος from which Latopolis took its name (see SBo 4, note 1). The text of G[1] is less clear than that of SBo and betrays a lack of local knowledge.

G[1] 4 [1]In fact Pachomius was pressed for the war between Maximinus Daia and Licinius in 313. See SBo 7, note 1.

G[1] 5 [1]Pachomius considered his conversion as a spiritual healing; one day, he will quote this text of Jn 17:3 saying: 'if a man is blind in his mind, because he does not see the light of God on account of his idolatry, but is subsequently guided by the faith in the Lord and receives sight to recognize *the only true God*, is this not healing and salvation?' (see below, ¶ 47).

G[1]6 [1]SBo 10 states that Pachomius spent a period of three years in Chenoboskion (Šeneset) before going to Palamon. During that period he dedicated himself to the service of the people dwelling in that village. See SBo 10, note 1.

G[1] 7 [1]In pachomian terminology, the *Passover* corresponds to our Holy Week; it is ended by the *Closing of the Passover*, which corresponds to our Easter Vigil, and is followed by the *Sunday of the Resurrection*, called here the Day of Joy. The *Passover* was preceeded by the *Forty Days* (of Lent), and the *Sunday of the Resurrection* was followed by the *Fifty Days* (of Eastertide).

[2]The tense of the verbs suggests that we have here a general information about the way of life of the anchorites of Upper Egypt.

[3]See SBo 201, note 4.

G[1] 8 [1]I.e. Palamon and Pachomius.

[2]Called Šmin in Coptic. See SBo 14, note 4.

G[1] 9 [1]With Festugière, p. 125, we read προσκοπῆς, instead of προκοπῆς, although MS Ath. 1015 (fol. 9v) also has προκοπῆς, like Halkins's edition.

[2]Col 1:5 is quoted in Am. Letter 2. Ammon says that, having heard from Athanasius about the way of life of the virgins and monks, and marvelling at the hopes *stored up for them in the heavens*, he decided to become a monk.

[3]This text is quoted also in Hors. Test. 33.

G[1] 10 [1]This is one of the ¶¶ in which G[1] states its sources. See also ¶¶ 46, 98 and 99. These references, absent from SBo and Ag, have been added by the author of G[1]. If they had been in the common source of SBo-G[1], we do not see why all the other Lives would have suppressed them.

G[1] 11 [1]Following Festugière's suggestion (p. 18), we place a comma after the word ἀνυπόδετος instead of before it.

G[1] 14 [1]On these reclining seats on which the pachomian monks used to sleep, see Pr. 87, n. 2, and Pr. 88; see also below, ¶ 79.

G[1] 15 [1]τῆς τότε ἐπαγγελίας τοῦ Cf. Rm 15:8, τὰς ἐπαγγελίας τῶν πατέρων: 'the promises made to the fathers.' It is a reference to the promise Pachomius made to God in the prison of Antinoe; see above, ¶ 5.

[2]We follow the text of G[3] (κατώγεον μικρὸν), which is better than that of Ms F. (κατάγεον μακρὰν). Unfortunately a folio of MS Ath. 1015 is missing at this point.

[3]This idea is frequently expressed by Pachomius. See v.g. G[1] 75 (= SBo 67c).

[4]There is another, more vivid, description of this incident in S[1] 7-9.

G[1] 16 [1]According to G[2] 16 John died not long afterward. This is supported by SBo 20 (end).

G[1] 17 [1]Horsiesios begins one of his instructions with this text; see Hors. Instr. 2.

G[1] 18 [1]See SBo 33, note 1.

[2]Cf. *Vit. Ant.* c. 5ff.

G[1] 19 [1]This is the only time we find the word ἀσκητήριον either in G[1] or in Paral., or in Am. Letter. It is not a pachomian term. We will find it again in H.L. c. 18, 12.

G[1] 20 [1]After Pachomius' death this Hieracapollon will be mentioned again (see below, ¶ 123) as one of the pillars of the *Koinonia*.

G[1] 21 [1]The text of Halkin's edition is corrupt and cannot be understood without some correction. We follow the text of MS Ath. 1015 (fol. 12r): καὶ ἐπὶ κροκοδείλων διαβαίνειν ἐν ὕδασιν καὶ θηρίων κατατολμᾶν. Except for MS F., which is corrupt, all the Greek Lives have this strange account of Pachomius crossing the river on crocodiles. This is probably an allusion to the incident related in SBo 20. In SBo 98 Pachomius instructs the brothers not to lose confidence if they tread on snakes, scorpions and other wild beasts. In Pach. Instr. 1: 42 we hear Christ reprimanding a negligent monk: 'Did I not give you the *power to tread underfoot, etc.*' In Paral. 12 Pachomius explains that it is the fear of God that prepares someone to tread serpents and scorpions underfoot; and in Paral 24, the demons themselves acknowledge that Pachomius received that power from the Word of God.

[2]In his first prayer in the prison, Pachomius had promised God *to serve his will* all the days of his life. To discover *the whole will of God* will remain his constant preoccupation; see below, ¶ 23.

G[1] 23 [1]The Greek text has 'with brothers', but this is probably a mistake, since the arrival of the first disciples will be related only in the next ¶. According to SBo 22, he was alone.

[2]The angel's statement about the will of God is very general and absolute. See SBo 22, note 2. It is difficult to see why, of all the apparitions of angels in Scripture, it is the one to Manoah and his wife that is explicitly mentioned. Is it to draw a parallel between the birth of a strong child (Samson) and the foundation of the *Koinonia*?

G[1] 25 [1]This text is quoted again below, ¶ 99 and in Hors. Test. 33.

G[1] 26 [1]Concerning the considerable discrepancy between our sources about Theodore's age at the time of his arrival at Tabennesi, see SBo 31, note 3.

G[1] 27 [1]On the importance of the 'rank' in the life of the community, see Pr. 1, n. 2.

G[1] 28 [1]If we compare this ¶ to its parallels in SBo and Am, we realize that G[1] has modified its source. The expression 'steward of all the bodily needs of the monastery' is surprising, since the housemaster had a role that was both spiritual and material, but first of all spiritual, as it appears even from the context of this ¶. It could be an unfortunate addition by the Greek author. The word οἰκόνομος had probably only the meaning of material administrator in his time, while at an earlier stage it had been used of the father of the monastery.

[2]The text of SBo 26 is clearer: 'If anyone wanted to abstain from what was served to the sick, there was no one to prevent him from doing so.' See SBo 26, note 2.

[3]τοῦ μεγάλου οἰκονόμου ἤτοι τοῦ πατρὸς τῆς μονῆς Festugière (p. 173) translates: 'selon l'avis de l'économe principal ou du supérieur du monastère,' as if they were two different persons. In fact, ἤτοι. . . μονῆς is simply an explanatory clause (absent from SBo). This is the normal meaning of ἤτοι, and the meaning it has in G[1] throughout: see v.g. Halkin, p. 1,4; 8,11; 74,16. The expression οἰκονόμος is found again at the end of this ¶, where it means clearly the father of the community. As for the expression 'Great Steward', in all the other instances it means the material steward or administrator on the whole *Koinonia*, residing in Phbow with Pachomius.

[4]ἐτάχθησαν ὑπ'αὐτοὺς in Halkin's edition is clearly a mistake of Ms F. We read ὑπ' αὐτοῦ in Ms Ath. 1015, fol. 16v.

[5]About the instructions, see SBo 26, note 7. The preceding sentence, referring to Leg. 6, is absent from SBo and Am.

G[1] 29 [1]I.e. Tabennesi.

[2]Sarapion is the form we find also in Coptic (S[1] 19; SBo 28). MS Ath. 1015 has Serapion, while G[2] and Den. have Aprion. The name of Nitentori in Greek is Τέντυρα; since this is not a Greek name but a transformation of the Coptic name, we shall always use Nitentori in our translation. Tabennesi belonged to the diocese of Nitentori.

[3]In SBo 25 the meaning is clear: Pachomius built a church in the village and went there every Saturday and Sunday to share in the celebration of the Eucharist with the villagers. Since they were poor, he took care of the offering himself. In G[1] the Eucharist is not mentioned; the people assembled to hear the Word of God; Pachomius took care of the expenses for them until a priest was appointed there. It does not hang together very well.

G[1] 30 [1]This is the meaning of αρχόμενος τῆς ἐπισκοπῆς, and it is confirmed by the parallel text in SBo 28: 'After his appointment as archbishop. . .' (Festugière, p. 174, translates: 'Athanase qui en ce temps-là était chef de l'épiscopat.') In fact, Athanasius became archbishop in 328, and this trip to the Upper Thebaid, up to Aswan (Συήνη, Syene in Greek), took place in 329-330.

[2]This last sentence is peculiar to G[1] and is not entirely consistent with chronology. Athanasius is a new bishop, and his real trials will come later, his first exile being in 335.

G[1] 31 [1]Actually Origen was condemned not by Heraclas but by Archbishop Demetrius in 230. Heraclas had been Origen's associate and his successor at the head of the School of Alexandria. He may have confirmed Demetrius' condemnation when he succeeded him in 231. Halkin's edition, following Ms F. has 'Arios and Melitios ‹who had uttered› blasphemy against the Church of Christ.' With Ms Ath. 1015, we read '. . . against Christ.' The rest of ¶ 31, ¶ 32, and the beginning of ¶ 33 do not appear in Halkin's edition, because of a *lacuna* both in the *Florentinus* and the *Ambrosianus* manuscripts. For these ¶¶ we shall translate from Ms Ath. 1015, a photocopy of which has kindly been sent to us by the *Centre National de la Recherche Scientifique* in Paris.

[2]τῶν ἀγνοούντων. In the short fragment of the Ms Ath. 1015 that he quotes in VC, p. 353, n. 8, Lefort has mistakenly written: τῶν ἀκουόντων; the manuscript gives very clearly ἀγνοούντων. In that same quotation by Lefort, the first line should read: Ἐμίσει δὲ. . ., οὐχ ὅτι μόνον ἐξεβλήθη κτλ.

[3]G[3] has considerably modified the meaning of this sentence: 'The holy Athanasius used to see the Saviour in his church upon the throne, as also did the holy Peter, the bishop and martyr of the same Church, as we have learned from the orthodox bishops his successors.' The meaning is that Pachomius recognized the Lord's presence in the bishop who occupied the throne.

[4]The Greek text gives the Greek form of the name: Μαρίας.

G[1] 32 [1]Pachomius' sister was called Mary according to SBo 27.

[2]σκέψαι: consider, think. But it seems to correspond to the Coptic *mošt* with its reflexive meaning: examine yourself. See SBo 27.

[3]εἰς τὸ ἡσυχάσαι: hesychastic vocabulary is very rare in the pachomian sources. Here ἡσυχάσαι corresponds to the Coptic *ôrb*, to be enclosed, to retire (ἀναχωρεῖν).

[4]Here G[3] introduces a change that makes the text incomprehensible: 'Their father Peter did not cease praying. . .' The two final sentences of G[3] 43 as well as G[3] 44 are borrowed directly from H.L. and do not belonging to G[1]; they are absent from Ms Ath. 1015.

G[1] 33 [1]τὰ αἰώνα: 'the eternal things' in general, or, more probably 'the eternal foods (βρωμάτα)'.

[2]We return to Halkin's text.

[3]About the age of Theodore, see SBo 31, note 3.

G[1] 35 [1]In SBo 30 Pecoš does not so easily agree to take Theodore along to Phbow.

G[1] 36 [1]In SBo 107 this text is applied by Pachomius to those who choose celibacy.

G[1] 37 [1]In SBo 37 it is a letter from the bishop of Sne.

[2]This story is found in the collections of *Apophthegmata*; see *Verba Seniorum*, n. 34b.

G[1] 38 [1]About the image of the darnel, see SBo 6, note 2. This is a summary of the vivid account we can read in S[1] 10-19 of Pachomius' failure to form a community with his first group of disciples. The account is reduced to two sentences in SBo 24. See SBo 24, note 2.

G[1] 40 [1]This text is used elsewhere in a very different sense. In Paral. 1, after Theodore's first instruction, Pachomius says to those who have left the assembly: 'I. . . was listening to him with all my soul as one who does not know his right hand from his left.' And in Pach. Letter 5:4, he writes: 'I want you to be like those who did not know their right hand and their left.'

G[1] 41 [1]Or a 'councillor'; see SBo 39, note 2.
[2]In SBo 189 this text is applied to Athanasius.

G[1] 42 [1]This text is quoted by Pachomius in Pach. Letter 7:3, in a series of texts concerning forgiveness.

G[1] 45 [1]The quotation of Mt 6:10 (26:42) recurs often (see SBo 7; 12; 17); by adding 'not mine', G[1] combines it with Lk 22:42.

G[1] 46 [1]This is another ¶ added by the author of G[1] to explain his sources.

G[1] 47 [1]See above G[1] 5, note 1.

G[1] 48 [1]G[1] 48-49-50 have no correspondent in SBo. They must come from a collection of Pachomius' instructions. See SBo 186, note 2.
[2]In Pach. Instr. 1:22 and 36, the expression 'image of God' means a neighbor; see also SBo 106.
[3]In Am. Letter 16 we hear the same doctrine, with the same reference to Gehazi, from the mouth of Ausonius.
[4]In SBo 184, this text is applied to Theodore.

G[1] 49 [1]Samuel is one of the O.T. saints given as models to the brothers by Pachomius (see Pch. Instr. 1:18). In SBo 32, Theodore's progress in virtue is assimilated to that of Samuel, and in SBo 118 Pachomius' last recommendations to the brothers on his deathbed are likened to those of Samuel to the people of Israel.
[2]Pr 24:30-31 is quoted also in Am Letter 24.
[3]We often find this expression; v.g. Pach. Fragm. 3:3; Hors. Test. 56.

G[1] 50 [1]We follow Halkin's punctuation, which seems to us to give a better sense than that proposed by Festugière, p. 125 (i.e. we keep the comma after ὀρθοῦ instead of putting it after μου).

G[1] 51 [1]About uniformity, see SBo 47, note 2.

G[1] 52 [1]This seems to be the meaning of ἐδοκίμαζεν τὰς κράσεις ὁποίαις εἶναι. The Mss A. and Ath. 1015 (fol. 27v) have tried to clarify the text, replacing τὰς κράσεις by τὰς διαφορὰς τῶν νόσων.

G[1] 53 [1]We have restored to ¶ 53 the last sentence of ¶ 52 in Halkin's edition. A comparison with the beginning of SBo 48 shows that this sentence (missing from the Mss A. and Ath. 1015, fol. 28r) belongs to ¶ 53 and is necessary for its understanding. When this adjustment is made, there is no need to suppose with Festugière (pp. 31 and 186) that something was lost at the beginning of ¶ 53.

[2]The reading of Ms F. (διὰ γνώμης ὑμῶν) gives a better sense than that of Mss A. and Ath. 1015, fol. 28v (δίχα γνώμης ἡμῶν).

[3]This reflection is probably a copist's gloss.

G[1] 54 [1]On Phbow, see SBo 49, note 3. The name has many forms in the Greek of G[1]. The most usual ones are Παβαῦ and Παβῶ. The Sahidic form is Pbow or Pboou, although we often find Pbau. Phbow is the Bohairic form.

[2]Nowhere else in pachomian sources is there reference to several 'seconds' assisting a steward. SBo has only the mention of the establishment of houses and of the appointment of housemasters and seconds. (Pachomius is for the time being the superior of both Tabennesi and Phbow.) The mention of a housemaster with seconds is another indication that the author of G[1] in its present form knew the original pachomian terminology and customs only imperfectly, although he makes a certain number of literary borrowings from the Rules of Pachomius. Here, Ms Ath. 1015, fol. 28v has corrected the illogism of Ms F. by putting everything in the plural form: 'he appointed stewards with seconds'; but who are those stewards and those seconds if not the housemasters and their seconds mentioned right afterwards?

[3]Both Horsiesios and Theodore give to the superiors the example of the Good Shepherd giving his life for his flock; see Theod. Instr. 3: 30; Hors. Test. 17.

[4]About this Ebonh—the Greek form of his name is 'Επώνυχος—see SBo 50, note 1.

[5]τῳ κοινοβίῳ; in SBo 50: 'the *Koinonia*'. In G[1] τὸ κοινόβιον corresponds always to the *Koinonia* of the parallel Coptic texts, and means either the whole pachomian congregation (see Halkin, pp. 11,21; 23,17; 25,9; 36,19; 54,11; 66,36; 74,1; 79,3; 81,4) or its way of life (see Halkin, pp. 16,15; 17,2; 77,32; 78,28). It never means a *coenobium* or local monastery. The word is absent from Am. Letter. In Paral. it is used as in G[1] (see Halkin, pp. 126,20; 132,10) except for one instance where it is used in the plural, but with the meaning 'the Koinonia' (Halkin, p. 141,21).

[6]Chenoboskion is the Greek name of Šeneset. See SBo 3, note 2.

[7]According to SBo 50 Pachomius appointed housemasters and seconds there, but not a 'steward of the monastery with his second'; Ebonh was already the superior of that monastery, and there is no indication that Pachomius replaced him. If this mention of the appointment of a steward and a second had been in the common source of SBo-G[1], it is difficult to see why SBo would have suppressed it; it is more likely one of the explanatory additions of G[1].

[8]About the site of Thmoušons called Μώνχωσις (Μουχονσίς, Μόγχωσις, Μογχοσή, κτλ.) in Greek, see SBo 51, note 1.

[9]Both here and in G[1] 79, Ms F. of G[1] writes *John*. The Coptic Lives and all the other Greek Lives have *Jonas*. Both Ms Ath. 1015 and G[3] omit mention of him here. In G[1] 79 Ms Ath. 1015 has simply the contraction ΙΩ that can mean either John or Jonas. Such a contraction in the original text of G[1]54 probably drew the scribe of our Ms F. into error. In G[1] 79 the mention of John follows on that of Titoue, after whose name Jonas appears in the list of G[1] 123. Moreover, the mention of John [Jonas] is followed in G[1]

79 by a story about monks dying on their seats; and that story has very much in common with the story of the death of Jonas, the gardener of Thmoušons, in Paral. 30. In fact, G^2, which closely follows G^1 up to this point, inserts here that story of Jonas borrowed from Paral 30. There is very little doubt, therefore, that we must read Jonas instead of John here.

[10]While SBo continues with the account of all the foundations, G^1 interrupts this account here, to resume it only much later (G^1 81 and 83).

G^1 55 [1]Col 3:2 is quoted again below, ¶ 78.

G^1 56 [1]This text is quoted also in Paral. 41.

[2]The second part of Is 53:10 is quoted in SBo 142 and Pach. Instr. 1: 31.

G^1 57 [1]This text came to Pachomius' mind when he was praying in the cave during the night after his wrangle with his brother John; see S^1 8.

[2]This long instruction (G^1 56-57), probably taken from a collection of Pachomius' instructions, is not found in SBo; neither are the next two ¶¶ (G^1 58-59),directly inspired by the Rules of Pachomius.

G^1 58 [1]μελετῶντες τὰ ἀπὸ στήθους. Cf. Pr 28: 'When the *synaxis* is dismissed, each one shall recite something from the Scripture while going either to his cell or to the refectory.' The verb μελετᾶν (= *meditari*, to meditate) expresses the action of reciting something—usually a text from Scripture—either in a low voice or within one's heart. Because the words 'meditation' and 'to meditate' have a very different connotation in our modern languages, we use 'to recite—reciting—recitation' to translate the words of the family μελετᾶν—*meditari.* About the meaning of meditation in early, especially pachomian monasticism see H. Bacht, '"Meditatio" in den ältesten Mönchquellen', Idem, *Das Vermächtnis des Ursprungs, Excursus* IV, pp. 244-264. The Pachomians spent most of their time reciting, and for that purpose they had to learn a great part of the Scripture by heart. They learned it by small sections. These sections were called μέρς or ἀποστήθους in the Coptic texts, this last word being transformed into a substantive that Lefort translates 'des par-coeurs' ('by-hearts'). The word *sôp* in the expression 'six sections of prayers' (or 'six times of prayers'?) seems to be the equivalent of *meros* and *apostêthous.* See A. Veilleux, *La liturgie. . .*, pp. 309-312.

[2]See Pr. 122 and 138. On the 'Six Prayers', see A. Veilleux, *La liturgie. . .*, pp. 306-313.

G^1 59 [1]See Pr. 112 (visit to a brother's cell); 70 (clothes); 82 and 101 (books); 81 (money). It is highly significant that at the end of these two chapters directly inspired from the *Praecepta*, the author of G^1 says that all that government or administration (κυβέρνησις) is written in detail in the book of the stewards (τῶν οἰκονόμων). Οἰκονόμος is the name given by the author of G^1, especially in his own additions, to the superior of the local community, elsewhere called the father of the community or the father of the monastery. Therefore we may conclude that, in his time, the *Praecepta* were considered as the Book of the fathers of the monasteries (we shall return to this in our introduction to the Rules). On the other hand, Lefort suggests ('La Règle de s. Pachôme. . .' *Muséon* 1935, p. 77, note 6) that ἐν τῳ βιβλίῳ. . . τῶν οἰκονόμων must be corrected to εὐ τῳ βιβλίῳ. . .τῶν οἰκοδομῶν. This could very well be, since οἰκοδομή, the exact equivalent of the Coptic *kôt*, is the Greek term for 'precept'. For example, the title of the *Praecepta* in the Greek *excerpta* is ἅυτη ἡ ἀρχὴ τῶν οἰκοδομῶν. Nevertheless, against that correction of the Greek text of G[1] 59 is the fact that Ms Ath. 1015 has also οἰκονόμων, just like Ms F.

G[1] 60 [1]A few words are missing in Ms F. We translate the text as it has been restored by Halkin from G[3]. Ms Ath. 1015 is a bit shorter, but with the same meaning: 'sleep a little and pray a little till morning.'
[2]The monastery in question was Thmoušons. This is explicitly stated in the parallel text of SBo 59, and is implicit in the mention of Cornelios below, in ¶ 61. Cornelios was the superior of Thmoušons (see G[1] 114). On the site of Thmoušons and its distance from Phbow, see SBo 51, note 1.

G[1] 62 [1]This text is applied to the resurrection from the death of sin in Pach. Inst. 1: 6; and Theod. Inst. 3: 29 and 37.
[2]The patriarch Joseph is often given as example to the brothers; see below ¶ 63 (his chastity and prudence); Pach. Instr. 1: 5 (his wisdom, submission and chastity); Pach. Letter 8: 2ff (his purity and his constancy in persecutions). On Theodore being likened to Joseph, see SBo 123, note 2.

G[1] 63 [1]According to the LXX; the Hebrew text is different.

G[1] 64 [1]The exact nature of the γαρέλαιον is not clear. It was probably a mixture of γάρος and oil. In the Greek *excerpta* of Pr. 45, γάρος corresponds to the *liquamen* of Jerome's translation, which is a dish reserved to the sick, like wine. In Pr. 46 Jerome specifies '*liquamen de piscibus*', which is exact since γάρος corresponds to the Coptic ϫr that Crum (*Coptic Dictionary*, pp. 780B-781A) translates by *brine, small salted fish* or *pickle*.
[2]See above, ¶ 7 (=SBo 11).

G[1] 65 [1]According to SBo 37 he came earlier, with his mother. In G[1] 37 the mother came alone.

G[1] 66 [1]Following Festugière (p. 126), we read πού ποτε (= G[3]) instead of πώποτε (= Ms F.). In Ms Ath. 1015 the text has been modified.

G[1] 67 [1]Cf. Pr. 54.

G[1] 68 [1]In SBo it is the same brother as in the preceding story.
[2]Here again, read πού ποτε instead of πώποτε.
[3]Following Lefort's suggestion (see VC, p. XLIII), we correct Halkin's punctuation in the following manner: ἐὰν γὰρ ἀπέλθῃ ἔνθεν, διὰ τοῦτο φήμη...

G[1] 69 [1]With Ms Ath. 1015, fol 35v, we read ὅτι instead of ὅ, τι (Ms F.).

G[1] 74 [1]On the theme of the bearing of the Cross in pachomian spirituality, see SBo 201, note 4.

G[1] 76 [1]The mention that Theodore was steward is peculiar to G[1], and it is an anachronism, since it is only in G[1] 78 (= SBo 70) that he will be appointed steward at Tabennesi.

[2]Another version of this story is found in S[10]. See SBo 68, note 3.

G[1] 77 [1]τῆς τραπέζης: Ms A. A folio of Ms Ath. 1015 is missing here.
[2]εἰς τὰς σκηνὰς αὐτῶν. This isolated mention of 'tents' is probably a blunder of the G[1] redactor. Even during the harvest the brothers lived in huts, not in tents. In G[1] 125, another text peculiar to G[1], we have τὰ σκηνώματα.
[3]About the age of Theodore at the time of his first instruction, see SBo, notes 31, 3 and 69, 1.

G[1] 78 [1]Ibidem.

G[1] 79 [1]ἡγουμένους καὶ πατέρας: this is a surprising expression, because in the pachomian terminology ἡγουμένος always designates the father of the monastery. But this ¶ is another addition of G[1]. This tends to prove once more that the author of G[1] in its present form was not conversant with traditional pachomian terminology and customs. There is another similar duplication of ἡγουμένοι and πατέρες peculiar to G[1], in G[1] 114 (cf. SBo 121).
[2]In Halkin's edition we find John; but Ms Ath. 1015, fol. 38v, has ιω, which can be a contraction for Jonas as well as for John. John is certainly a mistake; see above, note G[1] 54, 9.
[3]About these reclining seats, see Pr. 87.

G[1] 80 [1]The story of Petronios and of the foundation of Thbew is much more detailed in SBo 56. We learn in particular that this foundation was in the diocese of Hew (Diospolis parva). On the site of Thbew, see SBo 56, note 1.

G[1] 81 [1]The author of G[1] does not follow the chronological order in his account of the last foundations, but he gives the indications necessary to reconstruct that order.
[2]The Greek text has the plural (μοναστήρια), which is probably a mistake. SBo 54 and Am 569 have the singular, and the rest of the ¶ speaks only of one monastery. But the plural could be explained by the fact that there will be two more foundations in the region of Panopolis (Šmin): those of Tse and Tsmine (see below, ¶ 83).

G[1] 82 [1]With Ms Ath. 1015, fol. 40r, we read οὐχί instead of οὐχ.
[2]This Talmas is not named elsewhere. We do not need to correct ἐπυρώθη to ἐπηρώθη (Lefort's suggestion in VC, p. 118, n. 7).

G[1] 83 [1]G[1] mentions the last four foundations very rapidly: Tse (see SBo 52), Panopolis (SBo 54), Thbew (SBo 56), Tsmine (SBo 57) and Phnoum (SBo 58). All these foundations were made before the Synod of Latopolis (G[1] 112) in the autumn of 345.
[2]About the two annual meetings, see SBo 71, notes 2, 3 and 144, 3.

G[1] 84 [1]With Ms Ath. 1015, fol. 41v, we suppress καὶ ὅτι and we read διὰ γὰρ. . . , which is confirmed by G[3]. (Festugière, p. 126, corrects καὶ ὅτι in καθότι, which gives the same meaning.)
[2]In S[10] (= Ag, Am) there is a fragment of this story in which the temptation is in fact to pederasty.

G[1] 85 [1]There is a more detailed version of that story in Ag-Am (see the fragment of it in S[10] 7) and in Paral. 8-11.
[2]The same text is also quoted in Pach. Instr. 1: 59.

G[1] 86 [1]The negation is required by the context and the comparison with SBo 72.

G[1] 87 [1]We should have 'he' instead of 'they'. The scribe inadvertently wrote σκοποῦσιν because of the assonance with the immediately preceding ἐκλείπουσιν.

G[1] 88 [1]At this point, SBo 73 and S[10] give a description of the vision.
[2]In SBo 73 (end), this sentence is a reflection made by the ancient fathers who marvelled at what they heard.

G[1] 90 [1]The words quoted by Pachomius to Theodore here are quoted by Theodore to the brothers in SBo 183.

G[1] 91 [1]The example of the rich man of the Gospel is also given as a warning in Hors. Test. 22.
[2]This last paragraph likening Theodore to Pachomius is an addition of G[1].

G[1] 92 [1]The Greek text in Halkin's edition makes good sense, although we can also add ὁ Θεὸς συγχωρήσει σοι with Ms A. or συγχωρῆσαι σοι with Ms Ath. 1015.

G[1] 94 [1]I.e. Sahidic, the Coptic dialect of Upper Egypt.
[2]This reflection is an addition of the author of G[1], and shows clearly that he was writing after Athanasius' death (373), since he speaks of 'Athanasius who was *then* sitting...' G[1] 94 is an abbreviated adaptation of the much longer sotry that we find in SBo 89. According to P. Peeters ('A propos de la Vie sahidique...', p. 305), this ¶ shows that the author of G[1] was probably a cleric of the Church of Alexandria.
[3]This text about the Lord's presence in the midst of brothers assembled in his name is quoted also in SBo 184 and Hors. Reg. 2.

G[1] 95 [1]It is difficult to see how Theodore could have become housemaster in 333 (thirteen years before Pachomius' death), after being twelve years lector in the Church of Alexandria (see SBo 89) during the time of Athanasius, who became archbishop only in 328. Either the thirteen years as housemaster or the twelve years as lector is wrong. See SBo 91, note 4.

G[1] 97 [1]Cf. ¶ 48.

G[1] 99 [1]τοῖς μεγάλοις, the great ones. This expression usually means the superiors or the elders of the community. Here it means probably the ancient, early, brothers.
[2]In Halkin's text, p. 66,5, read ἀπ' αὐτοῦ πολλὰ νοήματα with Ms Ath. 1015, or πολλὰ παρ' αὐτου ν., with Lefort, VC, p. XXIV, n. 15.
[3]This text is quoted also above, ¶ 25, and Hors. Test. 33.
[4]This is a *verbatim* quotation of the title of Antony's Life by Athanasius,

written during the Archbishop's third exile (356-362). It gives us a *terminus a quo* for the date of G[1].

[5]In this ¶ the compiler of G[1] has enumerated the sources of his additions to his basic document. They are: the Rules, the Letters of Pachomius, collections of instructions and accounts of visions, and the Life of Antony.

G[1] 101 [1]In SBo 99, this brother is called Paul.

G[1] 102 [1]Text restored from G[3] (see Festugière, p. 51-52).

G[1] 104 [1]The story of Silvanos is found with very different details in Paral. 2-4. We read it also in Ag and S[5] 93, although Bo has omitted it (see Am 518ff).

G[1] 105 [1]'He became a living man': this is a beautiful expression of the aim of monastic conversion.

G[1] 106 [1]Here, as above, ¶¶ 66 and 68, read πού ποτε instead of πώποτε. Ms Ath. 1015, fo. 54v, has κατ' ἰδίαν.

G[1] 107 [1]According to pachomian spirituality, a sinner can *do penance*, but *metanoia*, repentance, is a gift he must receive from God. See A. Veilleux, *La liturgie...*, pp. 342-344.

[2]On the meaning of ἀδιάκριτον, see SBo 30, note 2.

G[1] 109 [1]Zacchaeus is the head of the boatmen; see SBo 96.

[2]On this trip to Alexandria, see SBo 96, note 3. About Theodore's rehabilitation, see SBo 97, note 3.

G[1] 110 [1]This ¶, with nothing in common with what precedes or what follows, is another addition of G[1], inspired directly from the text of the Rules; see Pr. 70, Leg. 15, etc. But there is something very similar in S[1] 5.

G[1] 111 [1]The *korsenilion* was a kind of sweet food distributed to the brothers after the meals. About this custom, see Pr. 37, n. 1, Pr. 38. About the etymology of the word, see L.-T. Lefort, 'Un mot nouveau', *Muséon* 26 (1923) 27-31; see also Festugière, p. 56, n. 1.

[2]In SBo this story is placed with the other stories about Theodore the Alexandrian, which is a more logical place than here.

G[1] 112 [1]About this moving account, absent from SBo but present in Ag, see SBo 96, note 3. Pachomius mentions this trial in G[1] 113, when Theodore comes back from Alexandria. This permits us to date this Synod of Latopolis in the autumn of 345, less than a year before Pachomius' death.

[2]Philo was made bishop of Thebes in 339. If our Mouei must be identified with the Masis spoken of by Athanasius in his *Festal Letter* n. 19, he was bishop of Latopolis at the time of these events. See D.J. Chitty, *The Desert a City*, p. 41, n. 57.

[3]We understand Magdolon as a name of town, although the meaning of the expression ὁ μαγδόλου τοῦ λεγομένου (F) or ὁ τοῦ λεγομένου μαγδόλου is not absolutely clear. It could also mean 'the one called "watch-tower"'. See Festugière, p. 56, n. 2.

[4]This text is quoted also in S[2] 7, and Hors. Test. 44.

[5]Phnoum was the last foundation made by Pachomius; it was also the one farthest upstream.

G[1] 113 [1]These two boats had been given to the *Koinonia* by a councillor of Kos and by bishop Arios of Šmin. See SBo 53 and 54. Later, each monastery will build its own boats; see G[1] 146 (= SBo 197). It seems to have been a custom to make a yearly journey to Alexandria; see G[1] 109 (SBo 96-97); G[1] 120 (SBo 124ff).

[2]Athanasius was in exile since 339; see SBo 96, note 3.

[3]Jm 1:12 is quoted also in Hors. Test. 50.

[4]This trip to Alexandria must be distinguished from the one made after Pachomius' death; see below, ¶ 120.

G[1] 114 [1]G[1] has not mentioned before that Petronios was the superior of Tsmine, but we know from SBo that after the foundation of Tsmine, Pachomius transferred Petronios from his monastery of Thbew and established him at Tsmine, with authority over the other two monasteries of the region of Šmin (Panopolis); see SBo 57, note 2.

G[1] 115 [1]οἰκονομεῖον; cf. Pr. 105, where the storeroom is called 'the place of the stewards' (*pma n̄noikonomos*).

[2]ὡς γὰρ δήποτε ἐκπλέκω; D.J. Chitty, 'Some Notes...', p. 266, translates: 'I will get through—extricate myself—somehow.'

G[1] 116 [1]We translate the text as we find it in Halkin's edition. Festugière, p. 121 and 126, proposes to correct κρύψωσιν to ἀποκρύψωσιν (if they discover my bones).

[2]The text of G[1] is abbreviated and obscure. It is clearer in SBo 122: Pachomius makes a recommendation to Theodore to stir up the brothers if they become negligent; Theodore wonders if Pachomius means that the brothers will be entrusted to him some day; and Pachomius tells him: 'Do not be hesitant. Do not waver. I am referring not only to what I am saying to you but to what you are thinking.'

[3]About the date of Pachomius' death, see SBo 123, note 1.

G[1] 117 [1]According to SBo Petronios died two days earlier; see SBo 130, note 1.

G[1] 118 [1]This long discourse by Horsiesios is placed by SBo at the beginning of his second period as superior of the *Koinonia*.

G[1] 120 [1]We know from SBo 124 and from an allusion in G[1] 136 that Theodore was on this trip too. About the trip itself, see SBo 124, note 2; about Antony's Outer Mountain, see SBo 126, note 1.

[2]We are in 346, ten years before Antony's death. If he really died at the age of one hundred and five, he was then ninety-five.

[3]One must see the text of SBo 126-127 in order to understand this dialogue, too abbreviated in G[1]. The verb ἀποπείθω, although normally constructed, is not recorded in any dictionary. Festugière translates 'Je vais te convaincre...' (p. 79); and D.J. Chitty ('Some Notes...', p. 267) translates: 'I dissuade thee from that.'

[4]Nothing else is known of this Aotas, who is not mentioned in SBo.

[5]D.J. Chitty finds two echoes of the language of Antony's *Letters* in these

few sentences here attributed to him: the fact that he calls Horsiesios 'the Israelite'; and the sentence where he expresses the desire he had to see Pachomius in the body. But we cannot argue a literary dependence.

[6]About the various applications of that title, see SBo 125, note 2.

G[1] 121 [1]This appointment of Theodore as housemaster is not mentioned in SBo. If Pachomius really restored Theodore to his function as his assistant, sending him to visit the monasteries, then his appointment by Horsiesios as housemaster—if it actually took place—must be seen as something of a demotion, and was bound to create some dissatisfaction among the ancient brothers who had remained faithful to Theodore.

G[1] 122 [1]Although the Greek sentence is not perfectly clear, it makes a good sense if we relate καὶ ἔταξεν αὐτοὺς to the various officers mentioned in the preceding sentence. Such appointment of the superiors at the two annual meetings is known from SBo 144; see SBo 144, note 3. Moreover the verb τάσσειν in G[1] is almost always (in thirty of thirty-two cases) used of the appointment of persons to offices.

G[1] 123 [1]This expression is applied to Theodore again in Am. Letter 9.

G[1] 124 [1]This Paphnouti, local superior of Phbow, is distinct from the other Paphnouti, Theodore's brother, who was the great material administrator of the whole *Koinonia* (also residing in Phbow), and who died during the great plague of 346, a few days before Pachomius. But since this ¶ 124 is peculiar to G[1] we may wonder whether this mention of Paphnouti as Great Steward of Phbow is not simply a mistake of G[1], misled by the ambivalent use of οἰκονόμος in pachomian texts. The young Paphnouti whose death is mentioned in SBo 181 would be a third monk of that name.

G[1] 125 [1]See above, ¶ 109.

G[1] 126 [1]This text is quoted also in Hors. Letter 1: 4.

[2]τα σκηνώματα: for another mention of the tents, see above, ¶ 77, note 2. The two other uses of σκῆνωμα are of a dead man's body; see below ¶¶ 147 and 149 (Halkin, pp. 93,22 and 94,26).

G[1] 129 [1]It is worth noting that Horsiesios introduces Theodore as someone who will take his place, not as an assistant. The biographers seem careful to exonerate Theodore of any possible accusation of ambition, but they do not hide the brothers' exultation at all. Both Petronios and Horsiesios were relatively new in the *Koinonia*. The return of Theodore to power after his demotion was a victory of the 'ancient brothers' over the new generation. Theodore will open what D.J. Chitty ('A Note on the Chronology...', p. 385) describes as 'his rallying call to the brothers' by the words Ποῦ εἰσιν οἱ ἀρχαῖοι;—'Where are the ancient brothers?' It is also significant that Horsiesios, who seemed to be too weak a superior during his first superiorship and preferred to retire to the background rather than be involved in tensions, will be able to 'govern the brothers in peace for a long time' (G[1] 149) after Theodore's death.

[2]The Greek sentence is grammatically incorrect and the exact meaning remains uncertain. Cf. SBo 140.

G[1] 130 [1]G[1] 116 (= SBo 122).

[2]διάδοχον... καὶ ὑπηρέτην. The conjunction of διάδοχον with ὑπηρέτην seems to call for a meaning like 'deputy' or 'assistant'. But the normal meaning of διάδοχος is 'successor', and it is the meaning the word has elsewhere in G[1]: the bishops are the *successors* of the apostles (Halkin, p. 17,17); the apostles are the *successors* of Jesus (85,29); the ancient brothers ask Theodore to be Pachomius' *successor* (69,29); Petronios on his deathbed asks the brothers whom they want as his *successor* (76,3); Antony asks the brothers whom Pachomius has appointed as his *successor* (82,26). Only when applied to Theodore, here and in ¶ 145 (where Theodore listens to Horsiesios as his assistant), is the meaning of the word somewhat qualified by the context. As a matter of fact, Theodore was Horsiesios' successor, his διάδοχος.

G[1] 131 [1]See above, G[1] 129, note 1.

[2]This text is quoted again below, G[1] 142 (= SBo 186).

G[1] 132 [1]Jn 16:33 is quoted in Hors. Test. 41.

[2]This text is quoted also in Theod. Instr. 3: 10 and 20, and in Hors. Test. 10.

[3]This same quotation, expressing the faith in God's will to save everyone, is found again in Pach. Letter 3: 13.

G[1] 134 [1]The foundation by Theodore of the two monasteries of Kaior and Oui in the region of Hermopolis is not recorded by SBo, but their existence is attested by SBo 202, where Oui is spelled Noui. The monastery of virgins founded by Theodore near Hermonthis is not recorded in SBo.

[2]This is the only mention of wool in the Lives of Pachomius, and it is a passage peculiar to G[1]. There is no doubt that it is an unfortunate addition of the last author of G[1] who was not conversant with pachomian customs. See SBo 183, note 1.

G[1] 135 [1]This is an allusion to the Synod of Latopolis, where Pachomius was summoned because of his 'clairvoyance'.

[2]We find many references to God's dwelling in man in our sources. I Co 3:13-17 is quoted in Pach. Fragm. 1: 2; other allusions in Theod. Instr. 3: 41; Hors. Test. 19; Hors. Letter 3: 2.

[3]Cf. above, ¶ 8 (= SBo 14).

[4]Pachomius often used the image of Christ as the Good Shepherd who came to gather the scattered sheep into his fold. See Pach. Instr. 1: 37; Pach. Instr. 2: 2. Cf. G[1] 54 (SBo 49) where Pachomius is said to be keeping watch over his monasteries as a servant of the Good Shepherd.

[5]We find a similar interpretation of this text in SBo 189. Cf. also Paral. 18 and Theod. Instr. 3: 32.

[6]See a similar application of Jn 21:15-16 in Hors. Test. 17.

G[1] 136 [1]We correct Halkin's punctuation: the second dash is more in place after παρῆν (p. 85,37) than after πλέον (86,1). ὅτε (85,37) refers to the antecedent τότε (85,36).

G[1] 137 [1]On this search of Artemios for Athanasius, see SBo 142, note 5. The mention of Constantius by G[1] is exact, since this perquisition took place in 360 and Constantius died in 361.

[2]In SBo 185 it is Theodore who wants to return and the brothers who do not.

G[1] 138 [1]This vision is not mentioned in the parallel text of SBo 185, but something almost identical happens in SBo 125, in another incident that is not recorded by G[1]. SBo and G[1] use their common source differently.

G[1] 139 [1]See SBo 180, note 3.

G[1] 140 [1]With Lefort (VC, p. 204, n. 2) and Festugière (p. 61), we read πηροῦσθαι instead of πυροῦσθαι, as required by the context and confirmed by a comparison with the Coptic version, although Ms Ath. 1015 also has πυροῦσθαι.

G[1] 142 [1]Theodore (or the author of G[1]) may be referring here to a collection of instructions of Pachomius. See SBo 186, note 2.

G[1] 143 [1]This trip of Athanasius to Upper Egypt took place in 363. He was then in flight from Julian the Apostate, having left Alexandria on 24 October 362.

G[1] 144 [1]About these reclining seats, see Pr. 87. Festugière (p. 65, n. 1) proposes to translate it by 'chaises percées' (lavatories); but there is no reason for giving to καθισμάτιον a meaning different than the one it has elsewhere in the Life (see G[1] 79, Halkin, pp. 53,21 and 54,1; also κάθισμα in G[1] 14, Halkin, p. 9,26). The argument that Festugière draws from the comparison with Am is without any value, since this part of Am is a late, free, translation of G[3], itself an adaptation of G[1]

[2]The fact that Athanasius calls the pachomian monks 'children of the Church' is an eloquent witness to the quality of their relations with the hierarchical Church. On this question, see A. Veilleux, *La liturgie...*, pp. 189-195; L. Ueding, 'Die Kanones von Chalkedon in ihrer Bedeutung für Mönchtum und Klerus', in A. Grillmeier and H. Bacht, *Das Konzil von Chalkedon. Geschichte und Gegenwart*, II (Würzburg, 1953) pp. 569-676, specially the section I: 'Hierarchie und Mönchtum bis zum Konzil von Chalkedon', pp. 570-600.

G[1] 145 [1]'For he was at Thmoušons': this information volunteered by G[1] is erroneous. In fact, Horsiesios retired to Šeneset after his resignation (G[1] 129-SBo 139), and there is no reason to believe he might have moved to another monastery afterwards. Moreover, the superior of Thmoušons was the same Apollonios who had stirred up the revolt against Horsiesios.

[2]We follow Halkin's punctuation rather than that proposed by Festugière (p. 66).

G[1] 146 [1]See above, ¶ 113, note 2.

[2]In SBo 197-198 this account comes before the account of Athanasius' visit and of Horsiesios' return to Phbow.

G[1] 147 [1]With Mss A. and Ms Ath. 1015, fol. 79v, we read πρὸ τοῦ πάσχα, instead of πρὸ τούτου (Ms F. and Halkin's edition). Cf. SBo 205.

G[1] 148 [1]According to SBo 206 the brothers of the monasteries in the area around Phbow came back when they were informed of Theodore's illness.

[2]About the date of Theodore's death see SBo 206, note 3.

G[1] 149 [1]In SBo 207, it is Horsiesios who does this, along with three brothers. Lefort (VC, p. 230, n. 2) mistakenly identified this Naphersaes, second of Phbow, with Psahref, the father of Phbow. Naphersaes and Psahref are two completely different Coptic names; see Chitty, 'Pachomian Sources Reconsidered', pp. 66-67.

G[1] 150 [1]The meaning is that Theodore is still alive in the person of Horsiesios. Cf. SBo 210.

[2]περὶ τῆς σεαυτοῦ...σωτηρίας: 'about your health', or 'about your salvation'.

THE FIRST SAHIDIC LIFE

(S[1])

FRAGMENT I

Text: VS 253,A, 12-254,B,36

Prologue

IT IS FOR US a good deed and it is God's will that the grace and gift which has come to us from God be manifested by us to everyone, and primarily to the brothers, to the descendants of our fathers and to their posterity who have not been in touch with the fathers in the body; that they may have knowledge, may strive to become sacrifices to God[1] through purity of body and heart, and may really be, both in the present age and in the age to come, sons of our fathers whose face they have not seen in the flesh. Cf. Rm 12:1; 1 P 2:5.

It is a good deed to write about our fathers

2. Likewise, Isaiah cries out to others who have not known their fathers, that they may know them, saying, *Consider Abraham your father and Sarah who gave you birth, for he was a chief and I called him, I blessed him, I loved him, and I increased him.* Is 51:2. Let us not venture to assert through ignorance that the Lord said in the Gospel, *Claim no father on earth; for one is your Father, who is in heaven.*[1] Mt 23:9. Our Lord indeed said this in the Gospel, because there are some *who mind the things of earth; but for us, our*

Ph 3:19-20. *dwelling is in heaven.* The Apostle, likewise, writing to others, says, *If we have fathers according to the flesh whom we respect, with even more reason shall we submit ourselves to the Father of*
Heb 12:19. *spirits, to be given life.* When he said, *If we have fathers according to the flesh,* he showed that these are not for them fathers of their own day; as it is written in the Gospel, *He who comes to me and does not hate his father and his mother, etc.*
Lk 14:26. *cannot be my disciple.*[2] This is so that we might know with certainty that a man who begets another in the work of God is his father after God, in this age and in the age to come. Paul says again in another place, *You might have ten thousand teachers in Christ, but not many fathers, for it was I who begot you in Christ Jesus through the*
1 Co 4:15. *Gospel.* And we know that he begot them not only through the Gospel but also through good and wonderful works. So he also instructed others saying, *Everything that is honorable, everything that is righteous, everything that is pure, everything that is good, all blessing, all praise, think upon these things. It is this that you have learned, and that you have received and heard and seen in me. Do this and the God of peace will be with*
Ph 4:8-9. *you.*[3]

Pachomius is our father

3. So it is indeed with our father Pachomius, for he deserves to be called father ⟨because our Father⟩ [1] who is in heaven dwells in him, as the Apostle confesses from his own mouth when he says, *It is not I who live, it is Christ who lives in*
Ga 2:20. *me.*[2] This is why through the divine goodness which was in him he encourages whoever wishes to obey him, saying, *Be imitators of me as I am of*
1 Co 11:1. *Christ.*[3] Therefore, all who imitate the Apostle

through their way of life deserve to be called fathers because of the Holy Spirit who dwells in them. Indeed, God the Lord of...

FRAGMENT II

Text: VS 102,A, 1-30

Pachomius' *ascesis*

4. ...hairshirt which [Pachomius] wore was tied around his loins so that the ashes would chafe him. He afflicted himself and he would only once in a while wear the tunic he had. From the time he instituted the *Koinonia,* he no longer wore the hairshirt except at night.

Pachomius' obedience to the common rule

5. Just as the brothers were established in separate houses and had in each house someone responsible for them as a father, [Pachomius] also belonged to a house. He was not any different from the brothers. He did not have the authority to go on his own to take a garment from the leader of the community. It was the housemaster of the house to which he belonged who took it for him, according to the regulations of the brothers he had established from God.[1]

FRAGMENT III

Text: VS 106,B, 35-107,B,23

Vision of Tabennesi *(Cf. SBo 22; G[1] 23)*

6. One day he and his brother were reaping the harvest on an island. They were close to the deserted village of Tabennesi to which they had withdrawn. During that night, after they had finished praying according to their custom, he went off a short distance from his brother and sat down alone. He was downcast and brokenhearted, desiring to know God's will. While it was

still dark, a luminous man appeared and stood before him. He said, 'Why are you downcast and broken-hearted?' He replied, 'I seek God's will.' The luminous man said to him, 'You really desire to know God's will?' [Pachomius] answered, 'Yes'. He said to him, 'God's will is to serve mankind and reconcile it to him.' He replied almost indignantly, 'I seek God's will, and you say to serve mankind!' The luminous man repeated three times, 'God's will is to serve men in order to call them to him.' After this [Pachomius] saw him no longer. Then he remembered the covenant he had made with God the day help had been brought to him, imprisoned with his companions. He had promised him, 'God, if you help me and deliver me from this distress I am in, I will serve mankind for your name's sake.'[1] Then his heart was satisfied that what had come into his

Text: VS 1,1-2, 21; = 107,B,23-109, B,1

heart was the work of the Lord's Spirit, for it was in accord with the words of the luminous man who had spoken before him. His brother who was not far from him and heard him speak, asked him, 'With whom are you speaking?' for he could not see the one who spoke to him. But Pachomius concealed the thing and answered, 'With no one'.

Wrangle between Pachomius and John

Col 1:22.

(Cf. SBo 19b; G[1] 15-16).

7. After the vision in which it was revealed to him that he should fashion the souls of men so as *to present them pure to God*[1]—for such was the will of God that he had sought—he and his brother began to expand the place where they lived to make it into a small monastery.[2] It was in accordance with the order he had been given to receive anyone who would come to him to stay with him and live the anchoritic life with him. It happened while they were building the monas-

tery's wall that they had a slight disagreement with each other.[3] His brother angrily retorted, 'Stop being so conceited!' Hearing this word his heart was agitated. When he saw that his heart was embittered at this little word, he was deeply distressed and said, 'I am not yet faithful,[4] and I am still far from God whose will I promised to follow.'

Pachomius' prayer during the night

8. That night he descended into an underground place in the deserted village where he lived. He placed a brick under his feet and stretched out his hands toward God crying the whole night, from evening until dawn, saying, 'Lord, help me; remove this fleshly thought so that I will no longer become angry in my heart even if someone slaps me in the face. Am I more honorable than my Lord, your beloved Son who became man to save us sinners? *For he was insulted and did not retaliate with insults; he suffered and did not grow bitter.*[1] How much more do I, a sinner, deserve to be humiliated seven times more than he? For he, a God without sin, suffered for us,* and I, a piece of clay fashioned by his hands,† why can I not suffer without bitterness?' And he cried out to God in these words all night long, so that the brick he stood on disintegrated under him because of the perspiration that rolled down onto it from his face. The place was very hot indeed, for it was summer. At daybreak he stopped praying and went again with his brother to work at their building.

1 P 2:23.

*1 P 2:21-22.

†Cf. Jb. 10:3.

Text: VS 2, 21-3,24

Another night in prayer

9. A few days later his brother hurled another remark at him. When he heard it, his heart was embittered and seeing the agitation of his heart he did as he had done the first time. He spent the

whole night in prayer so that the brick on which he stood turned to mud under his feet. From that day on, fleshly thoughts no longer made him angry, because God granted the request he had made to him. As James writes in his Epistle, *All that is good, every gift that is perfect is given us from heaven, coming down from the Father of lights.* Likewise, in the Gospel the Lord exhorts whoever loves him in these terms, *Ask and you shall receive, seek and you shall find, knock and it shall be opened to you; for whoever asks shall receive, and he who seeks shall find, and to him who knocks it shall be opened.* Likewise John, writing his Epistle to all the believers, says, *Such is the confidence that we have in him, that if we ask him for anything in accordance with his will, he will hear us.* And, his request heard by God, he became obedient to David who says, *Keep away from fury, abandon anger.* Truly indeed, from that day on he did not get angry again as fleshly men do, but if he happened once to be angry, he was angry as the saints are. He also eagerly asked the Lord to enable him to accomplish the other commandments that are written in the holy Scriptures. After that his brother died.

Jm 1:17.

Mt 7:7-8.

1 Jn 5:14.

Ps 37(36):8.

Cf. Ps 4:5; Eph 4:26.

Text: VS 3, 25-4,23; = 112,B,25-113,B,23

People gather around Pachomius

10. Then one by one, people from the surrounding villages came to him. They built dwellings for themselves in the place where he had retired and they gathered there to live the anchoritic life. Together they constituted a small group of men.[1]

Organization of the first group of disciples

11. When he saw the brothers gathering around him, he established for them the following rule: Each should be self-supporting and manage his own affairs, but they would provide

their share of all their material needs either for food or to provide hospitality to the strangers who came to them, for they all ate together. They brought their share to him and he administered it.[1] They did this freely and voluntarily so that he could see to all their needs, because they considered him trustworthy and because he was their father after God. This regulation he established was adapted to their weakness, in line with what the Apostle says, *To the weak I became weak, that I might gain the weak.* And writing to the Corinthians he says also, *I fed you with milk, not with solid food, for you were not yet ready for it.*[2] He proceeded this way because he could see that they were not yet ready to bind themselves together in a perfect *Koinonia* like that of the believers which Acts describes: *They were one heart and one soul and everything they owned was held in common; not one of them said that anything he possessed was his own.*[3] As the Apostle says again, *Do not forget communion and good works, for these are sacrifices that please God.*[4]

1 Co 9:22.

1 Co 3:2.

Ac 4:32.

Heb 13:16.

Text: VS 4, 24-7,14

Pachomius makes himself their servant

Pr 23:24(LXX).

12. Our father Pachomius nourished them as well as he could, as it is written, *A righteous father gives good food.*[1] That which he received from them according to this regulation, he administered in conformity with all their regulations. If they happened to bring him fish or other provisions, he received them and prepared them for them. Then when he had finished preparing their food and had given it to them to eat, if he has fasted the preceding day, he would put a bit of salt in his hand and would then eat bread on [the salt]. This is how he always dealt with them,

becoming their servant according to the covenant he had made before God, as Paul says, *For free though I was in everything, to all I have made myself a servant that I might win more.*

1 Co 9:19

Their contempt for Pachomius

13. Seeing his humility and obligingness, they treated him with contempt and great irreverence because of the lack of integrity of their hearts toward God. If he told them once to take care of some need they had, they would contradict him openly and insult him, saying, 'We will not obey you'. He did not punish them, however, but on the contrary, he bore with them with great patience saying, 'They will *see my humility and affliction* and they will return to God reforming themselves and fearing him.' This he did also according to what Paul says, *A servant of the Lord must not quarrel, but be kind to everyone, instructing and enduring evil, gently instructing those who dispute, so that God might give them repentance, that they might know the truth and recover from the snare of the devil, to whose will they are held captive.*[1]

Ps 25(24):7.

2 Tm 2:24-26.

They make fun of Pachomius

14. During harvest time they all went out together to hire themselves out as reapers. At mealtime Pachomius harnessed a donkey and went to fetch them something to eat. When he arrived, he set the table and they ate. When evening came, they stopped working. After work, some of them climbed on the donkey for fun while others chased the donkey and laughed saying, 'Pachomius, our servant, pack the utensils on your back and return them to the monastery.' Grieved and sighing, he took up the utensils and returned them to the monastery. His heart was grieved not on account of the affliction they

caused him, but because they were continuing their irreverence and because of the unworthiness of their souls.

Pachomius spends a night in prayer

15. He endured afflictions of this kind and pranks from them for a long time—not only for a year or two, but for four or five years. Then, seeing that they were not returning to God at all in spite of his patience and endurance with them, one evening he went off somewhere alone; he stood and prayed all night. His heart was broken over them, because they did not fear God in the work he was patiently doing with them.

Pachomius' prayer

16. In his prayer he invoked God saying:[1]

Lord, God Almighty, blessed God, blessed Father who is in the blessed Son, blessed Son who is in the blessed Father, in the blessed Holy Spirit; Cf. Jn 14:10-11.

You who fill every place by the power of your divinity, to whom nothing is hidden, for the universe was made by the Word of your mouth and created through the breath of your lips;[2] Cf. Ps 33(32):6.

Holy, Holy, Holy Lord Sabaoth; heaven and earth are full of your glory; Is 6:3.

You who, in the heaven, are seated on the Cherubim and Seraphim and whose eyes behold the depths; Dn 3:55.

You whom no man can bless, no man exalt or glorify as you deserve and as becomes the nature of your being, since you are invisible, invincible, and all blessing;

Lord, blessed God, of whose divinity no man can tell the power, since we are dust

Cf. Si 17:31.

and ashes, and you formed us from-nothingness into existence;

Text: VS 7, 14-28; = 114, A,1-34

You who with your beloved Son our Lord and your Holy Spirit are one, as it is written, Striving to preserve the unity of the Spirit;

Eph 4:3.

Holy God, sublime, living, patient, compassionate and good, abounding in mercy;

Lord God, faithful and righteous, truthful and sweet judge;

Lord God, the strong one among the powerful, the reliable, awesome one, who makes his angels spirits and his ministers a blazing fire;

Ps 105(104):4.

Lord, blessed God, you who created things both visible and invisible: archangels, principalities, powers, virtues, dominations, thrones, glories;

Cf. Col 1:16; Eph 1:21.

Lord, blessed God, you who created heaven and earth and the things which they contain: the light and darkness, the sun, moon and stars, the sea and rivers with all they contain;

Ps 146(145):6.

Text: VS 114,A, 34-115,B,38

Lord, blessed God, you who gave to man whom you created glory and beauty;[3]

You who took soil from the earth and in your own hands fashioned it into a man to your image and likeness, making him male and female, and breathed into his face the breath of life, so that man became a living soul; You gave him speech on earth, so that he would listen to your voice, obey your commandments, do all your will and bless you all the days of his life;

Cf. Gn 1:2-2:7.

Lord, blessed God, you who have made man his own master so that he could choose according to his own will, conscience, and discernment between good and evil;

Lord, blessed God, you who gave man whom you fashioned, wisdom, intelligence, knowledge, and skill;

Lord, blessed God, you who created all the races of men from a single man, so that they cover the face of the earth;

Lord, blessed God, you who put the fear and dread of man whom you created into all creatures: birds of the sky, beasts of the earth, fish and reptiles, and have established him as master of all the creatures of the earth;

Lord, blessed God, you who have created fecundity and sterility, as you taught us in the holy Scriptures;

Lord, blessed God, you who fashion us in the bosom and bring us forth from the womb;

Lord, blessed God, you who are the source of all our growth and nourish us from infancy to old age;

Lord, blessed God, you who through your will provide us with bread to eat, water to drink, and clothing to cover us;

Lord, blessed God, you who grant us varied and abundant goods: seed of the earth and of the fruit trees, and the things that we draw from beasts and birds, those we draw from the sea, rivers and the heavenly dew;

Lord, blessed God, you who help all who love you, seek you, keep your commandments in everything and are filled with all the fruits of righteousness of your holy Spirit according to the desire of their hearts;

Cf. Ph 1:11.

Lord, blessed God, you who have sent us in the world your holy Word, Truth and Life, the true Light, the Invisible who is conformed to your image in everything, our Lord your beloved Son Jesus Christ who died for us and is risen in order to raise us from the sins and offences through which we had died, and has bestowed upon us the eternal and imperishable life that he promised us;

Cf. Jn 14:6.

Lord, ⟨blessed⟩ God. . . .

Text: VS 116-117

FRAGMENT IV

Pachomius imposes a rule on the first disciples

17. '. . .easily;[1] and it was this that I had previously told you that you might repent and return to the Lord who created you, when you did not yet know him. Now when you are called to the *synaxis* you will all come and you will no longer treat me as you have every day. If often. . . until you. . . . Likewise, when you are called to eat you will come together and you will no longer act as you have every day. If you happen to be doing something necessary concerning our needs, you will all go together, and you will no longer be negligent as you have been up to now. If you do not want to obey the regulations I have given you, you are free, for *to the Lord belong the earth and*

all it holds. If you go somewhere else, do as you wish, for I will not put up with you from now on if you do not behave in accordance with all the regulations I have given you.' Ps 24(23):1.

He expels them

18. When he had finished speaking to them, they looked at one another sneeringly, laughing and saying, 'What is the matter with Pachomius today, with his sharp speech? We will never obey him when he speaks sharply to us.' So they left him, giving no heed to him, relying on their bodily strength. They were strong fellows indeed. Whereas they had been used to coming one by one when they were called to prayer, no one came after this. Actually they had agreed among themselves, 'Let us act this way and see what he does'. When he saw that in their obduracy and pride they did not have the fear of God and they had decided not to listen to His voice, he was emboldened through the grace of the Holy Spirit within him. Trusting in the word of the voice that spoke to him and had come to him, he rose without stick or weapons, holding a door bolt in his hand at that moment; he pursued them one by one in the name of God and chased them all out of the monastery. They went as if pursued by a troop or by a fire. In reality, it was not through an act of man that they were ousted from that place, but it was the Lord who treated them in such manner, as David says, *Let God arise and let his enemies be scattered.* Ps 68(67):1. Not only were the enemies scattered but they gave themselves up as slaves to be beaten. The man who clings to the spirit of God becomes as the Apostle says, *He who clings to the Lord is one spirit with him.*[1] 1 Co 6:17. This is why David likewise says, *Strike whoever is my enemy without cause.* Ps 3:7.

They go to the bishop

19. As for them, they ran in the blindness of their hearts to the bishop of the diocese of ⟨Hew⟩ [1] whose name was Sarapion. They accused Pachomius saying, 'He expelled us from the monastery.' The bishop looked at them and saw their build and their vigor. He told them, 'You are strong men. This is why Pachomius imposed ascetical practices upon you to soften you. If he chased you out of his monastery it was not he who did it but God. Surely he did this on account of evil deeds you did, for righteous men . . .'.[2]

Text: VS 8-9

FRAGMENT V

Temptations (*Cf. G[1] 17a*).

20. . . . testifies in the Scriptures against each temptation, putting the devil to shame.[1]

(*Cf. SBo 21; G[1] 19b*).
6 lines are missing

21. One day again a great throng of devils got together and brought before him . . . together, just in the same manner a group of men would strive to move a large stone. This also they did, so that perhaps he would laugh. . . .

11 lines are missing

22. When the devil saw that he could not deceive him with any of these wiles, he entered into a beautiful woman, who said with . . .

13 lines are missing

23. She got up, went and knocked at his dwelling place. He opened the door, and seeing her, he lowered his eyes. . . .

Text: VS 118-119

FRAGMENT VI

Pachomius expels his sister's son

24. He saw also his own sister's son doing evil deeds. The boy had also come to him and lived the anchoritic life in the *Koinonia*. When he

saw him, he remembered the word of the Gospel, *If your right hand scandalizes you, cut it off and cast it away,* and so he cast him away. He continued to act this way all the days of his life, in accordance with God's revelation that one should cast away from the house of the Lord scandals and obstacles. Mt 5:30.

Pachomius' care for the brothers

25. He acted like a true shepherd who takes care of his flock. The weak he nurtured in the pastures of righteousness. The vicious he fettered with the bonds of the Gospel. Those who went astray he brought back to the sheepfold. The fat and the first born, he offered on the altar as sacrifices to the Lord for Him to smell their fragrance, following the example of Noah who took clean animals and birds and offered them on the altar, and God smelled the fragrance.[1] Gn 8:20-21.
Likewise Paul says, *We are the fragrance of the Christ of God.*[2] Pachomius strove in every way to 2 Co 2:15.
avoid the reproach that the prophet Ezechiel adressed to the shepherds.[3] Indeed, the sheep Ez 34.
which the Lord had brought together for him, he nurtured according to the Apostle's command, *Instruct the ignorant, exhort the faint-hearted, help the weak, be patient with everyone.*[4] And 1 Th 5:14.
truly [the Apostle] urged the sheep of the Lord to eat good food, so that they would be a fragrance for the Lord as when he said, *I exhort you, my brothers, to offer your bodies as a living sacrifice, holy and pleasing to God,* not only to be a Rm 12:1.
fragrance from the purity of their bodies but also from the purity of their hearts, as David says, *The sacrifice to God is a broken spirit,* and he begged Ps 51(50):17.
them to become by their mouths a sacrifice of blessing. He dedicated himself to all whom the

Lord had gathered under his hands in every blessing and every good work. He also fashioned, as well as he could, each soul individually and he strove hard, so that if anyone did turn away from him, no one else would be better able to bring him back to the work of God. He acted in this way lest he lose someone he could not save while another person could, and lest he therefore in the age to come incur the following reproach, 'After you rejected me as having no value, another gave me life'. This is why he very carefully fashioned the brothers' souls. Some of them he reproached, others he prayed for, still others he chastized not only with words but also in the manner of Paul who says, *Shall I come to you with a stick or with*
1 Co 4:21. *love and a spirit of meekness?* Still others he admonished for the negligence in which they lived and instructed them *so that God might give them repentance, that they might know the truth, and*
2 Tm 2:25-26. *keep themselves from the snares of the devil.*[5] All kinds of people living in sin, he endeavored, in the fear of the Lord. . . .

Text: *Muséon* (1941) pp. 113-115,A,15

FRAGMENT VII

26. . . . think interiorly that you are taking care of me and that you continue to be saddened because I did not accept it from you. By no means, I tell you; on the contrary, do you not hate me? I do not know. If indeed I acted this way I would give you such scandal that you would act likewise
17 lines are missing
at a given moment, and that I would be subject to God's tribunal. In fact, many times. . . .

27. . . . [*I treat my body harshly and make it obey me for fear that having preached to*] *others, I myself would be disqualified.* Hearing these things, the brothers were afraid and they ceased to speak to him. The hair mantle he was wearing they got from him, as he had said, the day he died. . .

1 Co 9:27.

3 lines are missing

28. It happened again one day that one of the old men, housemaster of his house, became ill. He was a holy man. Our father Pachomius was overcome with constant sorrow and addressed continual prayers to the Lord. Then an angel spoke to him, 'How long will you go on being sorrowful and will you pray for this brother? If he dies, will you not find another?' He looked and saw three men, luminous, eminent, glorious, and grey-haired who came to take the sick man. As he was amazed, the angel told him, 'These are the patriarchs Abraham, Isaac, and Jacob.' And immediately they took the soul of the sick brother, carrying it up to heaven with great glory.

29. The Apostle also often spoke again with him and with the glorious one who conversed with him at the door. He said, 'Do you. . .*? He saw still other. . .† saint in a revelation.

*2 lines are missing
†2 lines are missing

Notes to the First Sahidic Life

S[1] 1. [1]Rm 12:1 is quoted again below, ¶ 25.

S[1] 2. [1]Cf. Theodore's statement at the time of his great trial: 'The thought never came into my heart that I should become their father. . .' (SBo 94).
[2]This text is quoted also in SBo 63 (= G[1] 68).
[3]Ph 4:8 is quoted in Hors. Instr. 7:3.

S[1] 3. [1]Words omitted by haplography; restored according to the context.
[2]This text is quoted also in Am. Letter 4.
[3]The same text is applied to the fathers of the *Koinonia* in Theod. Instr. 3:6.

S[1] 5. [1]Cf. Pr. 70; Leg. 15; etc. There is a similar ¶ in G[1] 110.

S[1] 6. [1]See SBo 7 (= G[1] 5).

S[1] 7. [1]Cf. SBo 141 (= G[1] 131), where Theodore complains to the brothers about the fact that they have abandoned Pachomius' rules, although they were not ignorant of everything he had suffered 'that he might present us holy to the Lord'.

[2]We already perceive here something of the tension between eremitism and cenobitism. Although the tension is still healthy in the pachomian texts, without any attacks against eremitism, our authors clearly express their faith in the superiority of common life.

[3]We follow the text of S[1]; S[3] is a little more elaborate here, possibly under the influence of SBo.

[4]Word omitted in S[1]; restored from S[3].

S[1] 8. [1]1 P 2:23 is quoted in an instruction of Pachomius in G[1] 57.

S[1] 10. [1]People gather around Pachomius because he is good to them, just as it had happened in Šeneset (see SBo 8). This is still a pre-monastic group, and in fact Pachomius will not succeed in transforming it into a monastic community.

S[1] 11. [1]'. . . they all *ate together*. They *brought their share* to him and he administered it. They did this *freely and voluntarily*. . .' Alfonso Levis establishes a parallel between this description and the 'summaries' of the Acts of the Apostles; see 'Koinonia e comunidad no monacato pacomiano', p. 299, n. 71.

[2]We find the same idea of food corresponding to a degree of growth, with the same quotation, in Theod. Instr. 3:43.

[3]Note the inversion of the last two members of the quotation. Ac 4:32 is quoted also in Hors. Reg. 51; (cf. SBo 194); Theod. Instr. 3:23. See above, S[1] 11 note 1.

[4]The sentence 'As the Apostle. . . God' is not in our manuscript of S[1], but is found in S[3] which follows closely S[1] in this section. The same quotation of Heb 13:16 along with Ac 4:32-33 is used in the same manner in Hors. Test. 50.

S[1] 12. [1]Horsiesios quotes also this text, applying it to Pachomius and Theodore, in Hors. Letter 3:1.

S[1] 13. [1]The same text is quoted again below, ¶ 25 and in SBo 182.

S[1] 16. [1]This prayer is certainly inspired by a liturgical model, but it has not been possible to identify its source. H. van Cranenburgh has published a good study of Pachomius' prayers; see H. van Cranenburgh, 'Les noms de Dieu dans la prière de Pachôme. . .

[2]See another allusion to Ps 33(32):6 in Hors. Instr. 6:2.

[3]The place of this sentence has been changed by S[3]; although S[1] is fragmentary, it permits us to re-establish the right order.

S[1] 17. [1]The next two pages of the manuscript are very mutilated; we translate the text as it has been restored by Lefort; but that restoration is hypothetical in many places.

S[1] 18. [1]This text is quoted also in SBo 194.

S[1] 19. [1]The name of the diocese is illegible on the manuscript, but there is no place for a name longer than three or four letters. The name of the bishop is Sarapion; and from SBo-G[1] we know of a Sarapion who was bishop of Nitentori. But there is no place for that long a name in the manuscript. Lefort suggests either Hew (Diospolis parva), where Phbow will later be founded, or Sne, diocese where Pachomius was born (see VC, p. 68, n. 76).

[2]Although incomplete, this account is much more vivid than the short veiled allusion to these difficulties in SBo 24 and G[1] 38.

S[1] 20. [1]This fragment is also severely mutilated.

S[1] 25. [1]Cf. the vision of SBo 76 when Pachomius offers Theodore to God. See also Pach. Letter 5:8, where Pachomius says that Moses offered some of the animals as victims to God because of their obedience.

[2]Cf. Theod. Instr. 3:5, where the monks are called to be *a sweet odor* for those outside; and Hors. Instr. 1:2, where Horsiesios says that 'the life of our holy father is an angelic life, perfuming the whole world'.

[3]Hors. Test. 8 reminds the superior of these reproaches.

[4]This text is quoted also in Hors. Test. 15 and Hors. Letter 3:5.

[5]This text is quoted above ¶ 13, and in SBo 182.

the second sahidic life (S[2])

Text: VS 12-15, B,3

FRAGMENT I

On discernment of spirits
2 Co 11:14-15.

IN FACT,[1] the Apostle instructs us about him saying, *For even Satan disguises himself as an angel of light. It is small wonder.* In a long exhortation on the same subject in his prophecy, John writes, *Do not trust every spirit but test the spirits to know which come from God; for many antichrists have come into the world. But distinguish God's spirit from deceiving spirits. For every spirit that fails to confess Jesus Christ is not good.* * And *the spirits of wickedness disguise themselves as apostles*[2] [*of Christ*] . . . . † Why then are some led astray by them, if not because they have performed works out of human desire and vainglory?

*1 Jn 4:1-3.
†2 Co 11:13; Cf. Eph 6:12.

Pachomius' love for God
*8 lines are missing

2. For Paul says, *The Lord*. . .* The Apostle tells us also, *Neither death nor life, no angel, no principality, nothing that exists, nothing still to come, neither power nor height, nor any other creature will be able to separate us from the Love of God which is in Christ Jesus Our Lord.* In the same manner, too, our father Pachomius loved God. With fear and in very great trembling he watched himself carefully.

Rm 8:38-39

3. And [God] gave him a sign to discern [spirits]. And first of all, to recognize with certainty that a man who...* and it was impossible for him ever to be deceived by the servants of the enemy. Secondly, to know with certitude if it was an impure spirit that was manifesting itself to him—for then his body would be terror-stricken—while if it was an angel of light, the members of his body ached and every thought vanished from his heart.[1] Through God's grace, he recognized [the spirits] and distinguished them from one another. He rebuked the evil ones and accepted the words of the angels of God. And he examined the words they imparted to him, to see if they conformed to the Scriptures. He kept in mind the word of Paul, *For even if we, or an angel from heaven, should preach to you something different from what you have received, let a curse be upon him.* And if he realized that their words accorded with those of the breath of the Spirit of God in the Scriptures, he consented to the revelation made to him by the angel of light.

How Pachomius discerned the spirits

*4 lines are missing (*Cf.* G^1 *87*).

Ga 1:8-9.

FRAGMENT II

Text: VS 17, A,2-16

Pachomius rebukes the demons

4. Many times again, wishing to deceive him, they appeared to him in various disguises but he recognized them through the gift he had received from God in whose name he rebuked them.

FRAGMENT III

Text: *Muséon* (1936) 225-226

The life of the saints

5. I tell you that *the world would not hold the*

Jn 21:25.

books that would be written. Just as this is true for Our Lord, so the same holds true for his servants, the saints, who resemble him in all things. What greater marvel, indeed, is there than that seen by Stephen? While still in the body, and although he was only a disciple of the apostles, he said, as we read in Acts, *I see the heavens open, and the Son of Man standing at the right hand of God.*

Ac 7:56.

Their faith

6. We say these things in response to those who are fainthearted in our presence because of Our Lord's words in the Gospels, that... and about the mustard seed, *If your faith were the size of a mustard seed, you would say to this mountain, 'Move from here to there', and it would move, or to this sycamore tree, 'Be uprooted and transplanted in the sea', and it would obey you.* For, as we have said that our father Pachomius was brought into the other age...[1] into the third heaven.* And it is not only into the other age that the saints are brought by the angels, but also on earth they are brought from one place to another according to the Lord's designs. Indeed, the angel addressed himself to Habakkuk the prophet, *Take the dinner you are carrying to Babylon, above the lion's pit* [*where is*] *Daniel.*[2] He answered, *Lord, I do not know Babylon nor the pit....*

5 lines are missing

Mt 17:20.

Lk 17:6.

5 lines are missing

*Cf. 2 Co 12:2.

Dn 14:34.

Dn 14:35.

Text: *Muséon* (1936) 227-228

FRAGMENT IV

Pachomius' virtues and love for God

1 Jn 3:9.

7. ... *born of God does not commit sin; because His seed abides in him,*[1] *and it is impossible for him to sin because he is born of God.* This therefore is how our father Pachomius lived:

in all those virtues, having given himself entirely to the Lord... great graces and many gifts; in him was fulfilled the word written in the Gospel, *With the measure you have used, it shall be measured out to you,* and again, *Full measure pressed down, shaken together, running over, will be poured into your lap.*[2] For the Lord is faithful and his words are unchanging, and *for two unalterable things, it is impossible for God to be lying.* And in the Gospels the Saviour also promises whoever will keep his commandments, *If anyone loves me, and keeps my words, then my Father will love him, and we shall come to him and make our dwelling place with him.*[3] What greater good than this is there then, to the point that... and what marvel, what great thing will not happen to him for having become the dwelling place of the creator of the universe? We know from what is written in the Scriptures, that *no one has ever seen God,* and again, that *He dwells in the light that nobody approaches....*

8 lines are missing

Mt 7:2.

Lk 6:38.

Heb 6:18.

Jn 14:23.

3 lines are missing

Jn 1:18; 1 Jn 4:12.

1 Tm 6:16.

FRAGMENT V

Text: VS 26-29

Pachomius' recommendation to Theodore

8. ... Theodore and two other brothers, at the time they were leaving for some place; and before they actually left the monastery, he had told him, 'Theodore, be mindful of this word written in the Gospel about the Saviour, *And the power of the Lord made him heal,* because He who worked healings in that time will still work some today, as it has been revealed to me...'.

Lk 5:17.

13 lines are missing

Healing of a dropsical man

9. A man who had dropsy came also to see him, and asked him to heal him. He had brought with

10 lines are missing

him a bit of oil for [Pachomius] to rub on him and anoint him with. He took the oil. . . .

Healing of a man bitten by a snake

10. After he had gone a bit further, they brought him a man who was suffering severely from a snake bite. The man was lying in a wagon. Those who brought him asked [Pachomius] to climb into the wagon to rub him for he was paralyzed. As he was climbing onto the wheel of the wagon and approached the sick man, the latter jumped up saying, 'Do not tire yourself, my father, for I was healed the moment you approached the wagon.'

Healing of another dropsical man

11. And it happened the same day, as he was coming back to the monastery, that he found a man with dropsy seated by the road, for he could no longer walk or go back to his house. As soon as he was blessed by Pachomius, his belly expelled the impurity of the disease that was in him. Coming to Pachomius, the man prostrated himself at his feet, thanking him for what had happened to him. And so [Pachomius] told him, 'Bless the Lord who healed you and watch that you do not sin against him all the days of your life . . .'.

Cf. Jn 5:14.

Pachomius' exhortation to those whom he healed

12. And this was the exhortation he gave all those whom the Lord healed through him, 'Hope in God who has healed you. From now on, do not sin against him, so that just as he has healed you from your diseases, so also he will give you courage until the day of your death.'

Pachomius' prayer concerning healings

13. Each time he spoke to God regarding healings, he expressed himself like this, as he told us: 'Lord, blessed God, you who have created the universe, things both visible and invisible, if this is your will, bring about the healing of this sick person, primarily so that your glorious name may

Cf. Col 1:16.

be glorified, and that this sick person may gain from what will happen to him, and that he may no longer sin against you... that your will be done.' If it happened that the sick person was healed while he applied a remedy to him, he did not pride himself on it, knowing that the power came not from him but from the Lord who dwelt in him. On the other hand, if he applied a remedy to someone without obtaining a cure, he was not saddened or disheartened, but blessed the Lord, [saying], 'No doubt, the profit...'.

FRAGMENT VI

Text: *Muséon* (1936) 229

14. ...[*dissensionsι, heresies, slander, drunkenness, orgies,* coarseness, jokes,† mockery, foolishness... back-biting‡...*

*Ga 5:20-21.
†Eph 5:4.
‡Cf.Rm 1:29-31; 2 Co 12:20; 1 P 2:1.

...flesh... no good abides in it, for the Holy Spirit of God is not in it.*

*Cf. Rm 7:18.

Notes to the Second Sahidic Life

S[2] 1. [1]This first fragment corresponds to page 47 of the manuscript. We do not translate the first few lines of column A which, apart from being very mutilated, come at the end of a sentence and do not give any real meaning.
[2]*ôs apostolos*; only the last three letters of the second word are legible on the manuscript. The dependence on 2 Co 11:13 and Eph 6:12 requires this restoration: *ôs apostolos* (see Lefort, VC., p. 7, n. 4) instead of *ôs aggelos* (Lefort, VS, p. 12,B,18).

S[2] 3. [1]Cf. SBo 113; G[1] 87.

S[2] 6. [1]Cf. SBo 114.
[2]See a reference to the same scene in Pach. Instr. 1:13.

S[2] 7. [1]This text is quoted also in Hors. Test. 20.
[2]See the same quotations in Inst. 18 and Hors. Test. 7 and 16.
[3]Jn 14:23 is quoted also in G[1] 112 and in Hors. Test. 44.

the tenth sahidic life

(S[10])

Text: *Muséon* (1941)137-138; Am 393

FRAGMENT I

Theodore wants to acquire true knowledge

ONE DAY, [Theodore] heard our father Pachomius instructing the brothers in these words: 'If a man possessed true knowledge, he would not sin either against God or against his neighbor.' After he heard these words, he was sad and he prayed to God, saying, 'O God in whom I took refuge, I thought I had found you; but behold, you are very far off, and I do not know you, because I did not find your knowledge for myself, as you have promised to whoever loves you, that I might do what is pleasing to you.'

When our father Pachomius learned that Theodore often wept over this matter, he prayed, and each time he met him he would tell him, 'Strive, my son, and acquire for yourself true knowledge.' Later, at a time when the moon was shining, he called him and he said to him, 'Raise your eyes, my son, and look at this light which shines on the entire earth, although it is a creature of God. The One who created it along with the sun and all creatures is invisible; and you see his brightness and his glory. Fear him all the days of your life; know that it is He who created us with all the other creatures and that we are in his hand. When you fear him and you believe that He sees you at every moment, be vigilant so as not to sin against him and you will receive true knowledge from him. So shall you bless him at all times all the days of your life.' As he was saying these things, they both wept copiously and prayed.

FRAGMENT II

Text: VS 33-36

How to form young monks

2. . . . he saw the Lord of the Universe, the Son of God made flesh for our salvation. Above all too we hear him in the Gospel saying, *Do not prevent . . .* *

*Mt 19:14.

About 12 lines are missing

. . . He set a little one in the midst of his disciples saying, *Anyone who shall receive a young child such as this in my name receives me.*[1] But as for other little ones who have acquired an evil bent in their [youth] . . .

Cf. Mt 18:2.

Mt 18:5.

About 12 lines are missing

. . . [as Solomon] says, *Anyone who lives wantonly from his youth shall become a slave.* And so, my brothers, every young child as well as those who are older whom the Lord has brought to us for the rebirth, let us be zealous . . .[2]

Pr 29:21.

About 20 lines are missing

. . . many times, let us teach them that it is God who has created them. And also concerning heaven and earth, the sun and moon . . .

A full column of 27 lines is missing

. . . teach them at all times to bless without ceasing him who created all these things, whether with their mouths or with their hearts saying, 'Blessed are you, Lord,' so that they too may become children of David who says, *I will bless the Lord at all times; at all times His blessing is in my mouth.* After that they will also be given

Ps 34(33):1.

psalms [to learn] by heart; and moreover they shall learn from the books of holy Scripture.[3] And afterwards the children shall be taught what is pleasing to God, and his will from his law and the rules that I drew from it for you, that they may love the Lord our God with all their heart, all their soul, and all their strength; and they may love their neighbor as themselves;[4] that they may know surely that which is written by the Holy Spirit; so that, if they keep their body pure from their youth up, they may become temples of the Lord and the Holy Spirit may dwell in them.

Mt 22:37-39; Lk 10:27.

1 Co 3:16.

Text: VS 37,A; Am 396

FRAGMENT III

Pachomius rebukes Theodore

3. One day, the brothers were eating, and the housemaster served them. It was during the time of the *khamsin*[1] and he gave them cheese to eat. When Theodore had finished, the housemaster gave him some more cheese to eat; but he did not want to take it and said, 'I do not want it'. As he was again constraining him to take some, he said to him, 'I will not'. And [Pachomius] said to him, 'What is this word you have said, "I will not", having given place in your heart to a demon of disobedience? Even if you do not wish to take some, say, "I wish none now" but take some and lay it down.' When Theodore heard this, he was very sad, and did not say it any more. This is how [Pachomius] used to edify Theodore and all the brothers in the fear of God and every good intention.

FRAGMENT IV

Text: VS 40-43; Am 402-403

(*Cf. SBo 33*).

Theodore wants to see God

4. And it happened, shortly after he had come to the brothers, that being still a boy, he came to our father Pachomius who asked him, 'Why are you weeping?'[1] For he was astonished to see him so often weeping, although he was young. Theodore told him, 'I wish you, father, to declare to me whether I shall see the Lord or not. If I am not worthy of seeing him who created me, what profit is there in having been born into this world? For it would have been good for me if I had not been born.' He said to him, 'Tell me, do you desire to see him here or in the age to come?' He said, 'There'. Pachomius said to him, 'Do all you can to observe the commandments written in the Gospel that says, *Blessed are the pure in heart, for they shall see God.*[2] If then an impure thought rises up in your heart, or hatred toward your brother or wickedness or envy or contempt for the brothers or vainglory, remember at once and say, "If I consent in my heart to one of these thoughts, I shall not see God." And if you want all these thoughts to diminish in you and not to have power over you, then recite in your heart without ceasing every fruit that is written in the Scriptures, having in yourself the resolution to walk in them, as it is written in Isaiah, *Your heart shall meditate on the fear* of the Lord, and all these things shall cease from you, little by little, and they shall grow weak, like the spider. For the Lord has placed in man conscience and freewill

Mt 5:8.

Is 33:18.

and judgement and understanding and wisdom. For even as the members of the body which are visible and with which man works, now with one now with the other according to his need. . .[3]

About 13 lines are missing

'. . . a house that has a door, which is the heart. And further, just as the door has a key and a bolt, a chain, a peg and every security, so it is with free-will, conscience, understanding, judgement and wisdom. . . .

About 15 lines are missing

'Now if a man is ignorant of the law, his conscience prompts him [saying], "This thing is not good". For to some it testifies according to the knowledge of the heart [saying], "You will sin against the Lord if you do this;" while to others again it testifies, "If you are discovered, you shall be in danger, or indeed they will slay you". . .

A few lines are missing

laws that are written after the prompting of this sort he received from it, he will destroy his own conscience and sear it until it shall not prompt him any more, as it is written concerning others of this sort *whose conscience is seared*[4]. . .

1 Tm 4:2.
A few lines are missing

Paul said concerning such as these that they should give themselves up to penance because they have not known the law. He wrote, *Our hearts being sprinkled clean from all evil conscience and our body washed with pure water*. . . .

Heb 10:22.
A few words are missing

They have a law through their conscience. This is what we are told by the herald of the Gospel. *When the Gentiles, who do not have the law, by nature do the things of the law, these men, although without the law, are a law unto themselves. They teach you the work of the law written in their heart, their conscience*. . .'.

Rm 2:14-15.

FRAGMENT V

Text: VS 72-73; Am 434

5. He remembered what he had seen in the vision he had received from the Lord on the day he was instructed to become a Christian; how in that revelation he had seen the dew of heaven descending upon him, condensing and becoming a honeycomb in his hand and falling to the ground. And he was told in the vision, 'Give heed to this word, for it shall be fulfilled in you after a time.' And later on he was informed by the Spirit that 'This honeycomb that condensed in your hand and fell to the ground, these are all the gifts that came to you from the Lord. And they shall come also upon your brothers, that is, the earth, when they are born again, cleansed from all pride and vainglory. Truly those who shall purify their hearts greatly from every evil thought shall discern between good and evil.'

(Cf. SBo 8; G[1] 5).

Pachomius remembers his first vision

FRAGMENT VI

Text: VS 74, B,5-75,A,14; Am 438-439

Pachomius' charity to the Church

6. It happened, as our father was praying, that an angel of the Lord appeared to him and said, 'What will you vow to give in charity, if the Lord ceases his wrath and holds back the barbarians?' He said, 'I will send to the Church of the city which the barbarians have laid waste one hundred measures of corn, with books and other things which they need.' Having heard this from the angel, he told the brothers what he had seen happening before it had actually taken place.

Thus the barbarians were conquered the next day and were driven back as he had been told.

Text: VS 75, A,15-77,B,7

FRAGMENT VII

(*Cf. G[1] 85; Paral. 8-11*).

Story of the monk who poured out a libation to the gods

7. While the barbarians were victorious they found a monk living as an anchorite some place and they took him captive. One day, when they came and wanted to drink wine, they said to him, 'Gird yourself and pour [wine] for us.' And when he began to pour them a drink, they told him, 'Make a libation before you give us a drink.' But he would not. When they saw he was not obeying them, they took a spear, saying to him, 'Pour out [a libation], or we will kill you.' Being afraid they would kill him, he poured out. Then he gave them a drink until they were drunk and slept; and the monk fled.

After that he was so heartbroken that he could not stretch out his hands to pray. 'How shall I pray to him whom I have disowned?' he said. For it is written, *The one who disowns me I will disown.* Then he thought to himself, 'I have heard that there is a man of God, father of the *Koinonia* of Tabennesi, called Pachomius. I will get up and go to him and tell him of everything I have done. If he gives me repentance, I believe that the Lord will also give it to me. But if he says, 'There is no repentance for you . . .'

Mt 10:33.

Cf. Lk 15:18.

About 15 lines are missing

. . . [there is no repentance for me] until I meet with you first and you show me the certainty of the matter.' He said to him, 'O wretched man, after the angel of the Lord had stood over you, with the crown...'

About 15 lines are missing

...He ordered him to fast every day and to abstain from all cooked foods, except in the event of sickness, and he said, 'If you do this, the saints will be the guarantees of your salvation before God, and I also with them, in the hour when the enemy shall accuse you.'[1]

Notes to the Tenth Sahidic Life

S[10] 2. [1]This text is quoted by Pachomius when Theodore gives his first instruction; see SBo 69 (= G[1] 77).
[2]See similar recommendations in G[1] 49.
[3]Cf. Pr. 139-140.
[4]This invitation to love our neighbor is quoted more than once; see SBo 70 (= G[1] 78) and SBo 204.

S[10] 3. [1]A scorching wind from the south which blows for a period of fifty days, from the end of March to the beginning of May (Amélineau's note).

S[10] 4. [1]The first part of this story is found almost word for word in SBo 33 (without parallel in G[1]), but the second part is much longer in S[10].
[2]About the use of Mt 5:8, see SBo 33, note 1.
[3]The Arabic text (Am) is too different here to be used for filling the gaps of our manuscript of S[10].
[4]Theod. Instr. 3, 1 uses this text differently: '[God] causes our conscience to burn us at every moment...'

S[10] 7. [1]See other versions of the same story in G[1] 85 and Paral. 8-11.

A SYNOPTIC TABLE of SBo and G¹

SBo			G¹
1			1
2			2a
3			2b
4			3a
5			
6			3b
7a			4
7b			5a
8			5b
9			
10			6
11			7
12			
13			
14			8
15a			9
			10
15b			11
16		13a	
17			12
	16		13a
18			13b
19a			14
19b			15
			16
20			
			17
21a			18
21b			19
21c		22	
			20
22		23	
	cf. 98		21
	21c		22
	22		23
23a		25a	
23b			24
	23a		25a
23c			25b
24			26a
25a		29	

SBo		*G*[1]	
25b			26b
25c			27
26			28
27		32	
	25a		29
28			30
			31
	27		32
	31		33
29			34
30a			35
30b			36a
31		33	
32			36b
33			
34			
35			
36		90	
37			37
38		65	
	cf. 24		38
39			39
40			40
41			41
42			42
43			43
44			44
45			45
			46
46			47
			48
			49
			50
47a			51
47b			52
48			53
49			54a
50			54b
51			54c
52			
53			
54		81a	
55a		82	
55b		81c	
56		80	

SBo		G^1	
57		83a	
58a		83b	
58b		81b	
58c		81d	
59a			55
			56
			57
	cf. 104		58
	cf. 104		59
59b			60
59c			61
			62
			63
60			
61			64
	38		65
62			66
63a			67
63b			68
64			69
65			70
66			71
67a			72
67b			73
			74
67c			75
68			76
69a			77
69b			78a
70			78b
			79
	56		80
71		83c	
	54		81a
	58b		81b
	55b		81c
	55a		82
	57		83a
	58a		83b
	71		83c
	58c		83d
	99b		84
			85
72a		96	
72b			86

SBo		*G^1*	
72c		97	
	113		87
73			88
74a			89
	36		90
74b			91
75			92
76			
77			
78			
79			
80			
81			
	83		93a
82			93b
83		93a	
84		96	
85			
86			
87			
88			
89a			94
89b			95a
90			95b
91a		111	
91b			95c
	72a		96
	72c		97
			98
	cf. 189		99
92			100
	99a		101
	103		102
93			103
93(bis)a			104
93(bis)b			105
94a			106
94b			107a
95a			107b
95b			108
96a			109a
96b		113	
97			109b
			110
	91a		111
			112

SBo		G^1	
	96b		113
98		cf. 21	
99a		101	
99b		84	
100			
101			
102			
103		102	
104		cf. 58-59	
105			
106			
107			
108			
109			
110			
111			
112			
113		87	
114			
115			
116			
117			
118			
119			114a
120		115	
121			114b
	120		115
122			116a
123			116b
124			117a
	130		117b
	209		118
	199		119
125			
126			120a
127			120b
128			
129			120c
130		117b	
131			
132			
133			120d
134a		136	
134b			120e
135		125	

SBo		*G¹*	
136			
137			121a
138			121b
			122
			123
			124
	135		125
			126
139a			127
139b			128
139c			129a
140			129b
			130
141			131a
142			131b
143			131c
144			
145			
146			
147			
148			
149			
150			
	cf. 191		132
151			133
152			
153			
154			
155			134
			135
	134a		136
....			
180		139	
181			
182			
183			
184			
185a			137
185b			138
	180		139
	187		140a
186a			140b
186b			141
186c			142
187		140a	

SBo		*G*[1]	
188			
189		cf. 99	
190			
191		cf. 132	
192			
193			
194			
195			
196			
197		146a	
198		146b	
199		119	
200			143a
201a			143b
201b			144a
202			144b
203			144c
204			145a
205a			145b
	197-198		146
205b			147
206			148
207			149a
208			149b
209		118	
210			150

CHRONOLOGICAL TABLE

(In the elaboration of this table we have borrowed much from D.J. Chitty, *The Desert a City*, pp. 208-210 and from H. Bacht, *Das Vermächtnis des Ursprungs*, pp. 287-291.)

Pachomian cenobitism	Monasticism in general
	c. 271 Antony becomes monk
c. 292 Pachomius' birth	
	c. 293 Macarios of Alex.'s birth
	c. 300 Macarios of Egypt's birth
	305 Antony assembles disciples
c. 312 Pachomius' conscription	
c. 313 Pachomius' baptism	
c. 316 Pachomius comes to Palamon	
c. 323 Pachomius settles in Tabennesi	
c. 324 Arrival of first disciples	
c. 328 Theodore's arrival	
c. 329 Foundation of Phbow and of other monasteries	

Church events	World events
	284 Diocletian becomes emperor
303 Persecution edict	
	305 Maximianus becomes emperor
	306 Constantine becomes emperor in the West
311 (24 Nov.) Archbishop Peter's martyrdom	
313 Edict of Milan	313 Maximin Daia's death
	320 Licinius' persecution
	324 Constantine gets control over the eastern empire
325 Council of Nicaea	
328 Athanasius becomes archbishop	
329-330 Athanasius' visit to the Thebaid	
335 Athanasius' first exile	

Pachomian cenobitism	Monasticism in general
c. 336-337 Theodore becomes steward of Tabennesi; Pachomius settles in Phbow	
	338 Antony visits Alexandria and Nitria
c. 340 Second group of foundations	
345 Synod of Latopolis	
346 (9 May) Pachomius' death (21 July) Petronios' death Horsiesios becomes superior of the *Koinonia*	
347 Theodore sent to Phnoum	
350 Crisis; Horsiesios resigns; Theodore becomes superior	
351 Ammon comes to Phbow	
	356 Antony's death
	357 Athanasius writes the *Vita Antonii*
360 Artemios searches for Athanasius in Phbow	
363 Athanasius visits the monasteries near Hermopolis	

Church events	*World events*
	337 Constantine's death; empire divided between Constans and Constantius
339 Athanasius' second exile	
345 Jerome's and Rufinus' birth	
346 (21 Oct.) Athanasius' return	
	350 Constans is murdered
353-354 Synod of Arles	353 Constantius rules over the whole empire
356 Athanasius' third exile (with the monks)	
357 Basil's baptism; he visits the monks	
361 Athanasius' return	361 Constantius' death; Julian becomes emperor
362 Athanasius' fourth exile	
363 Athanasius' return	363 Julian's death Jovian becomes emperor

Pachomian cenobitism	*Monasticism in general*
367 Theodore brings back Horsiesios to Phbow	
368 (27 April) Theodore's death; Horsiesios becomes superior again	
	373 Jerome becomes a monk
	379 Jerome becomes a priest
	382 Jerome comes to Rome
	383 Evagrius comes to Nitria
	384 Jerome comes to Bethlehem
	385 Evagrius comes to the "Cells"
after 387 Horsiesios' death	
391-392 Foundation of the monastery of Metanoia (Canope)	

Church events	*World events*
	364 Valens becomes emperor in the East
370 Basil becomes bishop	
373 Athanasius' death	
	378 Valens is murdered
379 Basil's death	379Theodosius becomes emperor
381 Council of Constantinople	
385 Theophilos becomes archbishop of Alexandria	
388 Palladius comes to Alexandria	
	391 Theodosius' edict against pagan cults
394 Quarrel between Jerome and Rufinus	
	395 Theodosius' death Arcadius becomes emperor

Pachomian cenobitism	*Monasticism in general*
	399 Evagrius' death; Origenist controversy
	400 Cassian becomes a deacon; Palladius becomes a bishop
	401 The Great Brothers go to appeal at Constantinople
404 Jerome translates the *Pachomiana latina*	404 Paula's death Composition of H.M.A.
	405 Cassian comes to Rome Euthymius comes to Jerusalem
	407-408 First devastation of Skete

Church events	*World events*
398 John Chrysostom becomes archbishop of Constantinople	
400 Synod of Alexandria against the Origenists	
403 Synod of the Oak against John Chrysostom	
404 John Chrysostom's exile	
407 John Chrysostom's death in exile	
	408 Arcadius' death Theodosius II becomes emperor
410 Rufinus' death	410 Devastation of Rome by Alaric
412 Theophilos' death	

GLOSSARY

Age (αἰών): term borrowed from Scripture and used to distinguish between the present earthly existence (this age) and the heavenly one (the other age).

Ancient (αρχαῖος): man of old age, but also one of the 'early' (pachomian) monks.

Ascesis: special way of life by which a monk realizes his struggle for conversion and sanctification.

Closing of the Passover: celebration corresponding to our Easter Vigil and concluding the six days of fast of the Passover.

Father of the monastery: superior of a local pachomian community.

Fifty Days (πεντηκοστή): the fifty days of Eastertide.

Forty Days (τεσσαρακοστή): the forty days of fast preceding the six days of the Passover, and corresponding to Lent.

Great one: 1) either a senior in community or, more specifically, a superior; 2) when used absolutely ('the Great One'), it means Pachomius.

House: one of the various groups into which a local pachomian community was divided. Each house had a specific service to fulfil in the community.

Housemaster: superior of one of the 'houses' into which a local pachomian commmunity was divided.

Instruction (κατήχησις): spiritual talk given by the superior of the community three times a week (on Saturday and twice on Sunday) and by the housemaster twice a week (on Wednesday and Friday).

Koinonia: technical name given to the whole congregation of pachomian monasteries. It is used also of their way of life.

Leader (ἡγούμενος, dux): name given to the superior of a monastery by some of our sources.

Little one: someone recently arrived in community or, in general, an ordinary monk without any charge.

Mountain: in Coptic the mountain is also the desert, and is the normal place for burial.

Old man (Coptic *hello, chello*; Greek γέρων): someone of long experience in monastic life; usually (but not always) advanced in age.

Passover: six days of fast preceding the celebration of the Resurrection.

Recitation, to recite (μελέτη, μελετᾶν, *meditatio, meditari*): reciting in a low voice of texts of the Scriptures learned by heart. We avoid using the word 'meditation' which has taken very different connotations in the Christian terminology of the last centuries as well as in the spiritual traditions of the East.

Second: name given to the assistant of the father of a local monastery (the 'second' of the monastery) and to the assistant of the housemaster (the 'second' of the house).

Six Prayers: technical name of an Office celebrated in the evening, at which six sections of the Scriptures were read, each one probably followed by a prayer.

Steward (οἰκονόμος): 1) name given in some of our sources to the superior of the local community. In other sources he is called 'leader', or 'father of the monastery', or 'the man of the community'; 2) name given to the material administrator (v.g. the Great Steward in charge of the material administration of the whole *Koinonia*).

Synaxis: name given 1) to the assembly of the brothers for prayer (prayer being accompanied by light manual work); 2) to the place where this assembly was held (also called 'assembly room' or 'celebration room'); 3) occasionally to the 'Office' of an anchorite.

Tabennesiots: name often given to pachomian monks in ancient monastic sources. Tabennesi was Pachomius' first monastery.

Thought (λογισμός): suggestion usually put in man's mind by the devil. It often has a meaning very close to 'temptation'.

SOURCES

Editions and Translations

A: *EDITIONS*

Coptic

Lefort, L.T. *S. Pachomii vita bohairice scripta, CSCO* 89. Louvain, 1925; rpt. 1953.

———. *S. Pachomii vitae sahidice scriptae, CSCO* 99/100. Louvain, 1933/34; rpt. 1952.

———. 'Glanures pachômiennes,' *Muséon* 54 (1941) 111-138. [S^{19}, S^{20}, and fragments of S^{3}, S^{3c}, and S^{4}].

———. 'Vies de S. Pachôme (Nouveaux fragments),' *Muséon* 49 (1936) 219-230. [Fragments of S^{2}].

———. *Oeuvres de s. Pachôme et de ses disciples, CSCO* 159. Louvain, 1956.

Quecke, Hans. *Die Briefe Pachoms. Griechischer Text der Handschrift W. 145 der Chester Beatty Library eingeleitet und herausgegeben von Hans Quecke. Anhang: Die koptischen Fragmente und Zitate der Pachombriefe. Textus Patristici et Liturgici* 11. Regensburg, 1975. [Coptic texts: pp. 111-118].

———. 'Ein Brief von einem Nachfolger Pachoms,' *Orientalia* 44 (1975) 426-433.

Greek

Halkin, F. Sancti Pachomii Vitae Graecae, Subsidia hagiographica 19. Brussels, 1932.

———. 'La vie abrégée de saint Pachôme dans le ménologe impérial (BHG 1401b),' *AnBoll* 96 (1978) 367-381.

———. 'Une vie inédite de saint Pachôme,' *AnBoll* 97 (1979) 5-55; 241-287.

Bousquet, J., and F. Nau. *Histoire de saint Pacôme (Une rédaction inédite des Ascetica) Texte grec des manuscrits Paris 881 et Chartres 1754 avec une traduction de la version syriaque et une analyse du manuscrit de Paris Suppl. grec. 480, PO* IV, 5. Paris, 1907.

Lefort, L.T. 'La Règle de S. Pachôme (2e étude d'approche),' *Muséon* 37 (1924) 1-28. [Text of the Greek *Excerpta* of the Rule of Pachomius. Rpt. in A. Boon, *Pachomiana latina. . ., p. 169-182*].

Draguet, R. 'Un morceau grec inédit des Vies de Pachôme apparié à un texte d'Evagre en partie inconnu,' *Muséon* 70 (1957) 267-306.

_______. 'Un Paralipomenon pachômien inconnu dans le Karakallou 251,' *Mélanges Eugène Tisserant*, Vol. II, *ST* 232. Vatican City, 1964. Pp. 55-61.

Quecke, Hans. *Die Briefe Pachoms. Griechischer Text der Handschrift W. 145 der Chester Beatty Library eingeleitet und herausgegeben von Hans Quecke. Anhang: Die koptischen Fragmente und Zitate der Pachombriefe, Textus Patristici et Liturgici* 11. Regensburg, 1975.

Latin

Boon, A. *Pachomiana latina. Règle et épîtres de s. Pachôme, épître de s. Théodore et 'Liber' de s. Orsiesius. Texte latin de s. Jérôme, Bibliothèque de la Revue d'histoire ecclésiastique* 7. Louvain, 1932.

Van Cranenburg, H. *La vie latine de saint Pachôme traduite du grec par Denys le Petit, édition critique, Subsidia hagiographica* 46. Brussels, 1969.

Arabic

Amélineau, A. *Monuments pour servir à l'histoire de l'Egypte chrétienne au IVe siècle.—Histoire de Saint Pakhôme et de ses communautés. Documents coptes et arabe inédits, publiés et traduits par E. Amélineau, ADMG* 17, 2 Vol. Paris 1889. [Arabic text: Vol. II, pp. 337-711].

Syriac

Budge, E.A.W. *The Book of Paradise*. London, 1904. [Syriac version of the *Paralipomena*, which Budge erroneously calls the Rule of Pachomius].

Ethiopic

Dillmann, A. *Chrestomatia Aethiopica*. Leipzig, 1866; 1941², pp. 57-69. [Ethiopic version of the Rules of Pachomius].

Löfgren, O. 'Zur Textkritik der äthiopischen Pachomiusregeln I, II,' *Le Monde Oriental* 30 (1936) 171-187. [Critical *apparatus* to be added to Dillman's edition].

Arras, V. *Collectio Monastica*, CSCO 238. Louvain, 1963. Pp. 141-143. [Ethiopic translation of the Greek *Excerpta* of the Rule of Pachomius].

B: *TRANSLATIONS*

From Coptic

Lefort, L.T. *Sancti Pachomii vita bohairice scripta, CSCO* 107. Louvain, 1936. [Latin translation].

________. *Les Vies coptes de Saint Pachôme et de ses premiers successeurs, Bibliothèque du Muséon* 16. Louvain 1943; rpt. 1966.

________. *Oeuvres de s. Pachôme et de ses disciples, CSCO* 160. Louvain 1956.

Draguet, R. *Les Pères du désert*. Paris, 1949. Pp. 87-126. [French translation of a Life of Pachomius reconstructed from the Coptic fragments].

Quecke, H. 'Briefe Pachoms in koptischer Sprache. Neue deutsche Übersetzung,' *Zetesis. Festschrift E. de Strycker*. Antwerp/Utrecht, 1973. Pp. 655-664.

Vögué, A. de. 'Epîtres inédites d'Horsièse et de Théodore,' *Commandements du Seigneur et Libération évangélique, SA* 70. Rome, 1977. Pp. 244-257.

From Greek

Athanassakis, A.N. *The Life of Pachomius* (*Vita Prima Graeca*). *Translated by Apostolos N. Athanassakis. Introduction by Birger A. Pearson*. Missoula, MT, 1975.

Festugière, A.-J. *Les Moines d'Orient, T. IV/2: La première Vie grecque de saint Pachôme. Introduction critique et traduction*. Paris, 1965.

Mertel, H. *Leben des hl. Pachomius, BKV* 31. Kempten, 1917. [German translation of the second Greek Life and of a few fragments of the fourth Greek Life].

From Latin

D'Andilly, A. *Les Vies des Saints Pères des Déserts*, Lyon, 1663. Pp. 175-276. [French translation of the Latin Life].

Bacht, H. *Das Vermächtnis des Ursprungs, Studien zum Frühen Mönchtum* I. Würzburg, 1972. [German translation of the *Liber Orsiesii*].

De Elizalde, M. *Libro de nuestro Padre San Orsisio. Introducción, traducción y notas de Martín de Elizalde. Cuadernos monásticos,* Nos. 4-5 (1967) 173-244.

Steidle, B. and O. Schuler. 'Der "Obern-Spiegel" im "Testament" des Abtes Horsiesi († nach 387),' *EuA* 43 (1967) 5-21. [German translation of the chapters 7-18 and 39-40 of the *Liber Orsiesii*].

From Arabic

Amélineau, E. *Monuments pour servir....* [French translation under the Arabic text].

From Syriac

Budge, E.A.W. *The Book of Paradise.* London, 1904. [English translation of the Syriac version of the *Paralipomena*]. Rpt. in *The Paradise or Garden of the Holy Fathers.* London, 1907, Vol. 1, pp. 283-315; and again in *Stories of the Holy Fathers,* Oxford, 1934, pp. 373-416.

Nau, F., in Bousquet J. and F. Nau, *Histoire de saint Pacôme* (Cited above). [A French translation of the Syriac version of the *Paralipomena* is given in front of the text of the sixth Greek Life].

From Ethiopic

Arras, V. *Collectio Monastica, CSCO* 239. Louvain, 1963. Pp. 104-105. [Latin translation of the Ethiopic version of the Greek Excerpta of the Rule.].

Basset, R. *Les apocryphes éthiopiens traduits en français,* fasc. 8. Paris, 1896. Pp. 28-40. [Translation of the Ethiopic Rules].

König, E. 'Die Regeln des Pachomius', *TSK* 51 (1878) 328-332.

Löfgren, O. 'Pakomius' etiopiska klosterregler. I svensk tokning.' *Kyrkohistorisk Årsskrift* 48 (1948) 163-184. [Swedish translation].

Schodde, G.H. 'The Rules of Pachomius translated from the Ethiopic,' *Presbyterian Review* 6 (1885) 678-689.

PACHOMIAN BIBLIOGRAPHY

Amand de Mendieta, A. 'Le système cénobitique basilien comparé au système cénobitique pachômien,' *RHR* 152 (1957) 31-80.

Amélineau, E. 'Etude historique sur St. Pachôme et le cénobitisme primitif dans la Haute-Egypte,' *Bulletin de l'Institut d'Egypte*, series 2,7 (1886) 306-309.

Bacht, H. 'Pakhome—der grosse "Adler",' *GuL* 22 (1949) 367-382.

________. 'Ein Wort zur Ehrenrettung der ältesten Mönchsregel,' *ZKT* 72 (1950) 350-359.

________. 'L'importance de l'idéal monastique de s. Pacôme pour l'histoire du monachisme chrétien,' *RAM* 26 (1950) 308-326.

________. 'Heimweh nach der Urkirche. Zur Wesensdeutung des frühchristlichen Mönchtums.' *LuM* 7 (1950) 64-78.

________. 'Vom gemeinsamen Leben. Die Bedeutung des christlichen Mönchideals für die Geschichte des christlichen Mönchtums,' *LuM* 11 (1952) 91-110.

________. '"Meditatio" in den ältesten Mönchsquellen,' *GuL* 28 (1955) 360-373.

________. 'Antonius und Pachomius. Von der Anachorese zum Cönobitentum,' in B. Steidle, *Antonius Magnus Eremita, SA* 38; Rome, 1956 Pp. 66-107.

________. 'Studien zum "Liber Orsiesii".'*HJ* 77 (1958) 98-124

________. 'Mönchtum und Kirche. Eine Studie zur Spiritualität des Pachomius,' in J. Daniélou and H. Vorgrimler, *Sentire Ecclesiam, Das Bewusstsein von der Kirche als gestaltende Kraft der Frömmigkeit.*Freiburg, 1961. Pp. 113-133.

________. 'Pakhôme et ses disciples,' in *Théologie de la vie monastique, Théologie* 49. Paris, 1961. Pp. 39-71.

________. 'La loi du "retour aux sources". (De quelques aspects de l'idéal monastique pachômien),' *RMab* 51 (1961) 6-25.

________. 'Ein verkanntes Fragment des koptischen Pachomius-Regel,' *Muséon* 75 (1962) 5-18.

________. 'Pachomius der Jüngere,' in *LTK*, 7^2 (1962) Col. 1331.

________. 'Zur Typologie des koptischen Mönchtums. Pachomius und Evagrius.' In *Christentum am Nil* (*Internationale Arbeitstagung zur Ausstellung 'koptische Kunst'*). Recklinghausen, 1964. Pp. 142-157.

________. 'Vom Umgang mit der Bibel im ältesten Mönchtum,' *Theologie und Philosophie* 41 (1966) 557-566.

________. '. . . Vexillum crucis sequi (Horsiesius). Mönchtum als Kreuzesnachfolge,' *Martyria.—Leiturgia—Diakonia. Festschrift für H. Volk, Bischof von Mainz, zum 65. Geburtstag*, Mainz, 1968. Pp. 149-162.

________. *Das Vermächtnis des Ursprungs* (*Studien zum Frühen Mönchtum I*). Würzburg, 1972.

________. 'Agrypnia. Die Motive des Schlafentzugs im frühen Mönchtum,' *Bibliothek—Buch—Geschichte* (*Kurt Köster zum 65. Geburtstag; herausgegeben von Günther Pflug, Brita Eckert und Heinz Friesenhahn*). Frankfurt am Main, 1977. Pp. 353-369.

Batlle, C.M. 'La vida religiosa comunitària a l'Egipte del segle IV.' Un nou plantejament des de les bases. *StMon* 12 (1970) 181-194.

Biedermann, H.M. 'Die Regel des Pachomius und die evangelischen Räte,' *OstKSt* 9 (1960) 241-253.

Chitty, D.J. 'Pachomian Sources Reconsidered,' *JEH* 5 (1954) 38-77.

________. 'A Note on the Chronology of Pachomian Foundations,' *Studia Patristica*, Vol. II, *TU* 64. Berlin, 1957. Pp. 379-385.

________. 'Some Notes, mainly Lexical on the Sources for the Life of Pachomius,' *Studia Patristica*, V, *TU* 80. Berlin, 1962. Pp. 266-269.

________. 'Pachomian Sources once more,' *Studia Patristica*, X. Berlin, 1970. Pp. 54-64.

Crum, W.E. *Theological Texts from Coptic Papyri edited with an Appendix upon the Arabic and Coptic Versions of the Life of Pachomius, Anecdota Oxoniensia, Semitic series* 12). Oxford, 1913.

________. *Der Papyruscodex saec. VI-VII der Phillipsbibliothek in Cheltenham. Koptische theologische Schriften. Mit einem Beitrag von A. Ehrhard. Schriften der Wissenschaftlichen Gesellschaft in Strassburg* 18. Strasbourg, 1915.

De Clercq, D. 'L'influence de la Règle de saint Pachôme en Occident,' *Mélanges d'Histoire du Moyen Age dédiés à la mémoire de Louis Halphen.* Paris, 1951. Pp. 169-176.

Delhougne, H. 'Autorité et participation chez les Pères du cénobitisme,' *RAM* 45 (1969) 369-394; 46 (1970) 3-32.

Deseille, P. *L'esprit du monachisme pachômien, suivi de la traduction française des Pachomiana latina par les moines de Solesmes, Spiritualité orientale* 2. Bellefontaine, 1968.

Draguet, R. 'Le chapitre de HL sur les Tabennésiotes dérive-t-il d'une source copte?' *Muséon* 57 (1944) 53-145; 58 (1945) 15-95.

Ehrhard, A. 'Zur literarhistorischen und theologischen Würdigung der Texte,' W.E. Crum, *Der Papyruscodex*. . . . Pp. 129-171. [Concerns the letter of Theophilos to Horsiesios].

Gindele, C. 'Die Schriftlesung im Pachomiuskloster,' *EuA*, 41 (1965) 114-122.

Gnolfo, P. 'Pedagogia Pacomiana,' *Sal* 10 (1948) 569-596.

Gribomont, J. 'Pachomios der Ältere,' *LTK* 7^2 (1962) Col. 1330-1331.

Grützmacher, O. *Pachomios und das älteste Klosterleben.* Freiburg, 1896.

Halkin, F. 'Les Vies grecques de S. Pacôme.' *AnBoll* 47 (1929) 376-388.

________. 'L'Histoire Lausiaque et les Vies grecques de S. Pacôme,' *AnBoll* 48 (1930) 257-301.

Hengstenberg, W. 'Pachomiana (mit einem Anhang über die Liturgie von Alexandrien),' in A.M. Königer, *Beiträge zur Geschichte des christlichen Altertums und der Byzantinischen Literatur. Festgabe Albert Ehrhard.* Bonn and Leipzig, 1922. Pp. 228-252.

Heussi, K. 'Pachomios,' in Pauly-Wissowa, *Realencyklopädie der classischen Altertumswissenschaft,* 18 (1942) Col. 2070 ff.

Ladeuze, P. 'Les diverses recensions de la vie de S. Pakhôme et leurs dépendances mutuelles,' *Muséon* (1897) 148-171; (1898) 145-168; 269-286; 378-395.

________. *Etude sur le cénobitisme pakhômien pendant le IVe siècle et la première moitié du Ve.* Louvain and Paris, 1898; rpt. 1962.

Leclercq, H. 'Pachôme, in *DACL* XIII/1 (1937) Col. 499-510.

Lefort, L.T. 'Théodore de Tabennêsi et la lettre pascale de S. Athanase sur le canon de la Bible,' *Muséon* 29 (1910) 205-216.

_______. 'Un texte original de la règle de saint Pachôme,' *Comptes rendus de l'Académie des Inscriptions et Belles-Lettres*, 1919. Pp. 341-348.

_______. 'La Règle de S. Pachôme (étude d'approche),' *Muséon* 34 (1921) 61-70.

_______. 'La Règle de S. Pachôme (2e étude d'approche),' *Muséon* 37 (1924) 1-28.

_______. 'La Règle de S. Pachôme (Nouveaux documents),' *Muséon* 40 (1927) 31-64.

_______. 'S. Pachôme et Amen-em-ope,' *Muséon* 49 (1927) 65-74.

_______. 'Littérature bohaïrique,' *Muséon* 44 (1931) 115-135.

_______. 'S. Athanase écrivain copte,' *Muséon* 46 (1933) 1-33.

_______. 'La Règle de S. Pachôme (nouveaux fragments coptes),' *Muséon* 48 (1935) 75-80.

_______. 'Les premiers monastères pachômiens. Exploration topographique,' *Muséon* 52 (1939) 379-408.

_______. 'Les sources coptes pachômiennes,' *Muséon* 67 (1954) 217-229.

Lehmann, K. 'Die Entstehung der Freiheitsstrafe in den Klöstern des heiligen Pachomius,' *Z. d. Savigny-Stift. f. Rechtsgesch., Kan. Abt.* 37 (1951). Pp. 1-94.

Leipoldt, J. 'Pachom,' *Bulletin de la Société de l'Archéologie Copte* 16 (1961-62) 191-229.

_______. 'Pachom,' *Koptologische Studien in der DDR. Wissenschaftliche Zeitschrift der Martin-Luther-Universität Halle-Wittenberg*. Sonderheft 1965, 236-249.

Levis, A. 'Koinonia e comunidade no monacato pacomiano,' *Claretianum* 15 (1975) 269-327.

Lozano, J.M. 'La comunità pacomiana: dalla comunione all'istituzione,' *Claretianum* 15 (1975) 237-267.

Monachino, V. 'Pacomio,' *Enciclopedia Cattolica* 9 (1952) Col. 511-514.

Morson, J. 'The sixteenth Centenary of St. Pachomius.' *Pax* 38 (1948) 65-74

Orlandi, T. 'Nuovi Testi copti pacomiani,' *Commandements du Seigneur et Libération évangélique, SA* 70. Rome, 1977. Pp. 241-243.

Peeters, P. 'A propos de la Vie sahidique de S. Pacôme.' *AnBoll* 52 (1934) 286-320.

________. 'L'édition critique des Vies coptes de S. Pacôme par le Prof. Lefort,' *Muséon* 59 (1946) 17-34.

________. 'Le dossier copte de S. Pacôme et ses rapports avec la tradition grecque,' *AnBoll* 64 (1946) 258-277.

________. 'L'oeuvre de L.T. Lefort,' *Muséon* 59 (1946) 41-62.

________. 'Un feuillet d'une Vie arabe de saint Pacôme,' *Muséon* 59 (1946) 399-412.

Pietschmann, R. 'Theodorus Tabennesiota und die sahidische Übersetzung des Osterfestbriefs des Athanasius vom Jahre 367,; *NGG* (1889) I, 87-104.

Quecke, H. 'Ein Pachomiuszitat bei Schenute,' *Probleme der koptischen Literatur. Wissenschaftliche Beiträge der Univ. Halle-Wittenberg*. 1968. Pp. 155-171.

________. 'Briefe Pachoms in koptischer Sprache. Neue deutsche Übersetzung,' *Zetesis* (*Festschrift E. de Strycker*). Antwerp and Utrecht, 1973. Pp. 655-664.

________. 'Ein neues Fragment der Pachombriefe in koptischer Sprache,' *Orientalia* 43 (1974) 66-82.

________. 'Die Briefe Pachoms,' *ZDMG*, Supp. II (1974) 96-108.

________. 'Die griechische Übersetzung der Pachombriefe,' *Studia Papyrologica* 15 (1976) 153-159.

________. 'Eine Handvoll Pachomianischer Texte,' *ZDMG*, Supp. III, 1 (1977) 221-229.

Revillout, E. 'Funérailles des moines égyptiens au temps de Saint Antoine et de Saint Pacome,' *Académie Delphinale*, Bull. s. 2,1 (1856-60) 374-386.

Řezáč, I. 'De forma unionis monasteriorum Sancti Pachomii,' *OCP* 23 (1957) 381-414.

Ruppert, F. *Das Pachomianische Mönchtum und die Anfänge klösterlichen Gehorsams. Münsterschwarzacher Studien* 20. Münsterschwarzach, 1971.

________. 'Arbeit und geistliches Leben im pachomianischen Mönchtum,' *OstKSt* 24 (1975) 3-14.

Samir, K. 'Témoins arabes de la catéchèse de Pachôme "A propos d'un moine rancunier". (CPG 2354.1),' *OCP* 42 (1976) 494-508.

Schiwietz, S. 'Geschichte und Organisation der pachomianischen Klöster im vierten Jahrhundert,' *Archiv für kathol. Kirchenrecht* 81 (1901) 461-490; 630-649.

Steidle, B. '"Der Zweite" im Pachomiuskloster,' *BM* 24 (1948) 97-104; 174-179.

________, and O. Schuler, 'Der "Obern-Spiegel" im "Testament" des Abtes Horsiesi († nach 387),' *EuA* 43 (1967) 22-38.

Steidle, B. 'Der Osterbrief unseres Vaters Theodor an alle Klöster. Zur 1600. Wiederkehr des Todesjahres (368-1968),' *EuA* 44 (1968) 104-119.

________. 'Der heilige Abt. Theodor von Tabennesi. Zur 1600. Wiederkehr des Todesjahres (368-1968),' *EuA* 44 (1968) 91-103.

Tamburrino, P. 'Koinonia. Die Beziehung "Monasterium"-"Kirche" im frühen pachomianischen Mönchtum,' *EuA* 43 (1967) 5-21.

________. 'Bibbia e vita spirituale negli scritti di Orsiesi,' in C. Vagaggini, ed., *Bibbia e spiritualità, Biblioteca di cultura religiosa* 79. Rome, 1967. Pp. 85-119.

________. 'Les saints de l'Ancien Testament dans la Ière catéchèse de saint Pachôme,' *Melto* 4 (1968) 33-44.

________. 'Die Heiligen des Alten Testaments in der 1. Katechese des heiligen Pachomius,' *EuA* 45 (1969) 50-56.

Van Cranenburgh, H. 'La "Regula Angeli" dans la Vie latine de saint Pachôme,' *Muséon* 76 (1963) 165-194.

________. 'Nieuw licht op de oudste kloostercongregatie van de christenheid: de instelling van Sint-Pachomius,' *TGL* 19 (1963) 581-605; 665-690; and 20 (1964) 41-54.

________. 'Actualiteitswaarde van het pachomiaanse kloosterleven,' *TGL* 24 (1968) 233-257.

________. 'Valeur actuelle de la vie religieuse pachômienne,' *VS* 120 (1969) 400-422.

________. 'Etude comparative des récits anciens de la vocation de saint Pachôme,' *RBén* 82 (1972) 280-308.

________. 'Les noms de Dieu dans la prière de Pachôme et de ses frères,' *RHS* 52 (1976) 193-212.

Van Molle, M.M. 'Essai de classement chronologique des premières règles de vie commune en chrétienté,' *VS Supplément* 84 (1968) 108-127.

________. "Confrontation entre les Règles et la littérature pachômienne postérieure,' *VS Supplément* 86 (1968) 394-424.

________. 'Aux origines de la vie communautaire chrétienne, quelques équivoques déterminantes pour l'avenir,' *VS Supplément* 88 (1969) 101-121.

________. 'Vie commune et obéissance d'après les intuitions premières de Pachôme et Basile,' *VS Supplément* 93 (1970) 196-225.

Van Rijen, A. 'Een regel van Pachomius,' *Ons geestelijk leven* 48 (1971) 334-344.

Veilleux, A. 'Le problème des Vies de Saint Pachôme,' *RAM* 42 (1966) 287-305.

________. *La liturgie dans le cénobitisme pachômien au quatrième siècle, SA* 57. Rome, 1968.

________. 'San Pacomio, abate di Tabennesi,' *Bibliotheca Sanctorum*, Vol. X (1968) Col. 10-20.

________. 'Pacomio il Giovane,' *Ibidem*, Col. 9-10.

________. 'Teodoro di Tabennesi,' *Ibidem* Vol. XII (1969) Col. 270-272.

________. 'Holy Scripture in the Pachomian Koinonia,' *Monastic Studies* 10 (1974) 143-153.

Vergote, J. 'L'oeuvre de L.T. Lefort,' *Muséon* 59 (1946) 41-62.

________. 'En lisant "Les Vies de saint Pakhôme",' *ChE* 22 (1947) 389-415.

________. 'La valeur des Vies grecques et coptes de S. Pakhôme,' *Orientalia Lovaniensia Periodica* 8 (1977) 175-186.

Vogüé, A. de 'Points de contact du chapitre XXXII de l'Histoire Lausiaque avec les écrits d'Horsièse,' *StMon* 13 (1971) 291-294.

________. 'Les pièces latines du dossier pachômien,' *RHE* 67 (1972) 26-67.

________. 'L'Anecdote pachômienne du "Vaticanus graecus" 2091. Son origine et ses sources,' *RSH* 49 (1973) 401-419.

________. 'Le nom du Supérieur de monastère dans la Règle pachômienne. A propos d'un ouvrage récent,' *StMon* 15 (1973) 17-22.

________. 'La vie arabe de saint Pachôme et ses deux sources présumées,' *AnBoll* 91 (1973) 379-390.

________. 'Saint Pachôme et son oeuvre d'après plusieurs études récentes,' *RHE* 69 (1974) 425-453.

________. 'Sur la terminologie de la pénitence dans la Règle de saint Pachôme', *StMon* 17 (1975) 7-12.

________. 'Les noms de la porte et du portier dans la Règle de Pachôme,' *StMon* 17 (1975) 233-235.

Wirszycka, E. 'Les terres de la congrégation pachômienne dans une liste de payements pour les apora,' *Le monde grec. Pensée, littérature, histoire, documents. Hommage à Claire Préaux*. Brussels, 1975. Pp. 625-636.

Zananiri, G. 'Saint Pacôme et le monachisme.' *Revue Confér. Franc. Or.* Cairo, 1948, 178-185.

* * * *Pachomiana. Commémoration du XVIème Centenaire de St Pacôme l'Egyptien* (348-1948). (*Publications du Centre d'Etudes Orientales de la Custodie Franciscaine de Terre-Sainte, Coptica* 3). Cairo, 1955.

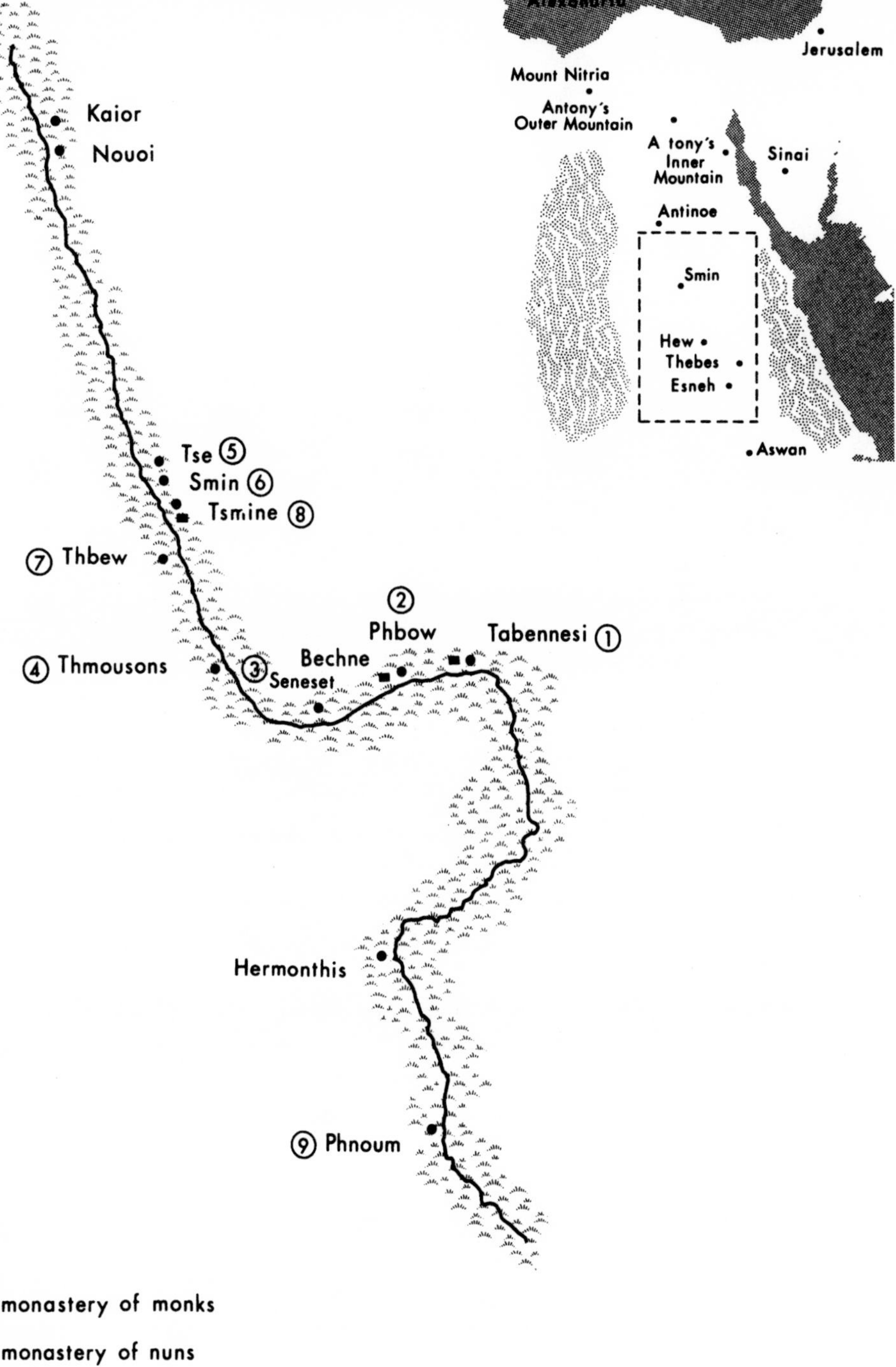

Map of

Pachomian Monasteries

ABBREVIATIONS

of names of periodicals and series

ADMG	*Annales du Musée Guimet*, Paris.
AnBoll	*Analecta Bollandiana*, Brussels.
BKV	*Bibliothek der Kirchenväter*, Kempten.
BM	*Benediktinische Monatschrift* (later: *Erbe und Auftrag*), Beuron.
ChE	*Chronique d'Egypte*, Brussels.
CSCO	*Corpus scriptorum Christianorum orientalium*, Louvain.
DACL	*Dictionnaire d'archéologie chrétienne et de liturgie*, Paris.
EuA	*Erbe und Auftrag* (formerly *Benediktinische Monatschrift*), Beuron.
GuL	*Geist und Leben. Zeitschrift für Aszese und Mystik*, Würzburg.
HJ	*Historisches Jahrbuch*, Munich-Freiburg.
JEH	*The Journal of Ecclesiastical History*, London.
LTK	*Lexikon für Theologie und Kirche*, Freiburg.
LuM	*Liturgie und Mönchtum. Laacher Hefte*, Maria Laach.
Muséon	*Le Muséon*, Louvain.
NGG	*Nachrichten der Gesellschaft der Wissenschaften zu Göttingen*, Göttingen.
OCP	*Orientalia Christiana Periodica*, Rome.
OGL	*Ons geestelijk leven.*
Orientalia	*Orientalia. Commentarii Periodici Pontificii Instituti Biblici*, Rome.
OstKSt	*Ostkirchliche Studien*, Würzburg.
PG	*Patrologia Graeca* of Migne, Paris.

PL	*Patrologia Latina* of Migne, Paris.
PO	*Patrologia Orientalis*, Paris.
RAM	*Revue d'ascétique et de mystique*, Toulouse.
RBén	*Revue bénédictine*, Maredsous.
RHE	*Revue d'histoire ecclésiastique*, Louvain.
RHR	*Revue de l'histoire des religions*, Paris.
RHS	*Revue d'Histoire de la Spiritualité*, Toulouse.
RMab	*Revue Mabillon*, Ligugé.
SA	*Studia Anselmiana*, Rome.
Sal	*Salesianum*, (Rome) Turin.
StMon	*Studia Monastica*, Montserrat.
TGL	*Tijdschrift voor geestelijk leven*, Nijmegen.
TSK	*Theologische Studien und Kritiken*, (Hamburg) Gotha.
TU	*Texte und Untersuchungen zur Geschichte der altchristlichen Literatur*. Archiv für die griechisch-christlichen Schriftsteller der ersten drei Jahrhunderte, Leipzig-Berlin.
VS	*La Vie Spirituelle*, Paris.
ZDMG	*Zeitschrift der deutschen morgenländischen Gesellschaft*, Leipzig.
ZKT	*Zeitschrift für katholische Theologie*, (Innsbruck) Vienna.

SIGLA

Ag	Arabic Life in Göttingen Ms.116.
Am	Arabic Life published by E. Amélineau.
Am. Letter	Letter of Bishop Ammon (*Epistula Ammonis*).
Apoph.	*Apophthegmata Patrum.*
Av	Arabic Life in Vatican Ms. 172.
Bo	Bohairic Life.
Den.	Latin Life translated by Denys (*Dionysius Exiguus*).
Draguet Fragm.	Fragment published by R. Draguet.
G^1, G^2, etc.	First Greek Life, Second Greek Life, etc.
H.L.	Lausiac History of Palladius (*Historia Lausiaca*).
H.M.A.	History of the Monks in Egypt (*Historia monachorum in Aegypto*).
Hors. Fragm.	Fragments from Horsiesios.
Hors. Instr.	Instruction of Horsiesios.
Hors. Letter	Letter of Horsiesios.
Hors. Reg.	Regulations of Horsiesios.
Hors. Test.	Testament of Horsiesios (*Liber Orsiesii*).
Inst.	Institutes (*Praecepta et Instituta*).
Jer. Pref.	Jerome's Preface to the *Pachomiana Latina.*
Jud.	Judgements (*Praecepta atque Judicia*).
Leg.	Laws (*Praecepta ac Leges*).
Pach. Fragm.	Fragments from Pachomius.
Pach. Instr.	Instruction of Pachomius.
Pach. Letter	Letter of Pachomius.
Paral.	*Paralipomena*

Pr.	Precepts (*Praecepta*).
S^1, S^2, etc.	First Sahidic Life, Second Sahidic Life, etc.
SBo	Recension of the Life represented by the group Bo, Av, S^4, S^5, S^6, S^7, etc.
Theod. Fragm.	Fragments from Theodore.
Theod. Instr.	Instruction of Theodore.
Theod. Letter	Letter of Theodore.
VB	L.-T. Lefort, *S. Pachomii vita bohairice scripta.*
VC	L.-T. Lefort, *Les vies coptes de saint Pachôme et de ses premiers successeurs.*
Vit. Ant.	Life of Antony by Athanasius (*Vita Antonii*).
VS	L.-T. Lefort, *S. Pachomii vitae sahidice scriptae.*

CISTERCIAN PUBLICATIONS INC.
Kalamazoo, Michigan

TITLES LISTING

Texts and Studies in the Monastic Tradition

THE CISTERCIAN FATHERS SERIES

THE WORKS OF BERNARD OF CLAIRVAUX

Treatises I: Apologia to Abbot William, On Precept and Dispensation .... CF 1
On the Song of Songs I–IV .... CF 4,7,31,40
The Life and Death of Saint Malachy the Irishman .... CF 10
Treatises II: The Steps of Humility, On Loving God .... CF 13
Magnificat: Homilies in Praise of the Blessed Virgin Mary [with Amadeus of Lausanne] .... CF 18
Treatises III: On Grace and Free Choice, In Praise of the New Knighthood .... CF 19
Sermons on Conversion: A Sermon to Clerics, Lenten Sermons on Psalm 91 .... CF 25
Five Books on Consideration: Advice to a Pope .... CF 37

THE WORKS OF WILLIAM OF SAINT THIERRY

On Contemplating God, Prayer, and Meditations .... CF 3
Exposition on the Song of Songs .... CF 6
The Enigma of Faith .... CF 9
The Golden Epistle .... CF 12
The Mirror of Faith .... CF 15
Exposition on the Epistle to the Romans .... CF 27
The Nature and Dignity of Love .... CF 30

THE WORKS OF AELRED OF RIEVAULX

Treatises I: On Jesus at the Age of Twelve, Rule for a Recluse, The Pastoral Prayer .... CF 2
Spiritual Friendship .... CF 5
The Mirror of Charity .... CF 17†
Dialogue on the Soul .... CF 22

THE WORKS OF GILBERT OF HOYLAND

Sermons on the Song of Songs I–III .. CF 14,20,26
Treatises, Sermons, and Epistles .... CF 34

THE WORKS OF JOHN OF FORD

Sermons on the Final Verses of the Song of Songs I–VII ...... CF 29,39,43,44,45,46,47

OTHER EARLY CISTERCIAN WRITERS

THE CISTERCIAN STUDIES SERIES

MONASTIC TEXTS

CHRISTIAN SPIRITUALITY

MONASTIC STUDIES

CISTERCIAN STUDIES

** Temporarily out of print*

† Forthcoming

Nicolas Cotheret's Annals of Citeaux (Louis J. Lekai) ..... CS 57

The Occupation of Celtic Sites in Ireland by the Canons Regular of St Augustine and the Cistercians (G. Carville) ..... CS 56

The Finances of the Cistercian Order in the Fourteenth Century (Peter King) ..... CS 85†

Medieval Religious Women

Distant Echoes: MRW, I (L.T. Shank and J.A. Nichols, edd.) ..... CS 71

Studies in Medieval Cistercian History sub-series

Studies I ..... CS 13

Studies II ..... CS 24

Cistercian Ideals and Reality (Studies III) ..... CS 60

Simplicity and Ordinariness (Studies IV) ..... CS 61

The Chimera of His Age: Studies on St Bernard (Studies V) ..... CS 63

Cistercians in the Late Middle Ages (Studies VI) ..... CS 64

Noble Piety and Reformed Monasticism (Studies VII) ..... CS 65

Benedictus: Studies in Honor of St Benedict of Nursia (Studies VIII) ..... CS 67

Heaven on Earth (Studies IX) ..... CS 68

Goad and Nail (Studies X) ..... CS 84

Studies in Cistercian Art and Architecture

Studies in Cistercian Art and Architecture, I (Meredith Lillich, ed.) ..... CS 66

Studies in Cistercian Art and Architecture, II (Meredith Lillich, ed.) ..... CS 69

THOMAS MERTON

The Climate of Monastic Prayer ..... CS 1

Thomas Merton on St Bernard ..... CS 9

Thomas Merton's Shared Contemplation: A Protestant Perspective (Daniel J. Adams) ..... CS 62

Solitude in the Writings of Thomas Merton (Richard Anthony Cashen) ..... CS 40

The Message of Thomas Merton (Brother Patrick Hart, ed.) ..... CS 42

Thomas Merton Monk (revised edition/ Brother Patrick Hart, ed.) ..... CS 52

Thomas Merton and Asia: His Quest for Utopia (Alexander Lipski) ..... CS 74

THE CISTERCIAN LITURGICAL DOCUMENTS SERIES

The Cistercian Hymnal: Introduction and Commentary ..... CLS 1

The Cistercian Hymnal: Text and Melodies ..... CLS 2

The Old French Ordinary and Breviary of the Abbey of the Paraclete: Introduction and Commentary ..... CLS 3†

The Old French Ordinary of the Abbey of the Paraclete: Text ..... CLS 4†

The Paraclete Breviary: Text ..... CLS 5-7†

The Hymn Collection of the Abbey of the Paraclete: Introduction and Commentary ..... CLS 8†

The Hymn Collection of the Abbey of the Paraclete: Text ..... CLS 9†

STUDIA PATRISTICA †

Papers of the Oxford Patristics Conference 1983 (Elizabeth A. Livingstone, ed.)

1. Historica-Gnostica-Biblica
2. Critica-Classica-Ascetica-Liturgica
3. The Second Century-Clement and Origen-The Cappodocian Fathers
4. Augustine-Post Nicene Latin Fathers-Oriental Texts-*Nachleben* of the Fathers

FAIRACRES PRESS, OXFORD

The Wisdom of the Desert Fathers

The Letters of St Antony the Great

The Letters of Ammonas, Successor of St Antony

A Study of Wisdom. Three Tracts by the author of *The Cloud of Unknowing*

The Power of the Name. The Jesus Prayer in Orthodox Spirituality (Kallistos Ware)

Contemporary Monasticism

A Pilgrim's Book of Prayers (Gilbert Shaw)

Theology and Spirituality (Andrew Louth)

Prayer and Holiness (Dumitru Staniloae)

Eight Chapters on Perfection and Angel's Song (Walter Hilton)

Creative Suffering (Iulia de Beausobre)

Bringing Forth Christ. Five Feasts of the Child Jesus (St Bonaventure)

Distributed in North America only for Fairacres Press.

DISTRIBUTED BOOKS

La Trappe in England

O Holy Mountain: Journal of a Retreat on Mount Athos

St Benedict: Man with An Idea (Melbourne Studies)

The Spirit of Simplicity

Vision of Peace (St. Joseph's Abbey)

The Animals of St Gregory (Paulinus Press)

Benedict's Disciples (David Hugh Farmer)

The Christmas Sermons of Guerric of Igny

The Emperor's Monk. A Contemporary Life of Benedict of Aniane

Journey to God:. Anglican Essays on the Benedictine Way

* *Temporarily out of print*

† *Forthcoming*

CPSIA information can be obtained at www.ICGtesting.com
Printed in the USA
LVOW042001141211

259485LV00002B/1/P